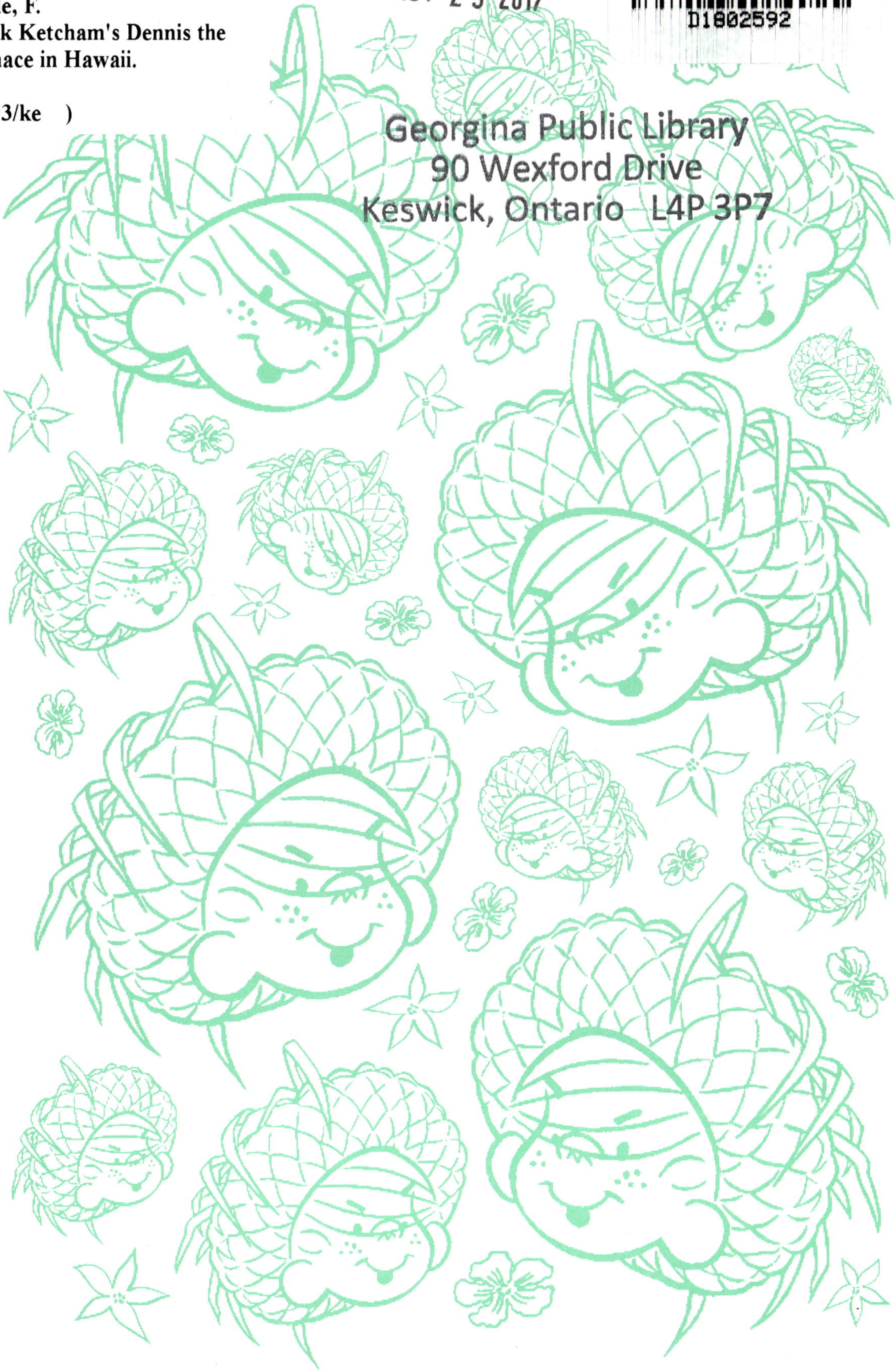

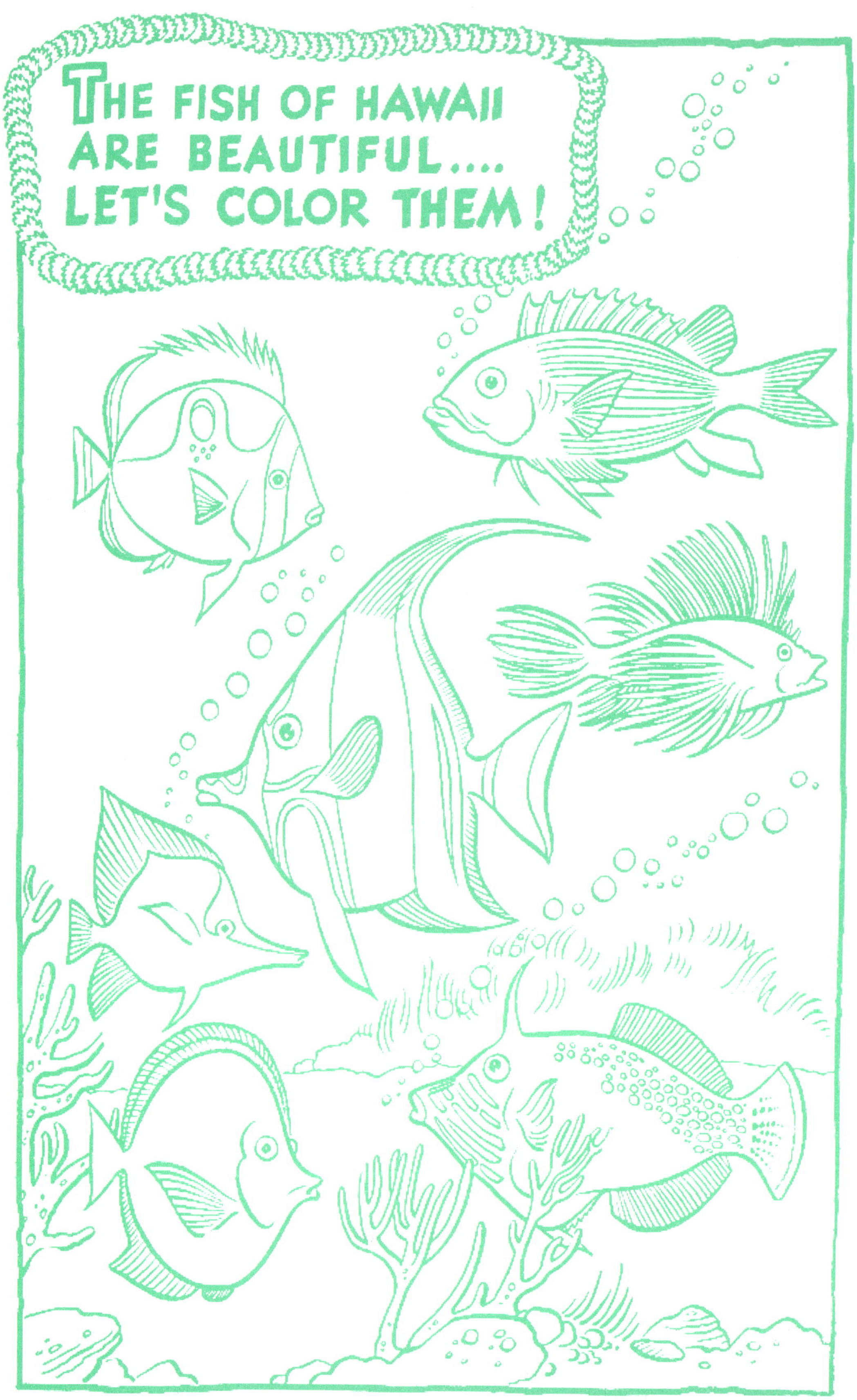
THE FISH OF HAWAII
ARE BEAUTIFUL....
LET'S COLOR THEM!

Hank Ketcham's Dennis the Menace in Hawaii

The Cult-Classic Comicbook
by Al Wiseman
& Fred Toole

ALOHA!

PAPERCUTZ

NOW ON SALE!

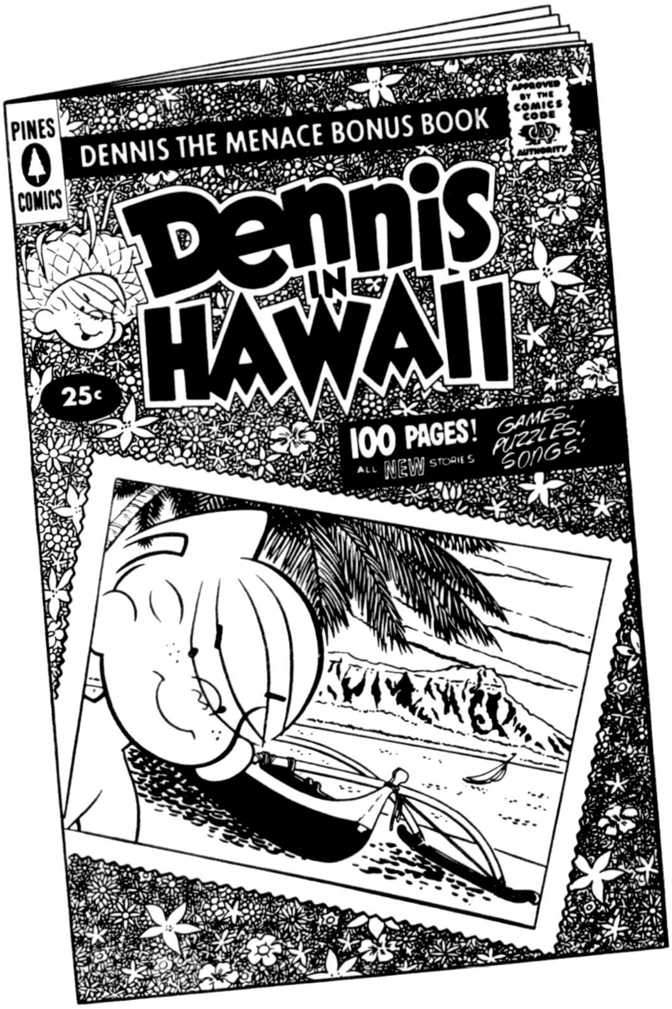
PINES COMICS
DENNIS THE MENACE BONUS BOOK
APPROVED BY THE COMICS CODE AUTHORITY
Dennis IN HAWAII
25¢
100 PAGES!
ALL NEW STORIES
GAMES! PUZZLES! SONGS!

SEE WHAT HAPPENS WHEN—

- Dennis goes down into a Volcano.
- Climbs a Mountain of Sugar.
- Rides a Catamaran.

YOU CAN LEARN TO HULA . . . EVEN TALK HAWAIIAN

Get DENNIS IN HAWAII at your newsstand TODAY

Advertisement for DENNIS IN HAWAII published in DENNIS THE MENACE #30 (Sept. 1958).

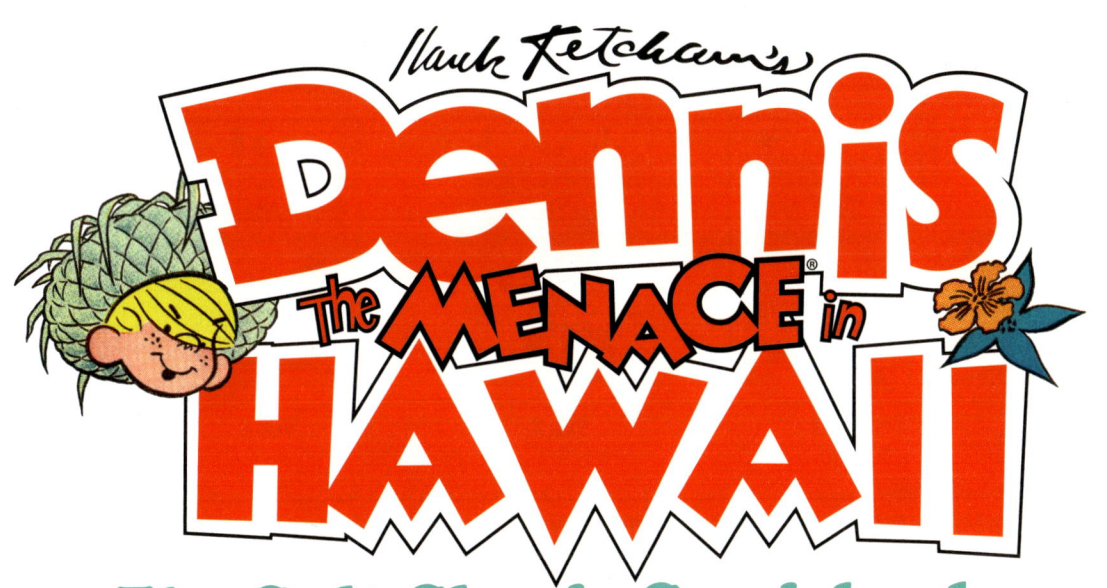

The Cult-Classic Comicbook
by Al Wiseman & Fred Toole

Introduction by Mark Arnold
Edited by Bill Alger

New York

DENNIS THE MENACE graphic novels available from PAPERCUTZ

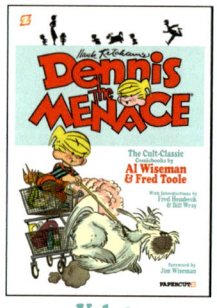 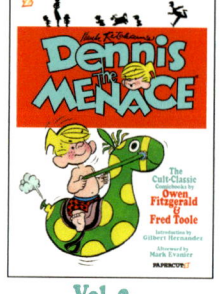 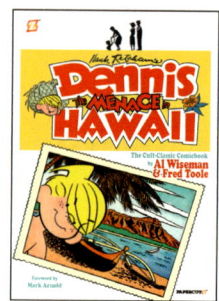

Vol. 1   Vol. 2   Vol. 3

DENNIS THE MENACE graphic novels vols. 1 and 2 are available for $19.99 in hardcover only. DENNIS THE MENACE IN HAWAII is $24.99 in hardcover only. Available from booksellers everywhere. You can order online from papercutz.com. Or call 1-800-886-1223 Monday through Friday, 9-5 EST. MC, Visa, and AmEx accepted. To order by mail, please add $5.00 for postage and handling for first book ordered, $1.00 for each additional book and make check payable to NBM Publishing. Send to: Papercutz, 160 Broadway, Suite 700, East Wing, New York, NY 10038

Special thanks to my brother Tom for transcribing my old interview tapes and editing the notes into some sort of logical order. And thanks to the following folks for help in scanning DENNIS comics for this volume: Jim & Teresa Wiseman, Tom Alger and Mark Arnold. Thanks also to Ron Ferdinand and Marcus Hamilton. This book is dedicated to these members of Al Wiseman's wonderful family who have always been patient with my endless barrage of questions about Al's life and career: Jim & Teresa Wiseman, Vadis Davis, Jan Wiseman Pisciotta, Merrily Wiseman Russo and Sue Dewer. Thanks also to Fred Toole's widow Mollie, who couldn't have been kinder when I spoke with her on the phone many years ago. — Bill Alger, Editor

Bill Alger – Design/Production/Artwork Cleanup & Restoration
Jeff Whitman – Assistant Managing Editor
Jim Salicrup
Editor-in-Chief

ISBN: 978-1-62991-768-9

Copyright © 2017 Hank Ketcham Enterprises, Inc.

Interviews with Hank Ketcham, Vadis Davis and Mollie Tool ©2017 William Alger

Papercutz books may be purchased for business or promotional use. For information on bulk purchases please contact Macmillan Corporate and Premium Sales Department at (800) 221-7945 x5442.

Printed in China
July 2017

Distributed by Macmillan

First Papercutz Printing

TABLE OF CONTENTS

Introduction by Mark Arnold 6
"Dennis The Menace To Try Isle Imping"
Article from *The Honolulu Star-Bulletin* August 27, 1956 10
DENNIS IN HAWAII (DENNIS THE MENACE GIANT #6) First Printing
Pines Comics, Summer 1958 (Written by Fred Toole & drawn by Al Wiseman) 11
Drawn From Life: Real Folks Who Snuck Into The DENNIS IN HAWAII Comic! 111
A Letter From Al 116
Interview: Hank Ketcham, Creator of DENNIS THE MENACE 118
Interview: Vadis Davis, Al Wiseman's First Wife 126
Interview: Mollie Toole, Fred Toole's Wife 138
"Artistry of Two Men Creates Dennis Comicbooks"
Article from *The Monterey Peninsula Herald* November 14, 1959............................... 156
"Comics Show What Fred Toole Thinks About"
Article from *The Monterey Peninsula Herald* May 18, 1980 159
1949: Al Wiseman Becomes Jack Chapman! (But Not Really, Probably.)
Article from *The American Cartoonist* Vol. 3 #7 Oct-Nov, 1949 160
1967: Al Wiseman Works For Boeing
Article from a 1967 issue of *The Everett Flyer* newsletter 161
Portfolio of Al Wiseman Original Art 162
Interview: Frank Hill by Greg Beda 175
DENNIS THE MENACE IN HAWAII (DENNIS THE MENACE GIANT #68)
Eighth Printing — Fawcett Publications, Inc., Summer, 1969 (Featuring additional
DENNIS IN HAWAII stories written by Fred Toole & drawn by Frank Hill)....................177
In The Year 2000: DENNIS Returns To Hawaii!
DENNIS newspaper comics by Ron Ferdinand & Marcus Hamilton.............................191

 **LOOK FOR THIS SEAL WHEN YOU BUY A COMIC MAGAZINE. IT GUARANTEES QUALITY AND WHOLESOME ENTERTAINMENT.**

INTRODUCTION

DENNIS THE MENACE IN HAWAII by Mark Arnold

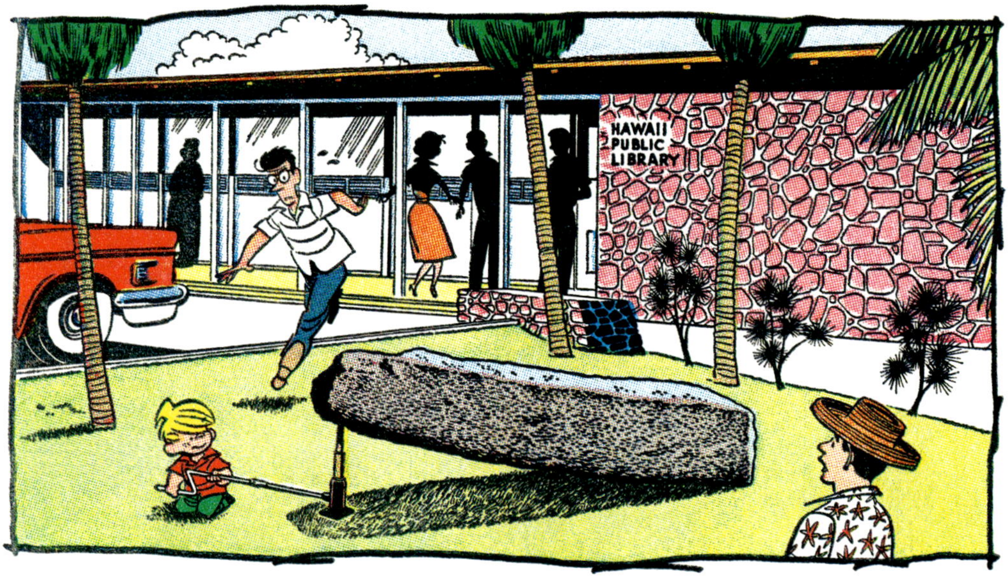
HAWAII
PUBLIC
LIBRARY

I am very pleased that Papercutz has decided to reprint this classic comic, DENNIS IN HAWAII. Even if you have read it multiple times or even own a few copies, this is the first time it has been presented in such a high quality edition, and the first time it has been reissued in its original, complete form since 1965, plus the 1969 addendum.

As you may know, Hank Ketcham created DENNIS THE MENACE in 1951 as a daily comic panel; a Sunday comic page in 1952 and a comicbook series in 1953. Initially, the comicbook stories, as written by Fred Toole and illustrated by Al Wiseman, were pretty straightforward, with Dennis harassing his parents or neighbor, Mr. Wilson, or playing with his friends, Tommy, Margaret, Joey and later, Gina. By the end of the decade, Toole and Wiseman were getting restless and wanted to expand upon the Dennis premise and also have a subject worthy of filling the 100-page template of the new DENNIS THE MENACE GIANT series, which up until this point were filled with new Christmas or generic vacation stories depending on the issue. Toole and Wiseman got the idea to have Dennis visit Hawaii and in the process, they got a paid vacation from Hank Ketcham out of the deal! It may or may not have been planned originally for the Hawaii stories to fill the entire 100-page issue, but they managed to do so in order to cover all the sights by having Dennis go to such places as Pearl Harbor and to attend an authentic Hawaiian luau.

Al Wiseman's son, Jim, comments on the Hawaii experience, "When my parents got back from Hawaii, I was fascinated by the fact that they had ridden on a JET airliner. I asked my dad, what it was like, and he replied, 'It was like listening to your mother vacuum the house ALL DAY!'

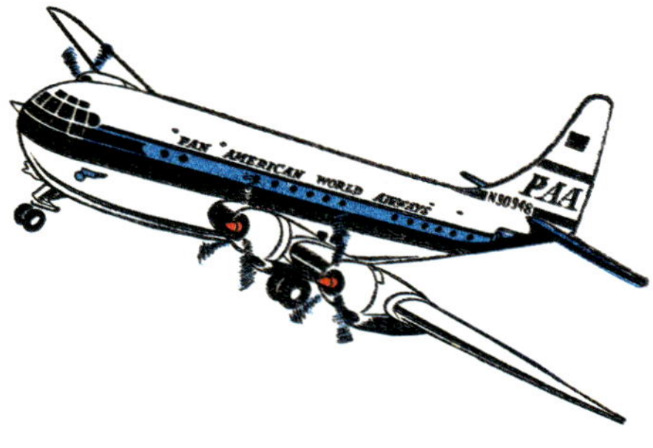
PAA

"The self-portraits were sorta close. If you look at the inside cover to HAWAII and MEXICO, you can see what he looked like. He had a crew cut, Buddy Holly glasses, smoked Chesterfields. Wore those short-sleeved shirts.

"The DENNIS THE MENACE travel books were the first comicbooks that took readers to places they might not otherwise see along with some historical or other cultural knowledge incorporated into the stories. I'm not sure how the destinations were chosen. I do know that my dad, mom, Fred and Mollie travelled to Hawaii for research and that their visit generated some local (Hawaiian) news coverage. I had the opportunity to travel to Mexico with my dad when he did the research on the DENNIS THE MENACE GOES TO MEXICO travel special and have many fond memories of that visit."

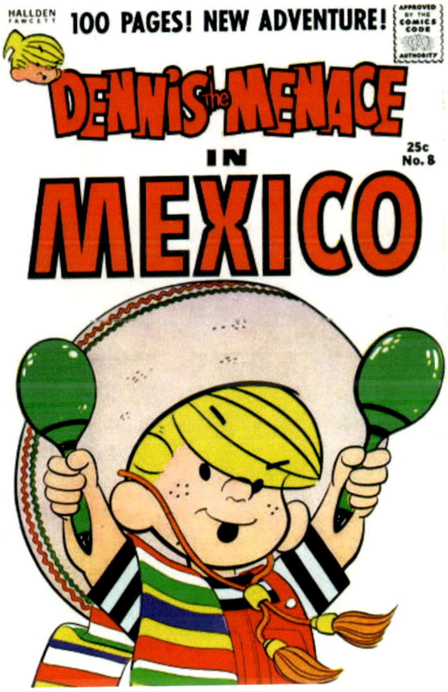
HALLDEN FAWCETT
100 PAGES! NEW ADVENTURE!
APPROVED BY THE COMICS CODE AUTHORITY
DENNIS the MENACE
IN
25c No. 8
MEXICO

What's interesting is that at the time of Wiseman and Toole's visit, Hawaii was still a US territory and not a state. This is reflected on the cover of the first printing of the comicbook where it's simply stated as "100 pages! All new stories!" It's changed to "Congratulations 50th State" on the third printing when Hawaii officially became our 50th state on August 21, 1959. Later printings continued to acknowledge this fact as they cut content and page counts as the DENNIS THE MENACE GIANTS decreased in size from 100 to 68 pages.

By 1969, some of the material contained in the HAWAII issue was deemed either out-of-date or reprinted too many times that Fred Toole wrote a few new stories. Al Wiseman had moved on from the DENNIS series a couple of years earlier, so artist chores were handed over to the then-current DENNIS THE MENACE comicbook artist, Frank Hill. Hill was not sent to Hawaii like Toole and Wiseman and so Toole provided Hill with photo references.

By this time, it is estimated that all printings of the HAWAII book sold were around 4.5 million copies, making it one of the most successful comicbooks ever published. In fact, DENNIS IN HAWAII'S nine printings would easily rank in at #3 in this listing of the best-selling comic books of the Moden Era:

TOP 10 BEST-SELLING COMICBOOKS OF THE MODERN ERA:
Zap-Kapow Comics Posted August 28, 2014

10. THE WALKING DEAD #100 - 384,000 copies
9. THE AMAZING SPIDER-MAN #583 - 530,000 copies
8. THE AMAZING SPIDER-MAN #1 (2014) - 533,000 copies
7. DEATHMATE (Prologue, Blue, and Yellow) - 700,000 copies each
6. THE FANTASTIC FOUR #60 (1998) - 752,000 copies
5. SPAWN #1 - 1.7 million copies
4. SPIDER-MAN #1 (1990) - 2.5 million copies
3. SUPERMAN #75 (1987) - 3 million copies
2. X-FORCE #1 - 5 million copies

1. X-MEN #1 (1991) - 7.1 million copies

The DENNIS THE MENACE string on the Internet postulated this, "The regular circulation figure of 800,000 also bolsters my argument that DENNIS IN HAWAII is the all-time best-selling comic. If you calculate six or seven printings at 600,000 each (and I think that's waaaay conservative), that pushes HAWAII past three million. According to Carlson's research, WALT DISNEY'S COMICS AND STORIES peaked at 2.8 million in the 50s. No other regular title from the 40s to the 60s even cracked two million. By the end of the 60s, comic circulation had fallen off dramatically."

DENNIS THE MENACE was one of the biggest best-sellers of its era. Here is a list posted for the early 1960s:

MAD Magazine: 1,048,550
WALT DISNEY'S UNCLE SCROOGE: 1,040,543
WALT DISNEY'S COMICS AND STORIES: 1,004,901
WALT DISNEY'S DONALD DUCK: 930,613
SUPERMAN: 810,000
DENNIS THE MENACE: 800,000
BUGS BUNNY: 615,552
WALT DISNEY'S MICKEY MOUSE: 568,803
WOODY WOODPECKER: 537,773
BATMAN: 502,000
THE LONE RANGER: 408,711
CASPER THE FRIENDLY GHOST: 399,985
BLACKHAWK: 316,000

Here are some publishing notes and a guide to help identify the various printings of DENNIS IN HAWAII:

First Printing: Summer 1958, Pines Comics (Hallden Comics, Inc.). Indicia says DENNIS IN HAWAII. Banner at top of cover says "Dennis the Menace Giant Vacation Special" and box says "100 pages! All New Stories! Games! Puzzles! Songs!"

Second Printing: Most likely occurred during the same summer with no notations on it to distinguish it from a first printing. Both first and second printings were published prior to Hawaii becoming a state on August 21, 1959 and both published by Pines. It is also possible that DENNIS THE MENACE GIANT CHRISTMAS ISSUE #6, Winter 1958, could actually be the second printing.

Third Printing: Summer 1959, Hallden Publications, Inc. Same as first printing but banner at top of cover reads "3rd Large Printing" and box reads "Congratulations, 50th State" and published in conjunction with Hawaii becoming a state. This and all subsequent printings are by Hallden. The Pines logo is replaced with a Hallden logo featuring Dennis's head.

Fourth Printing: Summer 1960, Hallden Fawcett (Hallden Publications, Inc.). Same as first printing but banner at top reads "4th Large Printing" and box reads "Congratulations, 50th State."

Fifth Printing: Summer 1962, Hallden Fawcett (Hallden Publications, Inc.). Same as first printing but banner at top reads "5th Large Printing" and box reads "Congratulations, 50th State". This is the final printing as issue #6. The 6th printing is DENNIS THE MENACE GIANT #18, Summer 1963.)

5th Large Printing
APPROVED BY THE COMICS CODE AUTHORITY
Dennis IN HAWAII
25c No. 6
Congratulations, 50th State

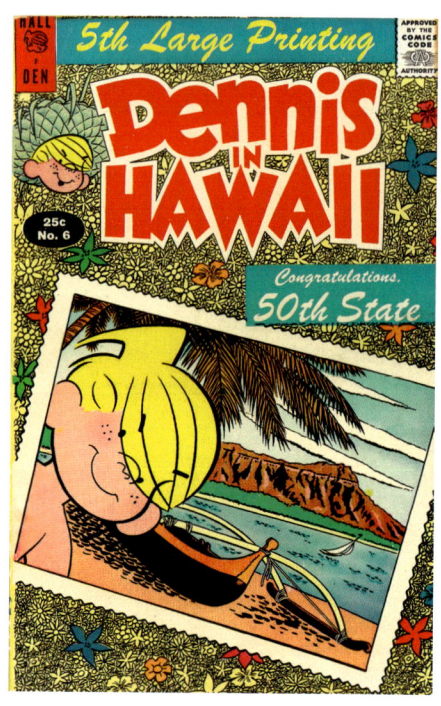

Sixth Printing: DENNIS THE MENACE IN HAWAII #18, Summer 1963, Hallden Fawcett (Hallden Publications, Inc.). Cover: Dennis is on a postcard from Hawaii. Subtitle: "6th Large Printing" and box reads "Congratulations, 50th State".

Seventh Printing: DENNIS THE MENACE IN HAWAII #30, Summer 1965, Fawcett Publications, Inc., last 100-page edition. Cover: Dennis is on a postcard from Hawaii. Blurbs: "7th Large Printing" and "1965" and a caption box reads "A Visit to The "Aloha" State."

Eighth Printing: DENNIS THE MENACE IN HAWAII #68, Summer 1969, Fawcett Publications, Inc., first 68-page edition. Cover: Dennis hides behind a tiki. Writer: Fred Toole; artist: Frank Hill

DENNIS THE MENACE BONUS MAGAZINE SERIES
FAWCETT
DENNIS the MENACE
1973
35c
06528
By HANK KETCHAM
IN HAWAII

MAGAZINE SERIES #114 (DENNIS THE MENACE IN HAWAII), March 1973, Fawcett Publications, Inc., 68 pages. Cover: Dennis dances the hula with a lei and a skirt. Writer: Fred Toole; artist: Frank Hill

There were two later DENNIS THE MENACE IN HAWAII issues where he visits Maui (BONUS MAGAZINE #174, March 1978) and Kauai (BONUS MAGAZINE #190, June 1979), both written by Toole and illustrated by Bill Williams. These issues fall outside the scope of the original DENNIS IN HAWAII issue, as they feature no reprints from any previous HAWAII edition.

The HAWAII issue is one of the reasons why DENNIS collecting can get frustrating: the numbering of the DENNIS THE MENACE GIANT issues is kind of wonky. This, coupled with the fact that DENNIS'S publishing imprint changed from Pines to Hallden Fawcett. This is why there are two GIANT #6s: a Hawaii and a Christmas issue. HAWAII was kind of its own thing after a while, while the GIANTS continued to be reserved for Vacation and Christmas issues.

The success of DENNIS IN HAWAII led to DENNIS IN MEXICO, DENNIS GOES TO HOLLYWOOD, DENNIS GOES TO CAMP and countless regular issues where Dennis visits many California destinations such as Solvang, Santa's Village, Frontier Village, Marine World, Marineland, Winchester Mystery House, The Exploratorium, Great America, the Dennis the Menace Playground and many, many more. Sadly, many of these destinations are long gone, but they live on in the pages of DENNIS THE MENACE comics. Fortunately, Hawaii is still around.

Note: This Introduction is composed of excerpts from Mark Arnold's book POCKET FULL OF DENNIS, published by BearManor Media in 2017, with some additional comments. Mark Arnold is an animation and comicbook historian who has written books about TTV (Underdog), Harvey Comics, Archie Comics, DFE (Pink Panther), The Beatles, and CRACKED MAGAZINE. He is currently working on a book about The Monkees and a book about Harvey Comics artist Warren Kremer.

F06528 1978 / 35c
DENNIS THE MENACE ★ BIG BONUS SERIES
Dennis the Menace
by HANK KETCHAM
in HAWAII
MAUI

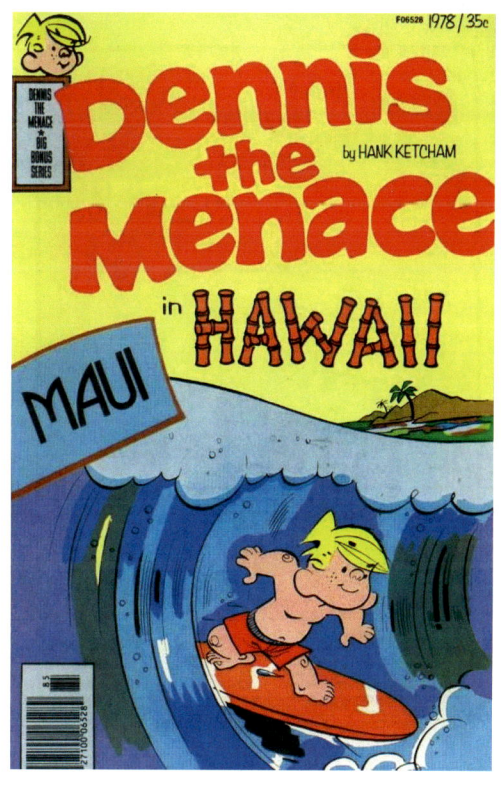

Star-Bulletin

1956 ★ PAGE 13

Dennis the Menace To Try Isle Imping

Hawaii will hit the comic book stands sometime next year via the adventures of the persistently incorrigible Dennis the Menace.

Fred Toole and Al Wiseman, writer and cartoonist of the nation's largest selling single comic book, are here for two weeks gathering background material for the little imp's adventures.

Hank Ketcham, creator of the cartoon which appears exclusively in Hawaii in the Star-Bulletin, recently surprised the duo with round-trip tickets for the trip.

Ketcham was here last year and thought this locale would make a good setting for the comic.

SELLS OVER A MILLION

Toole and Wiseman have been with Ketcham for four and one-half years producing the 100 page comic book which sells about 1¼ million copies each issue.

Last year at the 50th anniversary of the Boys Clubs of America, the book was given an award for providing consistently wholesome entertainment.

Toole, who dreams up Dennis the Menace comic situations, has no children himself but admits he can turn out the copy easily "being a child at heart myself."

Wiseman has a seven-year-old son, whom he claims resembled the famed cartoon child "until he started growing new teeth."

Both men, accompanied by their wives, are staying at the Hawaiian Village on their first Island trip.

Today they are leaving for a tour of Kauai and Hawaii.

Having found the Islands a fertile place for brain-storms, they expect to remain until September 3 or 4.

Volunteer Helpers Needed This Week

Registration Aides: Temporary registration aides are needed starting September 6.

Clerical Help: Clerical Aides for stamping, stuffing and sorting can find work immediately.

Phone or visit the Volunteer Service Bureau, 420 South Hotel Street.

Star-Bulletin Photo

Hawaii imps Glen Higuchi, left, and Roddy Lee, menace Fred Toole, right, staff writer for Dennis the Menace, while cartoonist Al Wiseman captures event on paper.

Racing Cars Force Policeman Off Street Into Lamp Post

In the fight between speeders and the police, yesterday's score stood at:

One police car wrecked.

One speeder's car wrecked.

Sergeant Francis K. Apoliona of the Patrol Division told investigators, after his car smashed into a lamp post on Dole Street, that two speeding autos were bearing down on him from the opposite direction at 2:45 a.m.

Sergeant Apoliona said the cars were racing side by side.

The officer, who was off-duty, said he had intentions of turning around and giving chase, but his car went up the curbing and butted the post.

He was treated at Emergency Hospital for bruises on his knee and chest and then released to his home.

The speeding cars got away.

Earlier, at 12:35 a.m., Motor Patrolman William Funn gave chase to a car he observed traveling at high speed on Ala Moana.

Officer Funn chased the car along the waterfront and up Nuuanu Avenue to Kuakini Street, where the fleeing auto went out of control while turning and crashed into a parked car.

The driver, Harold T. Uchima, 1156 19th Avenue, was booked for reckless driving and sent to the Detention Home.

Damage to his car was placed at $900 and another $200 to the parked car owned by Dr. Herbert Dang, 32 South Kuakini Street.

Above: A newspaper article reporting on Al and Fred's fact-finding mission to Hawaii, in preparation for writing and drawing the DENNIS IN HAWAII comic. From *The Honolulu Star-Bulletin* August 27, 1956. (Courtesy of Jim and Teresa Wiseman.)

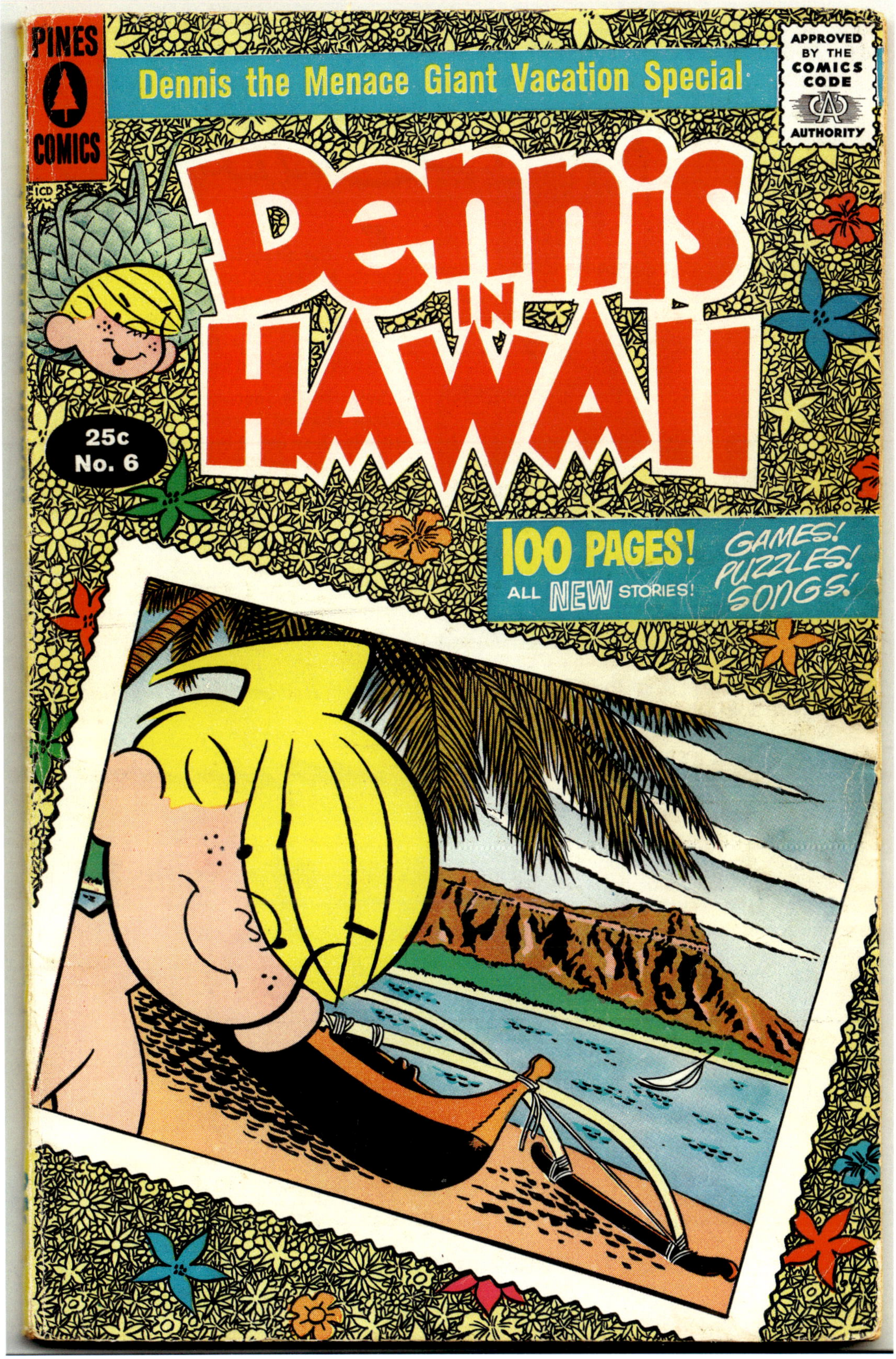
PINES COMICS
Dennis the Menace Giant Vacation Special
APPROVED BY THE COMICS CODE AUTHORITY
Dennis in Hawaii
25c
No. 6
100 PAGES!
ALL NEW STORIES!
GAMES! PUZZLES! SONGS!

ALOHA!

*F*or the first time in the history of comic books, an artist-writer team has been sent "on location" to gather authentic material. This book is the result of a special trip to the Hawaiian Islands by artist Al Wiseman and writer Fred Toole.

Their on-the-spot sketches, photos, and notes enabled them to draw and write this book as could only be done by people who had actually visited the Islands.

I hope you will agree with me that their trip has resulted in one of the most beautiful and entertaining comic books **ever** published.

Robert M. Hall

Robert M. Hall, President
Hallden Publications, Inc.

*A*nxious to get to the "Paradise of the Pacific", writer Fred Toole lends a hand as artist Al Wiseman tries to start their plane.

*F*red and Al get ideas from a pair of native Hawaiian "menaces". The team reported that, even more impressive than the beautiful scenery and lovely climate, was the wonderfully warm hospitality and friendliness of the Hawaiian people.

DENNIS IN HAWAII, a magazine published and copyright 1958 by Hallden Publications, Inc., 163 Pratt Street, Meriden, Conn. All rights reserved. Names of all characters used in cartoons, stories and articles are fictitious. If the name of any living person or existing institution is used, it is a coincidence. Summer, 1958. PRINTED IN THE U.S.A.

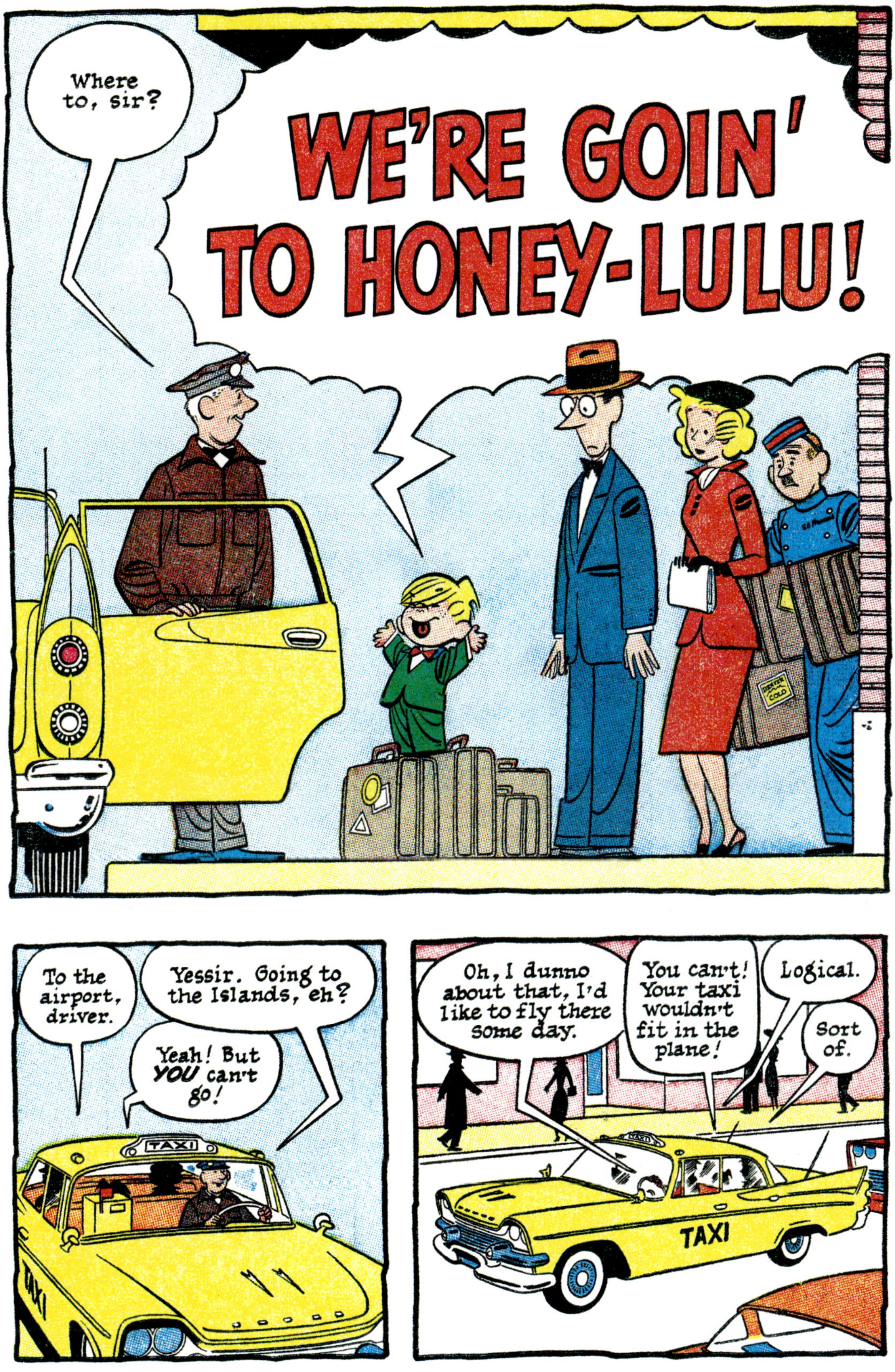
Where to, sir?
WE'RE GOIN' TO HONEY-LULU!
To the airport, driver.
Yessir. Going to the Islands, eh?
Yeah! But YOU can't go!
TAXI
TAXI
Oh, I dunno about that, I'd like to fly there some day.
You can't! Your taxi wouldn't fit in the plane!
Logical.
Sort of.
TAXI
TAXI

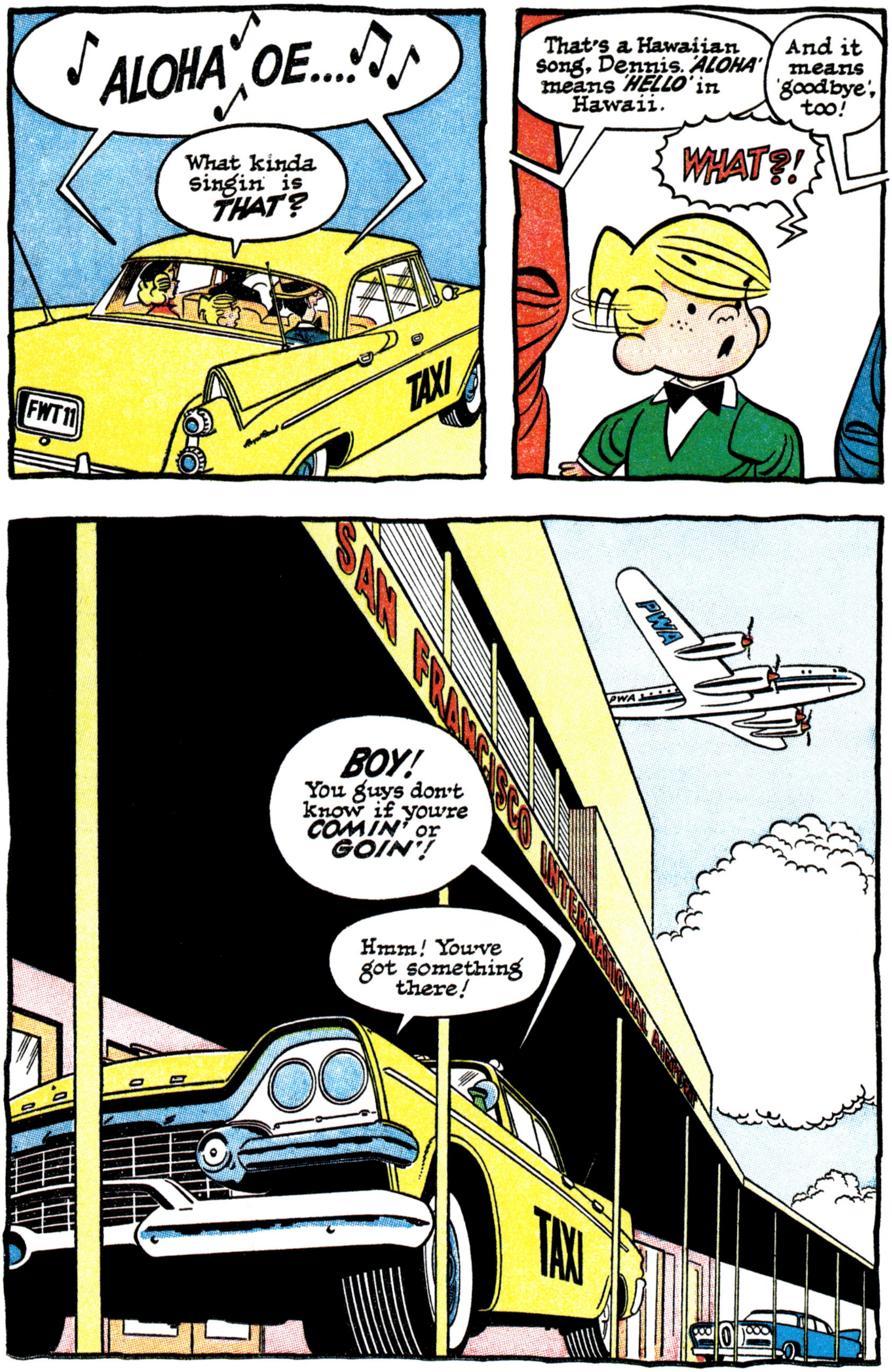
ALOHA OE....!
What kinda singin' is THAT?
That's a Hawaiian song, Dennis. 'ALOHA' means 'HELLO' in Hawaii.
And it means 'goodbye', too!
WHAT?!
TAXI
FWT 11
SAN FRANCISCO INTERNATIONAL AIRPORT
PWA
BOY! You guys don't know if you're COMIN' or GOIN'!
Hmm! You've got something there!
TAXI

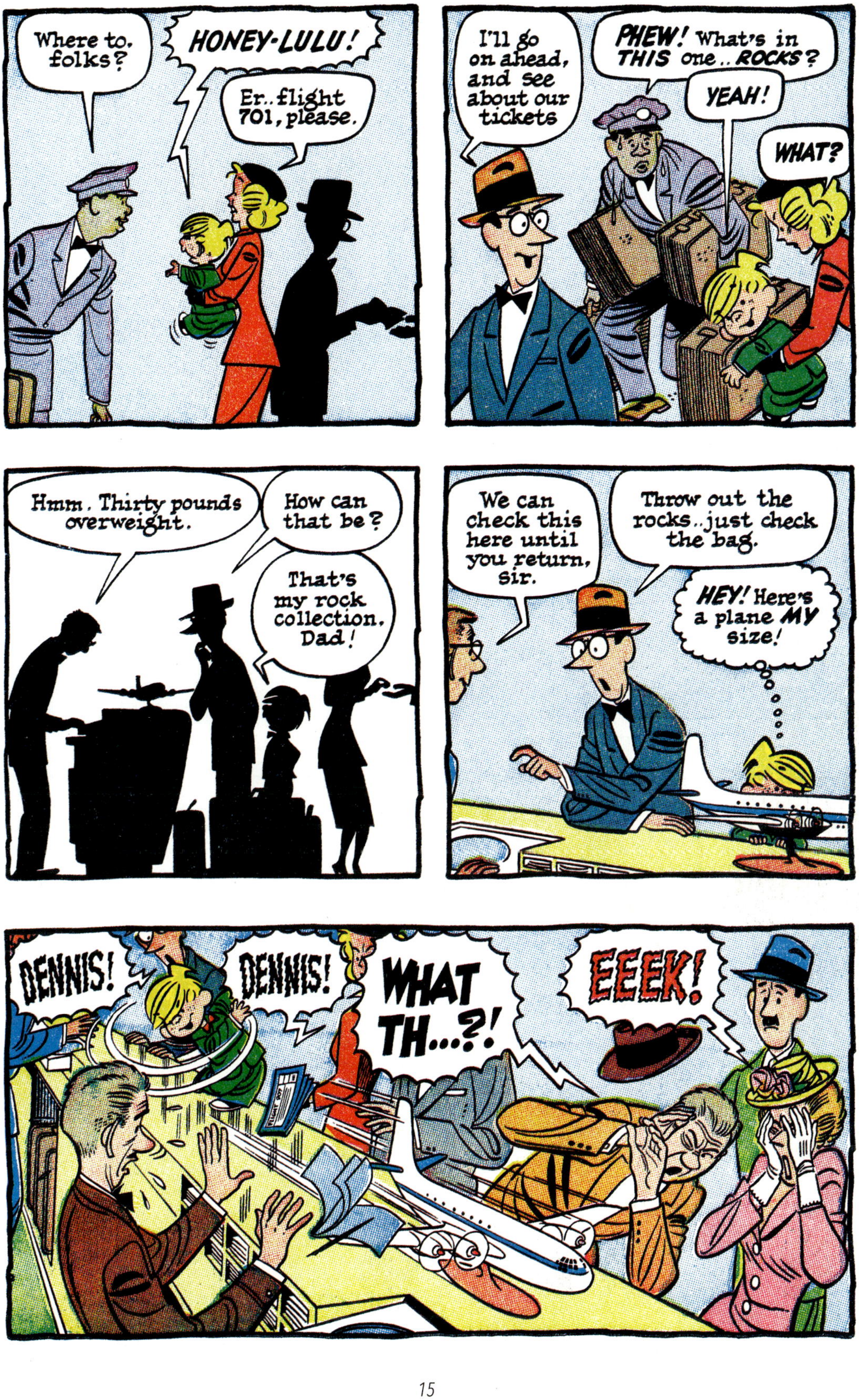
Where to, folks?
HONEY-LULU!
Er.. flight 701, please.
I'll go on ahead, and see about our tickets
PHEW! What's in THIS one.. ROCKS?
YEAH!
WHAT?
Hmm. Thirty pounds overweight.
How can that be?
That's my rock collection, Dad!
We can check this here until you return, sir.
Throw out the rocks.. just check the bag.
HEY! Here's a plane MY size!
DENNIS!
DENNIS!
WHAT TH...?!
EEEK!

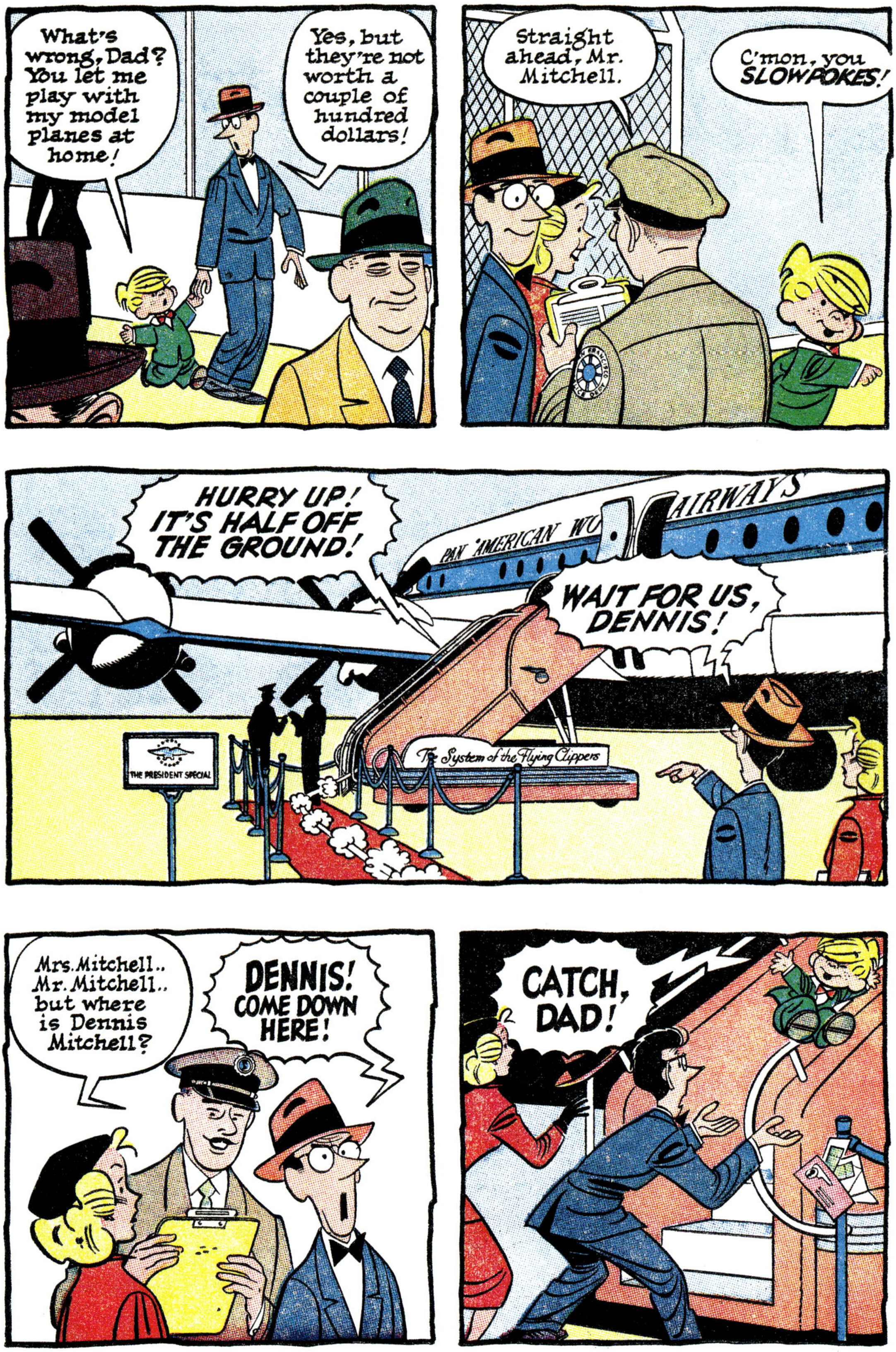
What's wrong, Dad? You let me play with my model planes at home!
Yes, but they're not worth a couple of hundred dollars!
Straight ahead, Mr. Mitchell.
C'mon, you SLOWPOKES!
HURRY UP! IT'S HALF OFF THE GROUND!
AIRWAYS
WAIT FOR US, DENNIS!
The System of the Flying Clippers
THE PRESIDENT SPECIAL
Mrs. Mitchell.. Mr. Mitchell.. but where is Dennis Mitchell?
DENNIS! COME DOWN HERE!
CATCH, DAD!

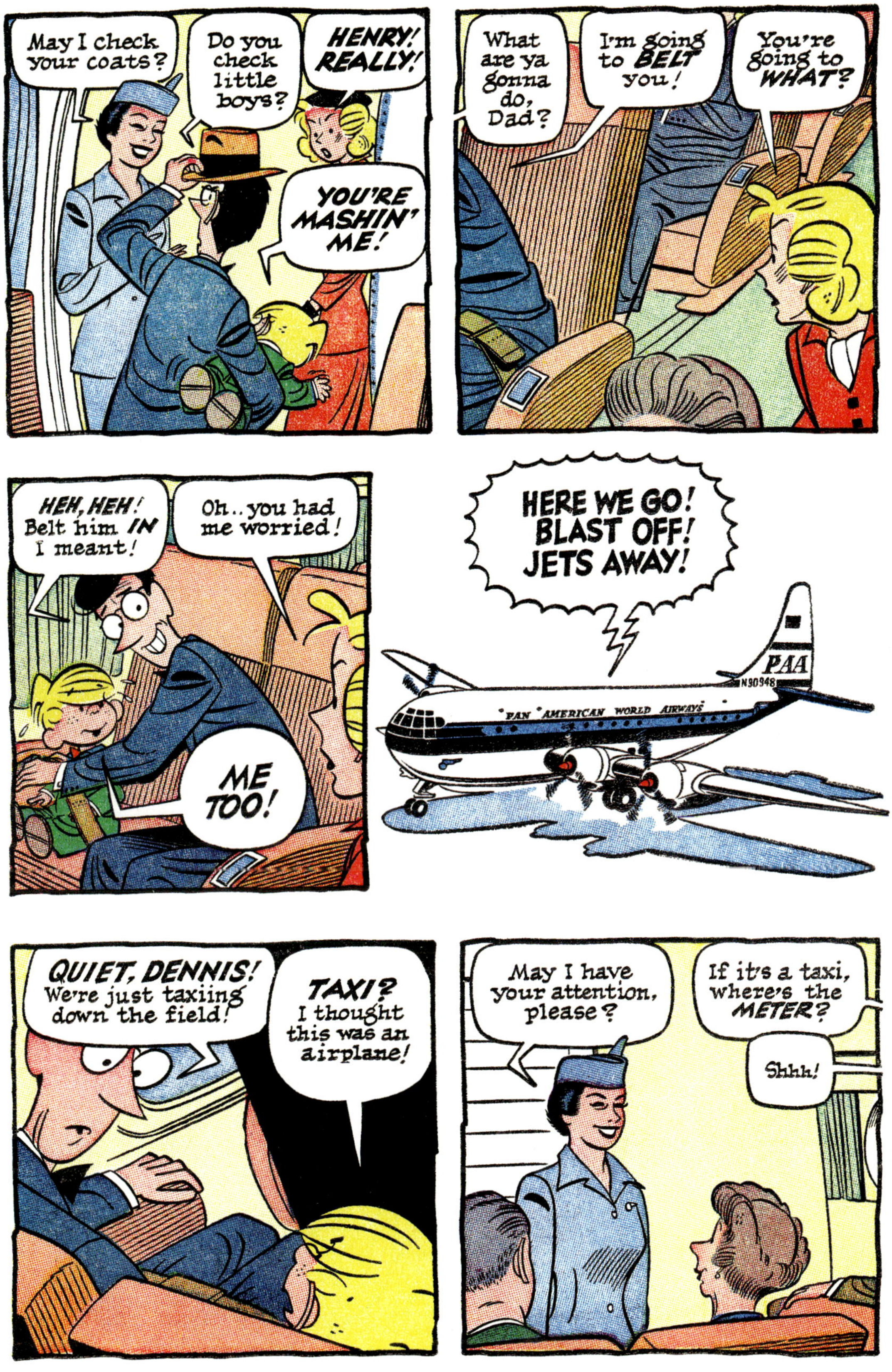
May I check your coats?
Do you check little boys?
HENRY! REALLY!
YOU'RE MASHIN' ME!
What are ya gonna do, Dad?
I'm going to BELT you!
You're going to WHAT?
HEH, HEH! Belt him IN I meant!
Oh.. you had me worried!
ME TOO!
HERE WE GO! BLAST OFF! JETS AWAY!
PAA
N90948
PAN AMERICAN WORLD AIRWAYS
QUIET, DENNIS! We're just taxiing down the field!
TAXI? I thought this was an airplane!
May I have your attention, please?
If it's a taxi, where's the METER?
Shhh!

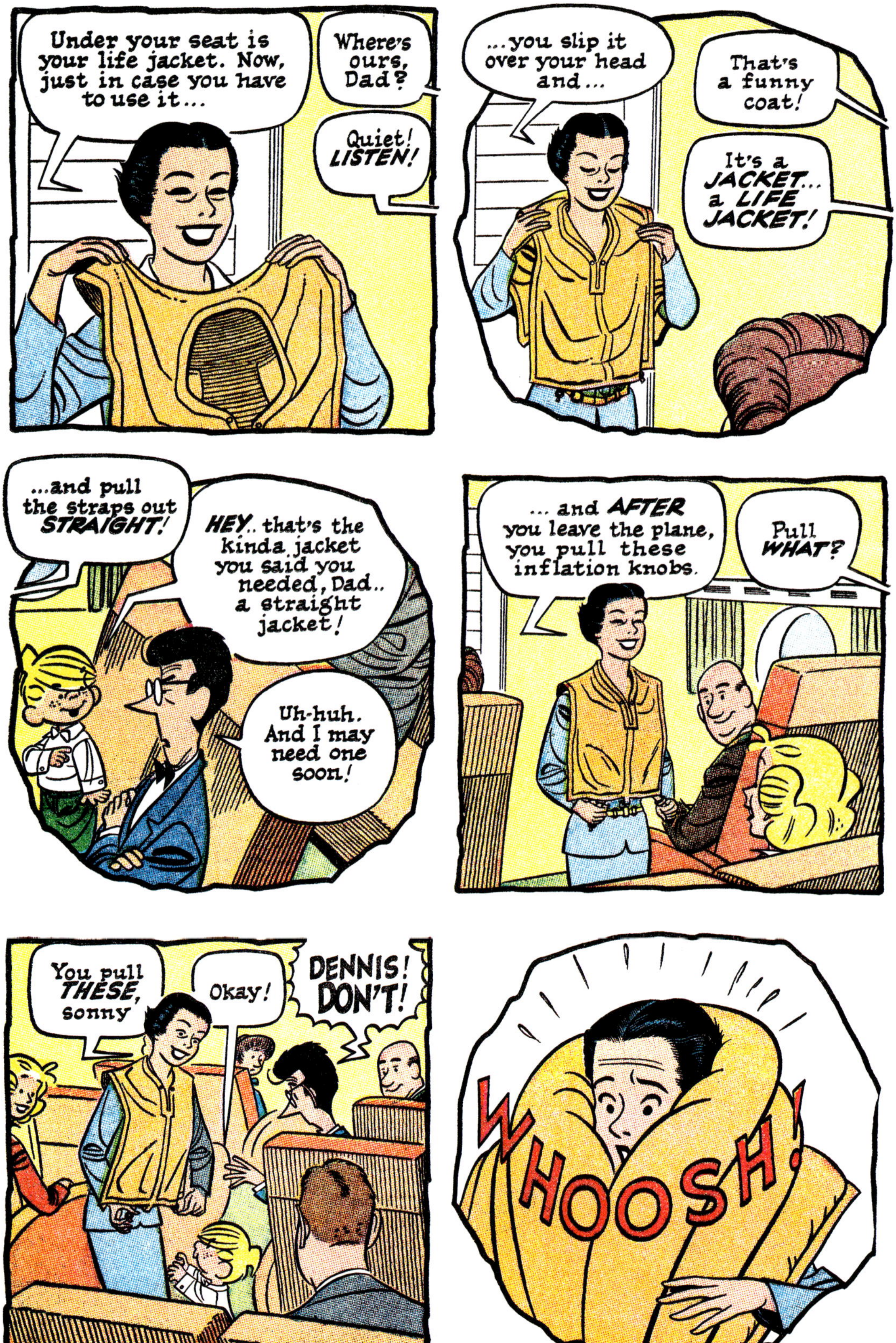
Under your seat is your life jacket. Now, just in case you have to use it...
Where's ours, Dad?
Quiet! LISTEN!
...you slip it over your head and...
That's a funny coat!
It's a JACKET... a LIFE JACKET!
...and pull the straps out STRAIGHT!
HEY.. that's the kinda jacket you said you needed, Dad.. a straight jacket!
Uh-huh. And I may need one soon!
... and AFTER you leave the plane, you pull these inflation knobs.
Pull WHAT?
You pull THESE, sonny
Okay!
DENNIS! DON'T!
WHOOSH!

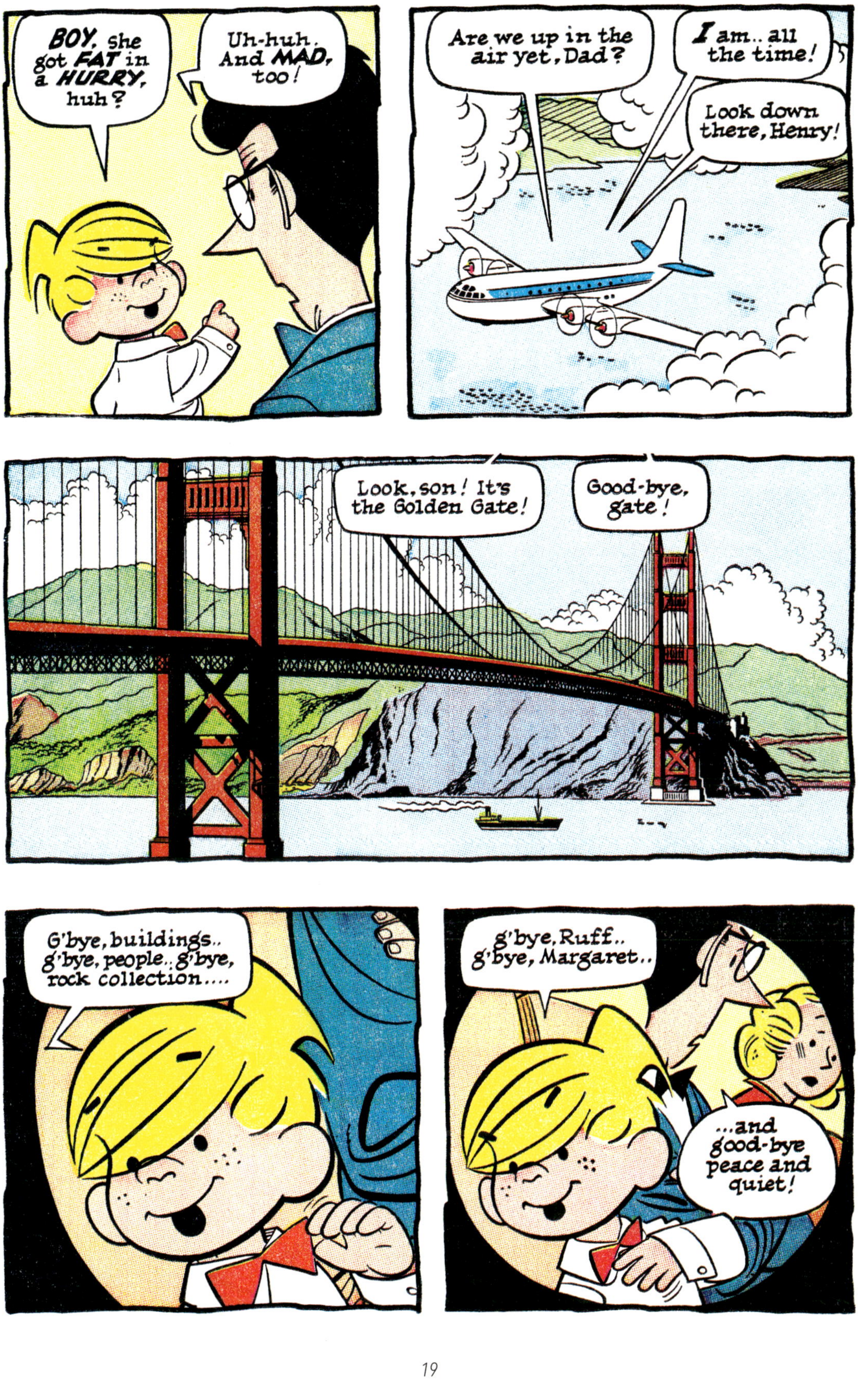
BOY, she got FAT in a HURRY, huh?
Uh-huh. And MAD, too!
Are we up in the air yet, Dad?
I am.. all the time!
Look down there, Henry!
Look, son! It's the Golden Gate!
Good-bye, gate!
G'bye, buildings.. g'bye, people.. g'bye, rock collection....
g'bye, Ruff.. g'bye, Margaret..
...and good-bye peace and quiet!

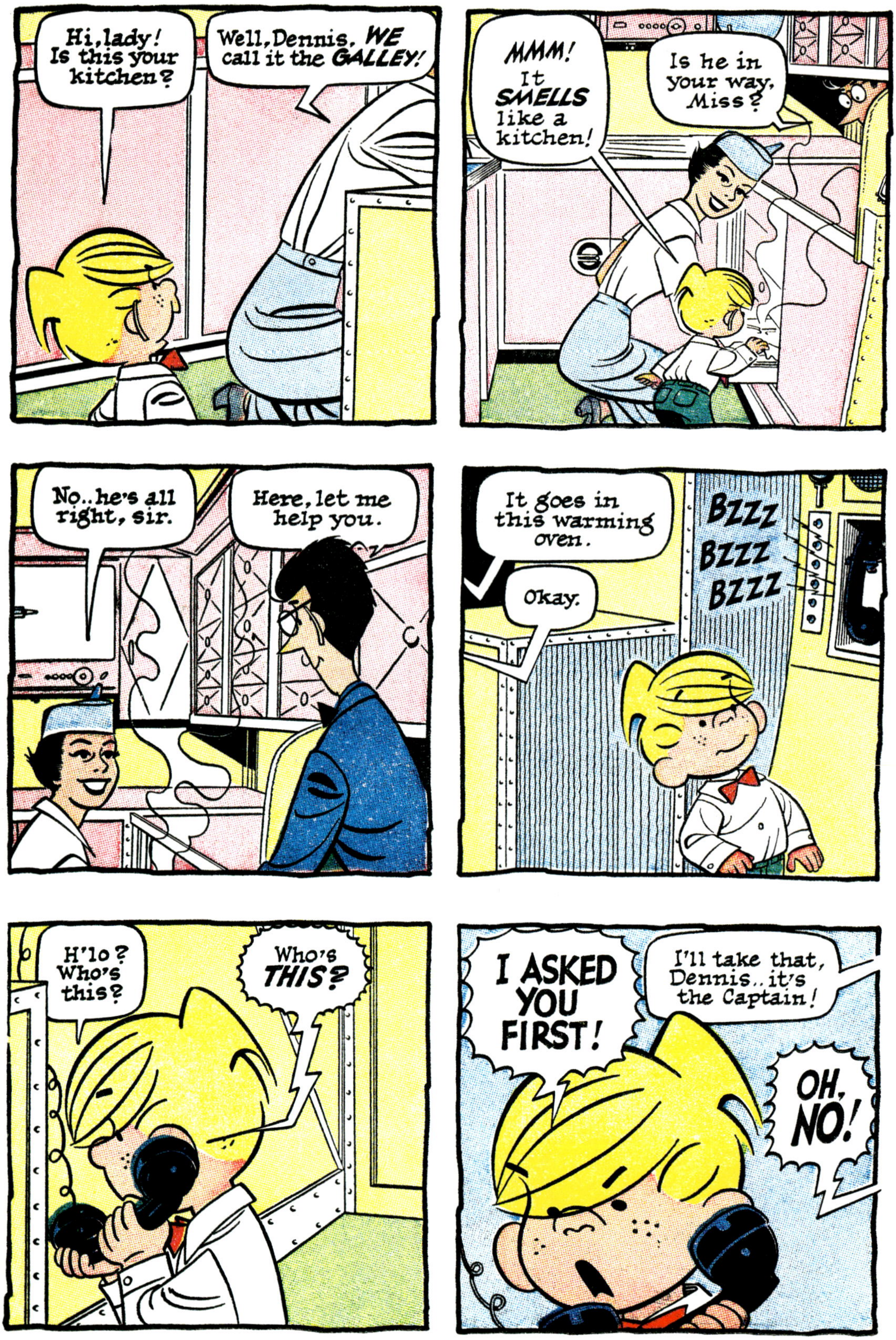
Hi, lady! Is this your kitchen?
Well, Dennis, WE call it the GALLEY!
MMM! It SMELLS like a kitchen!
Is he in your way, Miss?
No.. he's all right, sir.
Here, let me help you.
It goes in this warming oven.
Okay.
BZZZ
BZZZ
BZZZ
H'lo? Who's this?
Who's THIS?
I ASKED YOU FIRST!
I'll take that, Dennis.. it's the Captain!
OH, NO!

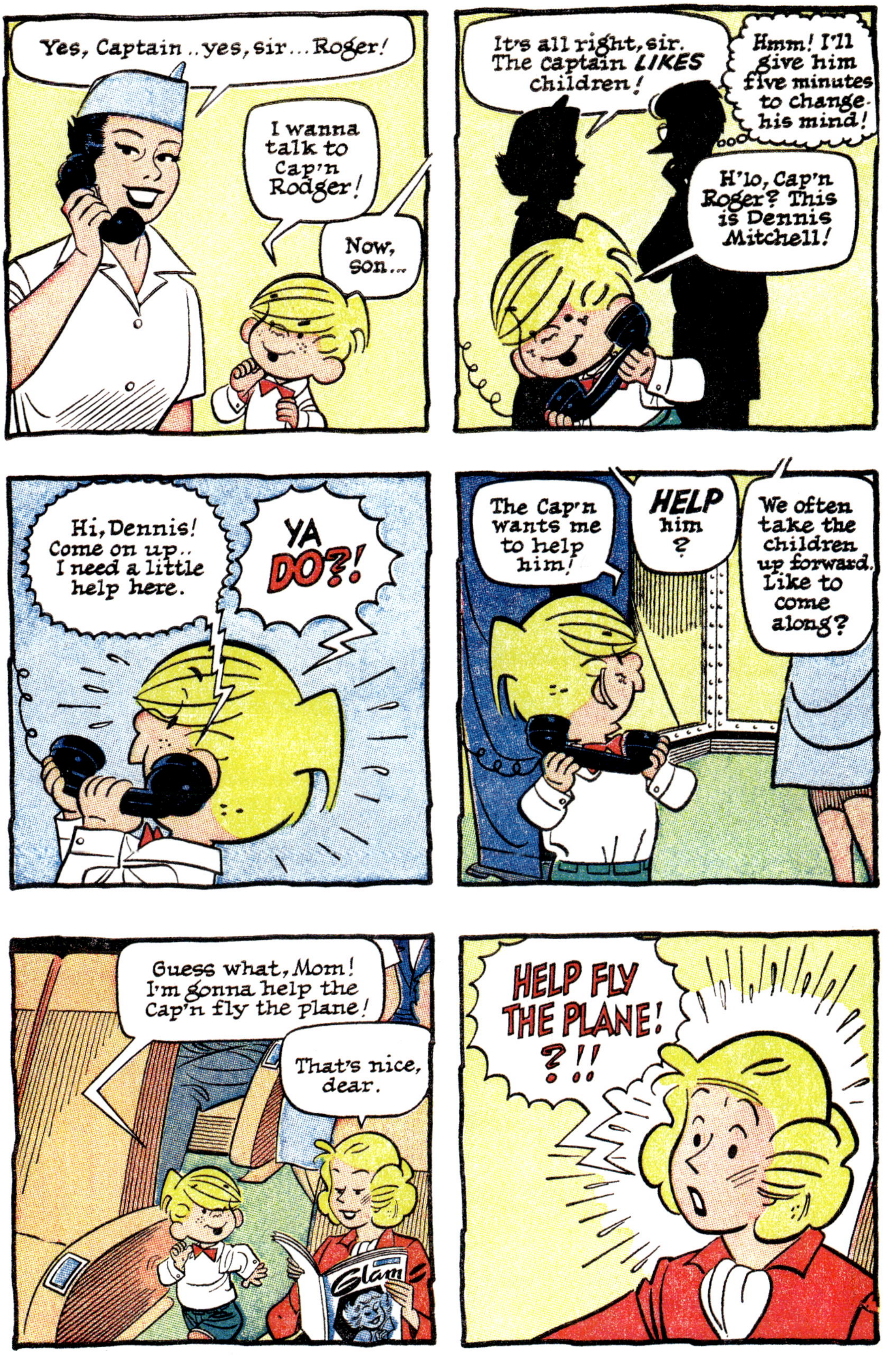
Yes, Captain .. yes, sir... Roger!
I wanna talk to Cap'n Rodger!
Now, son...
It's all right, sir. The captain LIKES children!
Hmm! I'll give him five minutes to change his mind!
H'lo, Cap'n Roger? This is Dennis Mitchell!
Hi, Dennis! Come on up.. I need a little help here.
YA DO?!
The Cap'n wants me to help him!
HELP him?
We often take the children up forward. Like to come along?
Guess what, Mom! I'm gonna help the Cap'n fly the plane!
That's nice, dear.
Glam
HELP FLY THE PLANE! ?!!

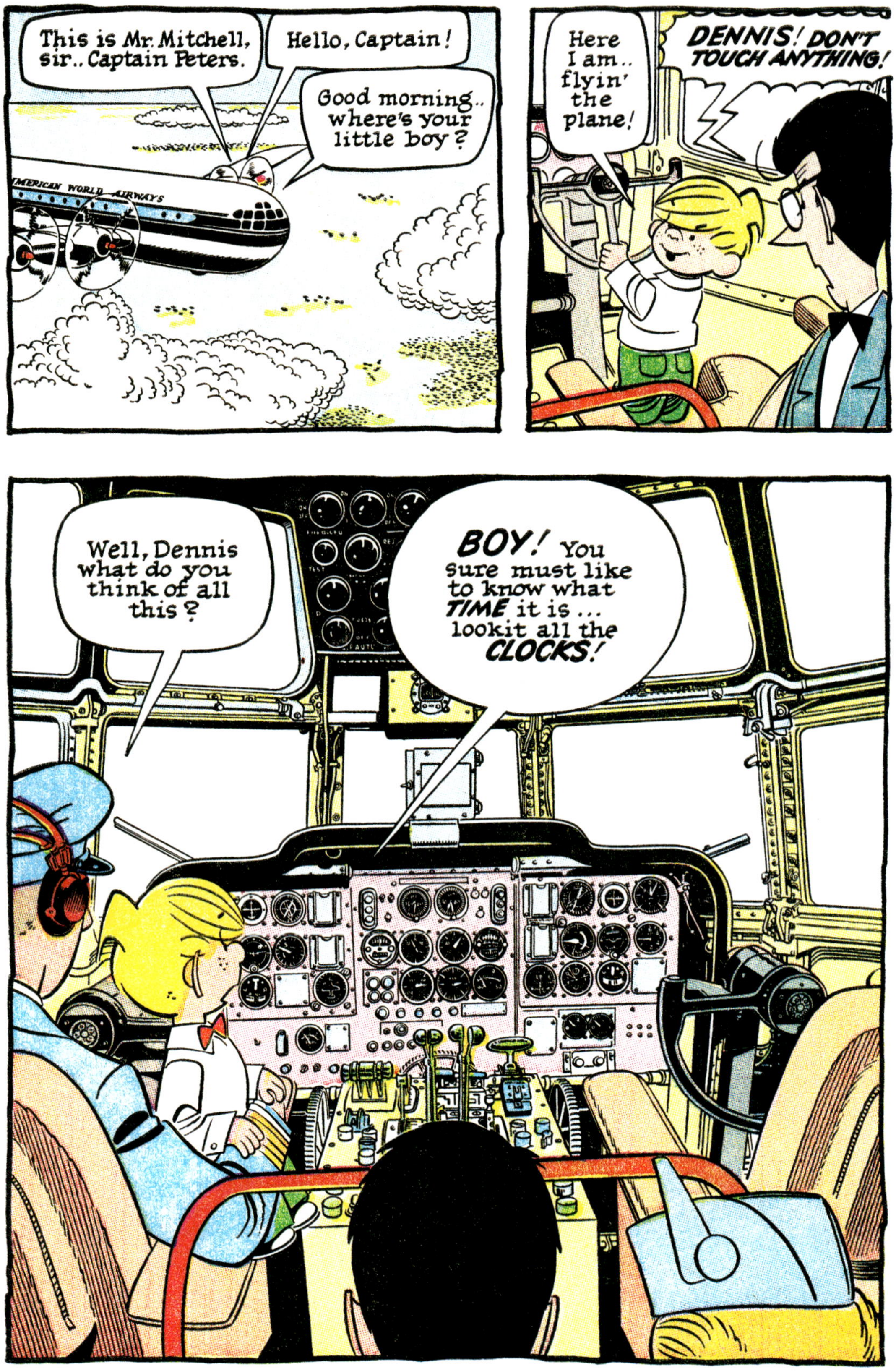
This is Mr. Mitchell, sir.. Captain Peters.
Hello, Captain!
Good morning.. where's your little boy?
Here I am.. flyin' the plane!
DENNIS! DON'T TOUCH ANYTHING!
Well, Dennis what do you think of all this?
BOY! You sure must like to know what TIME it is... lookit all the CLOCKS!

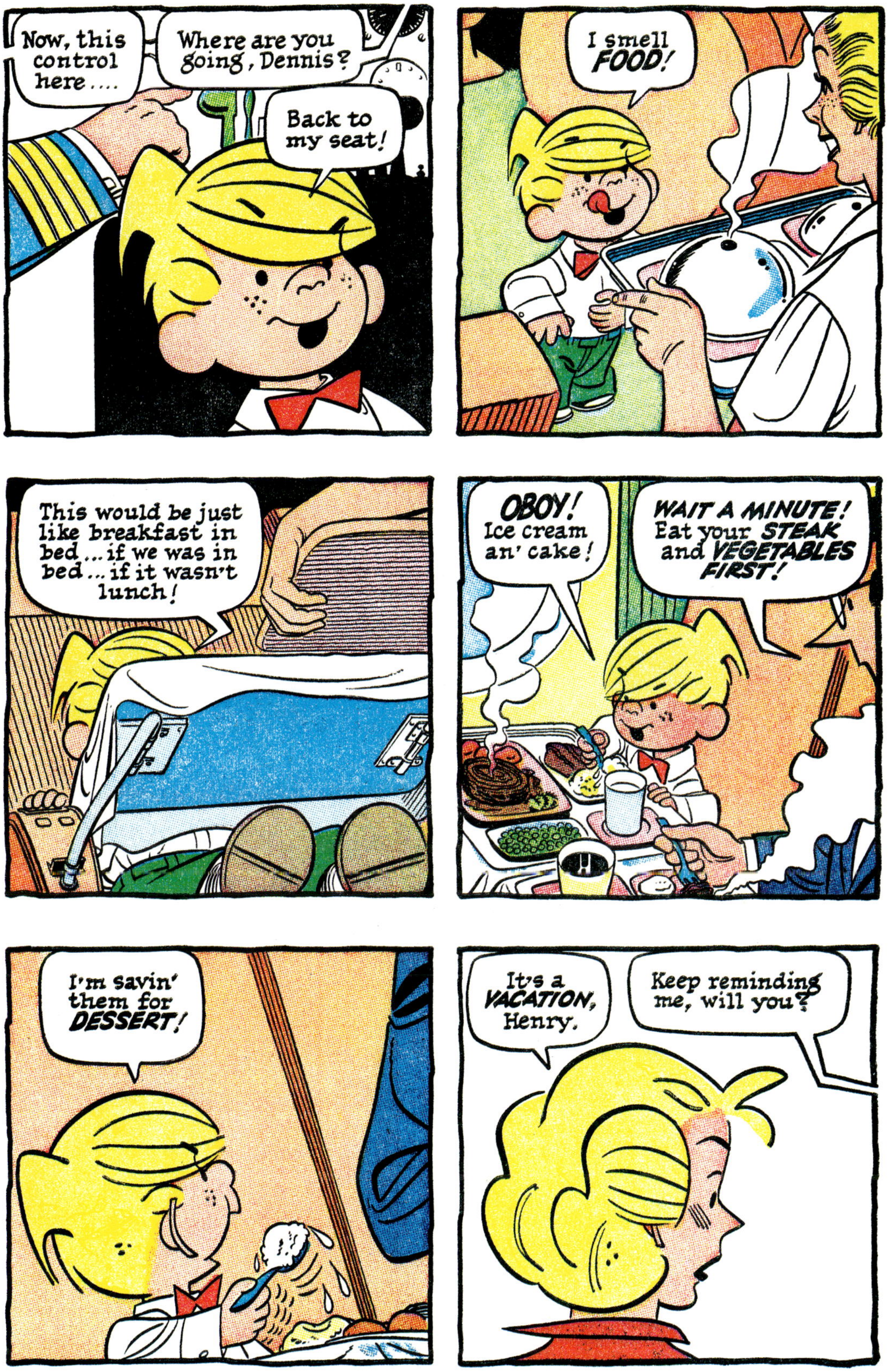
Now, this control here....
Where are you going, Dennis?
Back to my seat!
I smell FOOD!
This would be just like breakfast in bed...if we was in bed...if it wasn't lunch!
OBOY! Ice cream an' cake!
WAIT A MINUTE! Eat your STEAK and VEGETABLES FIRST!
I'm savin' them for DESSERT!
It's a VACATION, Henry.
Keep reminding me, will you?

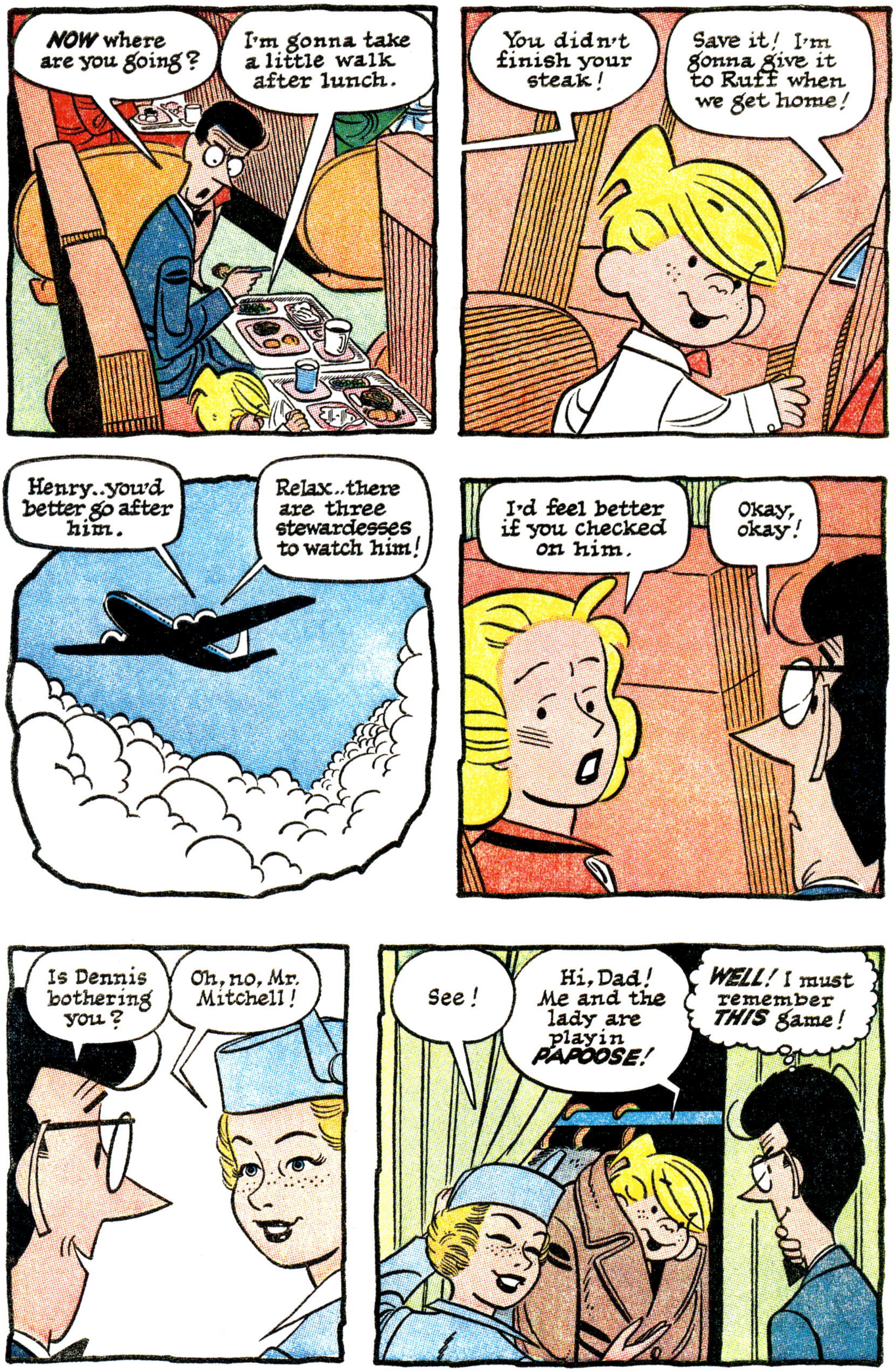

NOW where are you going?
I'm gonna take a little walk after lunch.
You didn't finish your steak!
Save it! I'm gonna give it to Ruff when we get home!
Henry..you'd better go after him.
Relax..there are three stewardesses to watch him!
I'd feel better if you checked on him.
Okay, okay!
Is Dennis bothering you?
Oh, no, Mr. Mitchell!
See!
Hi, Dad! Me and the lady are playin PAPOOSE!
WELL! I must remember THIS game!

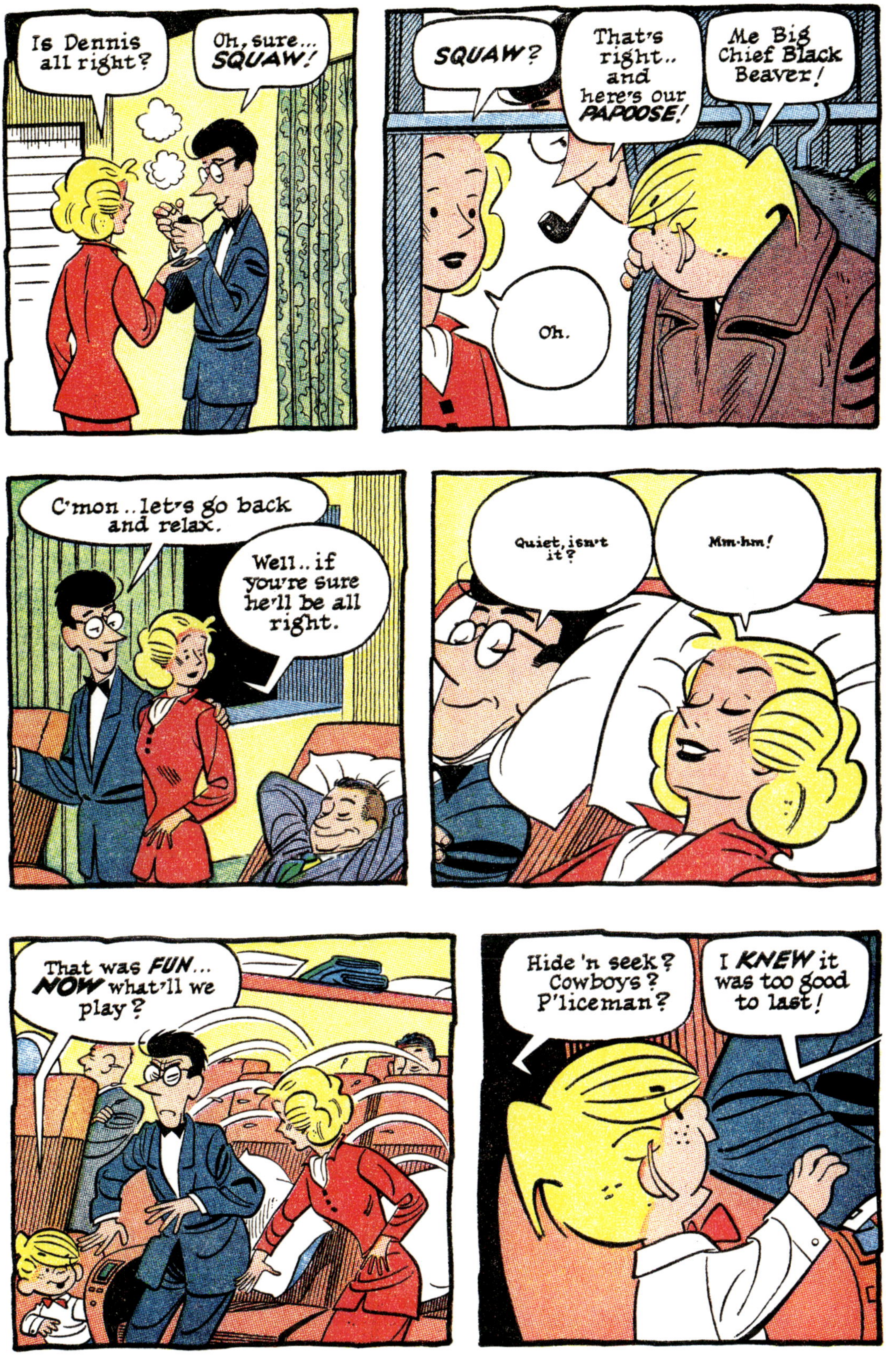
Is Dennis all right?
Oh, sure... SQUAW!
SQUAW?
That's right.. and here's our PAPOOSE!
Me Big Chief Black Beaver!
Oh.
C'mon .. let's go back and relax.
Well .. if you're sure he'll be all right.
Quiet, isn't it?
Mm-hm!
That was FUN... NOW what'll we play?
Hide 'n seek? Cowboys? P'liceman?
I KNEW it was too good to last!

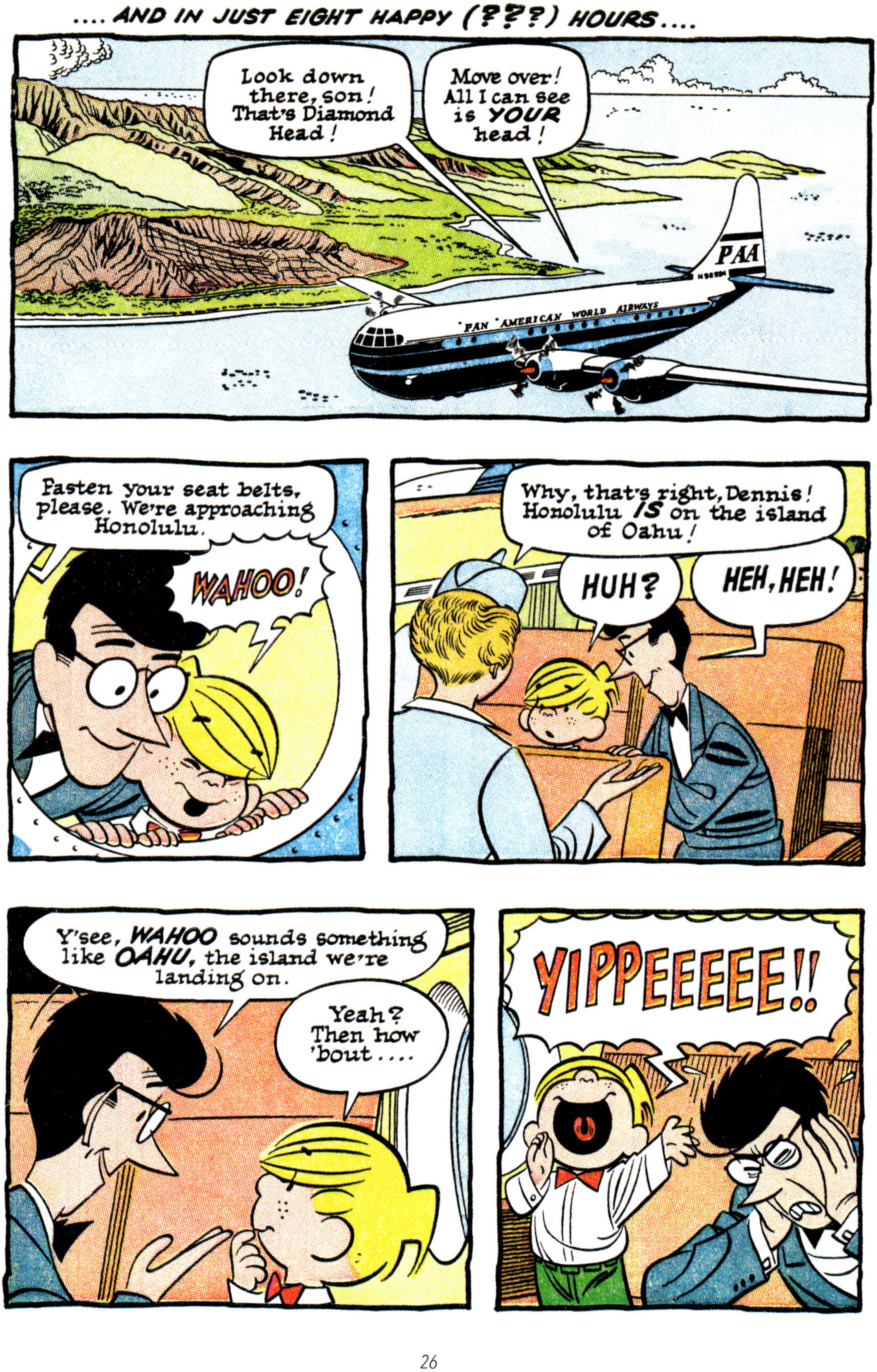
....AND IN JUST EIGHT HAPPY (???) HOURS....
Look down there, son! That's Diamond Head!
Move over! All I can see is YOUR head!
PAA
PAN AMERICAN WORLD AIRWAYS
Fasten your seat belts, please. We're approaching Honolulu.
WAHOO!
Why, that's right, Dennis! Honolulu IS on the island of Oahu!
HUH?
HEH, HEH!
Y'see, WAHOO sounds something like OAHU, the island we're landing on.
Yeah? Then how 'bout....
YIPPEEEEE!!

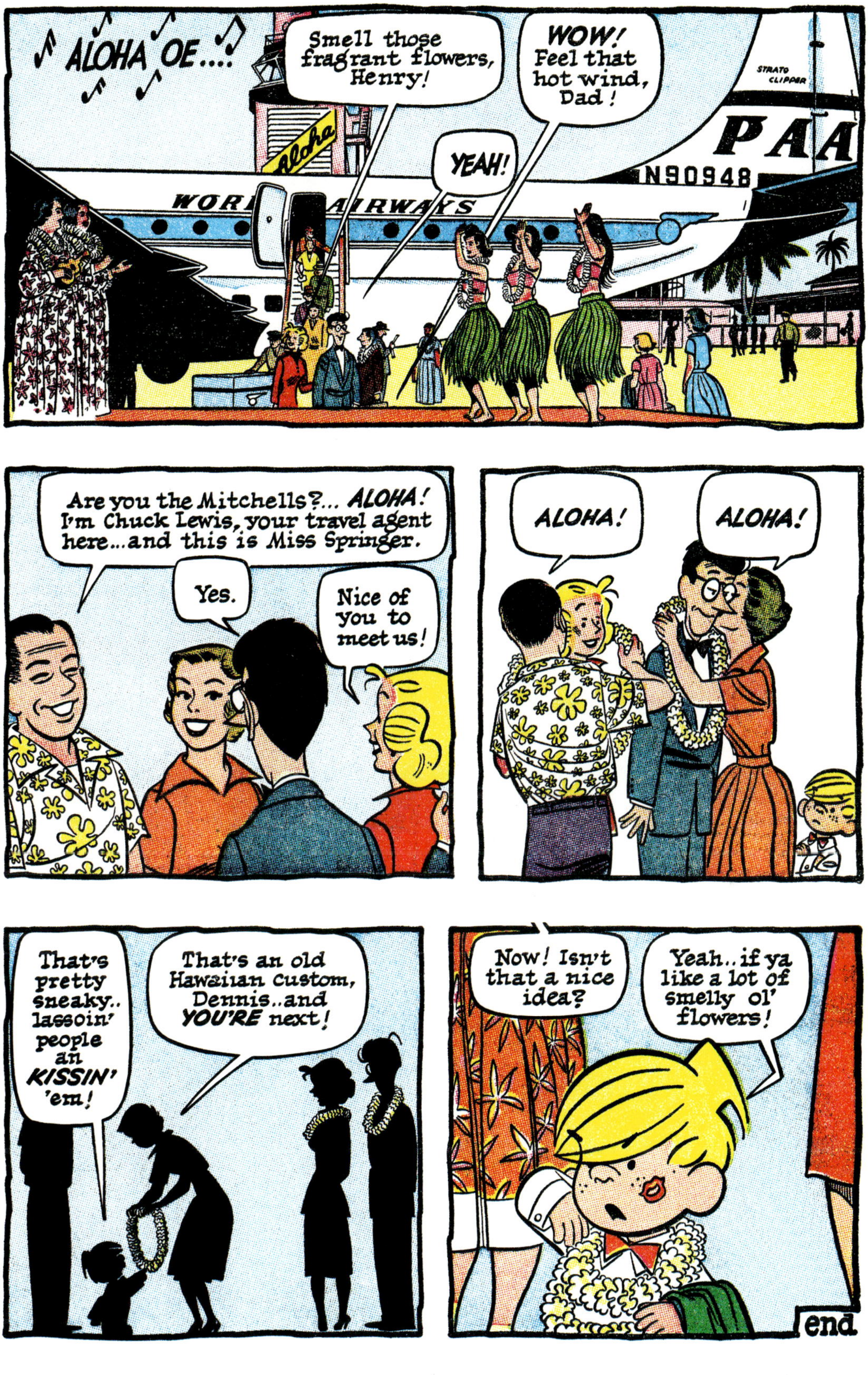
ALOHA OE...!
Smell those fragrant flowers, Henry!
WOW! Feel that hot wind, Dad!
YEAH!
STRATO CLIPPER
PAA
N90948
Aloha
Are you the Mitchells?... ALOHA! I'm Chuck Lewis, your travel agent here...and this is Miss Springer.
Yes.
Nice of you to meet us!
ALOHA!
ALOHA!
That's pretty sneaky.. lassoin' people an KISSIN' 'em!
That's an old Hawaiian custom, Dennis..and YOU'RE next!
Now! Isn't that a nice idea?
Yeah.. if ya like a lot of smelly ol' flowers!
end

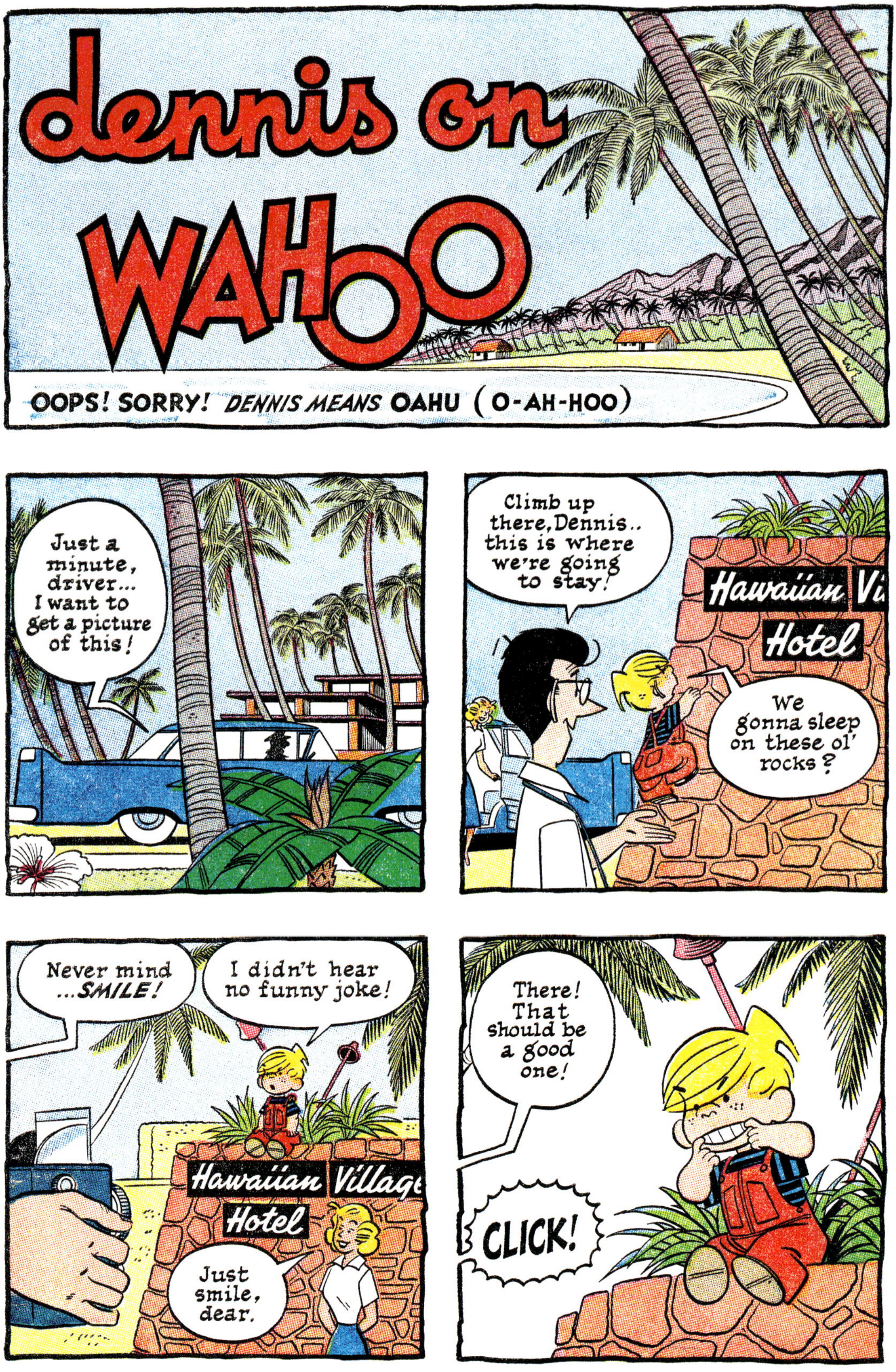
dennis on WAHOO
OOPS! SORRY! DENNIS MEANS OAHU (O-AH-HOO)
Just a minute, driver... I want to get a picture of this!
Climb up there, Dennis.. this is where we're going to stay!
Hawaiian Vi
Hotel
We gonna sleep on these ol' rocks?
Never mind ...SMILE!
I didn't hear no funny joke!
Hawaiian Village
Hotel
Just smile, dear.
There! That should be a good one!
CLICK!

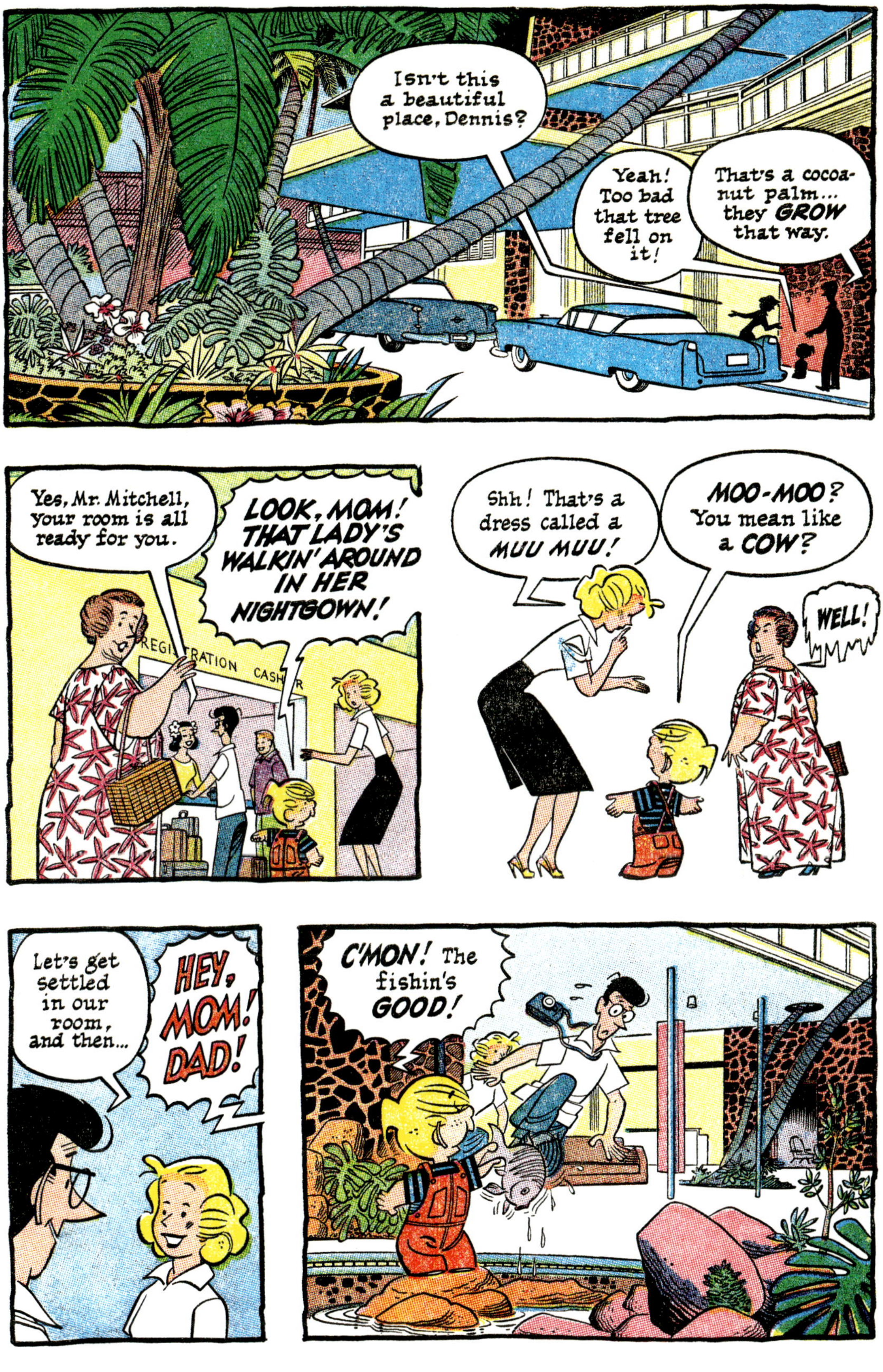
Isn't this a beautiful place, Dennis?
Yeah! Too bad that tree fell on it!
That's a cocoa-nut palm... they GROW that way.
Yes, Mr. Mitchell, your room is all ready for you.
LOOK, MOM! THAT LADY'S WALKIN' AROUND IN HER NIGHTGOWN!
REGISTRATION
CASHIER
Shh! That's a dress called a MUU MUU!
MOO-MOO? You mean like a COW?
WELL!
Let's get settled in our room, and then...
HEY, MOM! DAD!
C'MON! The fishin's GOOD!

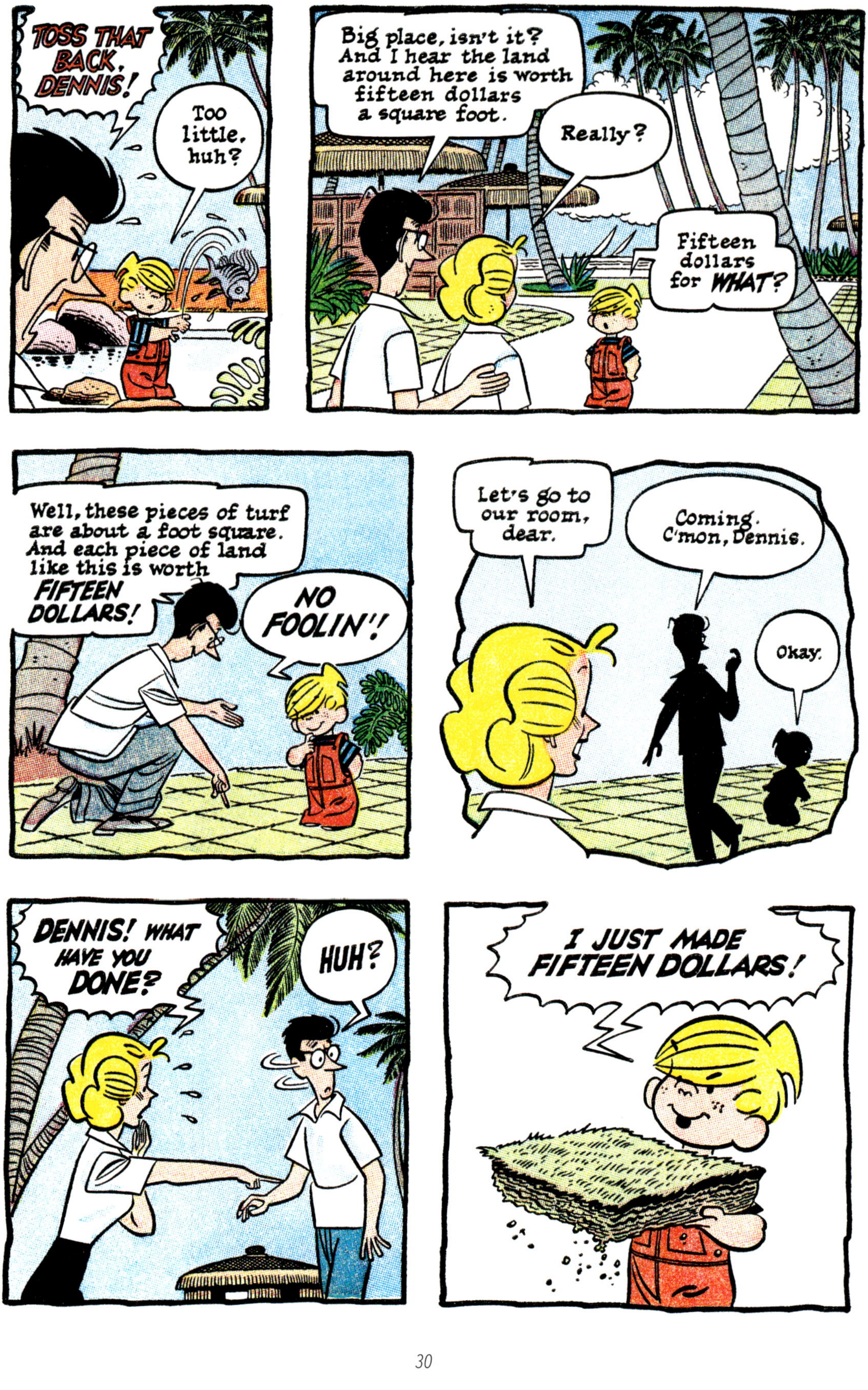
TOSS THAT BACK, DENNIS!
Too little, huh?
Big place, isn't it? And I hear the land around here is worth fifteen dollars a square foot.
Really?
Fifteen dollars for WHAT?
Well, these pieces of turf are about a foot square. And each piece of land like this is worth FIFTEEN DOLLARS!
NO FOOLIN'!
Let's go to our room, dear.
Coming. C'mon, Dennis.
Okay.
DENNIS! WHAT HAVE YOU DONE?
HUH?
I JUST MADE FIFTEEN DOLLARS!

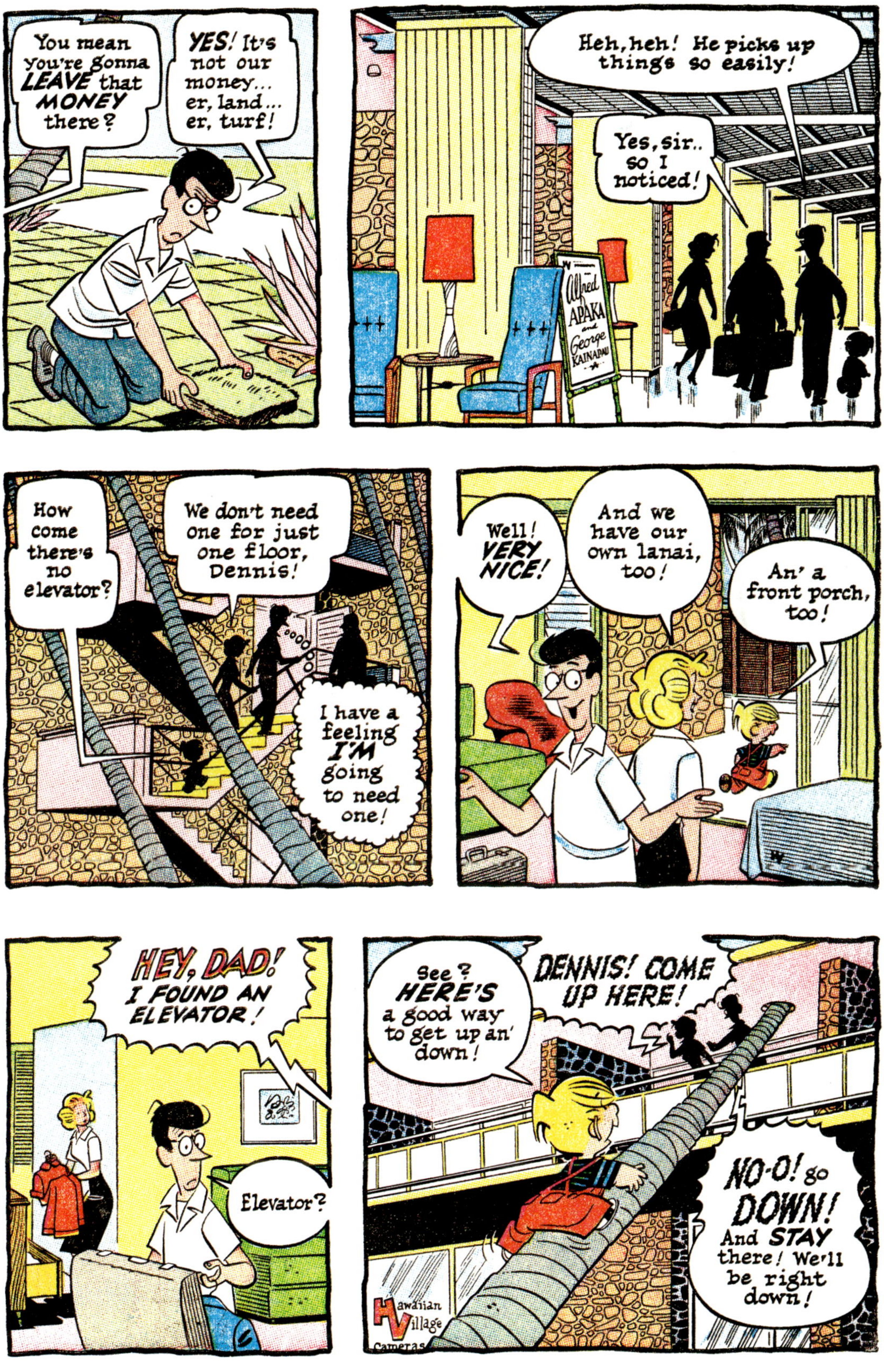
You mean you're gonna LEAVE that MONEY there?
YES! It's not our money... er, land... er, turf!
Heh, heh! He picks up things so easily!
Yes, sir.. so I noticed!
Alfred APAKA and George KAINAPAU
How come there's no elevator?
We don't need one for just one floor, Dennis!
I have a feeling I'M going to need one!
Well! VERY NICE!
And we have our own lanai, too!
An' a front porch, too!
HEY, DAD! I FOUND AN ELEVATOR!
Elevator?
See? HERE'S a good way to get up an' down!
DENNIS! COME UP HERE!
NO-O! go DOWN! And STAY there! We'll be right down!
Hawaiian Village Cameras

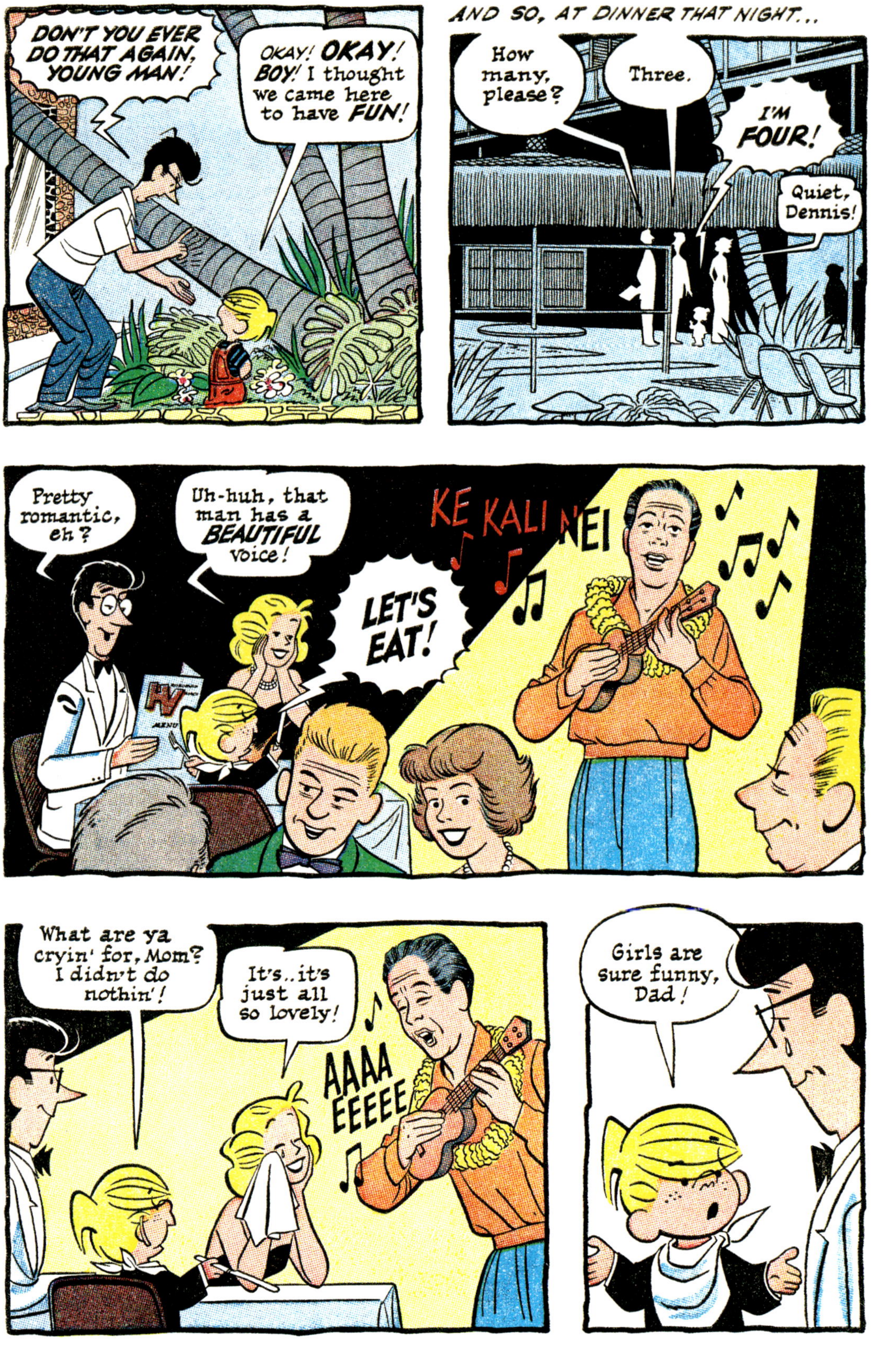
DON'T YOU EVER DO THAT AGAIN, YOUNG MAN!
OKAY! OKAY! BOY! I thought we came here to have FUN!
AND SO, AT DINNER THAT NIGHT..
How many, please?
Three.
I'M FOUR!
Quiet, Dennis!
Pretty romantic, eh?
Uh-huh, that man has a BEAUTIFUL voice!
KE KALI NEI
LET'S EAT!
What are ya cryin' for, Mom? I didn't do nothin'!
It's..it's just all so lovely!
AAAA EEEEE
Girls are sure funny, Dad!

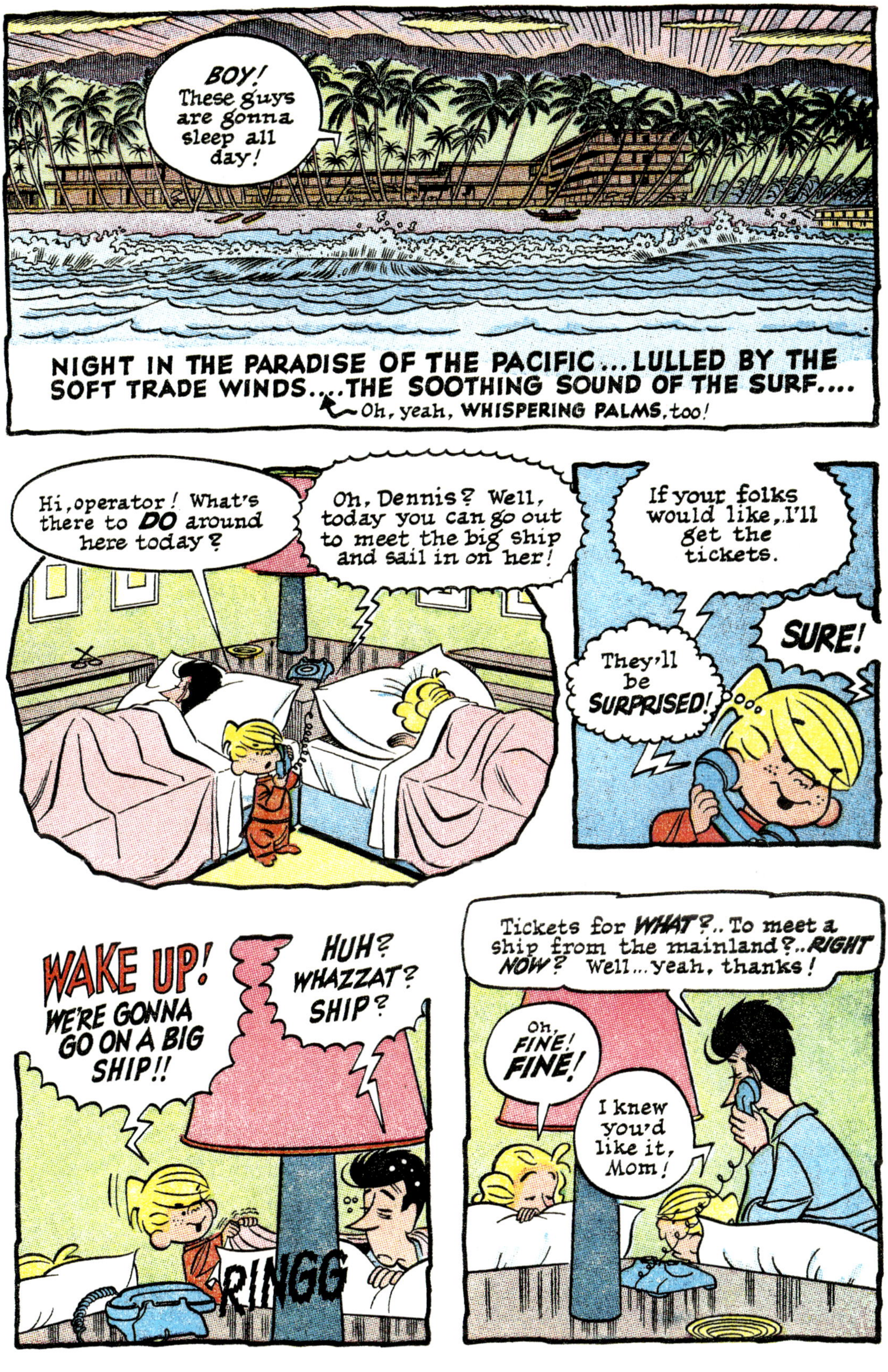
BOY! These guys are gonna sleep all day!
NIGHT IN THE PARADISE OF THE PACIFIC... LULLED BY THE SOFT TRADE WINDS.... THE SOOTHING SOUND OF THE SURF....
Oh, yeah, WHISPERING PALMS, too!
Hi, operator! What's there to DO around here today?
Oh, Dennis? Well, today you can go out to meet the big ship and sail in on her!
If your folks would like, I'll get the tickets.
SURE!
They'll be SURPRISED!
WAKE UP! WE'RE GONNA GO ON A BIG SHIP!!
HUH? WHAZZAT? SHIP?
RINGG
Tickets for WHAT?.. To meet a ship from the mainland?.. RIGHT NOW? Well... yeah, thanks!
Oh, FINE! FINE!
I knew you'd like it, Mom!

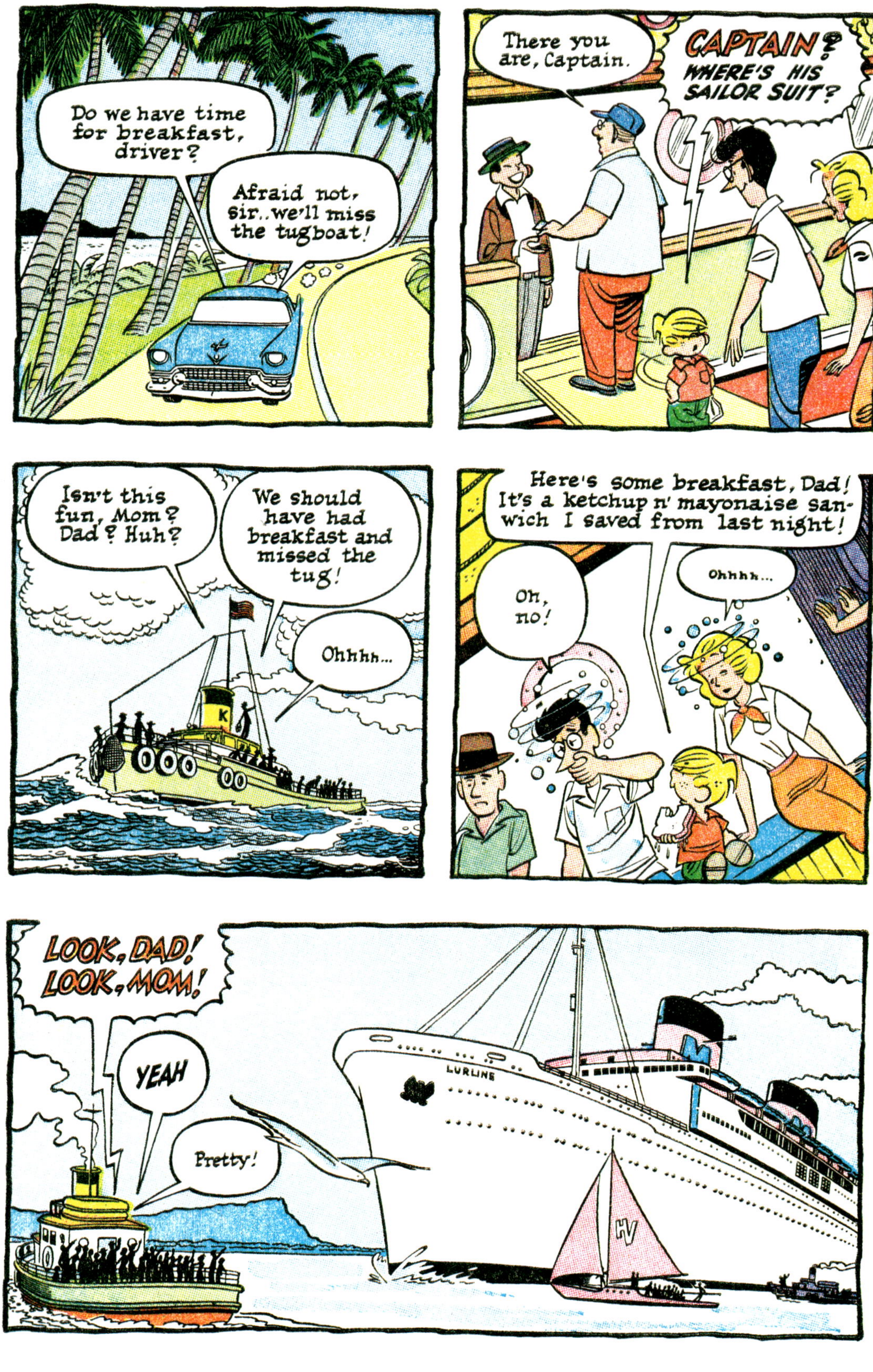
Do we have time for breakfast, driver?
Afraid not, sir..we'll miss the tugboat!
There you are, Captain.
CAPTAIN? WHERE'S HIS SAILOR SUIT?
Isn't this fun, Mom? Dad? Huh?
We should have had breakfast and missed the tug!
Ohhhh...
Here's some breakfast, Dad! It's a ketchup n' mayonaise san-wich I saved from last night!
Oh, no!
Ohhhh...
LOOK, DAD! LOOK, MOM!
YEAH
Pretty!
LURLINE
HV

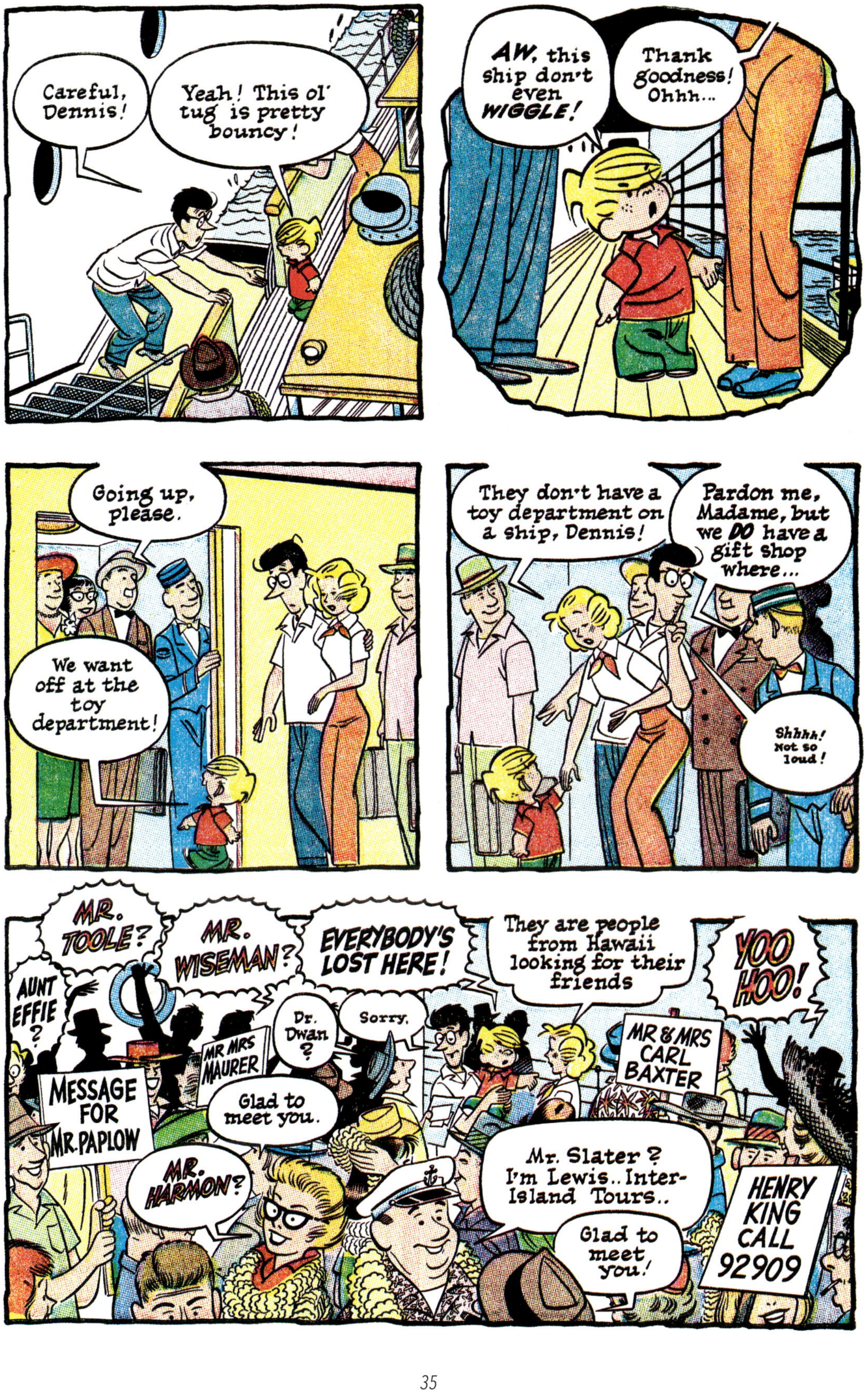

Careful, Dennis!
Yeah! This ol' tug is pretty bouncy!
AW, this ship don't even WIGGLE!
Thank goodness! Ohhh...
Going up, please.
We want off at the toy department!
They don't have a toy department on a ship, Dennis!
Pardon me, Madame, but we DO have a gift shop where...
Shhhh! Not so loud!
AUNT EFFIE?
MR. TOOLE?
MR. WISEMAN?
EVERYBODY'S LOST HERE!
They are people from Hawaii looking for their friends
YOO HOO!
MESSAGE FOR MR. PAPLOW
MR MRS MAURER
Dr. Dwan?
Sorry.
Glad to meet you.
MR & MRS CARL BAXTER
MR. HARMON?
Mr. Slater? I'm Lewis.. Inter-Island Tours..
Glad to meet you!
HENRY KING CALL 92909

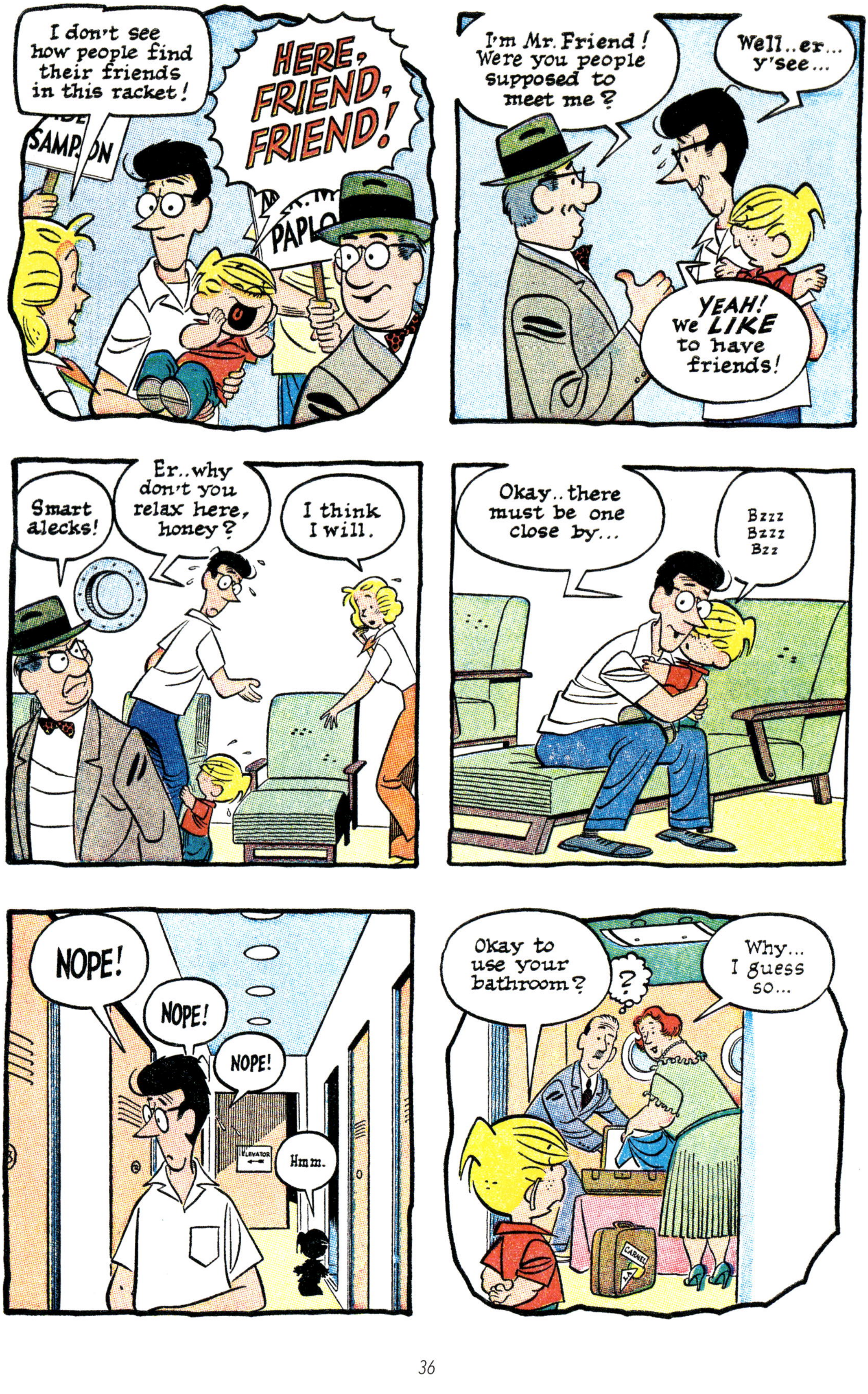
I don't see how people find their friends in this racket!
HERE, FRIEND, FRIEND!
I'm Mr. Friend! Were you people supposed to meet me?
Well..er... y'see...
YEAH! We LIKE to have friends!
Smart alecks!
Er..why don't you relax here, honey?
I think I will.
Okay..there must be one close by...
Bzzz Bzzz Bzz
NOPE!
NOPE!
NOPE!
ELEVATOR
Hmm.
Okay to use your bathroom?
?
Why... I guess so...

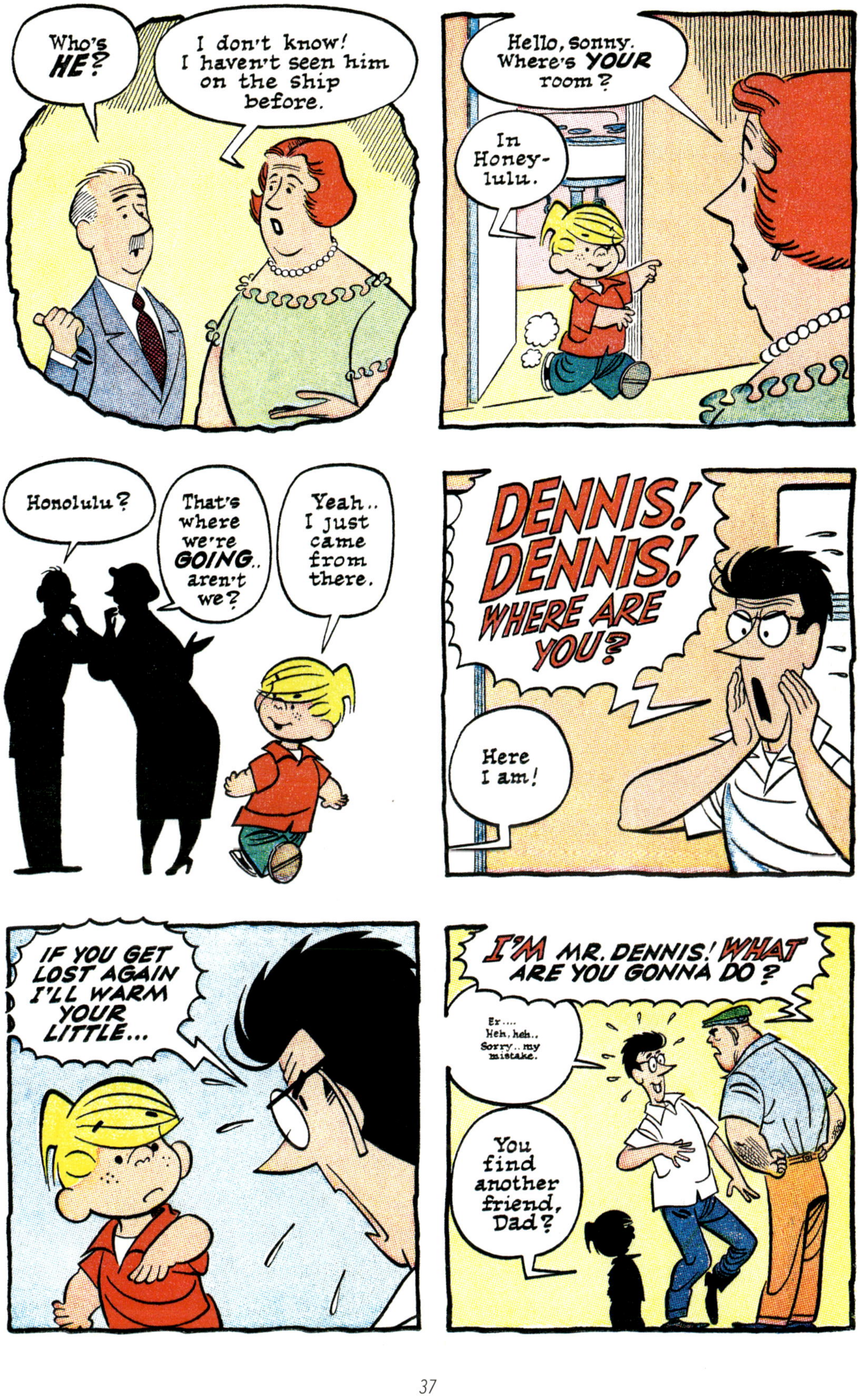
Who's HE?
I don't know! I haven't seen him on the ship before.
Hello, sonny. Where's YOUR room?
In Honey-lulu.
Honolulu?
That's where we're GOING.. aren't we?
Yeah.. I just came from there.
DENNIS! DENNIS! WHERE ARE YOU?
Here I am!
IF YOU GET LOST AGAIN I'LL WARM YOUR LITTLE...
I'M MR. DENNIS! WHAT ARE YOU GONNA DO?
Er.... Heh, heh.. Sorry.. my mistake.
You find another friend, Dad?

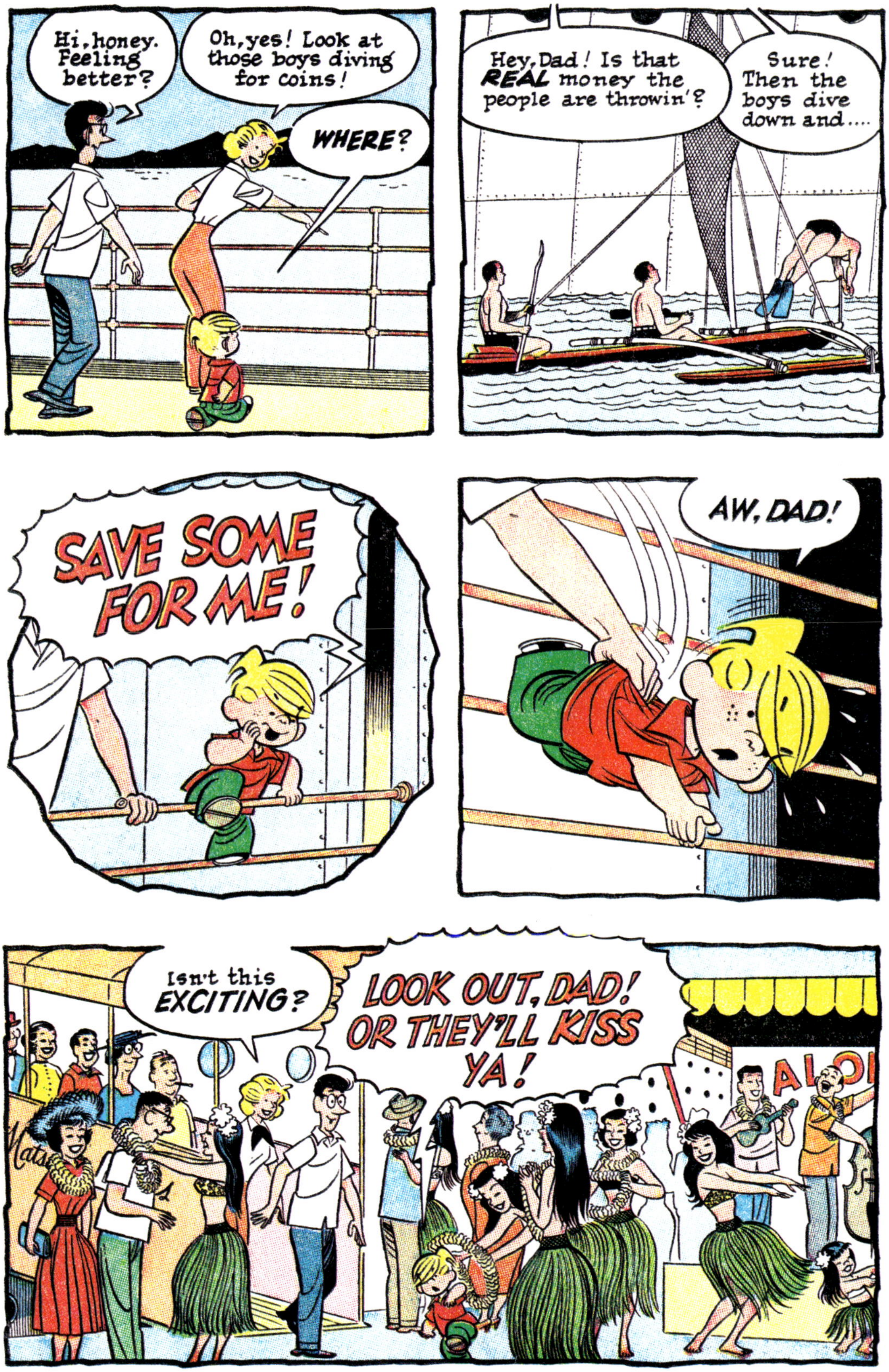
Hi, honey. Feeling better?
Oh, yes! Look at those boys diving for coins!
WHERE?
Hey, Dad! Is that REAL money the people are throwin'?
Sure! Then the boys dive down and....
SAVE SOME FOR ME!
AW, DAD!
Isn't this EXCITING?
LOOK OUT, DAD! OR THEY'LL KISS YA!
ALO

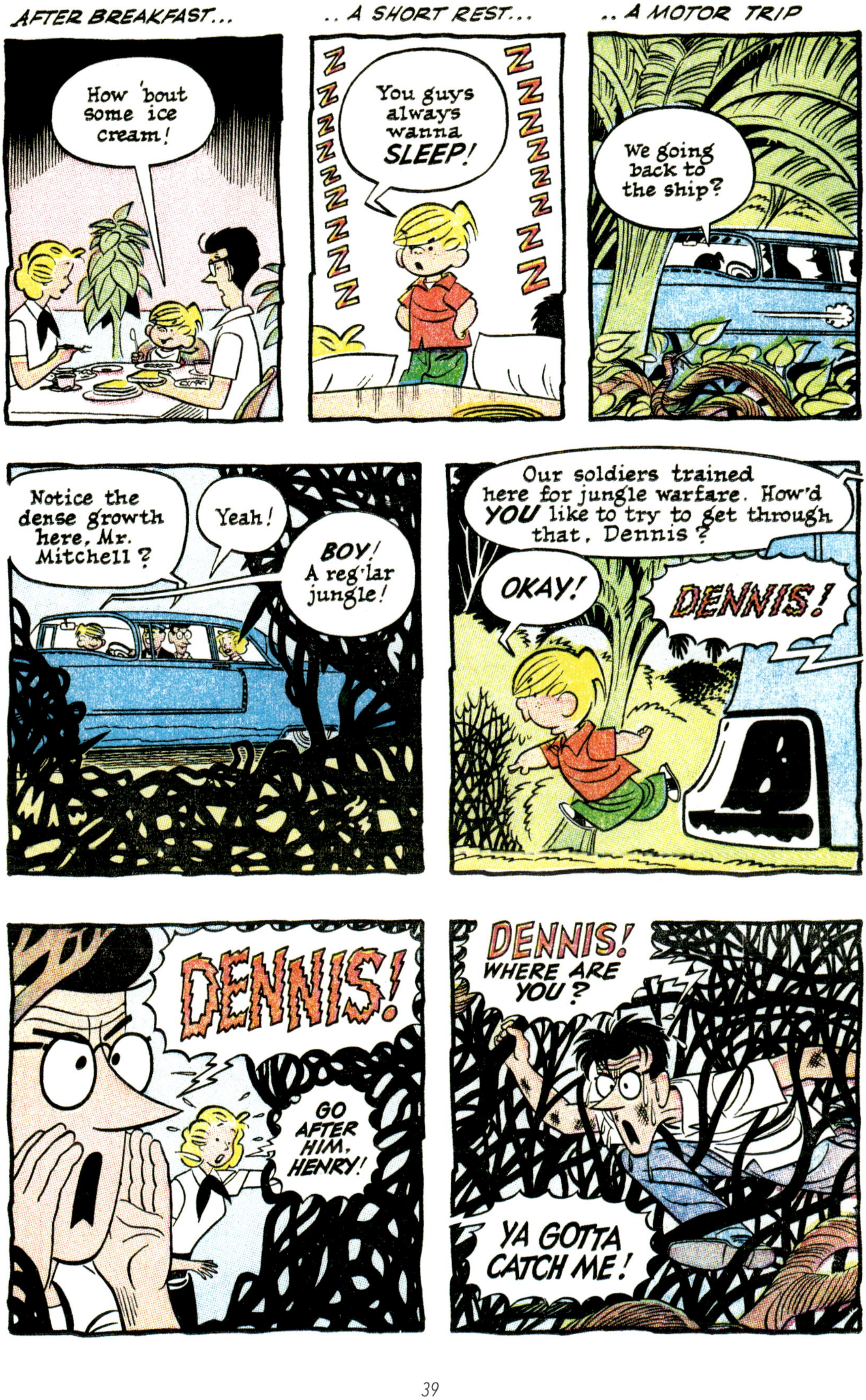
AFTER BREAKFAST...
How 'bout some ice cream!
.. A SHORT REST...
You guys always wanna SLEEP!
.. A MOTOR TRIP
We going back to the ship?
Notice the dense growth here, Mr. Mitchell?
Yeah!
BOY! A reg'lar jungle!
Our soldiers trained here for jungle warfare. How'd YOU like to try to get through that, Dennis?
OKAY!
DENNIS!
DENNIS!
GO AFTER HIM, HENRY!
DENNIS! WHERE ARE YOU?
YA GOTTA CATCH ME!

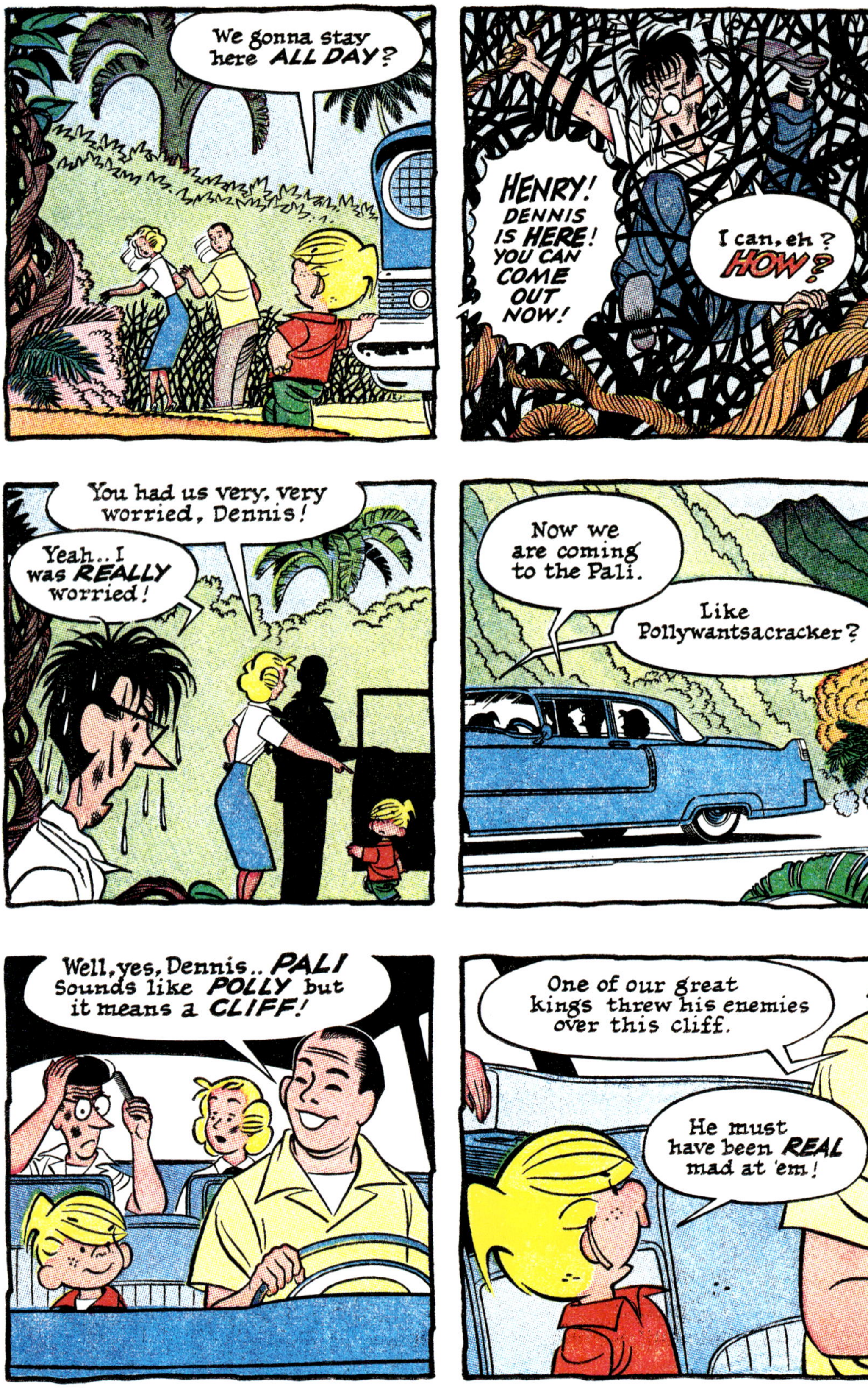
We gonna stay here ALL DAY?
HENRY! DENNIS IS HERE! YOU CAN COME OUT NOW!
I can, eh? HOW?
You had us very, very worried, Dennis!
Yeah.. I was REALLY worried!
Now we are coming to the Pali.
Like Pollywantsacracker?
Well, yes, Dennis.. PALI Sounds like POLLY but it means a CLIFF!
One of our great kings threw his enemies over this cliff.
He must have been REAL mad at 'em!

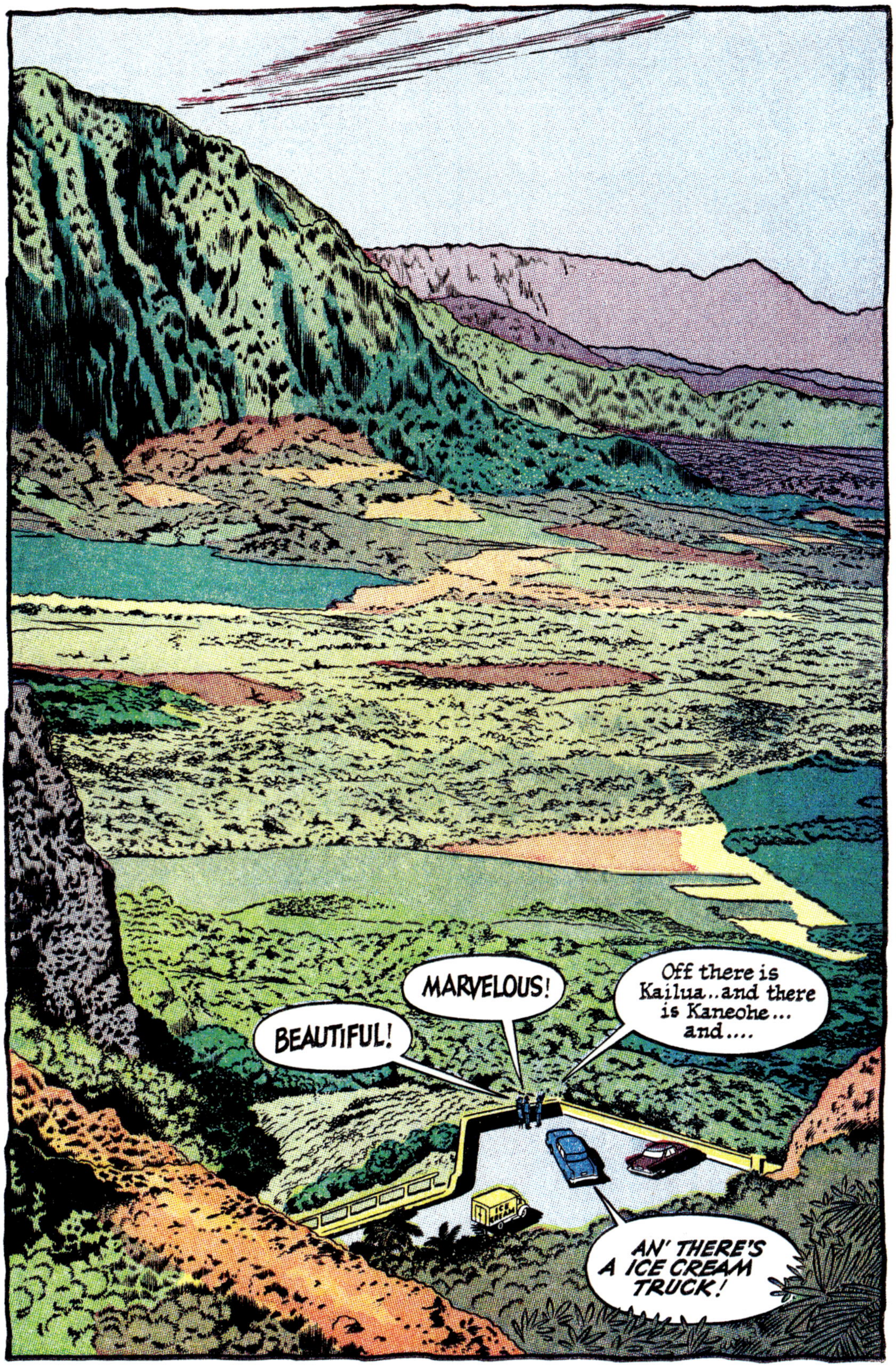
BEAUTIFUL!
MARVELOUS!
Off there is Kailua..and there is Kaneohe... and....
AN' THERE'S A ICE CREAM TRUCK!

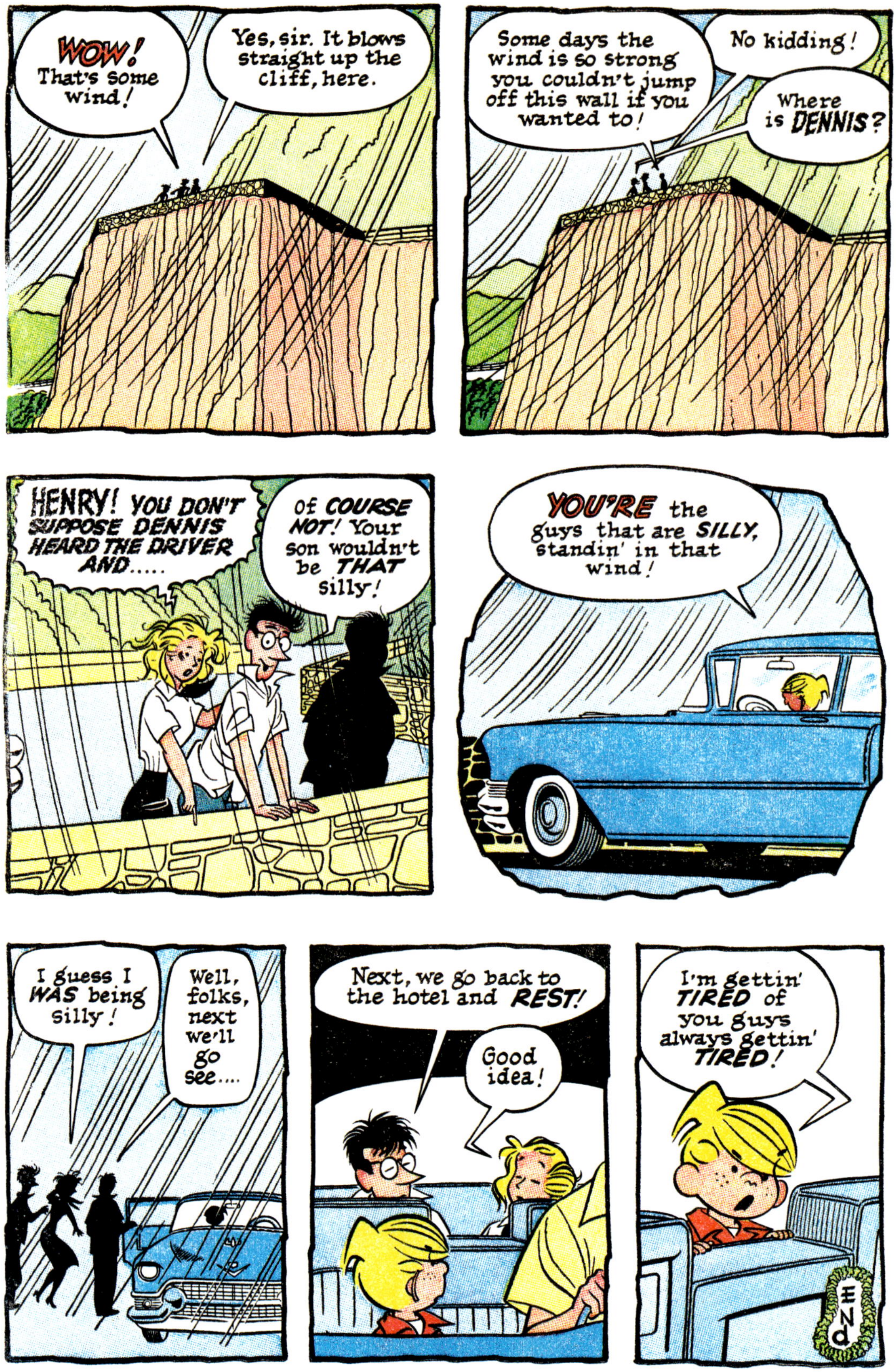
WOW! That's some wind!
Yes, sir. It blows straight up the cliff, here.
Some days the wind is so strong you couldn't jump off this wall if you wanted to!
No kidding!
Where is DENNIS?
HENRY! YOU DON'T SUPPOSE DENNIS HEARD THE DRIVER AND.....
Of COURSE NOT! Your son wouldn't be THAT silly!
YOU'RE the guys that are SILLY, standin' in that wind!
I guess I WAS being silly!
Well, folks, next we'll go see....
Next, we go back to the hotel and REST!
Good idea!
I'm gettin' TIRED of you guys always gettin' TIRED!
END

LITTLE GRASS SHACK PUZZLE

IMPORTANT.. An ✻ indicates a ***HAWAIIAN*** word, which you can look up on the inside back cover.

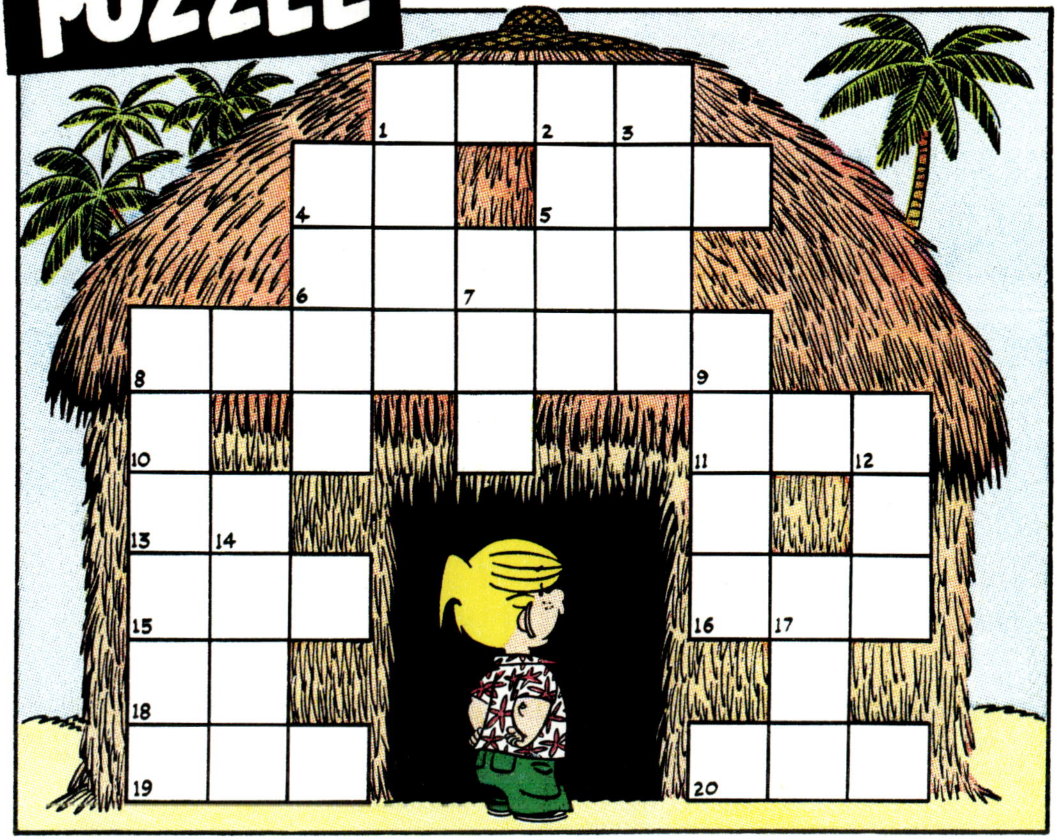

Down

1. Game played on horseback
2. Island on which Honolulu is located
3. Actual: not imaginary
4. Man (*)
7. Opposite of young
8. Happy (*)
9. On
12. Necklace of flowers
14. Metal clothes fastener
17. United States of America

SOLUTION

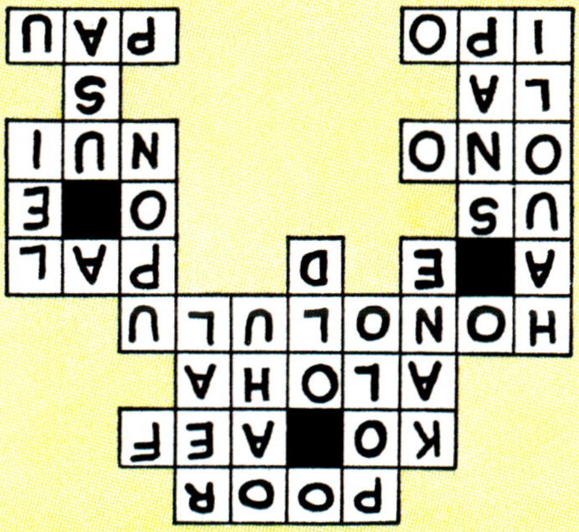

Across

1. Opposite of rich
4. Knockout (abbr.)
5. American Expeditionary Force (abbr.)
6. Hello, goodbye (*)
8. Largest city in Hawaiian Islands
11. Friend, buddy
13. You and I
15. Tastes good (*)
16. Very much (*)
18. Los Angeles (abbr.)
19. Sweetheart (*)
20. Finished (*)

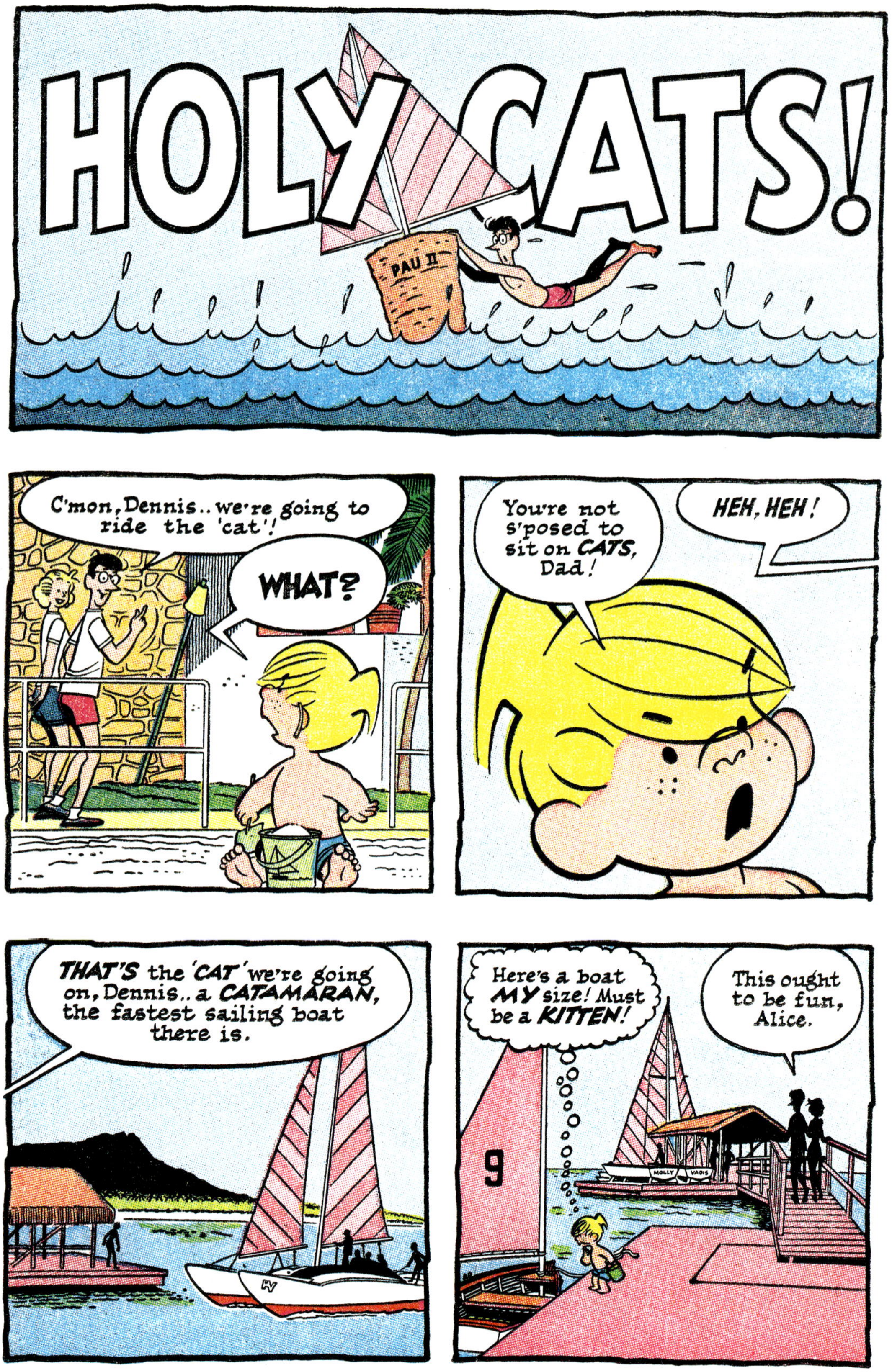
HOLY CATS!
PAU II
C'mon, Dennis.. we're going to ride the 'cat'!
WHAT?
You're not s'posed to sit on CATS, Dad!
HEH, HEH!
THAT'S the 'CAT' we're going on, Dennis.. a CATAMARAN, the fastest sailing boat there is.
Here's a boat MY size! Must be a KITTEN!
This ought to be fun, Alice.
9
MOLLY
VADIS

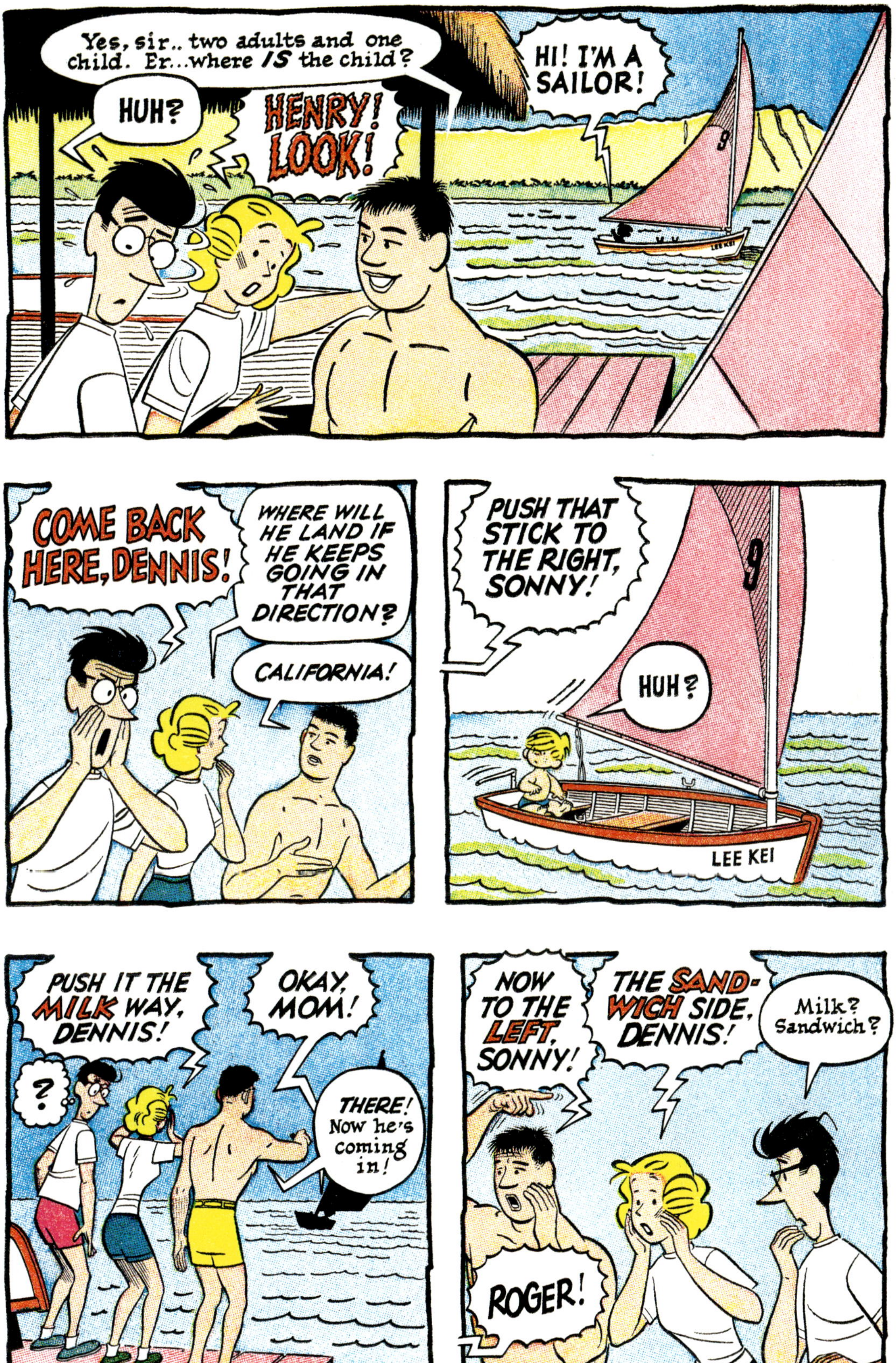
Yes, sir.. two adults and one child. Er...where IS the child?
HUH?
HENRY! LOOK!
HI! I'M A SAILOR!
LEE KEI
COME BACK HERE, DENNIS!
WHERE WILL HE LAND IF HE KEEPS GOING IN THAT DIRECTION?
CALIFORNIA!
PUSH THAT STICK TO THE RIGHT, SONNY!
HUH?
LEE KEI
PUSH IT THE MILK WAY, DENNIS!
OKAY, MOM!
?
THERE! Now he's coming in!
NOW TO THE LEFT, SONNY!
THE SAND-WICH SIDE, DENNIS!
Milk? Sandwich?
ROGER!

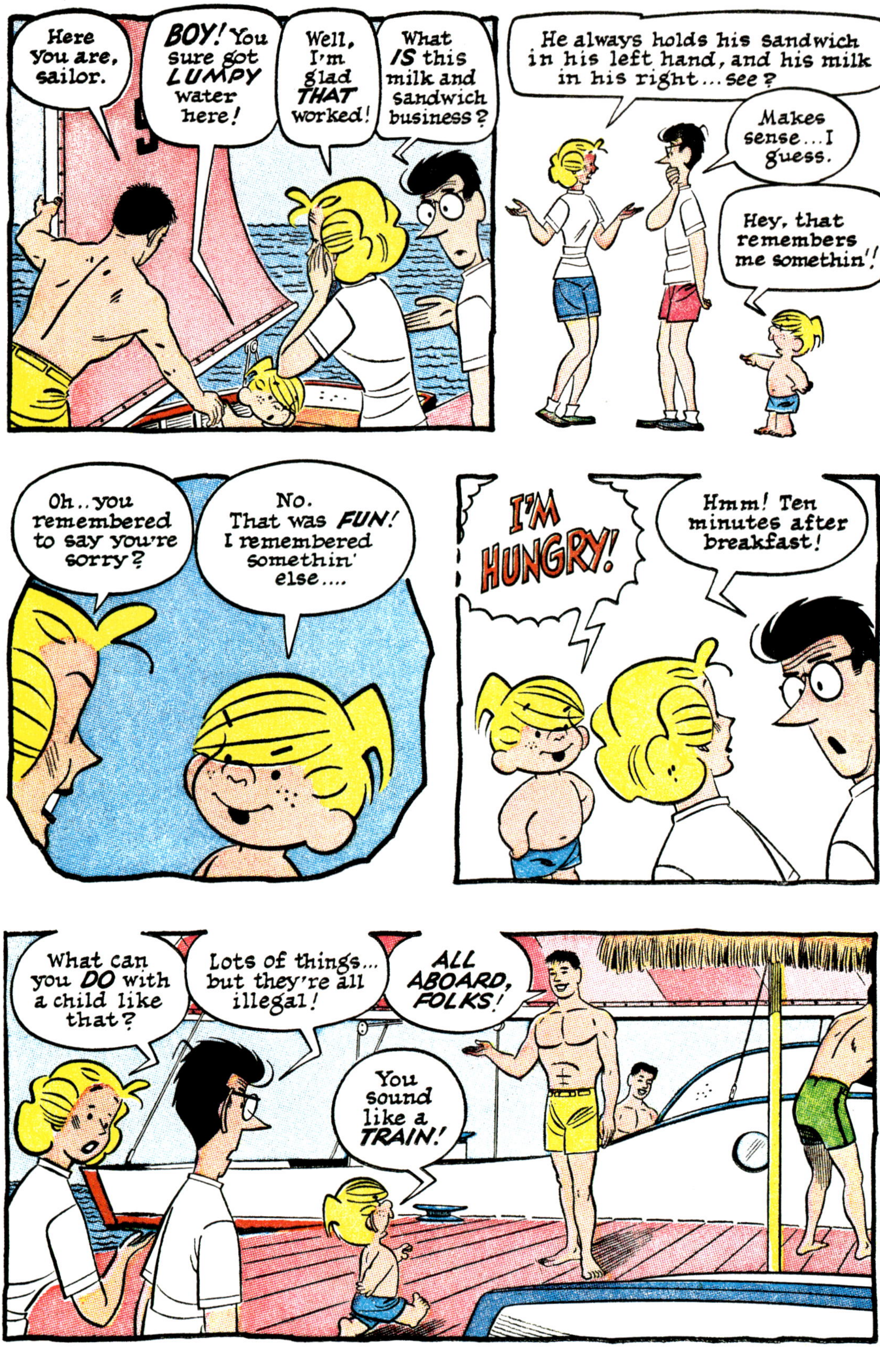
Here you are, sailor.
BOY! You sure got LUMPY water here!
Well, I'm glad THAT worked!
What IS this milk and sandwich business?
He always holds his sandwich in his left hand, and his milk in his right... see?
Makes sense... I guess.
Hey, that remembers me somethin'!
Oh.. you remembered to say you're sorry?
No. That was FUN! I remembered somethin' else....
I'M HUNGRY!
Hmm! Ten minutes after breakfast!
What can you DO with a child like that?
Lots of things... but they're all illegal!
ALL ABOARD, FOLKS!
You sound like a TRAIN!

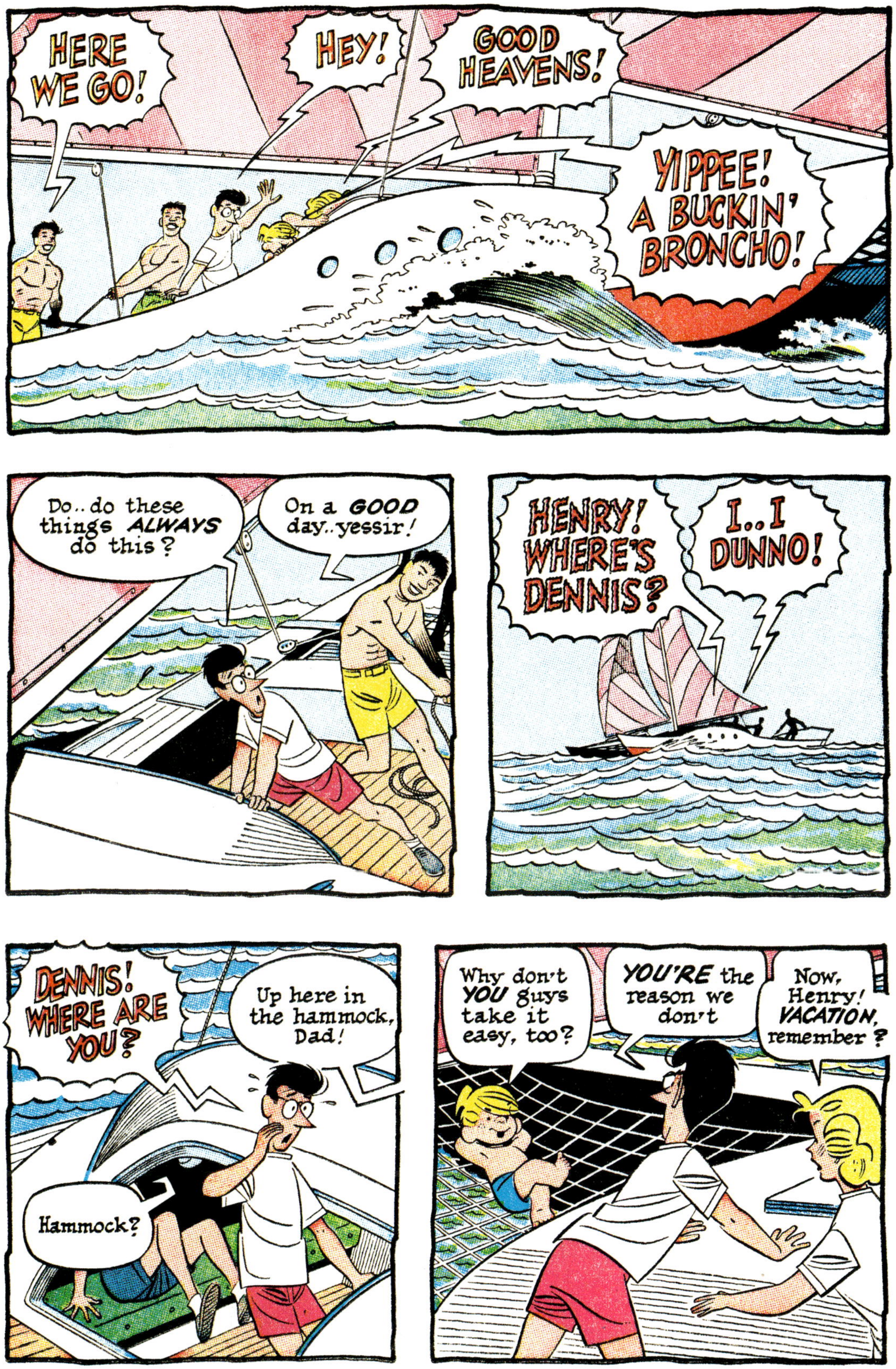
HERE WE GO!
HEY!
GOOD HEAVENS!
YIPPEE! A BUCKIN' BRONCHO!
Do.. do these things ALWAYS do this?
On a GOOD day.. yessir!
HENRY! WHERE'S DENNIS?
I..I DUNNO!
DENNIS! WHERE ARE YOU?
Up here in the hammock, Dad!
Hammock?
Why don't YOU guys take it easy, too?
YOU'RE the reason we don't
Now, Henry! VACATION, remember?

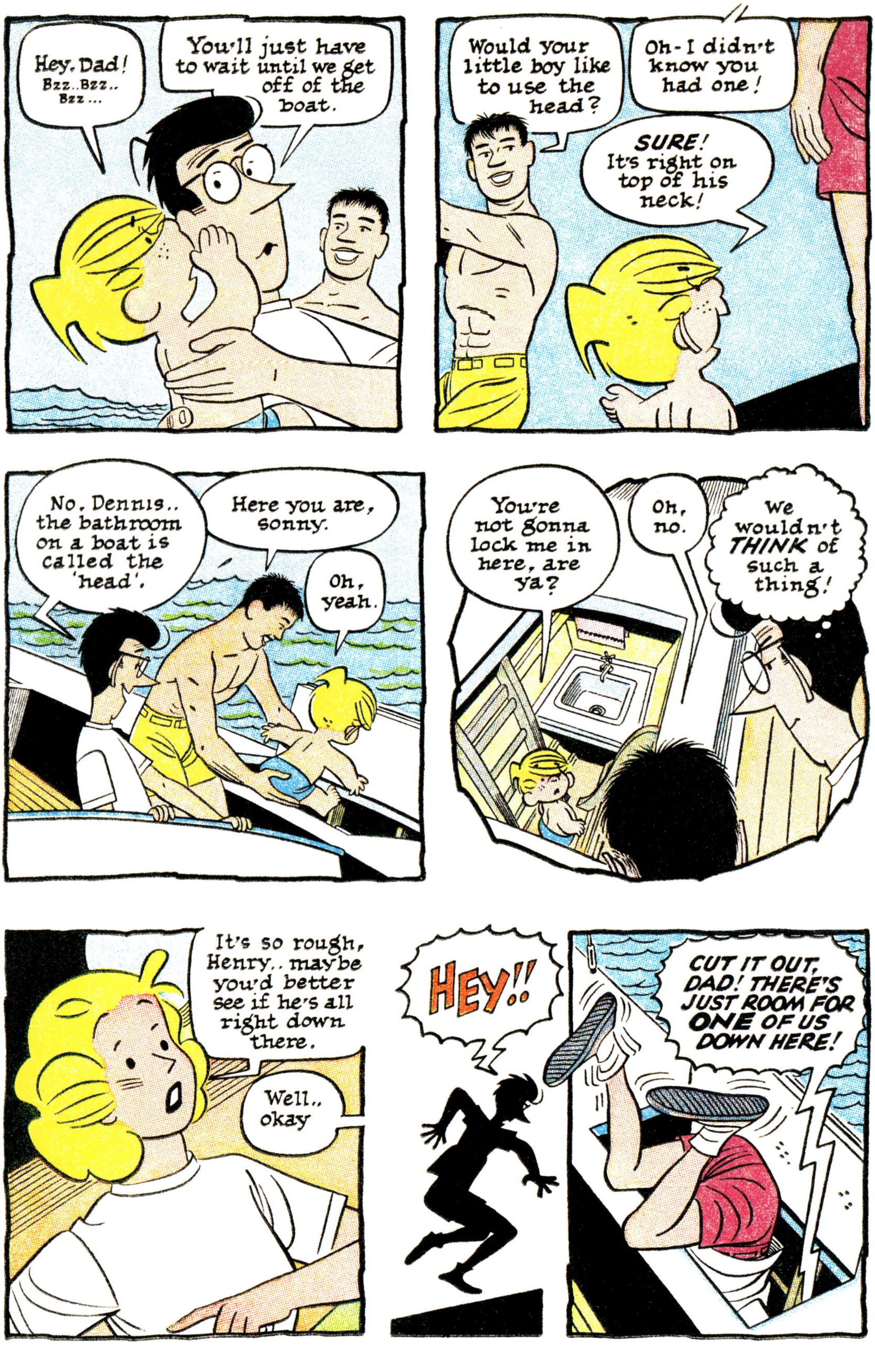
Hey, Dad! Bzz..Bzz.. Bzz...
You'll just have to wait until we get off of the boat.
Would your little boy like to use the head?
Oh-I didn't know you had one!
SURE! It's right on top of his neck!
No, Dennis.. the bathroom on a boat is called the 'head'.
Here you are, sonny.
Oh, yeah.
You're not gonna lock me in here, are ya?
Oh, no.
We wouldn't THINK of such a thing!
It's so rough, Henry.. maybe you'd better see if he's all right down there.
Well.. okay
HEY!!
CUT IT OUT, DAD! THERE'S JUST ROOM FOR ONE OF US DOWN HERE!

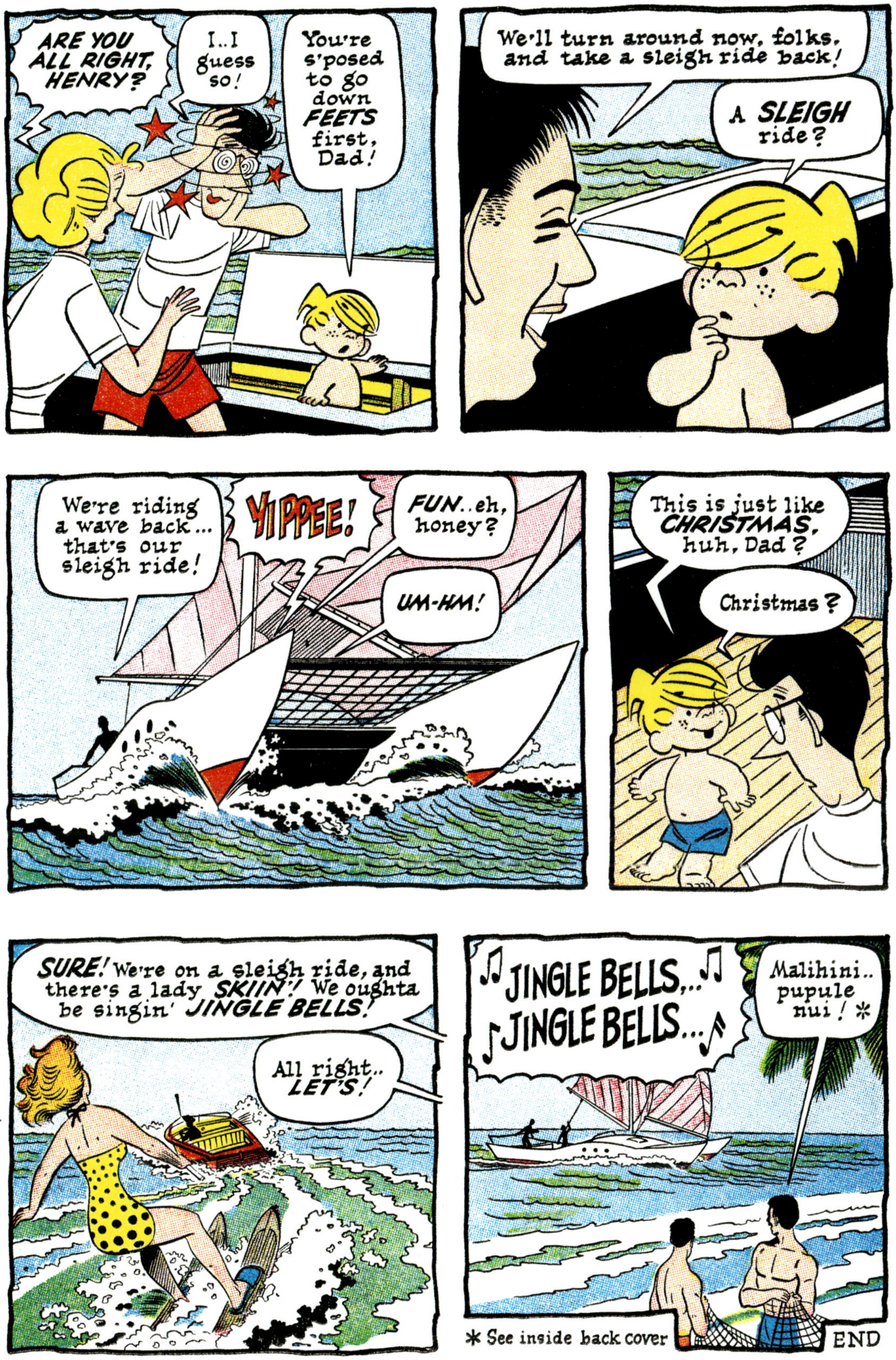
ARE YOU ALL RIGHT, HENRY?
I..I guess so!
You're s'posed to go down FEETS first, Dad!
We'll turn around now, folks, and take a sleigh ride back!
A SLEIGH ride?
We're riding a wave back... that's our sleigh ride!
YIPPEE!
FUN..eh, honey?
UM-HM!
This is just like CHRISTMAS, huh, Dad?
Christmas?
SURE! We're on a sleigh ride, and there's a lady SKIIN'! We oughta be singin' JINGLE BELLS!
All right.. LET'S!
JINGLE BELLS,.. JINGLE BELLS...
Malihini.. pupule nui! *
* See inside back cover
END

* Which is reproduced on page 109.

WHAT'S YOUR NAME
BOYS' NAMES

English	Hawaiian	Pronunciation
Alexander	Alika	Ah-**lee**-ka
Alfred	Alapaki	Ah-la-**pa**-kee
Anthony	Akoni	Ah-**ko**-nee
Arthur	Aka	**Ah**-ka
Benjamin	Beiamina	Bay-ah-**mee**-na
Bernard	Belenaka	Bay-lay-**na**-ka
Calvin	Kalawina	Kah-la-**wee**-na
Carl	Kala	**Kah**-la
Charles	Kale	**Kah**-lee
Daniel	Kaniela	Kah-nee-**ay**-la
David	Kawika	Kah-**wee**-ka
Dennis	Keniki	Ken-**ee**-kee
Edward	Eluwene	Ay-loo-**way**-nay
Edwin	Eluene	Ay-loo-**ay**-nay
Ernest	Eneki	Ay-**nay**-kee
Francis	Palani	Pa-**la**-nee
Frank	Palakiki	Pa-la-**kee**-kee
Fred	Peleke	Pay-**lay**-kay
George	Keoki	Kay-**oh**-kee
Henry	Hanale	Ha-**na**-lay
Isaac	Iaikake	Ee-eye-**kah**-kay
Jack	Keaka	Kay-**ah**-kah
James	Iakepo	Ee-ah-**kay**-po
Jimmy	Kimo	**Kee**-mo
John	Keoni	Kay-**oh**-nee
Joseph	Iokepa	Ee-oh-**kay**-pa
Kenneth	Keneke	Kay-**nay**-kay
Lawrence	Lapaki	La-**pa**-ki
Moses	Moke	**Mo**-kay
Norman	Nomana	No-**ma**-nah
Oliver	Oliwa	Oh-**lee**-va
Patrick	Palika	Pa-**lee**-kah
Paul	Paulo	**Pow**-lo
Peter	Peteo	Pay-**taye**-oh
Philip	Pilipo	Pee-**lee**-po
Richard	Likelike	**Lee**-kay-**lee**-kay
Robert	Lopaka	Loh-**pa**-ka
Roy	Loe	**Lo**-ay
Samuel	Kamuela	Kah-moo-**ay**-la
Stephen	Setepano	Say-tay-**pon**-oh
Theodore	Teo	**Tay**-oh
Thomas	Kamaki	**Kah**-**ma**-kee
Victor	Viki	**Vee**-kee
Walter	Wala	**Wah**-la
William	Wiliama	**Wee**-lee-**ah**-ma

(These names were furnished by The Hawaii Visitors Bureau, in Honolulu.)

IN HAWAIIAN ??? GIRLS' NAMES

English	Hawaiian	Pronunciation
Alice	Alika	Aa-**lee**-ka
Anna	Ana	**Ah**-nah
Barbara	Babara	**Bah**-bah-ra
Betty	Bete	**Bay**-tay
Carol	Kalole	Kah-**loh**-lay
Claire	Kalea	Kah-**lay**-ah
Cynthia	Kinikia	Kee-nee-**kee-ah**
Diana	Kina	**Kee**-na
Doris	Korisa	Koh-**ree**-sa
Dorothy	Kaloke	Kah-**loh**-kay
Edith	Edie	**Ay**-dee
Elizabeth	Elikapeka	Ay-lee-ka-**pay-ka**
Esther	Ekekela	Ay-kay-**kay**-la
Ethel	Ekela	Ay-**kay**-la
Florence	Felorena	**Fay**-loh-ray-na
Frances	Palani	Pah-**la**-nee
Gertrude	Gerekuke	Gay-ray-**coo**-kay
Grace	Lokomaikai	Loh-koh-ma-ee-kye
Harriet	Hariaka	Ha-ree-**ah**-ka
Helen	Helena	Hay-**lay**-nah
Ida	Ida	**Ee**-dah
Jane	Kini	**Kee**-nee
Janet	Ianete	Ee-ah-**nay**-tay
Joan	Ioana	Ee-oh-ah-nah
Josephine	Kapina	Kay-**pee**-nah
Judith	Tukiki	Too-**kee**-kee
Kathleen	Kakalina	Kah-kah-ah-**leena**
Laura	Lola	**Loa**-la
Lily	Lilia	**Lee**-lee-ah
Lois	Loika	**Loh**-ee-kah
Louise	Luika	Lou-**ee**-kah
Mabel	Mapela	Mah-**pay**-lah
Margaret	Makaleka	Mah-ka-**lay**-kah
Marion	Mariana	Mah-ree-**ah**-nah
Marjorie	Makoli	Mah-**koh**-lee
Mary	Malia	Mah-**lee**-ah
Nancy	Ane	**Ah**-nay
Olive	Olivia	Oa-**lee**-via
Pearl	Momi	**Moh**-mee
Rose	Loke	**Loh**-kay
Ruth	Luka	**Loo**-kah
Sarah	Kalai	Kah-**la**-ee
Susan	Suse	**Soo**-say
Thelma	Kama	**Kah**-mah
Victoria	Wikolia	**Week**-oh-lee-ah
Violet	Waioleka	Why-oh-**lay**-kah
Virginia	Veginia	Vay-gee-**nee**-ah
Winifred	Winileleke	**Wee**-nee-lay-lay-kay

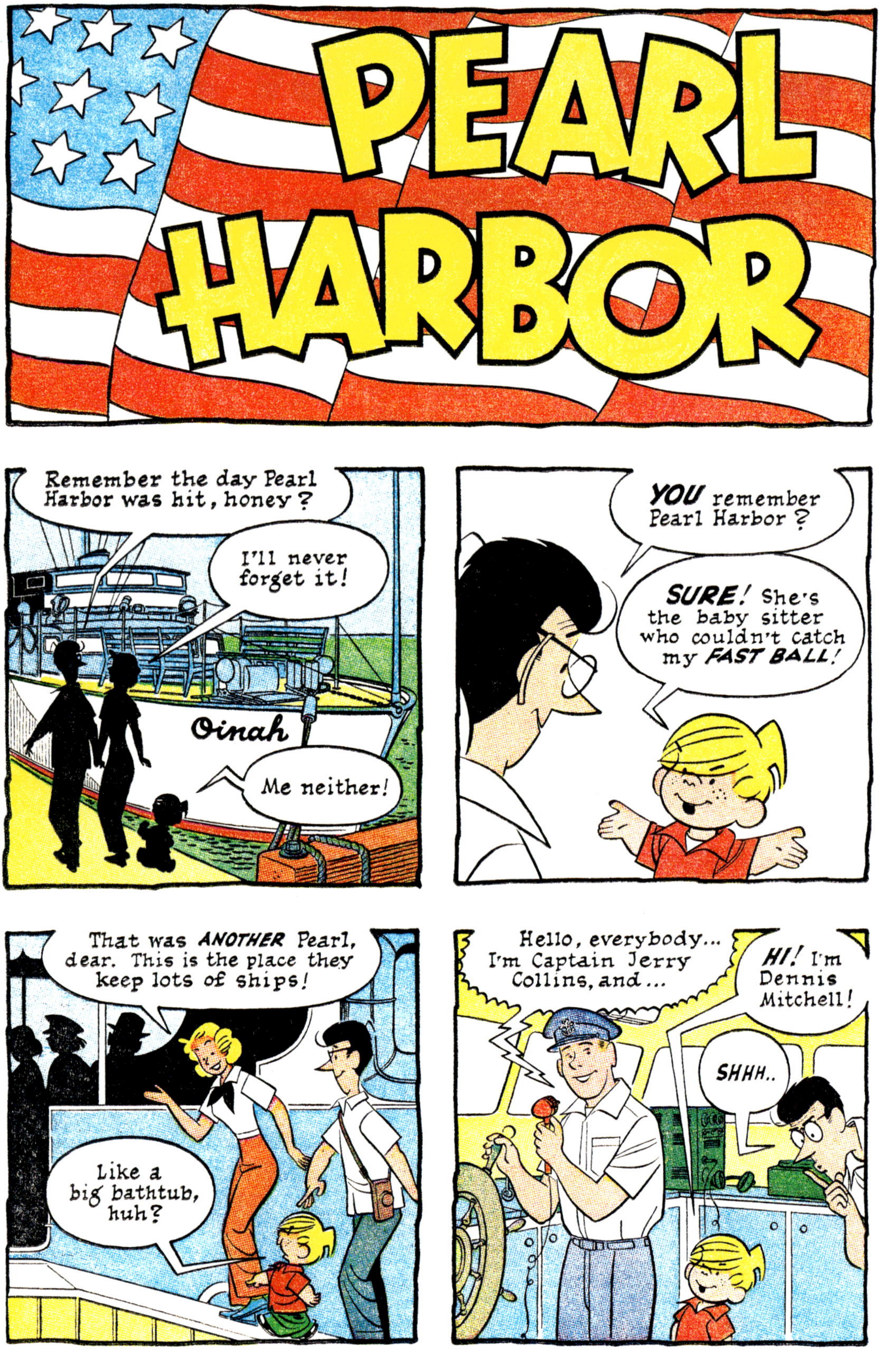
PEARL HARBOR
Remember the day Pearl Harbor was hit, honey?
I'll never forget it!
Oinah
Me neither!
YOU remember Pearl Harbor?
SURE! She's the baby sitter who couldn't catch my FAST BALL!
That was ANOTHER Pearl, dear. This is the place they keep lots of ships!
Like a big bathtub, huh?
Hello, everybody... I'm Captain Jerry Collins, and...
HI! I'm Dennis Mitchell!
SHHH..

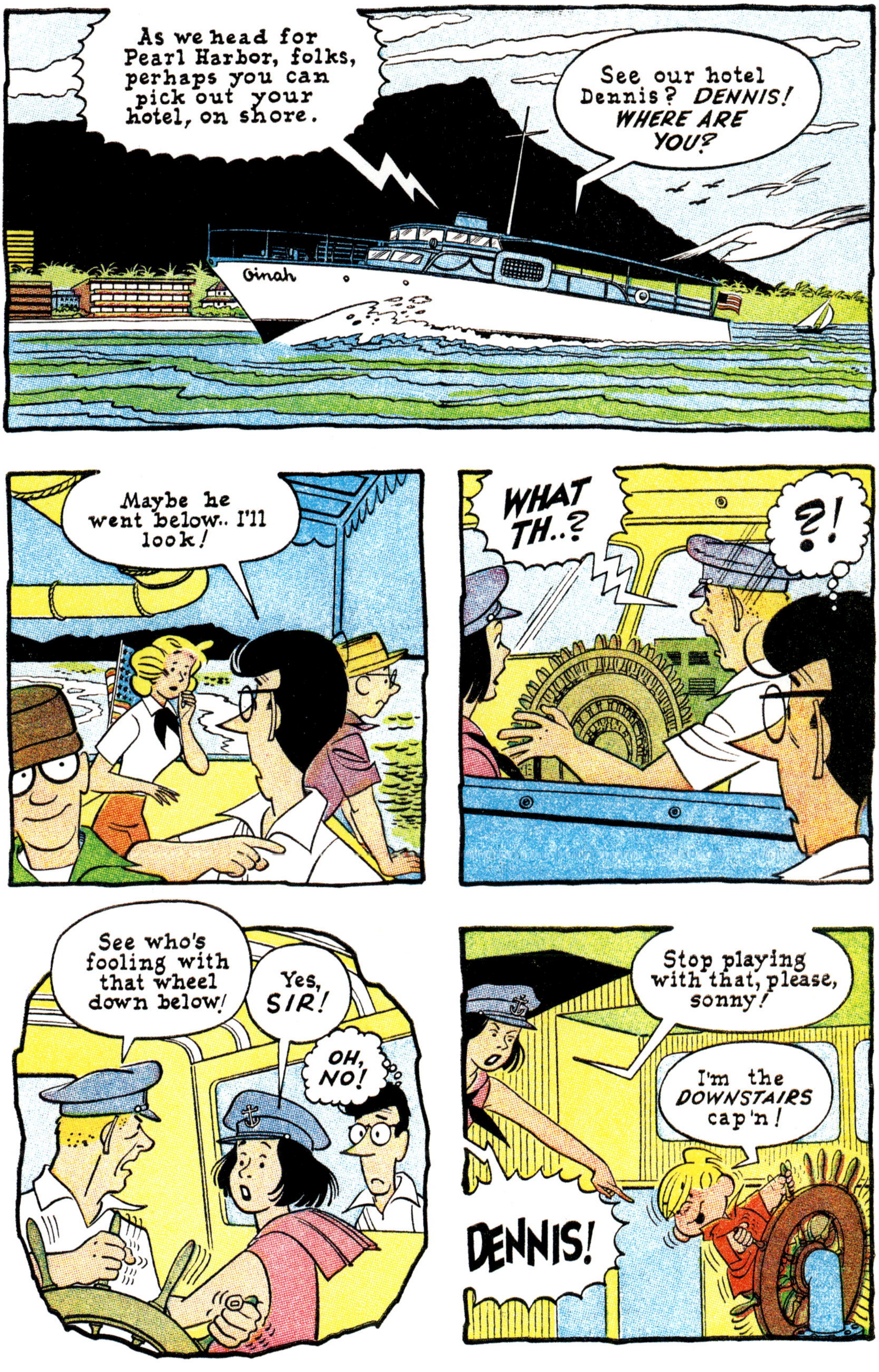
As we head for Pearl Harbor, folks, perhaps you can pick out your hotel, on shore.
See our hotel Dennis? DENNIS! WHERE ARE YOU?
Oinah
Maybe he went below.. I'll look!
WHAT TH..?
?!
See who's fooling with that wheel down below!
Yes, SIR!
OH, NO!
Stop playing with that, please, sonny!
I'm the DOWNSTAIRS cap'n!
DENNIS!

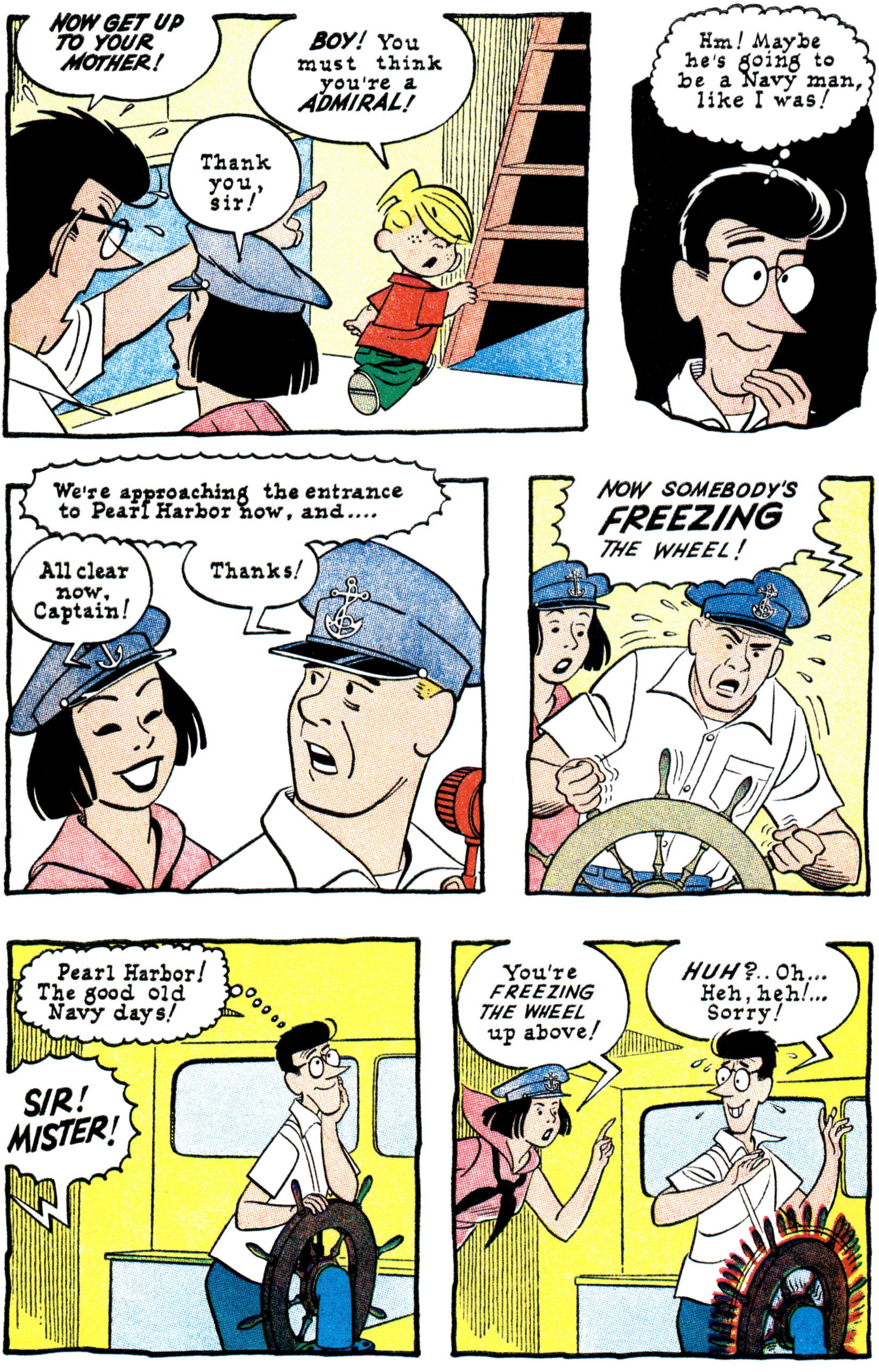
NOW GET UP TO YOUR MOTHER!
BOY! You must think you're a ADMIRAL!
Thank you, sir!
Hm! Maybe he's going to be a Navy man, like I was!
We're approaching the entrance to Pearl Harbor now, and....
All clear now, Captain!
Thanks!
NOW SOMEBODY'S FREEZING THE WHEEL!
Pearl Harbor! The good old Navy days!
SIR! MISTER!
You're FREEZING THE WHEEL up above!
HUH?.. Oh... Heh, heh!... Sorry!

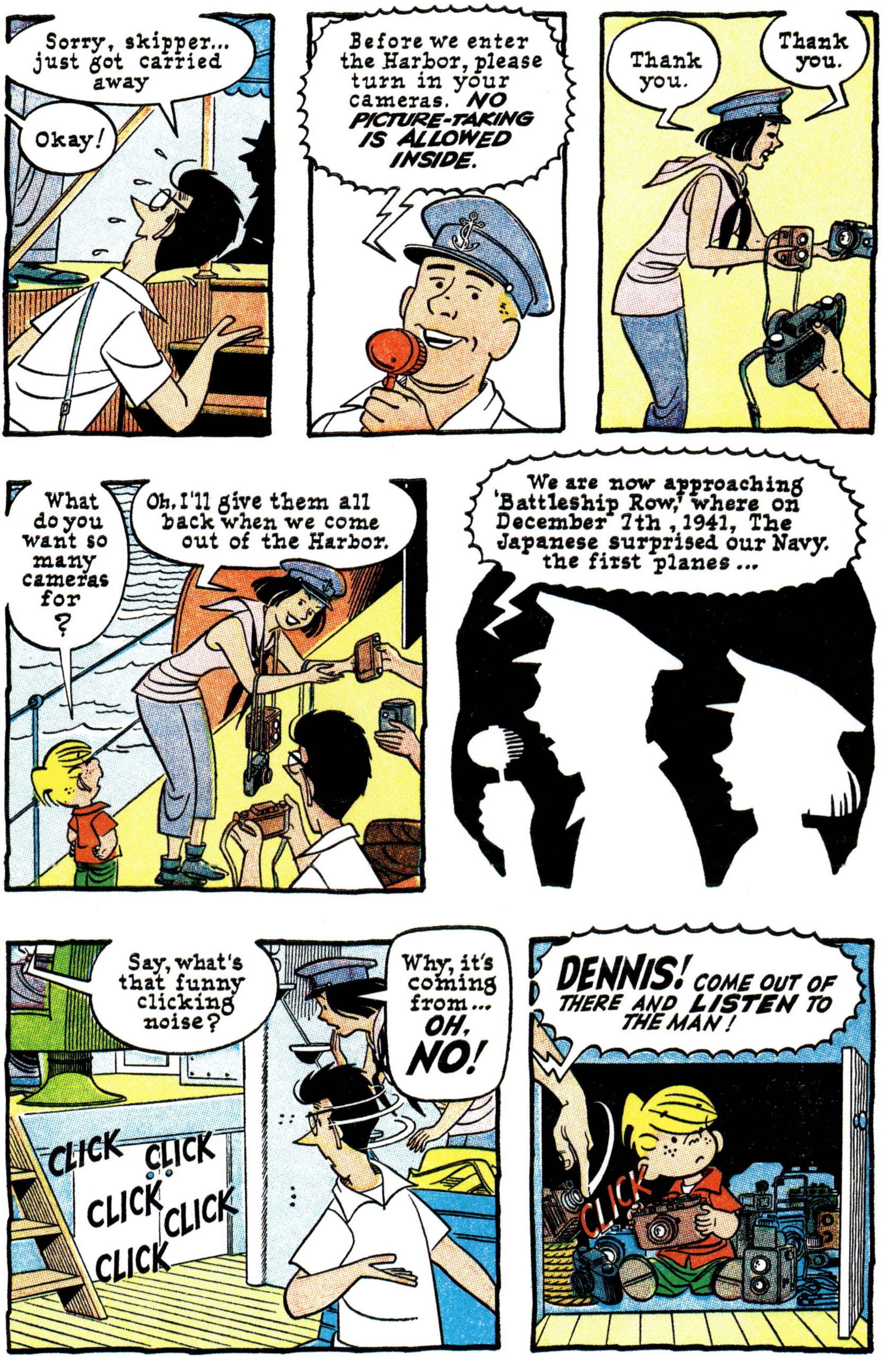
Sorry, skipper... just got carried away
Okay!
Before we enter the Harbor, please turn in your cameras. NO PICTURE-TAKING IS ALLOWED INSIDE.
Thank you.
Thank you.
What do you want so many cameras for ?
Oh, I'll give them all back when we come out of the Harbor.
We are now approaching 'Battleship Row,' where on December 7th, 1941, The Japanese surprised our Navy. the first planes ...
Say, what's that funny clicking noise?
Why, it's coming from... OH, NO!
CLICK CLICK CLICK CLICK CLICK
DENNIS! COME OUT OF THERE AND LISTEN TO THE MAN!
CLICK

"On Sunday morning, December 7, 1941, a Japanese task force of 33 ships, including six aircraft carriers, arrived about 250 miles north of Pearl Harbor, and at 6 A.M. they launched their first wave of planes.

"They swept in over the Islands at 7:40 A.M., completely surprising us. Fighters and dive-bombers led the attack, and within a matter of minutes, they had destroyed or damaged all of the 450 planes we had on the ground. With our air defense destroyed, they began the attack on 'Battleship Row', a channel one mile long where eight battleships were tied up.

"At this time there were 97 ships in the Harbor; 18 were sunk or damaged, including all eight battleships. The Japanese, out of 353 planes, lost 29, as well as several submarines. But of our 18 ships sunk or damaged, all but three were back in action before the end of World War II."

PEARL HARBOR
DECEMBER 7, 1941
HIGH LEVEL BOMBING 0805
TORPEDO ATTACK 0800
PEARL CITY
"BATTLESHIP ROW"
FORD ISLAND
NAVY YARD
HIGH LEVEL BOMBING 0805
SOLACE
NEVADA
ARIZONA
VESTAL
HICKAM FIELD
AIEA
FLEET LANDING
0900 TORPEDO ATTACK
SUBMARINE BASE
F.P.O.
0900 DIVE BOMBER ATTACK
0755 DIVE BOMBER ATTACK
OIL TANK FARM
HONOLULU 8 MILES
CINCPAC
HEADQUARTERS
COMMANDER-IN-CHIEF
PACIFIC FLEET

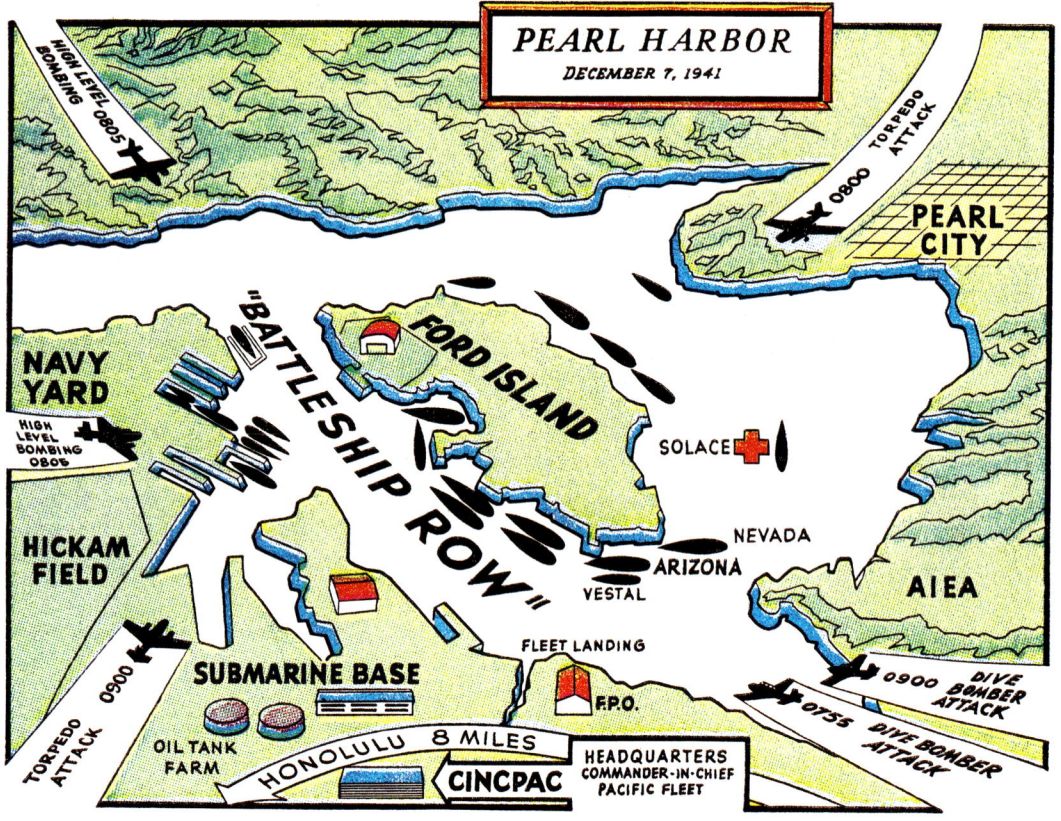

"The Japanese made three big mistakes in their attack. They did not destroy our oil tanks; they did not destroy our submarines; and they did not destroy our shipyard. Our submarines, burning that oil and repaired in our shipyard, were the only attacking weapon we had for almost a year.

"Four days after the attack, our submarines sank a Japanese transport. That was the first of over 1,300 ships sent to the bottom by our submarines during the war—65% of the Japanese fleet."

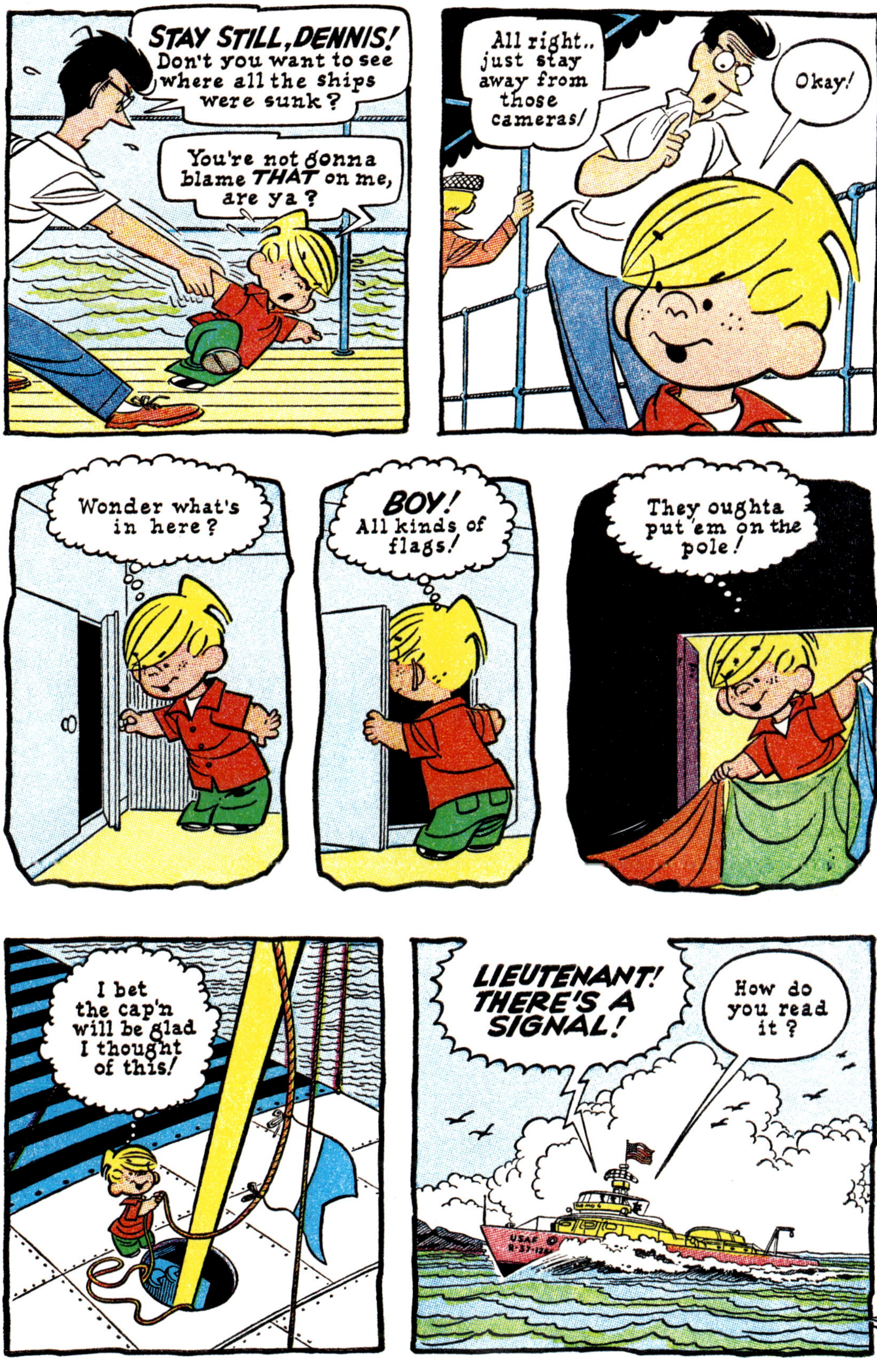
STAY STILL, DENNIS! Don't you want to see where all the ships were sunk?
You're not gonna blame THAT on me, are ya?
All right.. just stay away from those cameras!
Okay!
Wonder what's in here?
BOY! All kinds of flags!
They oughta put 'em on the pole!
I bet the cap'n will be glad I thought of this!
LIEUTENANT! THERE'S A SIGNAL!
How do you read it?

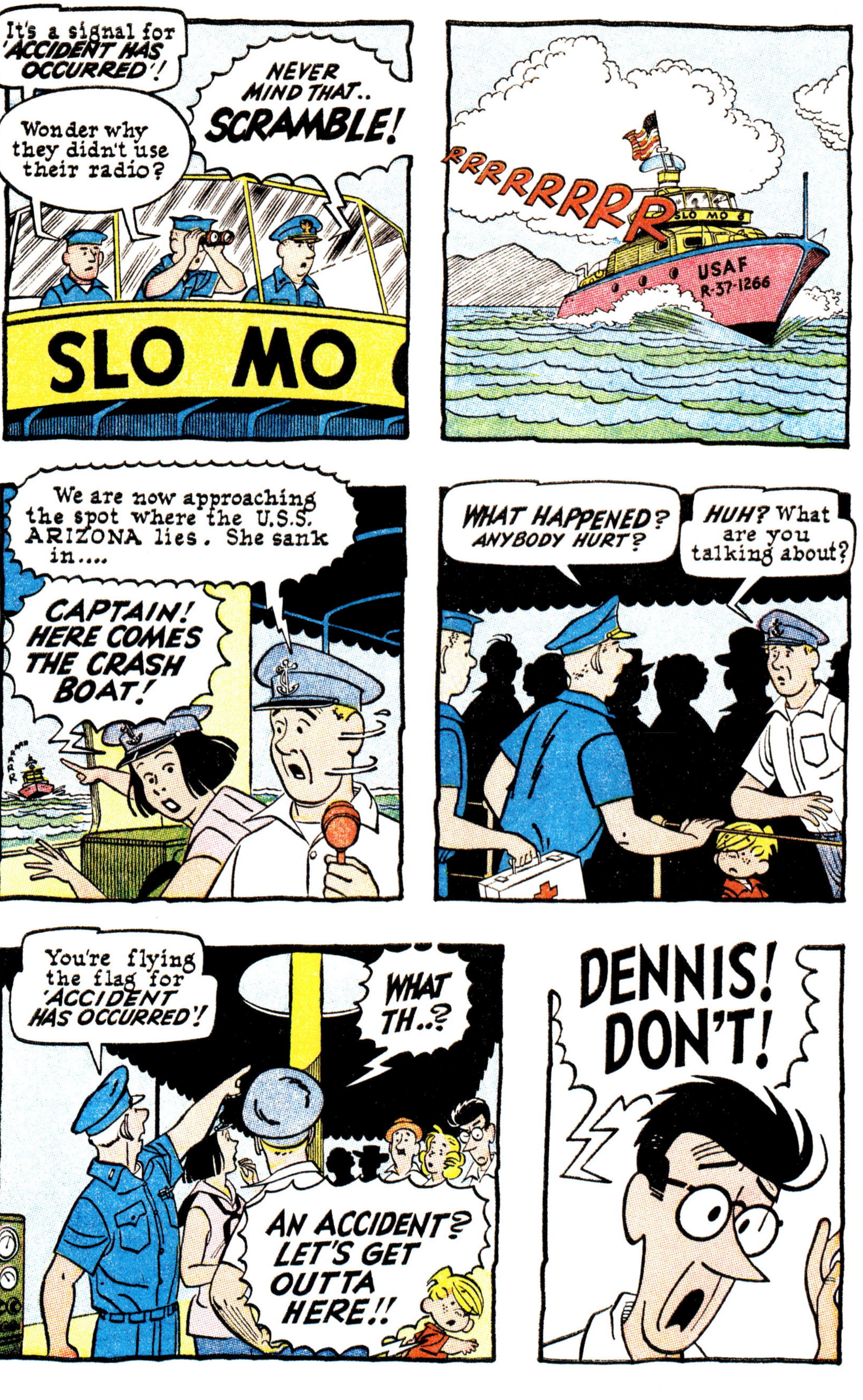
It's a signal for 'ACCIDENT HAS OCCURRED'!
Wonder why they didn't use their radio?
NEVER MIND THAT.. SCRAMBLE!
RRRRRRRRR
SLO MO
USAF R-37-1266
We are now approaching the spot where the U.S.S. ARIZONA lies. She sank in....
CAPTAIN! HERE COMES THE CRASH BOAT!
WHAT HAPPENED? ANYBODY HURT?
HUH? What are you talking about?
You're flying the flag for 'ACCIDENT HAS OCCURRED'!
WHAT TH..?
AN ACCIDENT? LET'S GET OUTTA HERE!!
DENNIS! DON'T!

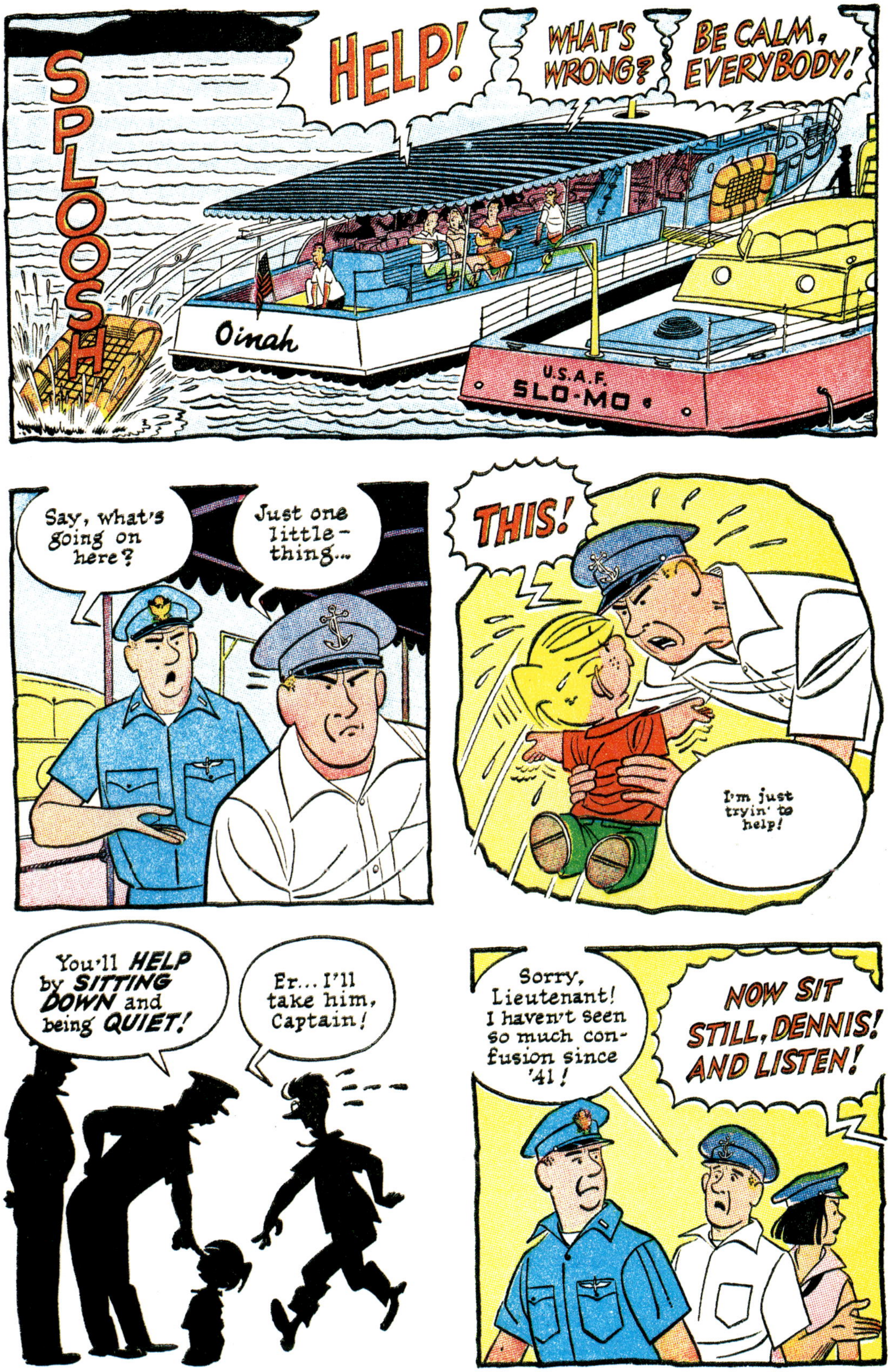
SPLOOSH
HELP!
WHAT'S WRONG?
BE CALM, EVERYBODY!
Oinah
U.S.A.F. SLO-MO
Say, what's going on here?
Just one little-thing...
THIS!
I'm just tryin' to help!
You'll HELP by SITTING DOWN and being QUIET!
Er... I'll take him, Captain!
Sorry, Lieutenant! I haven't seen so much confusion since '41!
NOW SIT STILL, DENNIS! AND LISTEN!

...and here is all we can see of the Arizona. During the attack, a Japanese bomb went down her smokestack and she blew up and sank in eight minutes. Still within this ship are the bodies of over one thousand gallant officers and men who went down with her. Because of this, the Navy has never taken the Arizona off its books, and in 1950, a plaque was placed on her by the Commander-In-Chief of the Pacific Fleet. It reads:

"From today on the USS Arizona will again fly our country's flag just as proudly as she did on the morning of 7 December1941. I am sure the Arizona's crew will know and appreciate what we are doing. May God make His face to shine upon them and grant them peace."

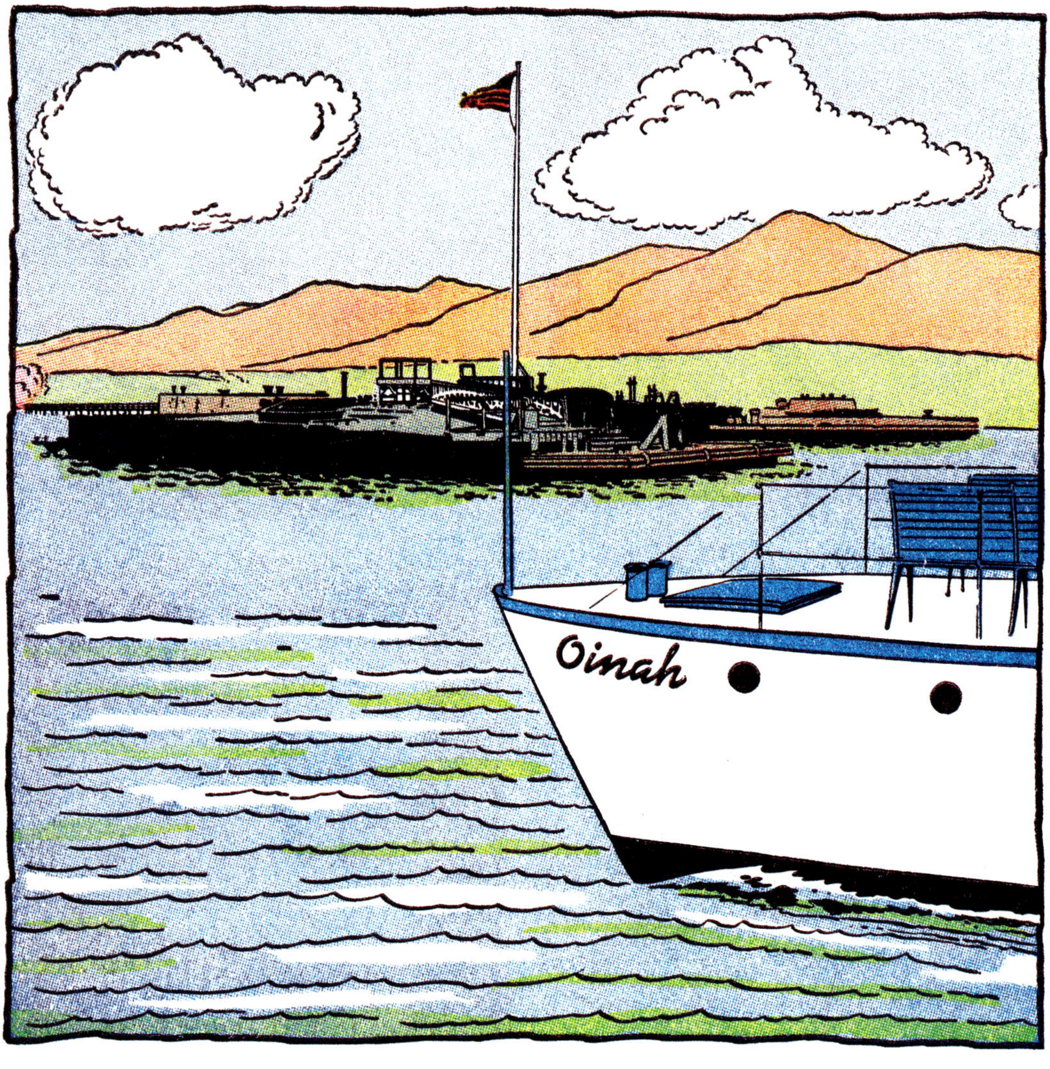
Oinah

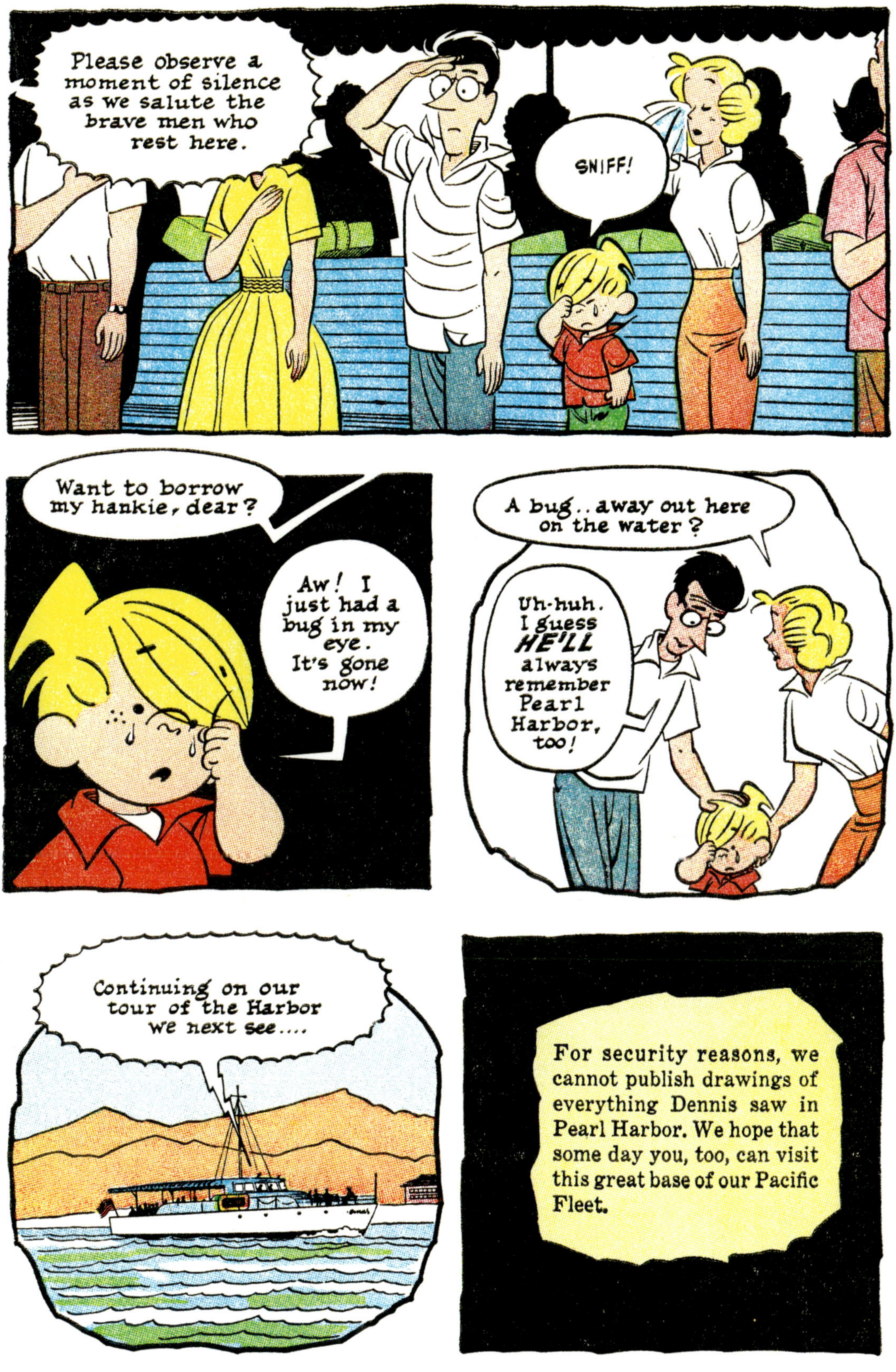
Please observe a moment of silence as we salute the brave men who rest here.
SNIFF!
Want to borrow my hankie, dear?
Aw! I just had a bug in my eye. It's gone now!
A bug.. away out here on the water?
Uh-huh. I guess HE'LL always remember Pearl Harbor, too!
Continuing on our tour of the Harbor we next see....
For security reasons, we cannot publish drawings of everything Dennis saw in Pearl Harbor. We hope that some day you, too, can visit this great base of our Pacific Fleet.

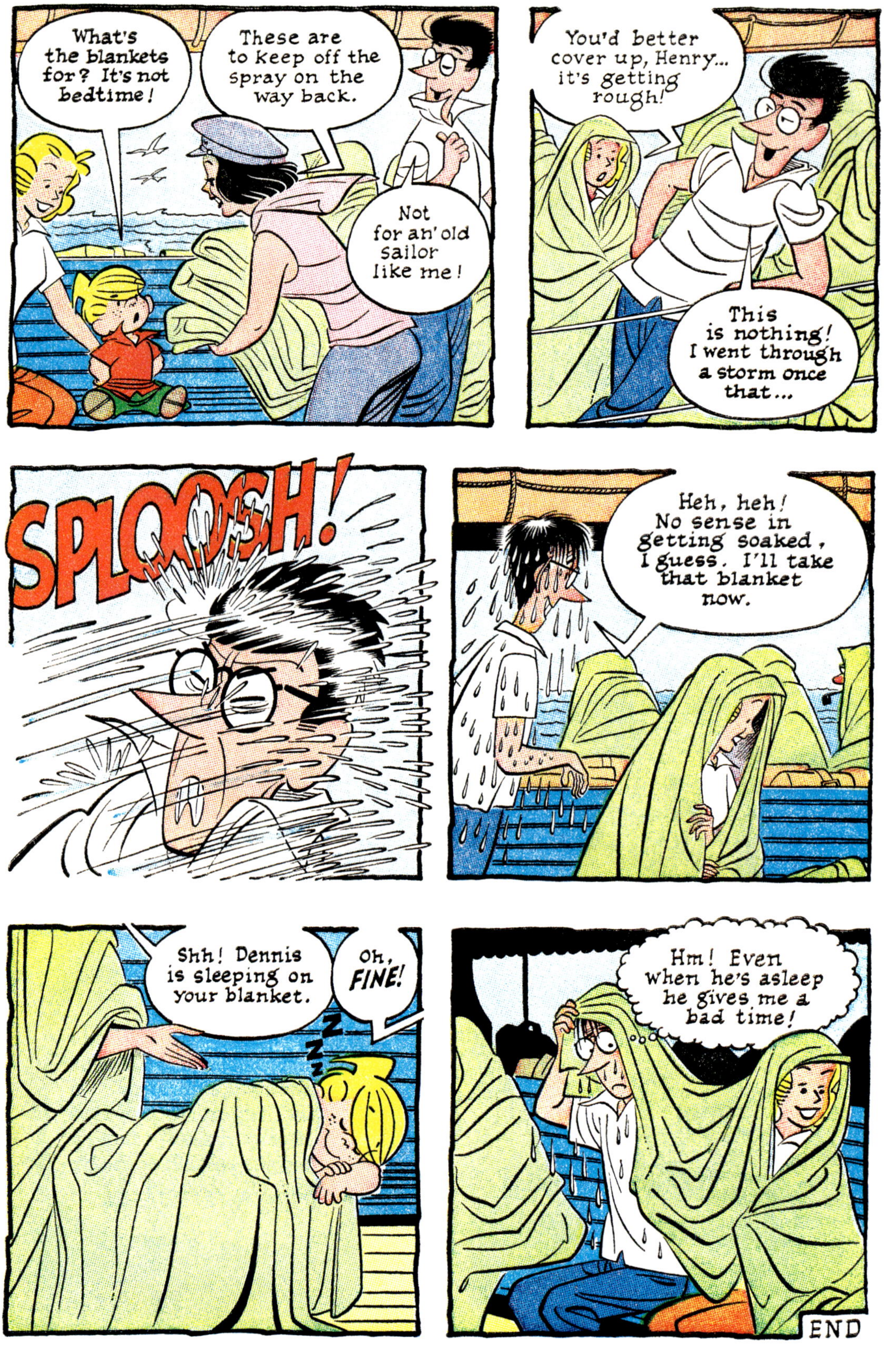
What's the blankets for? It's not bedtime!
These are to keep off the spray on the way back.
Not for an' old sailor like me!
You'd better cover up, Henry... it's getting rough!
This is nothing! I went through a storm once that...
SPLOOSH!
Heh, heh! No sense in getting soaked, I guess. I'll take that blanket now.
Shh! Dennis is sleeping on your blanket.
Oh, FINE!
Z Z Z
Hm! Even when he's asleep he gives me a bad time!
END

CATAMARAN

THE FASTEST BOAT UNDER SAIL!

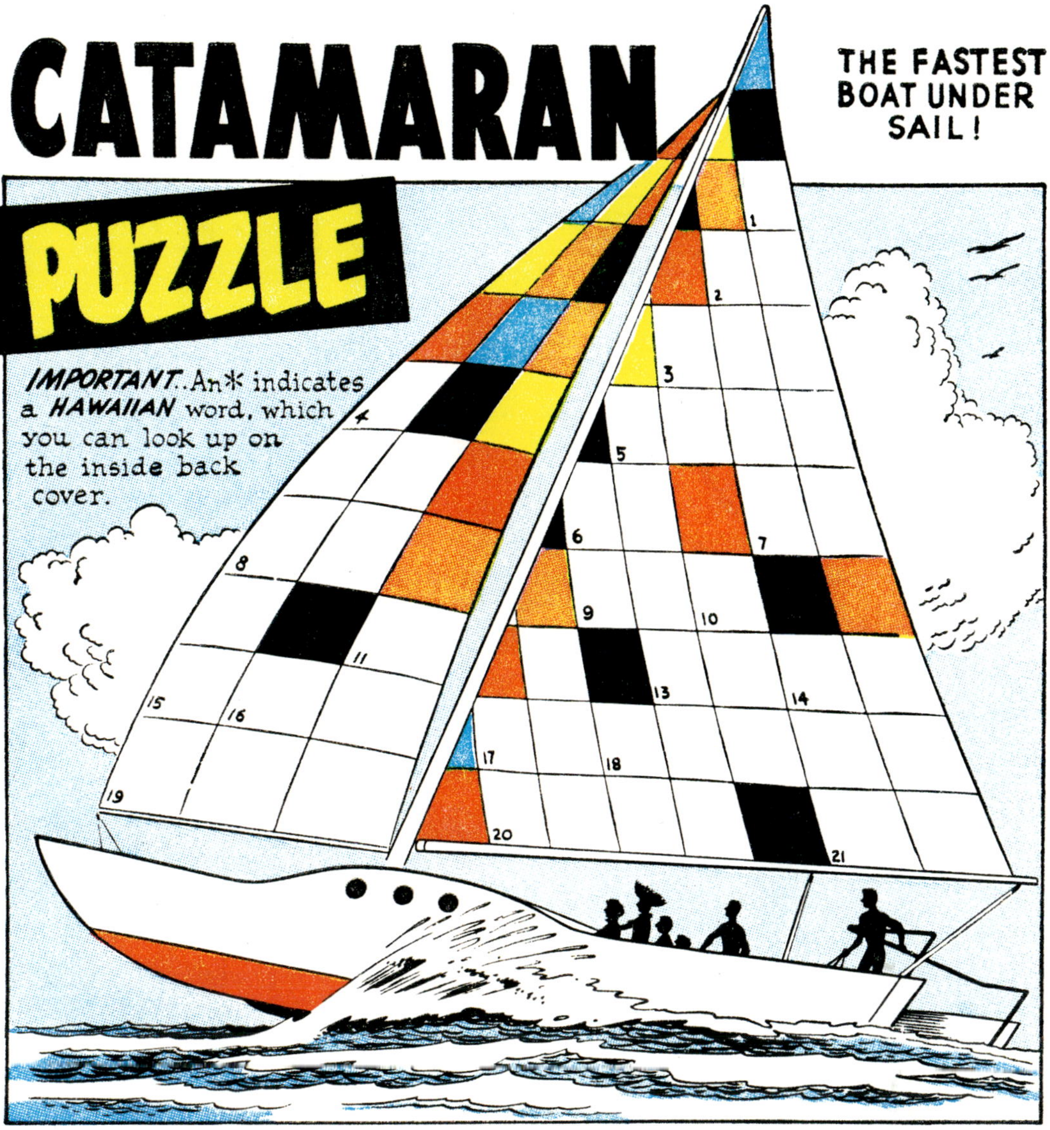
PUZZLE
IMPORTANT..An * indicates a HAWAIIAN word, which you can look up on the inside back cover.

Down

1. Waterway for ships, like the Panama, the Suez
2. No (*)
3. Mom
4. Friend (*)
5. Food: to eat (*)
6. Street (abbr.)
10. Girl (slang)
11. Top for a pot
12. Finished (*)
14. Cooking utensil
16. United Nations (abbr).
17. Matson Line (abbr.)
18. Ha ——

SOLUTION

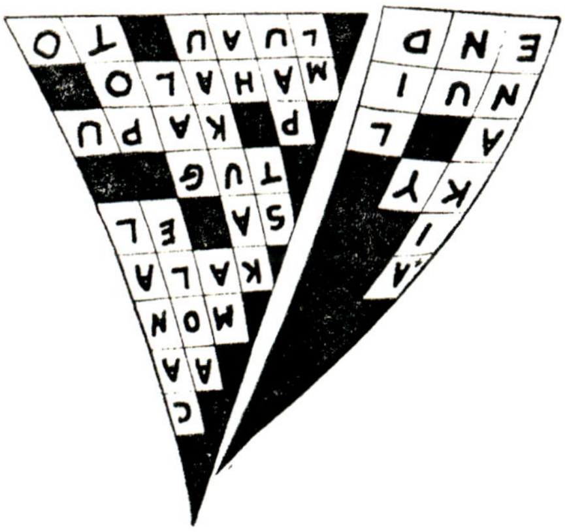

Across

2. Automobile Association (abbr.)
3. Monday (abbr.)
5. Money (*)
6. South America (abbr.)
7. Elevation (abbr.)
8. Kentucky (abbr.)
9. A hard pull
13. Forbidden: Keep out (*)
15. Very much (*)
17. Thank you (*)
19. Finish
20. Big meal: feast (*),
21. Toward

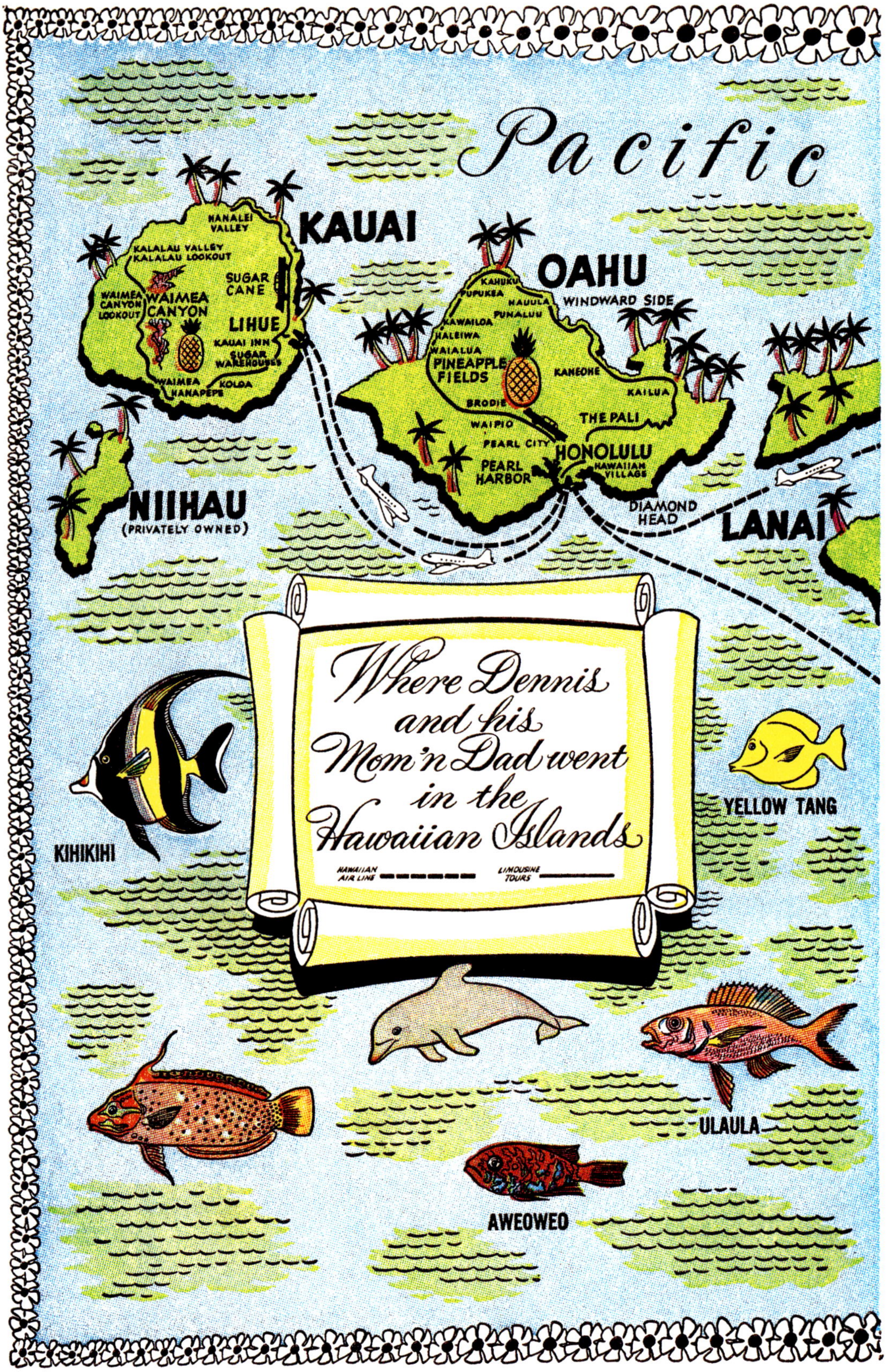
Pacific
KAUAI
HANALEI VALLEY
KALALAU VALLEY
KALALAU LOOKOUT
WAIMEA CANYON LOOKOUT
WAIMEA CANYON
SUGAR CANE
LIHUE
KAUAI INN
SUGAR WAREHOUSES
WAIMEA
HANAPEPE
KOLOA
OAHU
KAHUKU
PUPUKEA
HAUULA
PUNALUU
WINDWARD SIDE
KAWAILOA
HALEIWA
WAIALUA
PINEAPPLE FIELDS
KANEOHE
KAILUA
BRODIE
WAIPIO
THE PALI
PEARL CITY
HONOLULU
PEARL HARBOR
HAWAIIAN VILLAGE
DIAMOND HEAD
NIIHAU
(PRIVATELY OWNED)
LANAI
Where Dennis and his Mom'n Dad went in the Hawaiian Islands
HAWAIIAN AIR LINE
LIMOUSINE TOURS
KIHIKIHI
YELLOW TANG
ULAULA
AWEOWEO

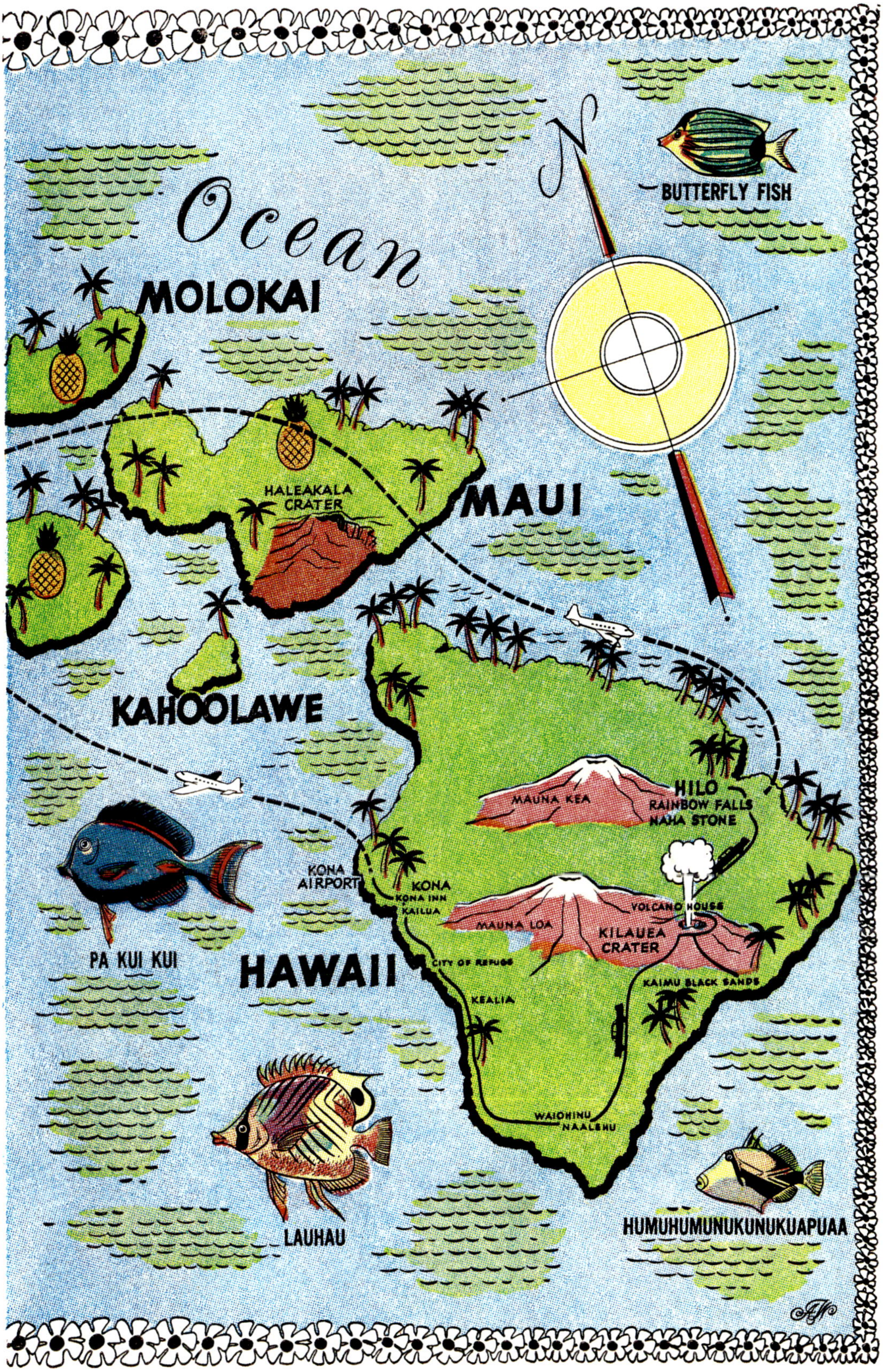

Ocean
N
BUTTERFLY FISH
MOLOKAI
HALEAKALA CRATER
MAUI
KAHOOLAWE
MAUNA KEA
HILO
RAINBOW FALLS
NAHA STONE
KONA AIRPORT
KONA
KONA INN
KAILUA
MAUNA LOA
VOLCANO HOUSE
KILAUEA CRATER
PA KUI KUI
HAWAII
CITY OF REFUGE
KEALIA
KAIMU BLACK SANDS
WAIOHINU
NAALEHU
LAUHAU
HUMUHUMUNUKUNUKUAPUAA

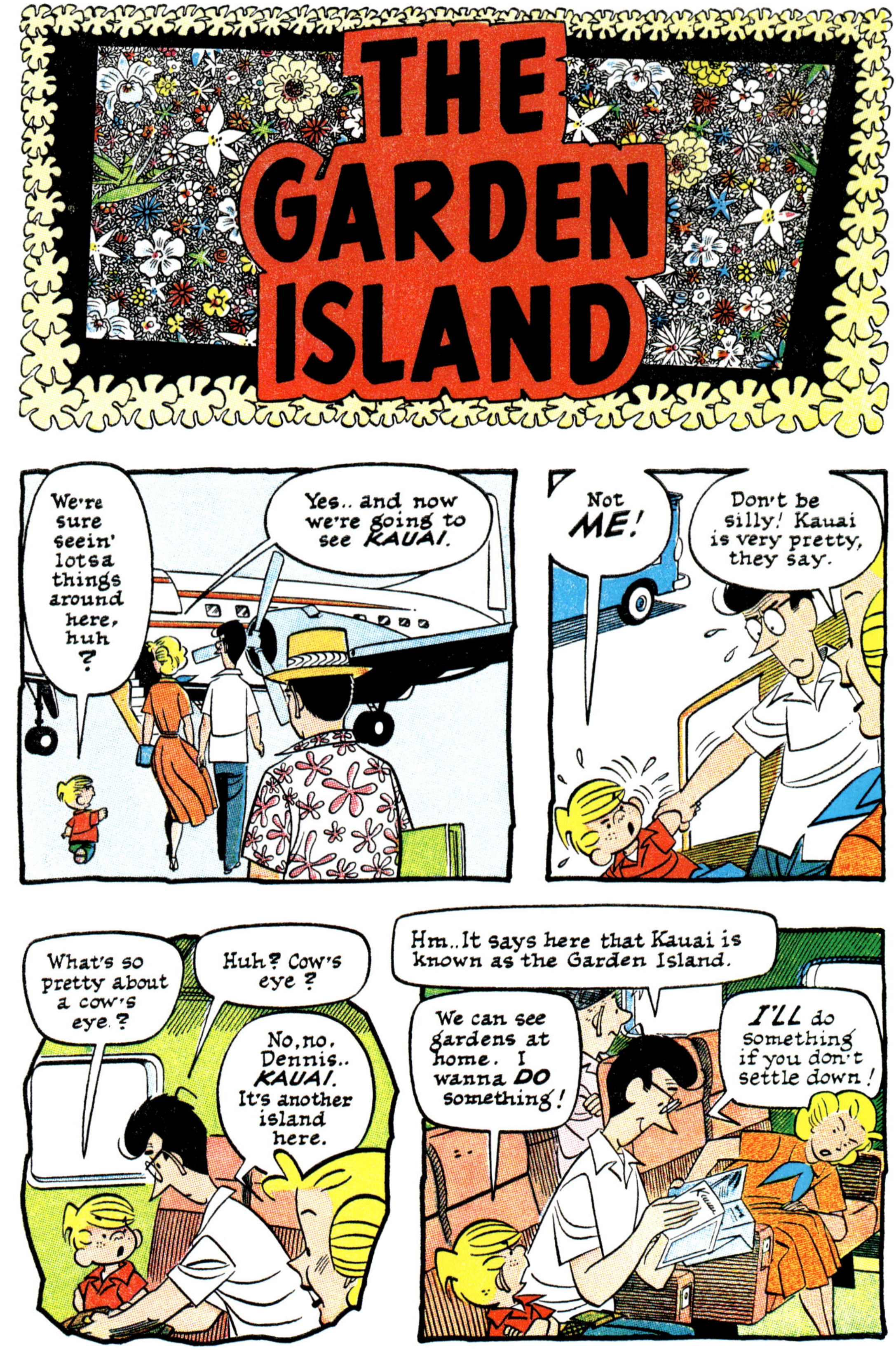
THE GARDEN ISLAND
We're sure seein' lotsa things around here, huh?
Yes.. and now we're going to see KAUAI.
Not ME!
Don't be silly! Kauai is very pretty, they say.
What's so pretty about a cow's eye?
Huh? Cow's eye?
No, no. Dennis.. KAUAI. It's another island here.
Hm..It says here that Kauai is known as the Garden Island.
We can see gardens at home. I wanna DO something!
I'LL do something if you don't settle down!

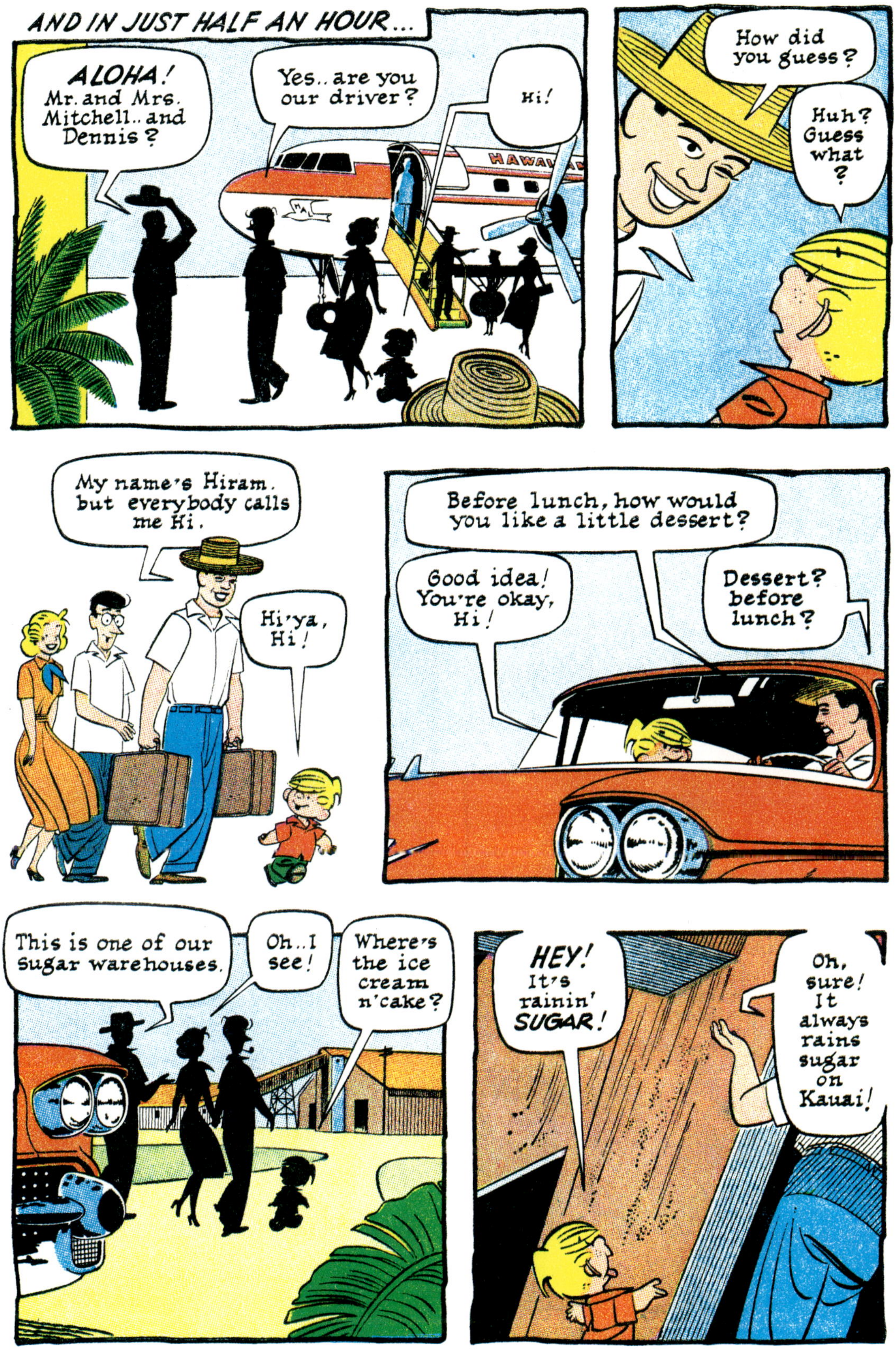
AND IN JUST HALF AN HOUR...
ALOHA! Mr. and Mrs. Mitchell.. and Dennis?
Yes.. are you our driver?
Hi!
HAWAI
How did you guess?
Huh? Guess what?
My name's Hiram. but everybody calls me Hi.
Hi'ya, Hi!
Before lunch, how would you like a little dessert?
Good idea! You're okay, Hi!
Dessert? before lunch?
This is one of our sugar warehouses.
Oh..I see!
Where's the ice cream n'cake?
HEY! It's rainin' SUGAR!
Oh, sure! It always rains sugar on Kauai!

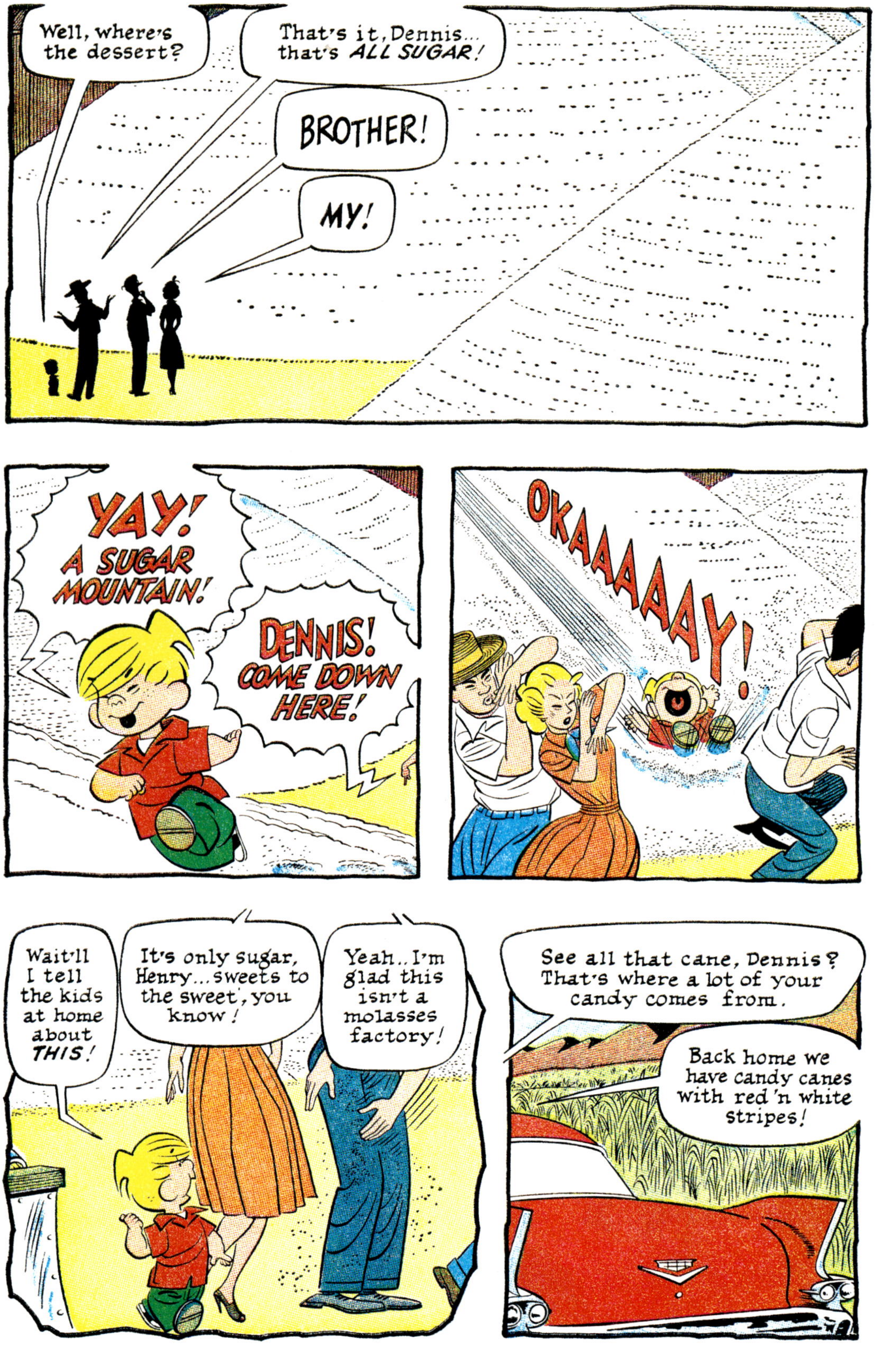
Well, where's the dessert?
That's it, Dennis... that's ALL SUGAR!
BROTHER!
MY!
YAY! A SUGAR MOUNTAIN!
DENNIS! COME DOWN HERE!
OKAAAAAAY!
Wait'll I tell the kids at home about THIS!
It's only sugar, Henry... sweets to the sweet, you know!
Yeah.. I'm glad this isn't a molasses factory!
See all that cane, Dennis? That's where a lot of your candy comes from.
Back home we have candy canes with red 'n white stripes!

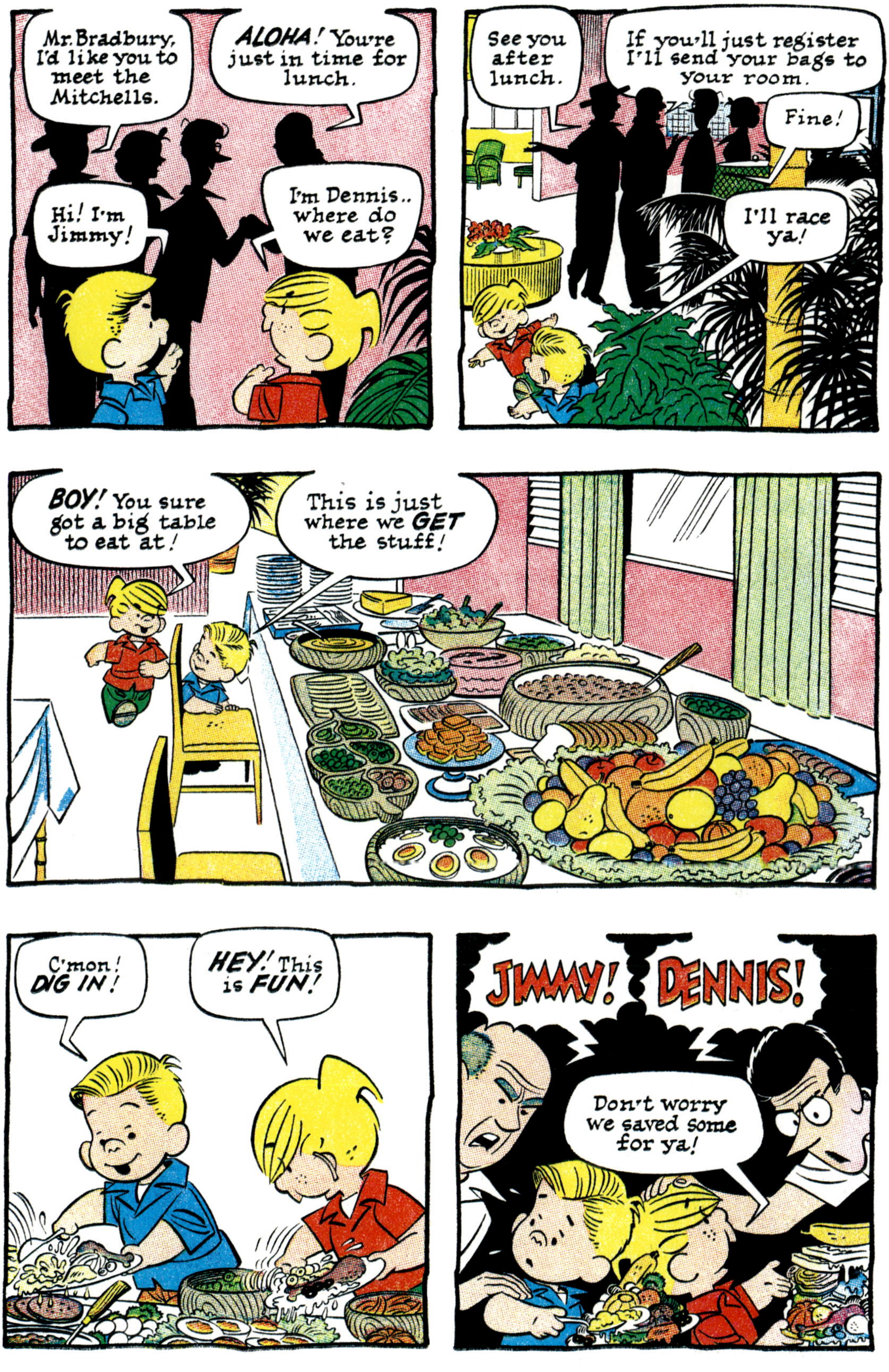
Mr. Bradbury, I'd like you to meet the Mitchells.
ALOHA! You're just in time for lunch.
Hi! I'm Jimmy!
I'm Dennis.. where do we eat?
See you after lunch.
If you'll just register I'll send your bags to your room.
Fine!
I'll race ya!
BOY! You sure got a big table to eat at!
This is just where we GET the stuff!
C'mon! DIG IN!
HEY! This is FUN!
JIMMY! DENNIS!
Don't worry we saved some for ya!

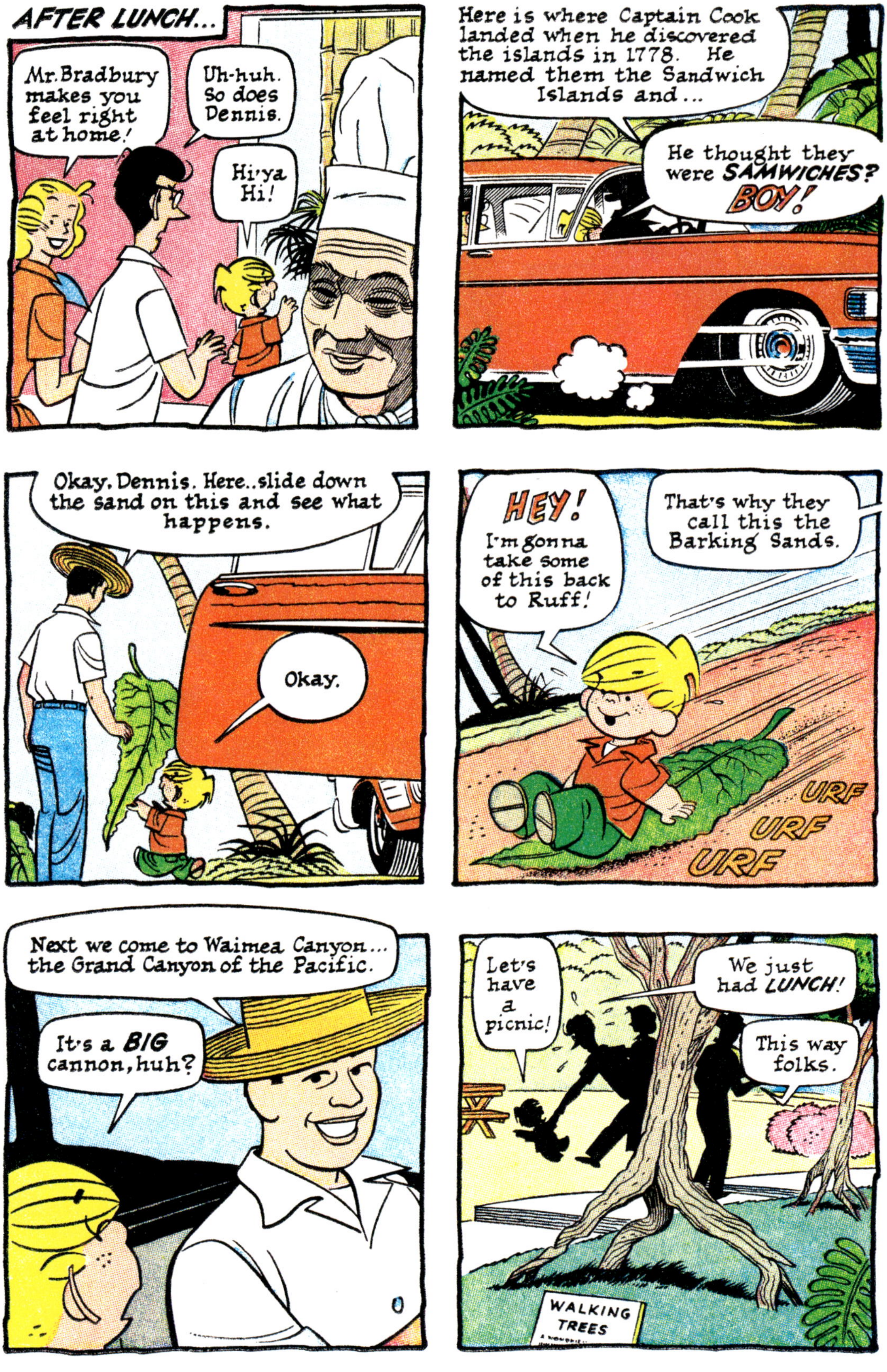
AFTER LUNCH...
Mr. Bradbury makes you feel right at home!
Uh-huh. So does Dennis.
Hi'ya Hi!
Here is where Captain Cook landed when he discovered the islands in 1778. He named them the Sandwich Islands and...
He thought they were SAMWICHES? BOY!
Okay, Dennis. Here..slide down the sand on this and see what happens.
Okay.
HEY! I'm gonna take some of this back to Ruff!
That's why they call this the Barking Sands.
URF
URF
URF
Next we come to Waimea Canyon... the Grand Canyon of the Pacific.
It's a BIG cannon, huh?
Let's have a picnic!
We just had LUNCH!
This way folks.
WALKING TREES

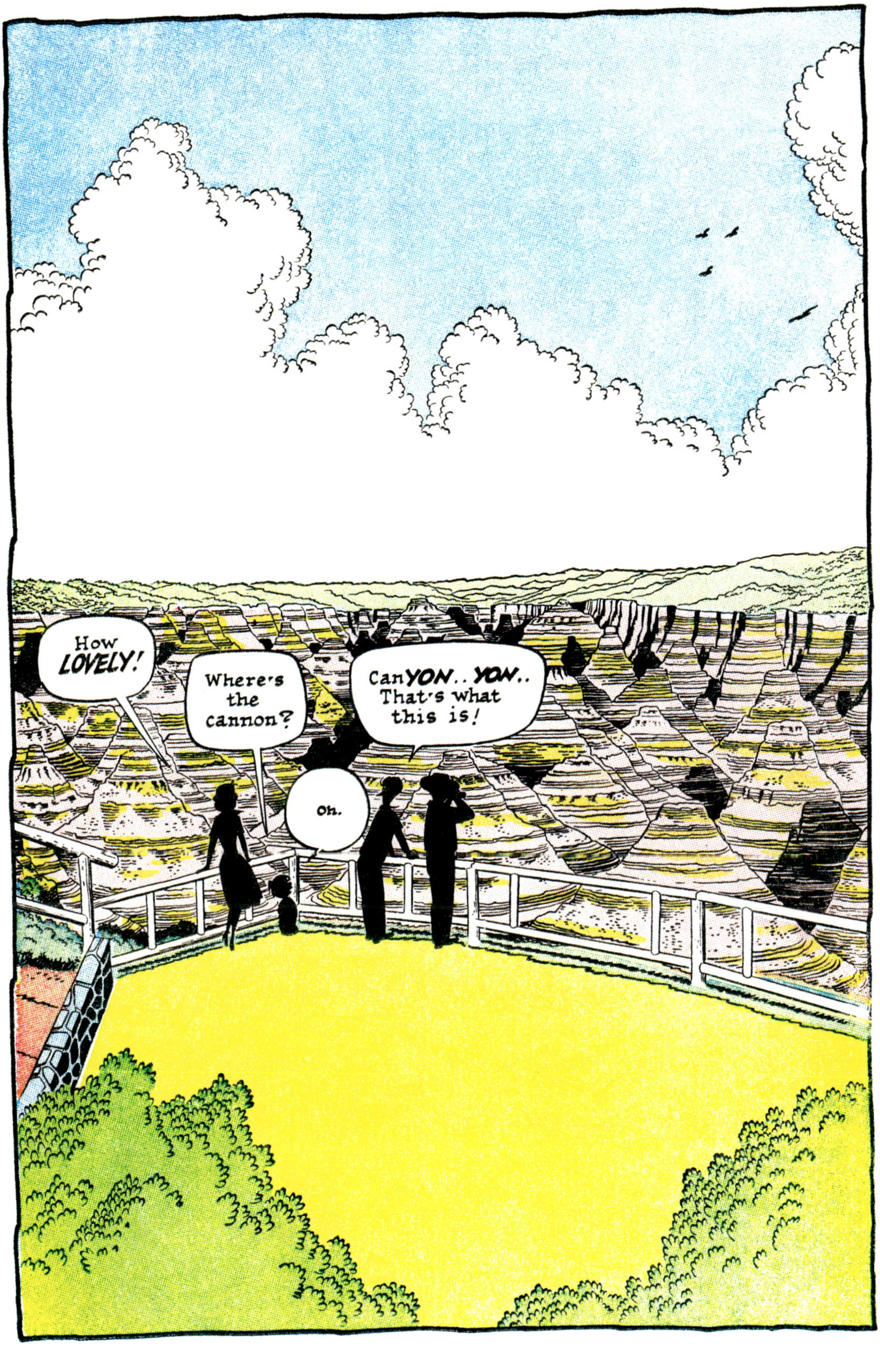
How LOVELY!
Where's the cannon?
Oh.
CanYON.. YON.. That's what this is!

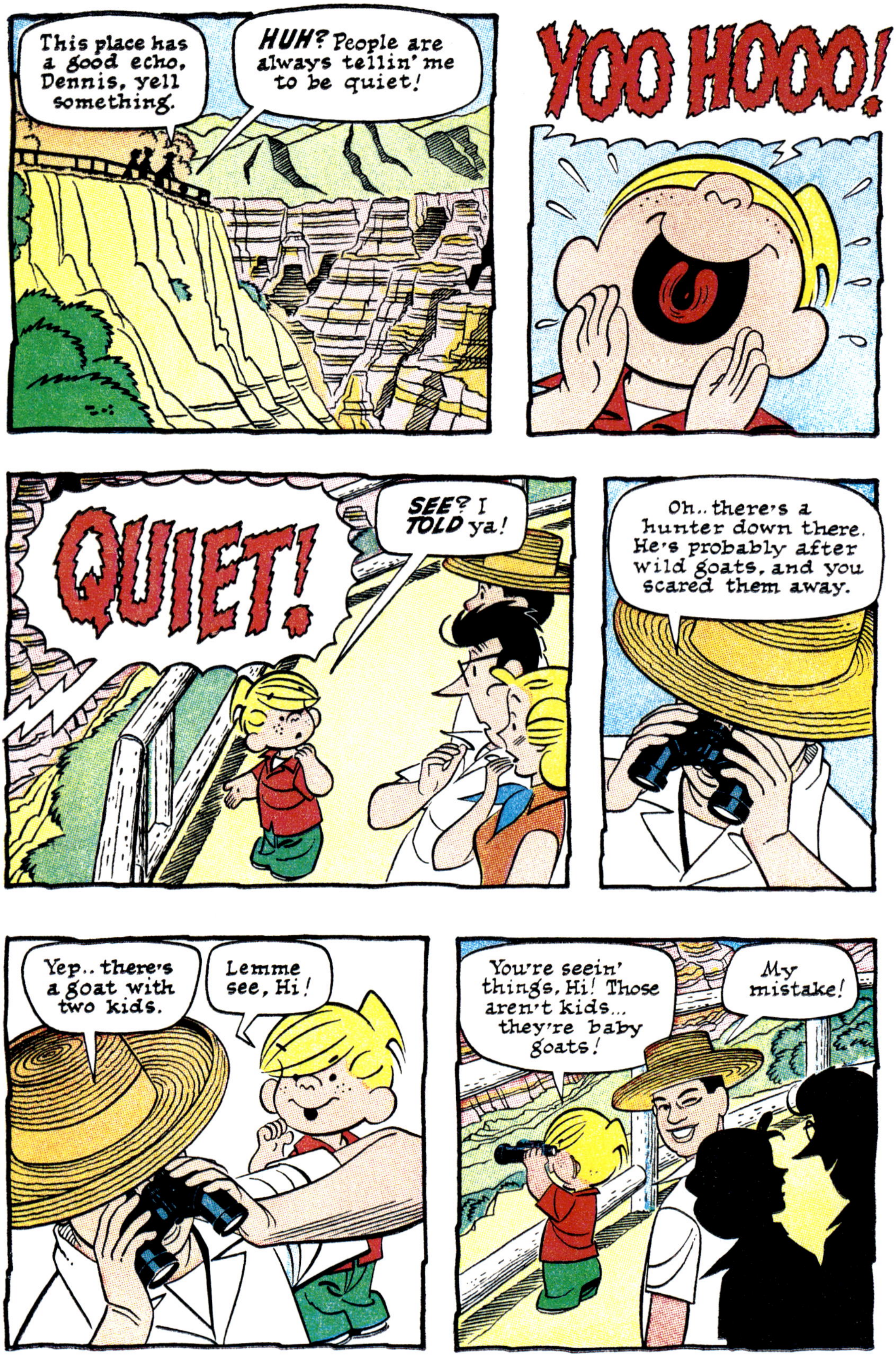
This place has a good echo, Dennis, yell something.
HUH? People are always tellin' me to be quiet!
YOO HOOO!
QUIET!
SEE? I TOLD ya!
Oh.. there's a hunter down there. He's probably after wild goats, and you scared them away.
Yep.. there's a goat with two kids.
Lemme see, Hi!
You're seein' things, Hi! Those aren't kids... they're baby goats!
My mistake!

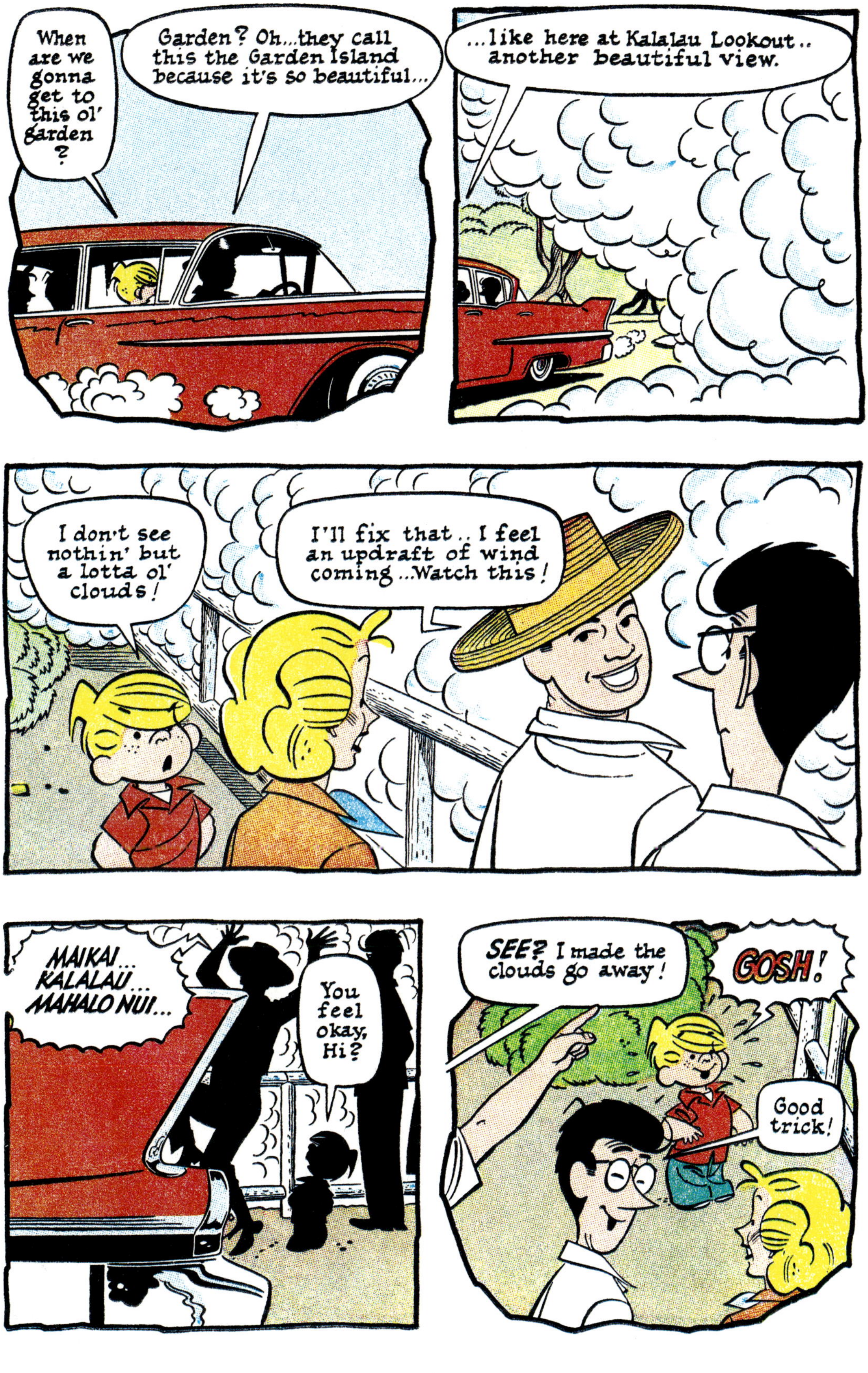
When are we gonna get to this ol' garden?
Garden? Oh...they call this the Garden Island because it's so beautiful...
...like here at Kalalau Lookout.. another beautiful view.
I don't see nothin' but a lotta ol' clouds!
I'll fix that.. I feel an updraft of wind coming...Watch this!
MAIKAI... KALALAU... MAHALO NUI...
You feel okay, Hi?
SEE? I made the clouds go away!
GOSH!
Good trick!

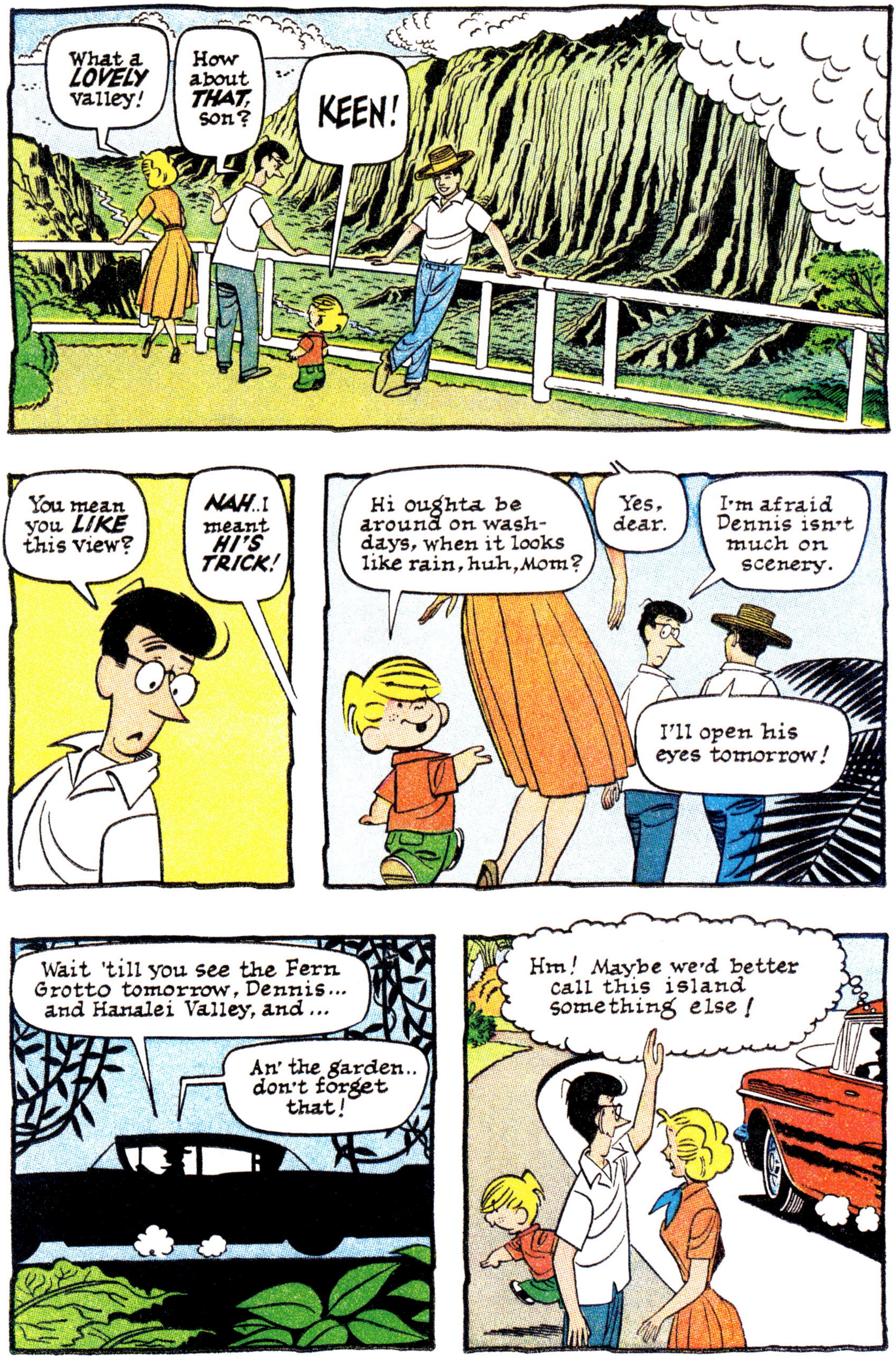

What a LOVELY valley!
How about THAT, son?
KEEN!
You mean you LIKE this view?
NAH..I meant HI'S TRICK!
Hi oughta be around on wash-days, when it looks like rain, huh, Mom?
Yes, dear.
I'm afraid Dennis isn't much on scenery.
I'll open his eyes tomorrow!
Wait 'till you see the Fern Grotto tomorrow, Dennis... and Hanalei Valley, and ...
An' the garden.. don't forget that!
Hm! Maybe we'd better call this island something else!

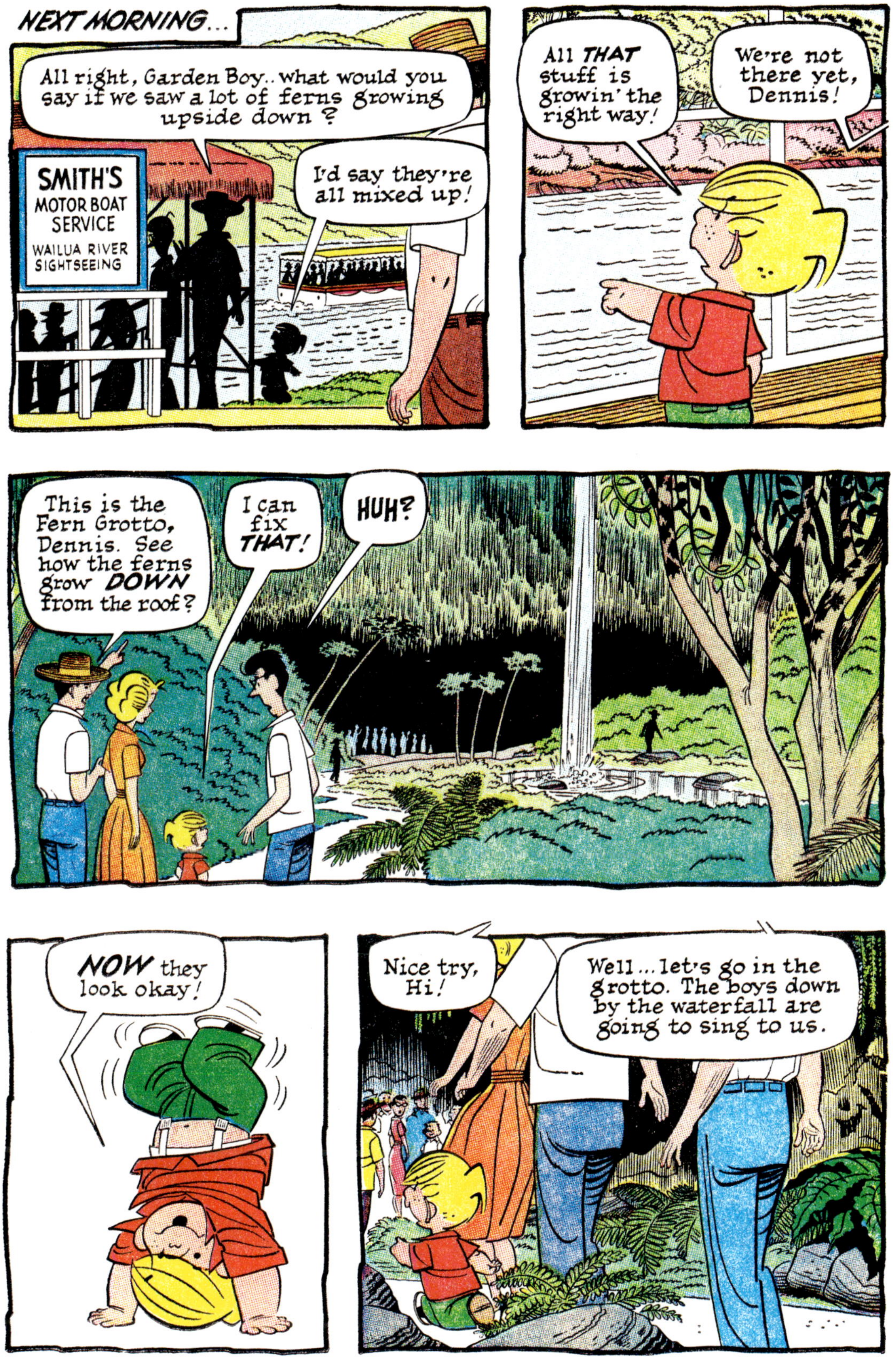
NEXT MORNING...
All right, Garden Boy.. what would you say if we saw a lot of ferns growing upside down?
SMITH'S MOTOR BOAT SERVICE WAILUA RIVER SIGHTSEEING
I'd say they're all mixed up!
All THAT stuff is growin' the right way!
We're not there yet, Dennis!
This is the Fern Grotto, Dennis. See how the ferns grow DOWN from the roof?
I can fix THAT!
HUH?
NOW they look okay!
Nice try, Hi!
Well... let's go in the grotto. The boys down by the waterfall are going to sing to us.

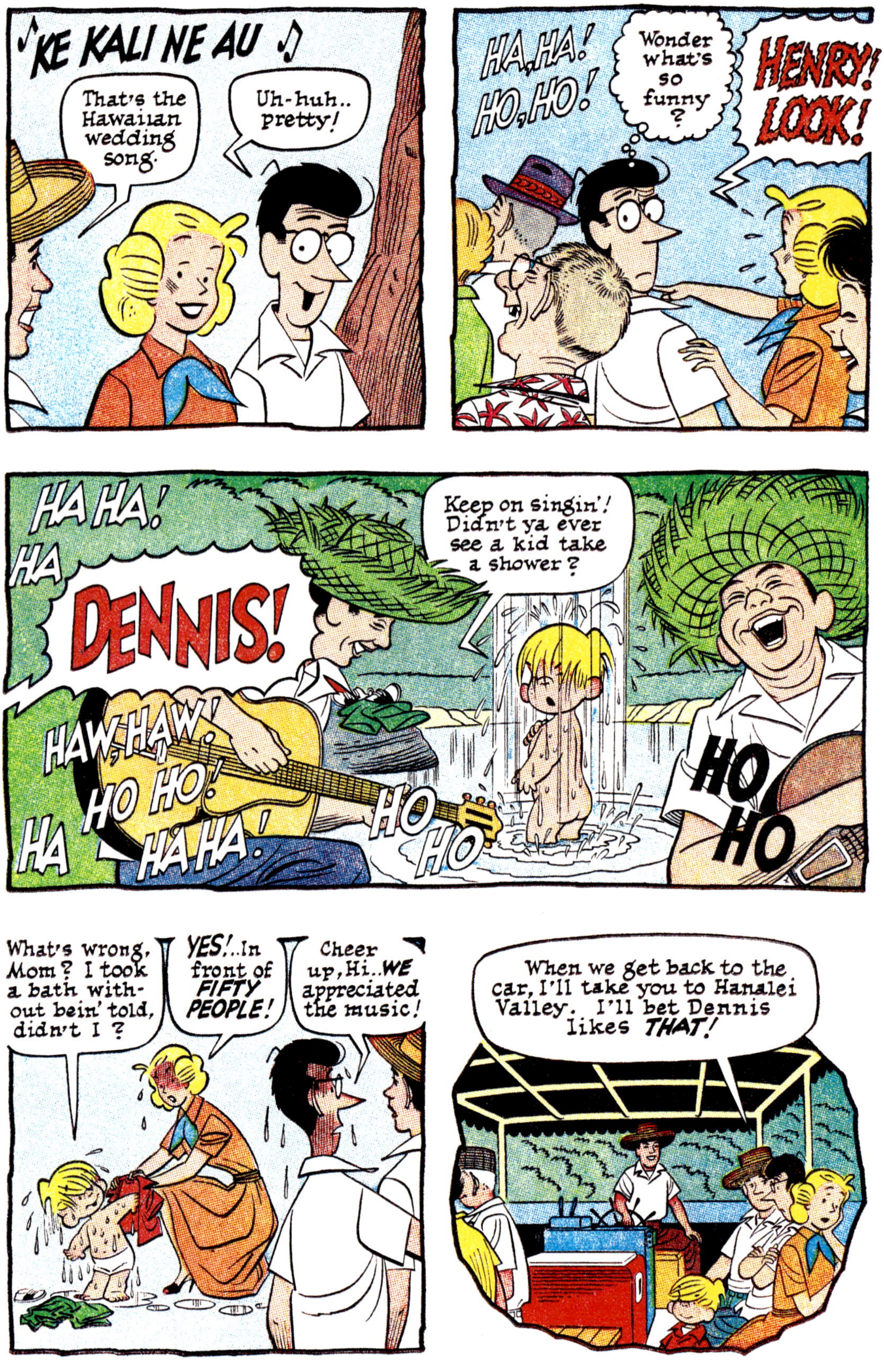
♪ KE KALI NE AU ♫
That's the Hawaiian wedding song.
Uh-huh.. pretty!
HA,HA! HO,HO!
Wonder what's so funny?
HENRY! LOOK!
HA HA! HA
DENNIS!
Keep on singin'! Didn't ya ever see a kid take a shower?
HAW,HAW! HO HO! HA HA HA!
HO HO
HO HO
What's wrong, Mom? I took a bath with-out bein' told, didn't I?
YES!..In front of FIFTY PEOPLE!
Cheer up, Hi.. WE appreciated the music!
When we get back to the car, I'll take you to Hanalei Valley. I'll bet Dennis likes THAT!

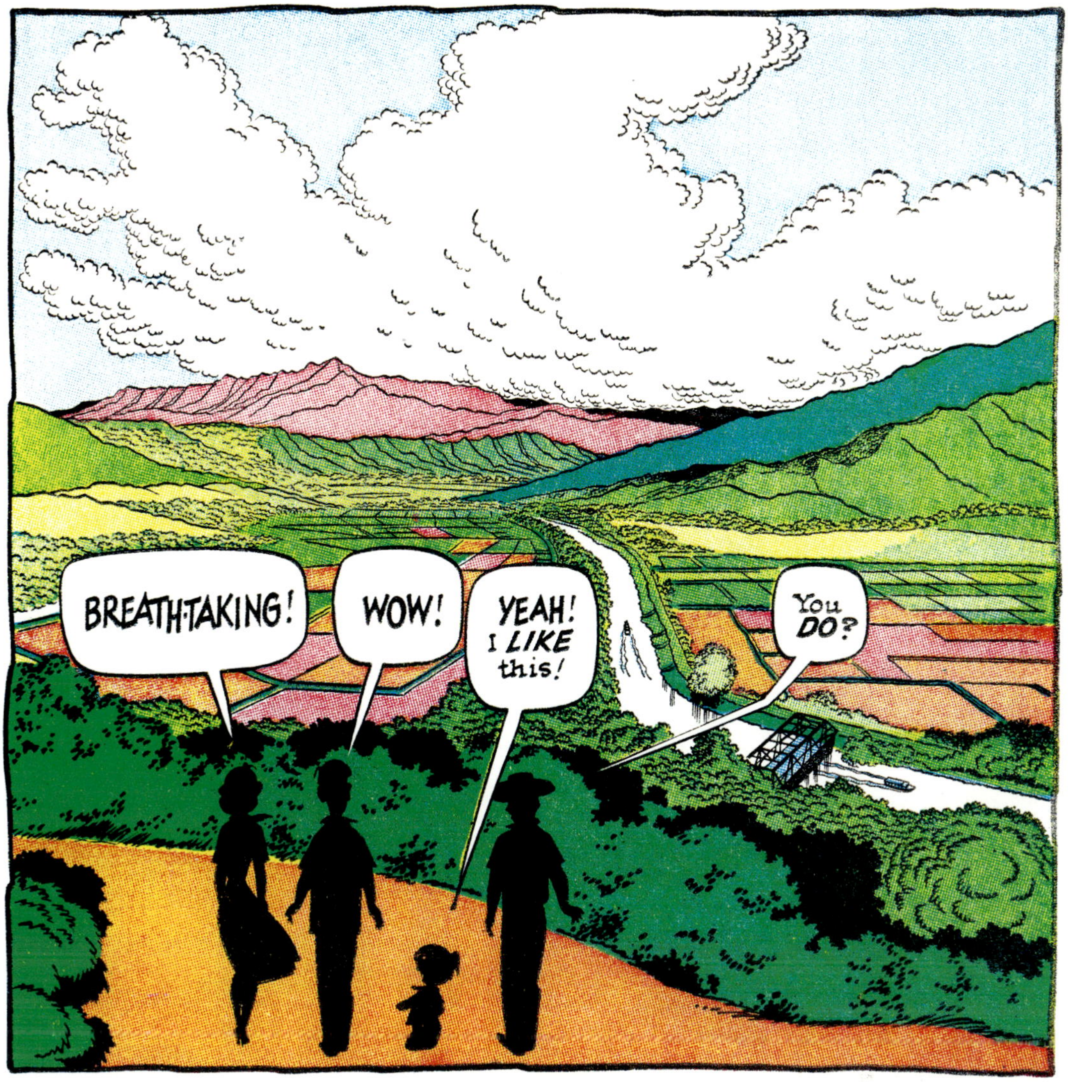
BREATH-TAKING!
WOW!
YEAH! I LIKE this!
You DO?

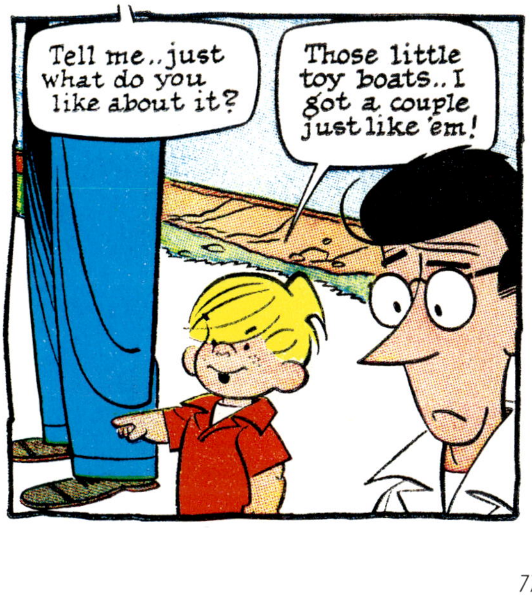
Tell me..just what do you like about it?
Those little toy boats..I got a couple just like 'em!

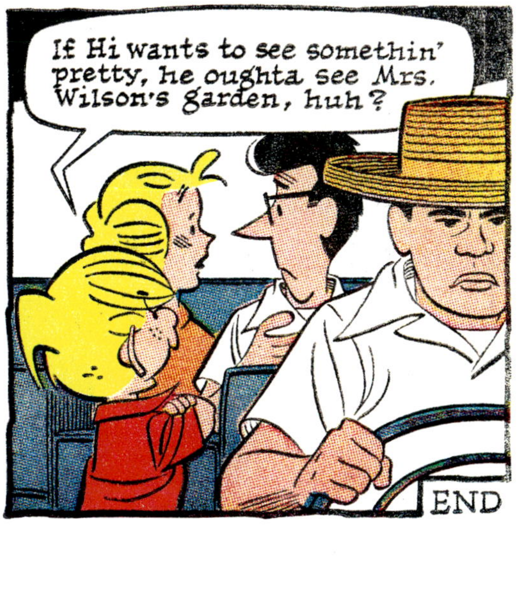
If Hi wants to see somethin' pretty, he oughta see Mrs. Wilson's garden, huh?
END

NOW YOU CAN

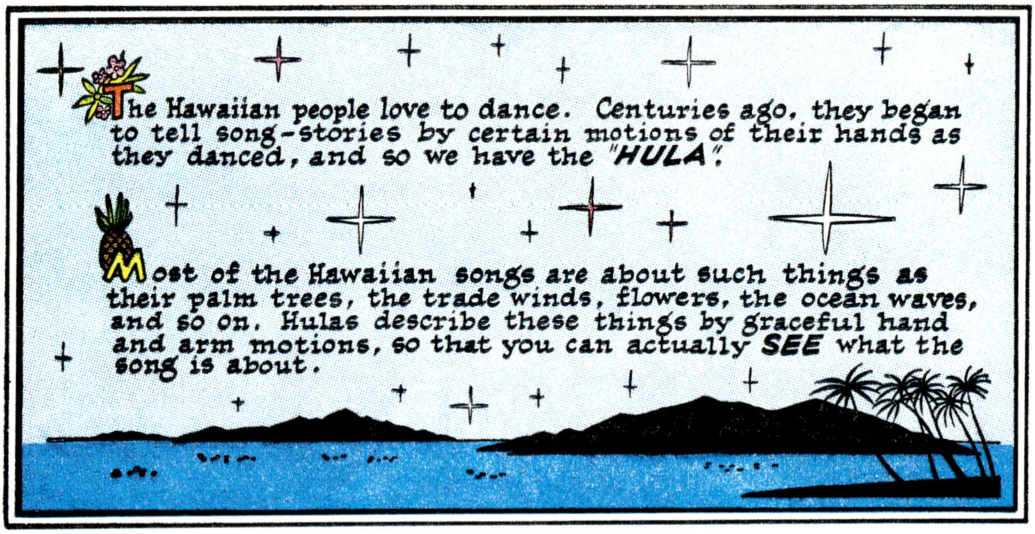
The Hawaiian people love to dance. Centuries ago, they began to tell song-stories by certain motions of their hands as they danced, and so we have the "HULA".
Most of the Hawaiian songs are about such things as their palm trees, the trade winds, flowers, the ocean waves, and so on. Hulas describe these things by graceful hand and arm motions, so that you can actually SEE what the song is about.

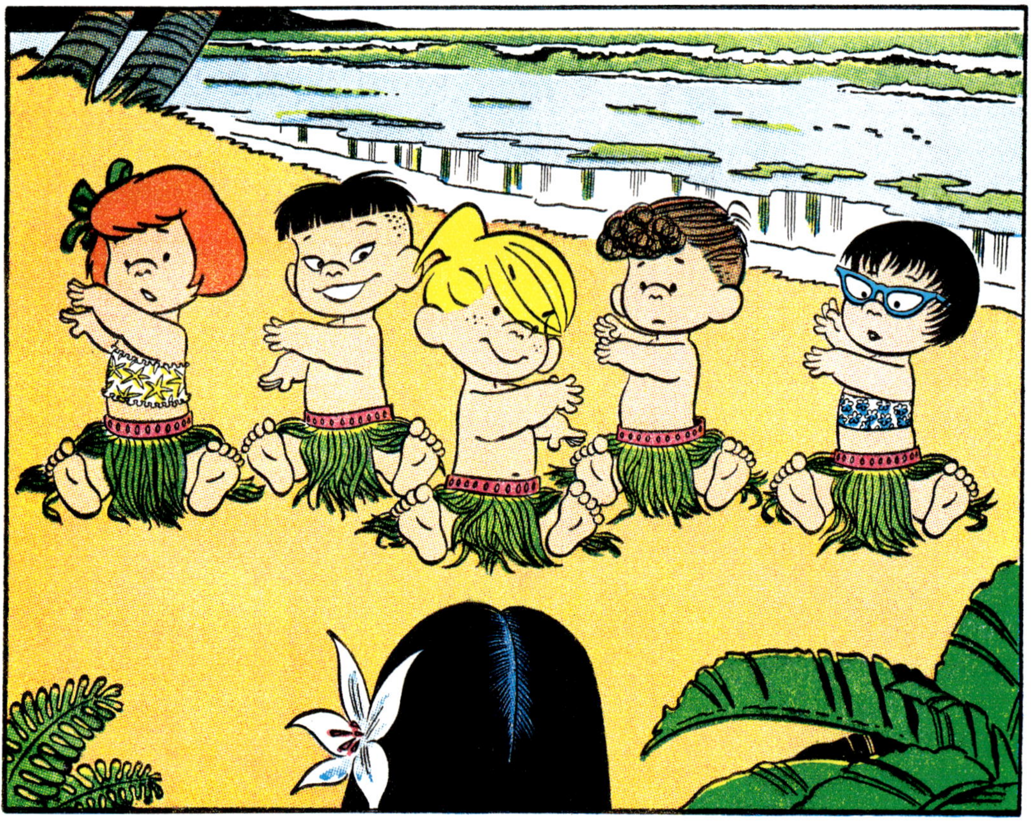

DO THE HULA!

Here is a simple little hula YOU can do to the tune of "Twinkle, Twinkle, Little Star." You do this with just your hands and arms, while sitting cross-legged on the floor or ground. It's a lot of fun if several of you do it together, sitting in a circle, singing the song as you do it.

This was taught us by NONA KAPUA BEAMER, one of the most famous teachers of the hula in Hawaii.

"TWINKLE, TWINKLE, LITTLE STAR"

① (STARTING POSITION) OH... ②

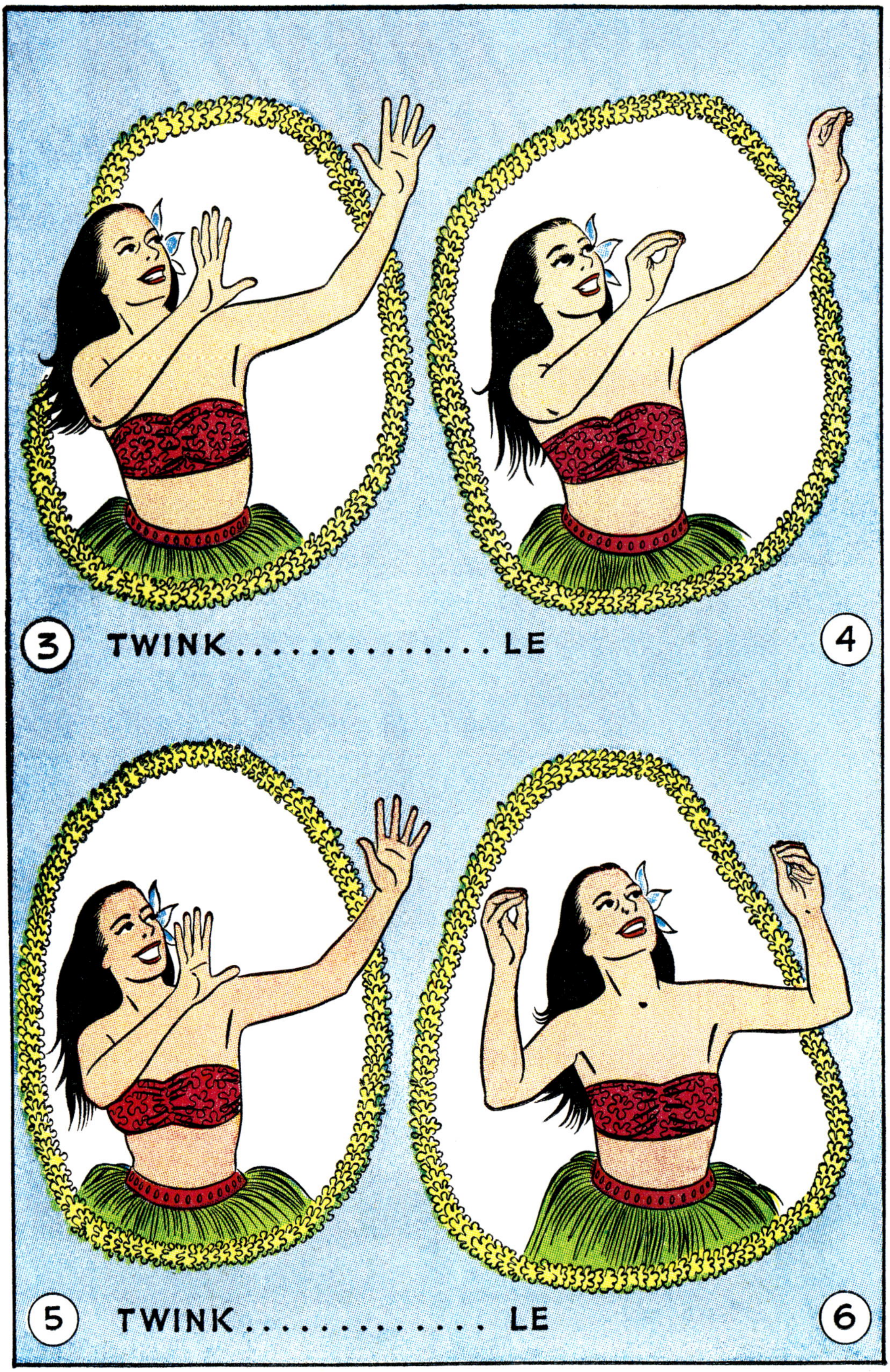
3
TWINK............LE
4
5
TWINK............LE
6

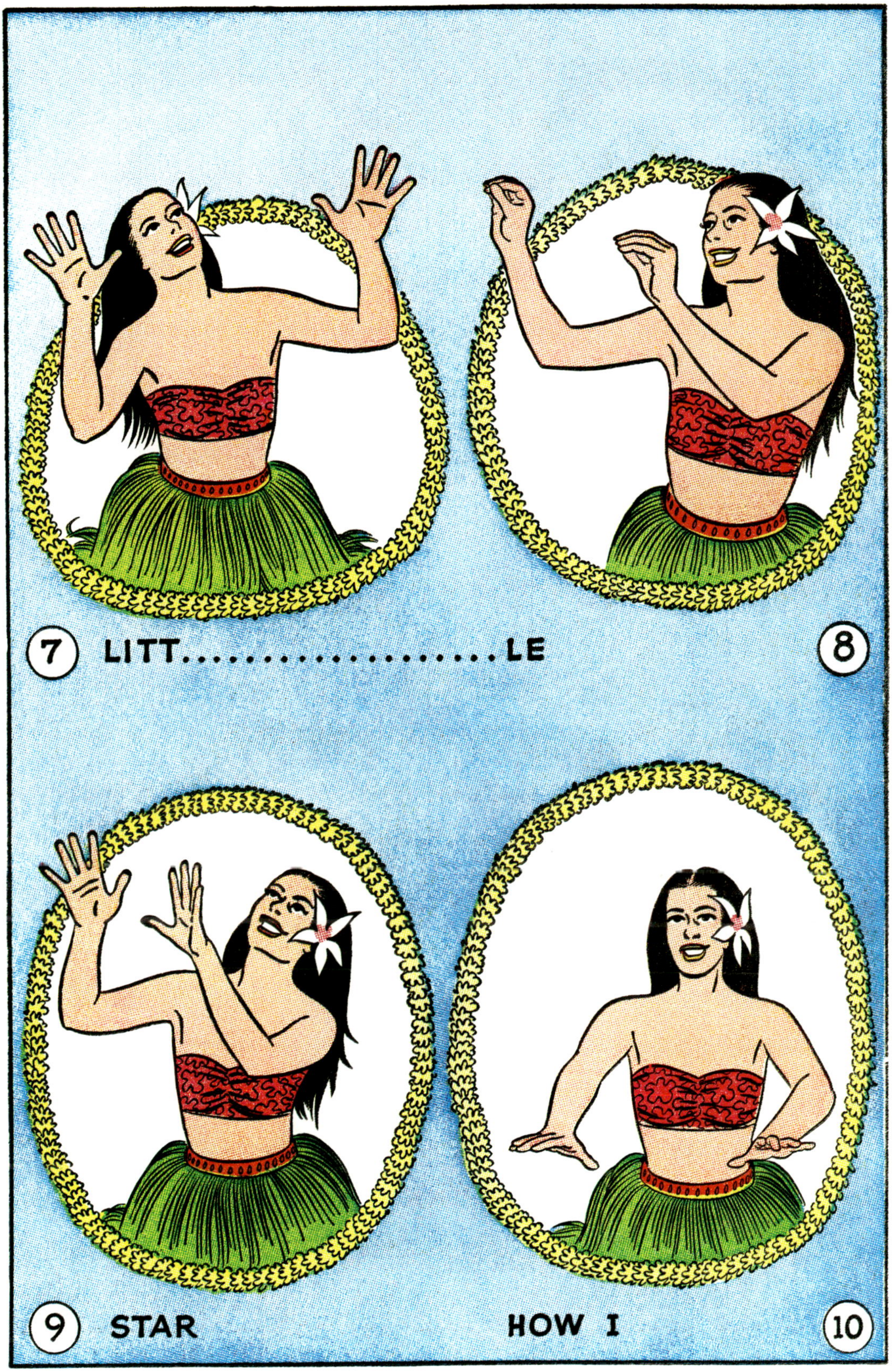
7 LITT.....................LE
8
9 STAR
HOW I
10

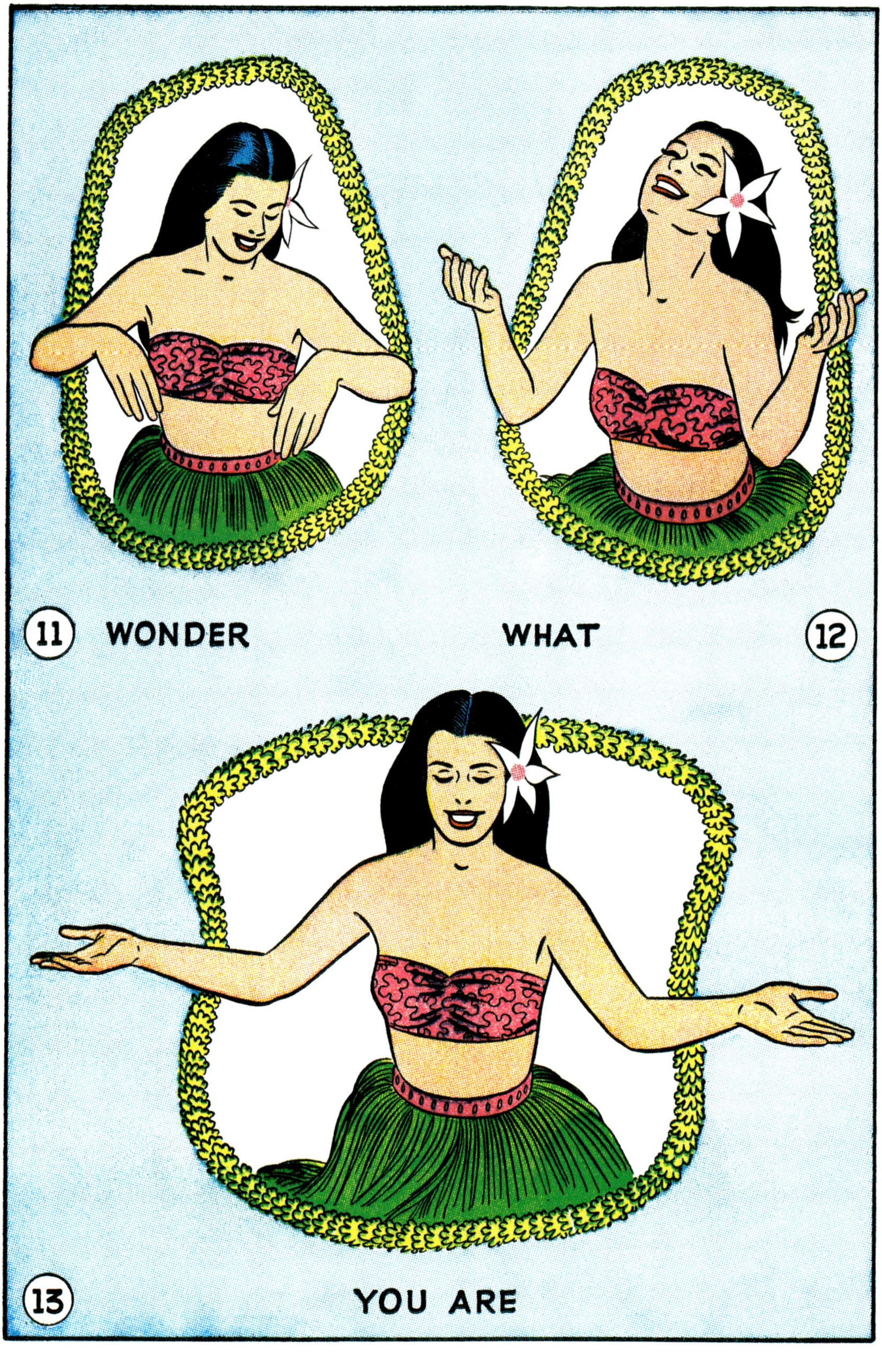
11 WONDER
WHAT 12
13 YOU ARE

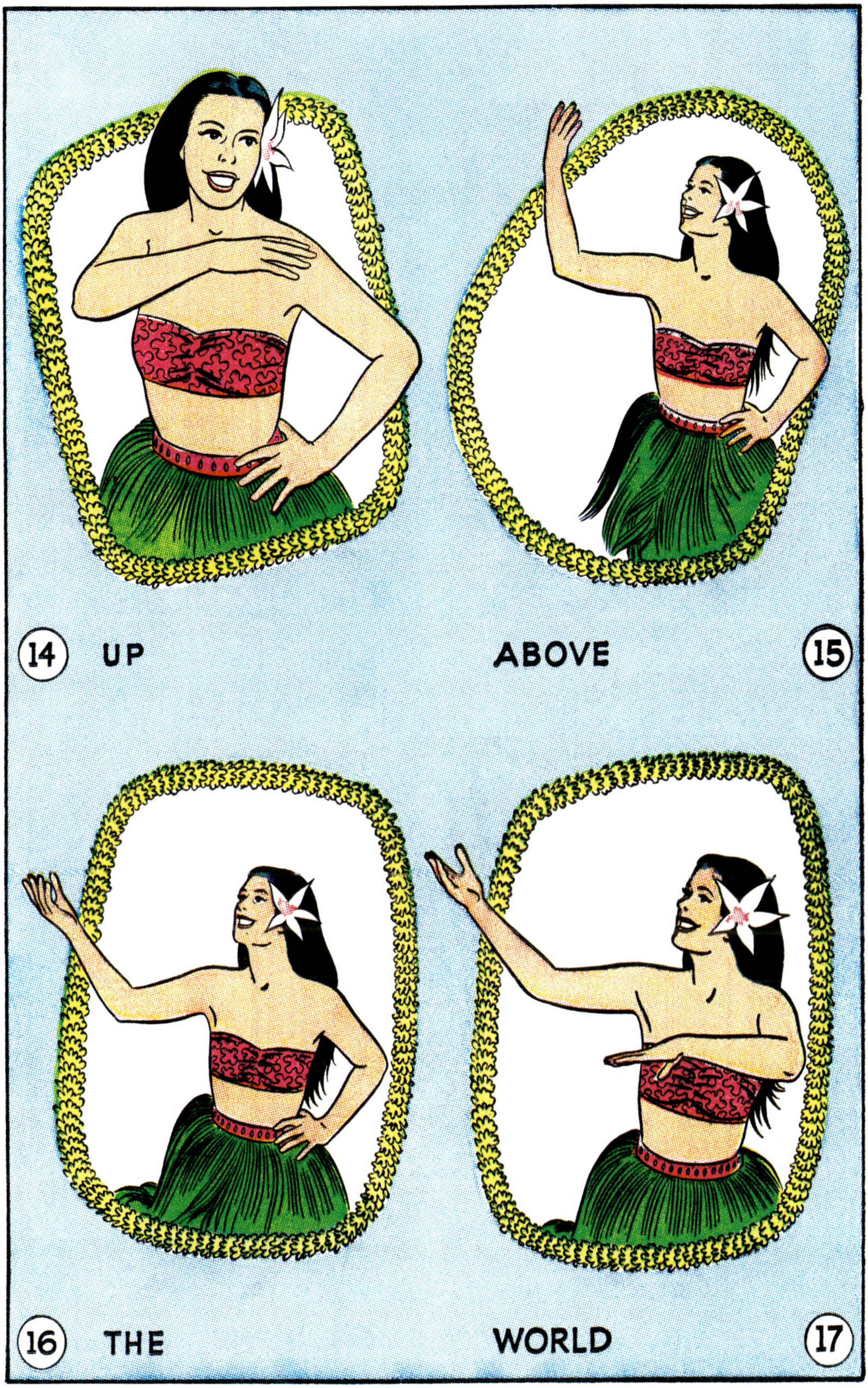
14 UP
ABOVE 15
16 THE
WORLD 17

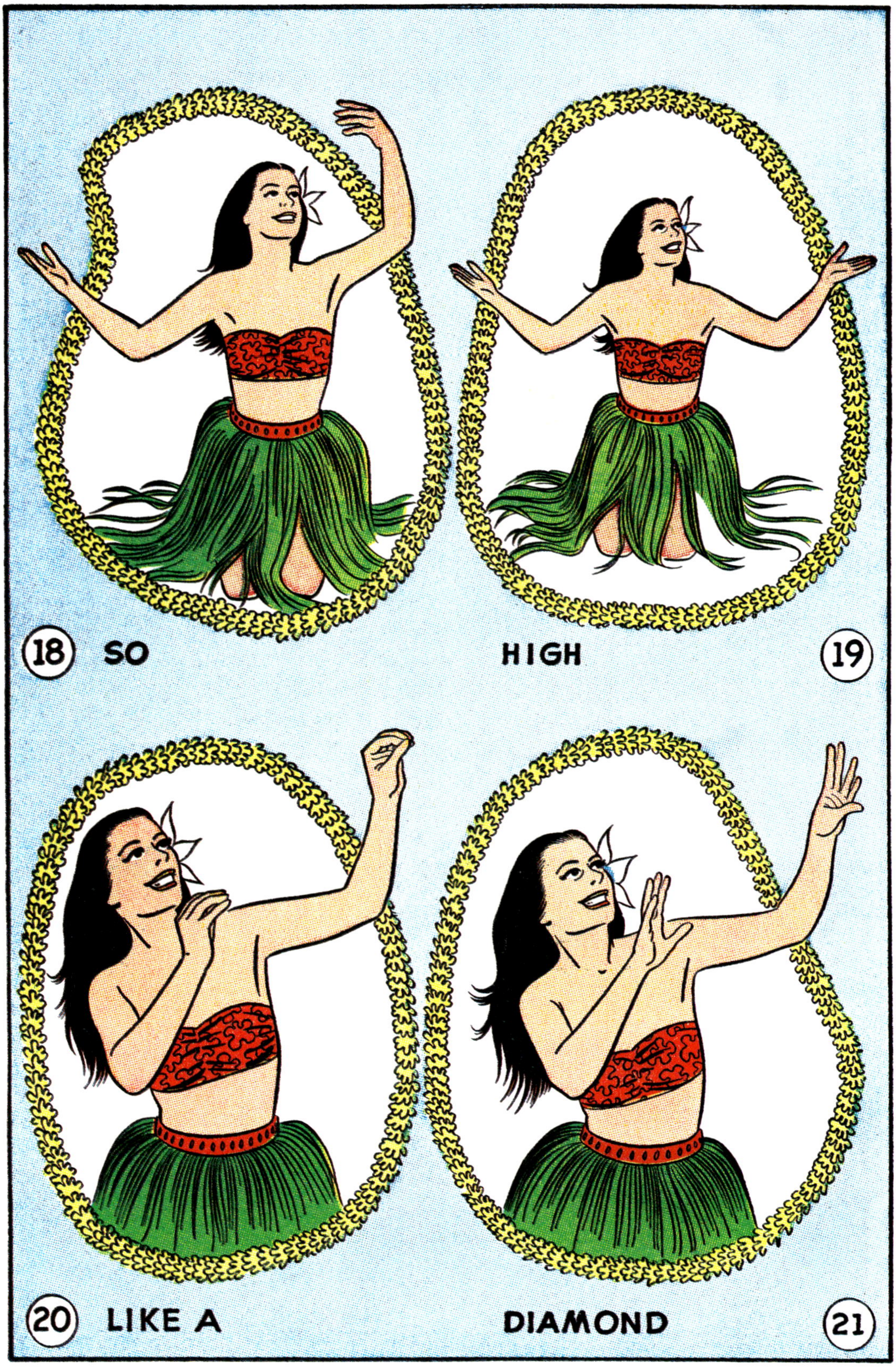
18 SO
HIGH 19
20 LIKE A
DIAMOND 21

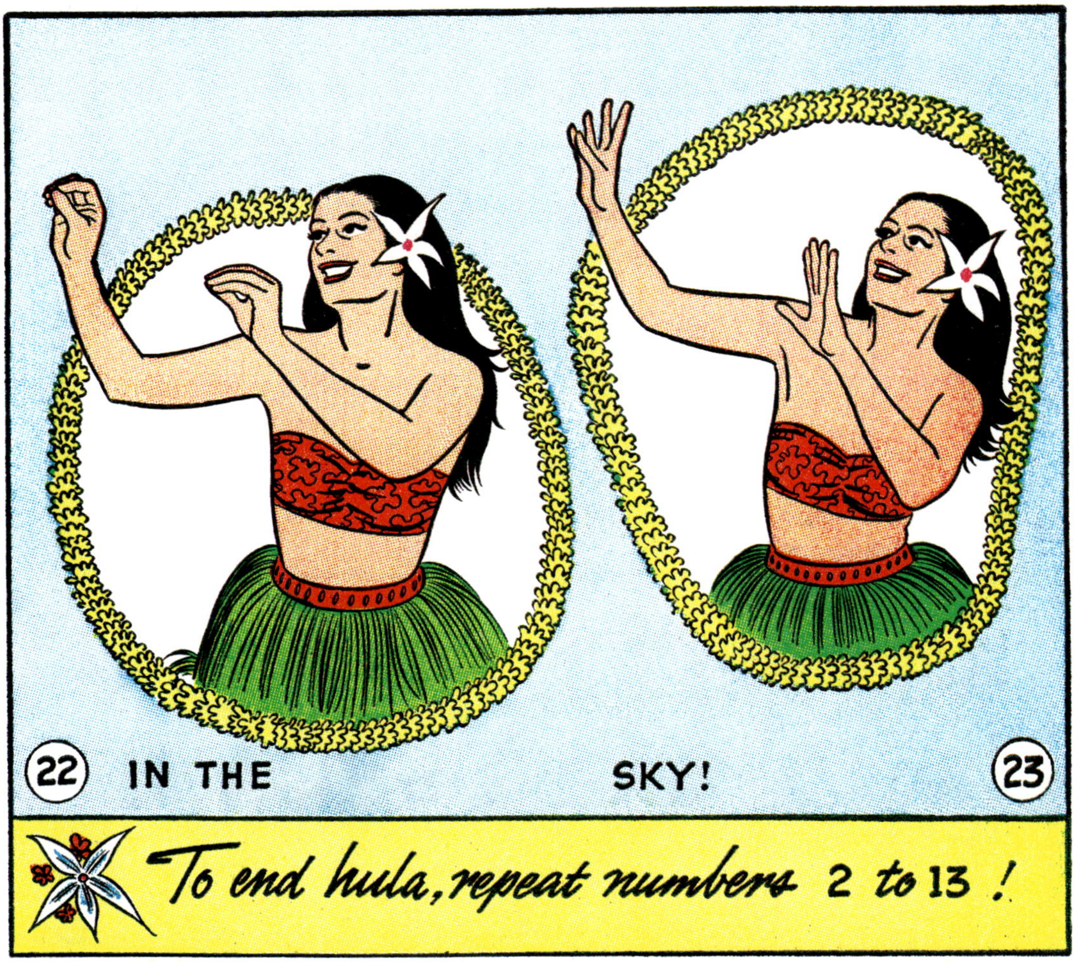

22
IN THE
SKY!
23
To end hula, repeat numbers 2 to 13 !

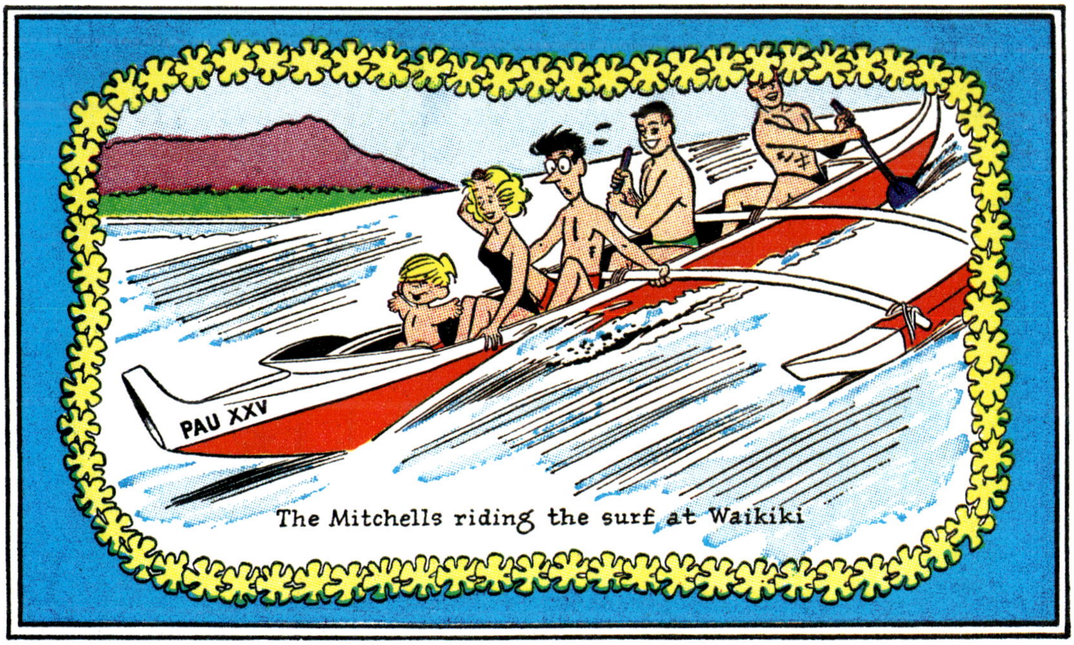

PAU XXV

The Mitchells riding the surf at Waikiki

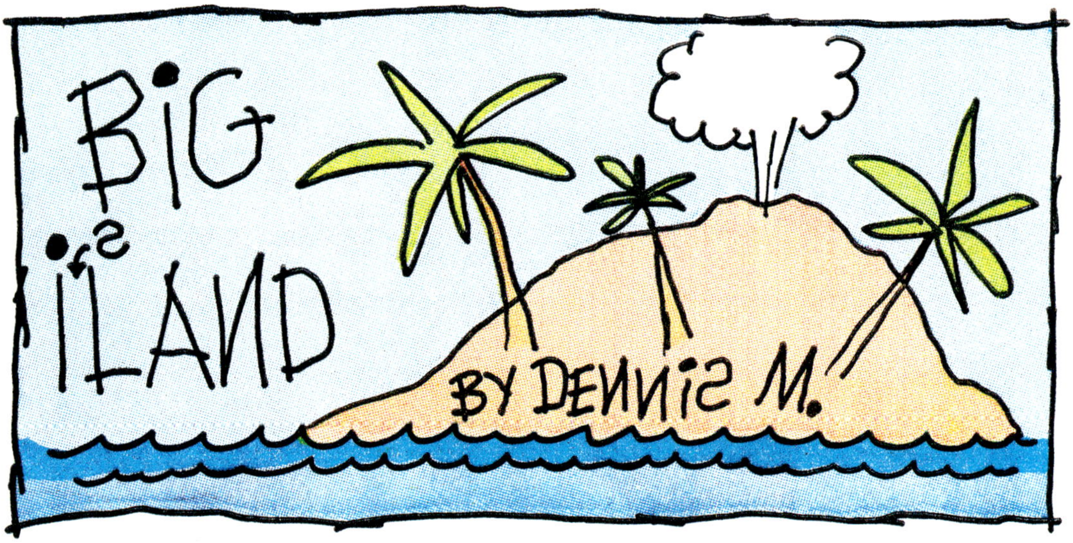
BIG ILAND
BY DENNIS M.

HEY, YOU GUYS! I WANNA TELL YA ALL 'BOUT THE LAST ILAND WE ~~VIST~~ ~~VIZIT~~ SAW! IT'S CALLED HAWAII, AN IT'S A BIG ONE. THEY GOT VOL-CANOES ON IT.... THAT'S MOUNTAINS THAT BLOW THEIR TOPS.... LIKE DAD DOES.

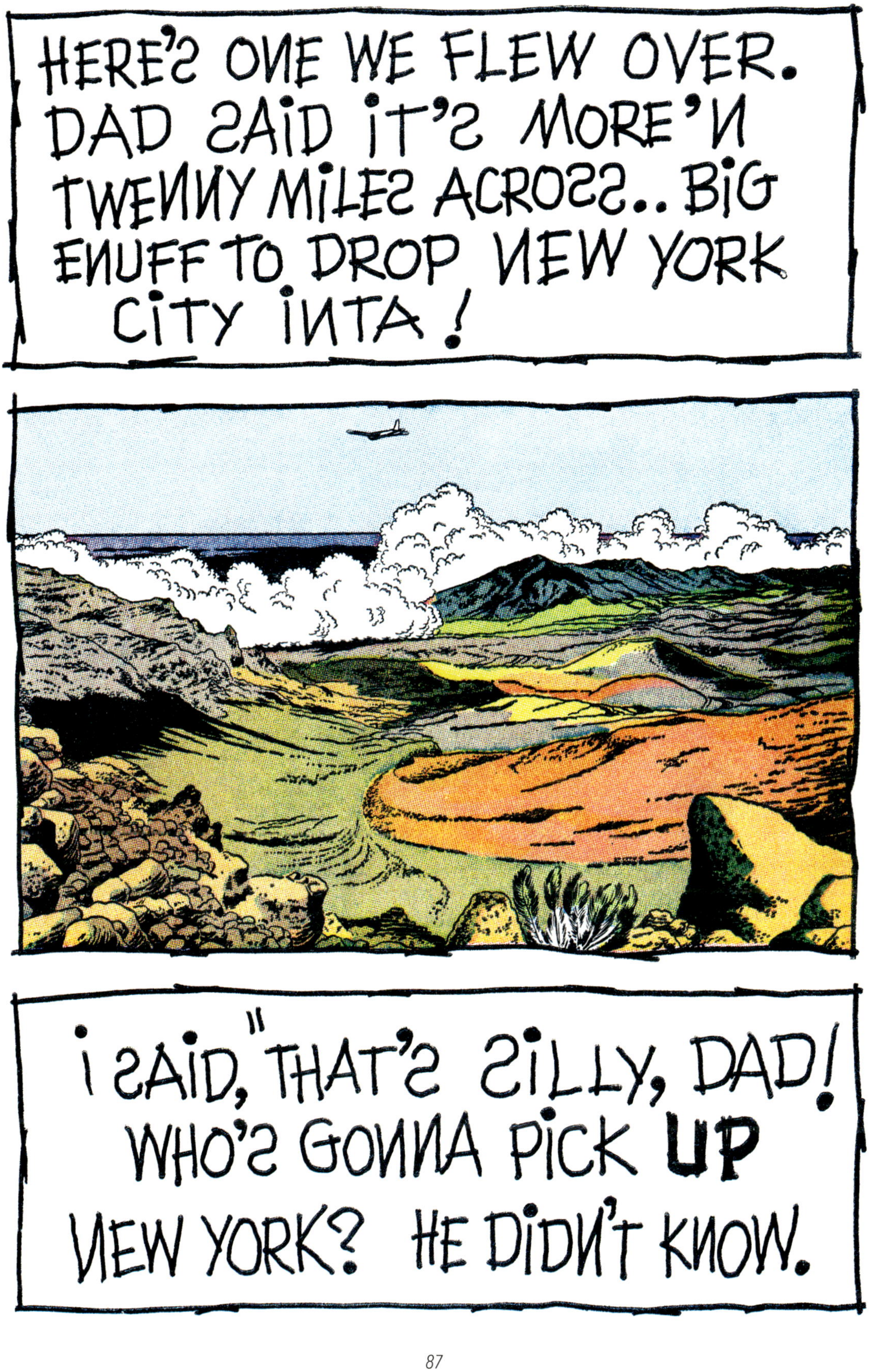
HERE'S ONE WE FLEW OVER. DAD SAID IT'S MORE'N TWENNY MILES ACROSS.. BIG ENUFF TO DROP NEW YORK CITY INTA!
I SAID, "THAT'S SILLY, DAD! WHO'S GONNA PICK **UP** NEW YORK? HE DIDN'T KNOW.

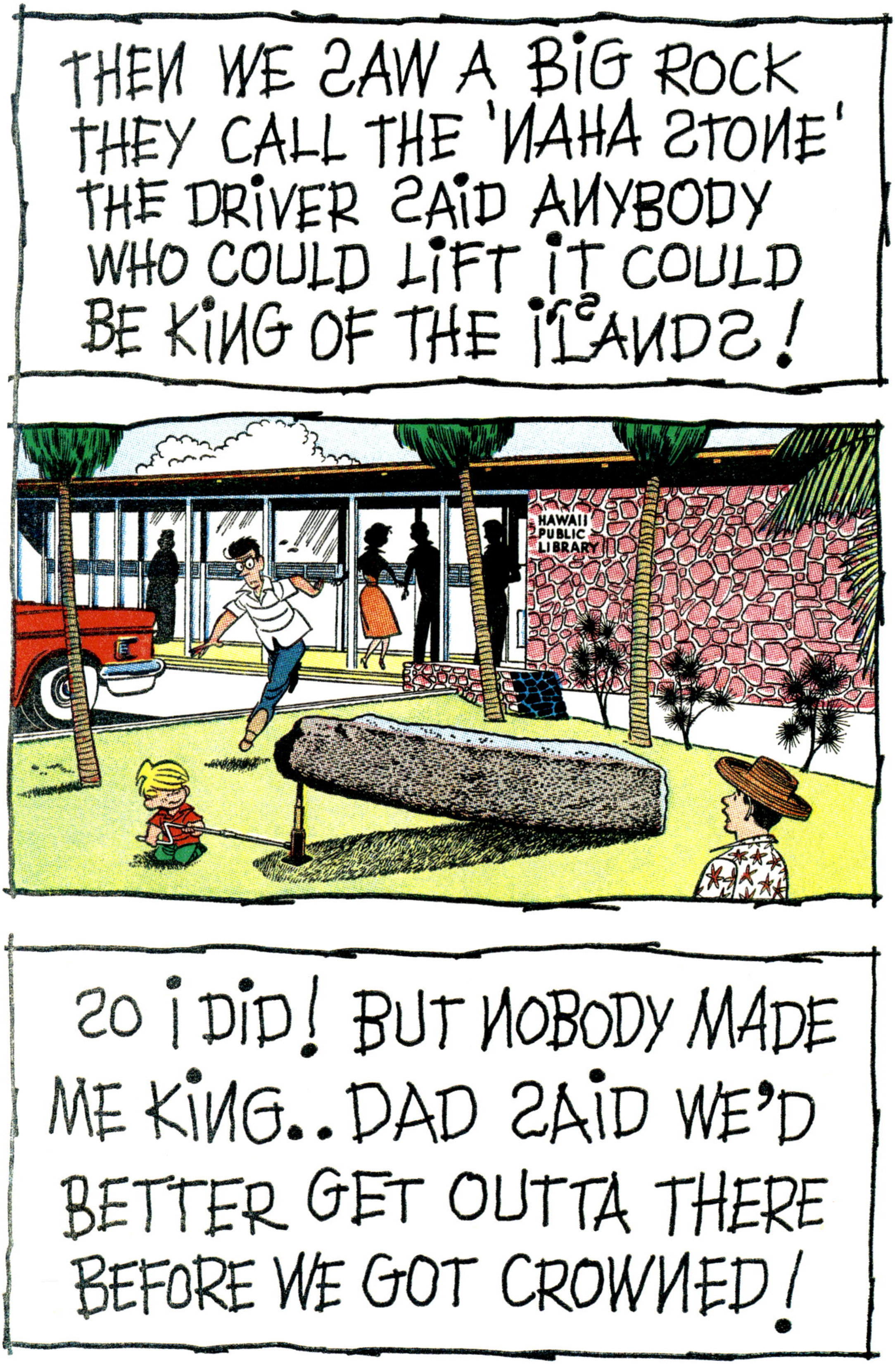
THEN WE SAW A BIG ROCK THEY CALL THE 'NAHA STONE' THE DRIVER SAID ANYBODY WHO COULD LIFT IT COULD BE KING OF THE ISLANDS!
HAWAII PUBLIC LIBRARY
SO I DID! BUT NOBODY MADE ME KING.. DAD SAID WE'D BETTER GET OUTTA THERE BEFORE WE GOT CROWNED!

WHEN WE SAW RAINBOW FALLS, DAD GOT NERVOUS.

BECAUSE IT REMEMBERED ME... MAYBE.... MAYBE I LEFT THE WATER RUNNIN' IN THE BATHROOM BACK HOME! (THEN I REMEMBERED I DIDN'T)

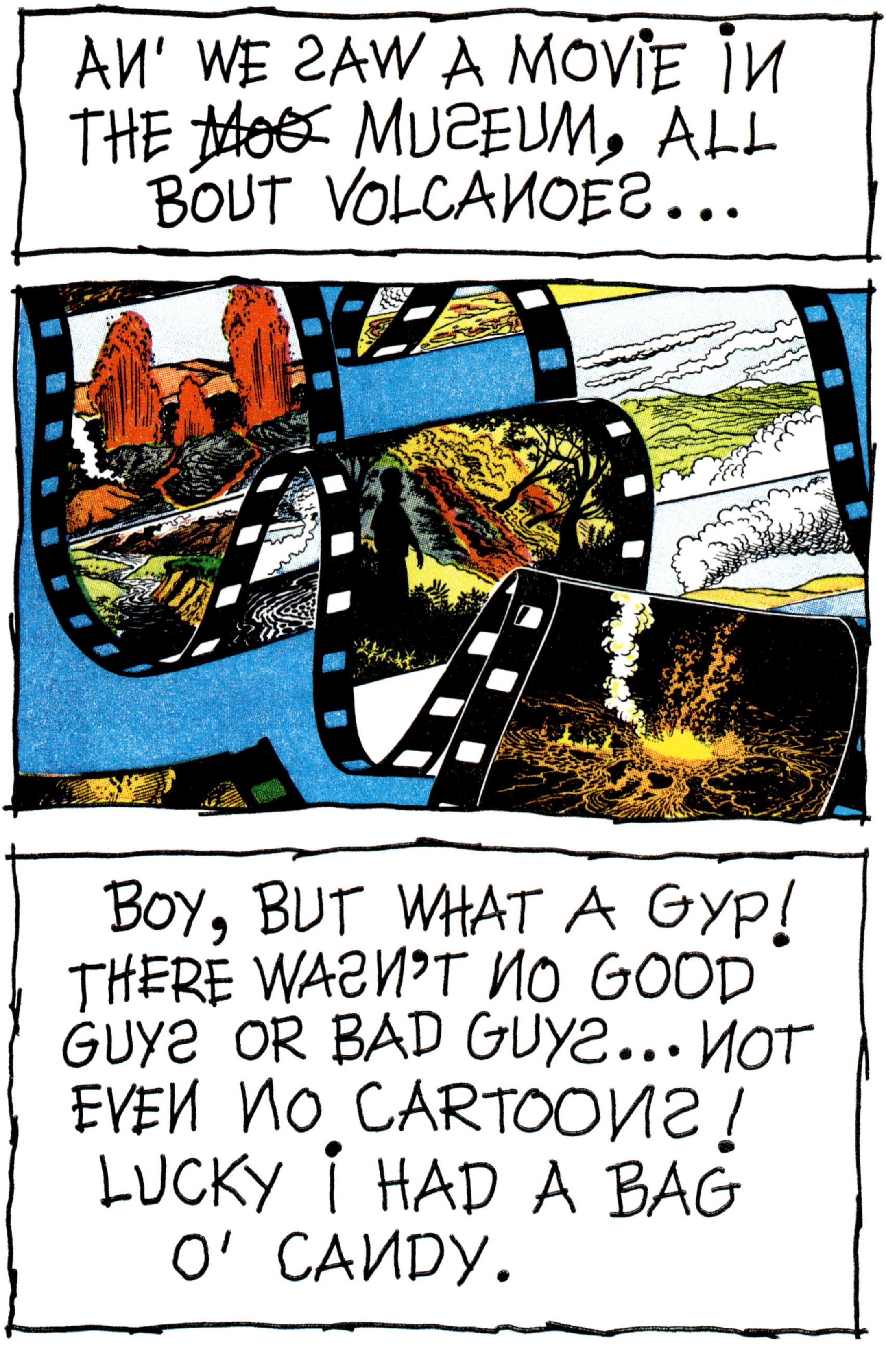
AN' WE SAW A MOVIE IN THE ~~Moo~~ MUSEUM, ALL BOUT VOLCANOES...
BOY, BUT WHAT A GYP! THERE WASN'T NO GOOD GUYS OR BAD GUYS... NOT EVEN NO CARTOONS! LUCKY I HAD A BAG O' CANDY.

THEN DAD SAID "C'MON! WE'RE GONNA DRIVE DOWN INTA THAT VOLCANO WE JUST SAW!"

I SAID "HECK NO! I DON'T WANNA GET BURNED UP!" AN' HE TOLD ME—"COME ALONG BEFORE I GET BURNED UP!"

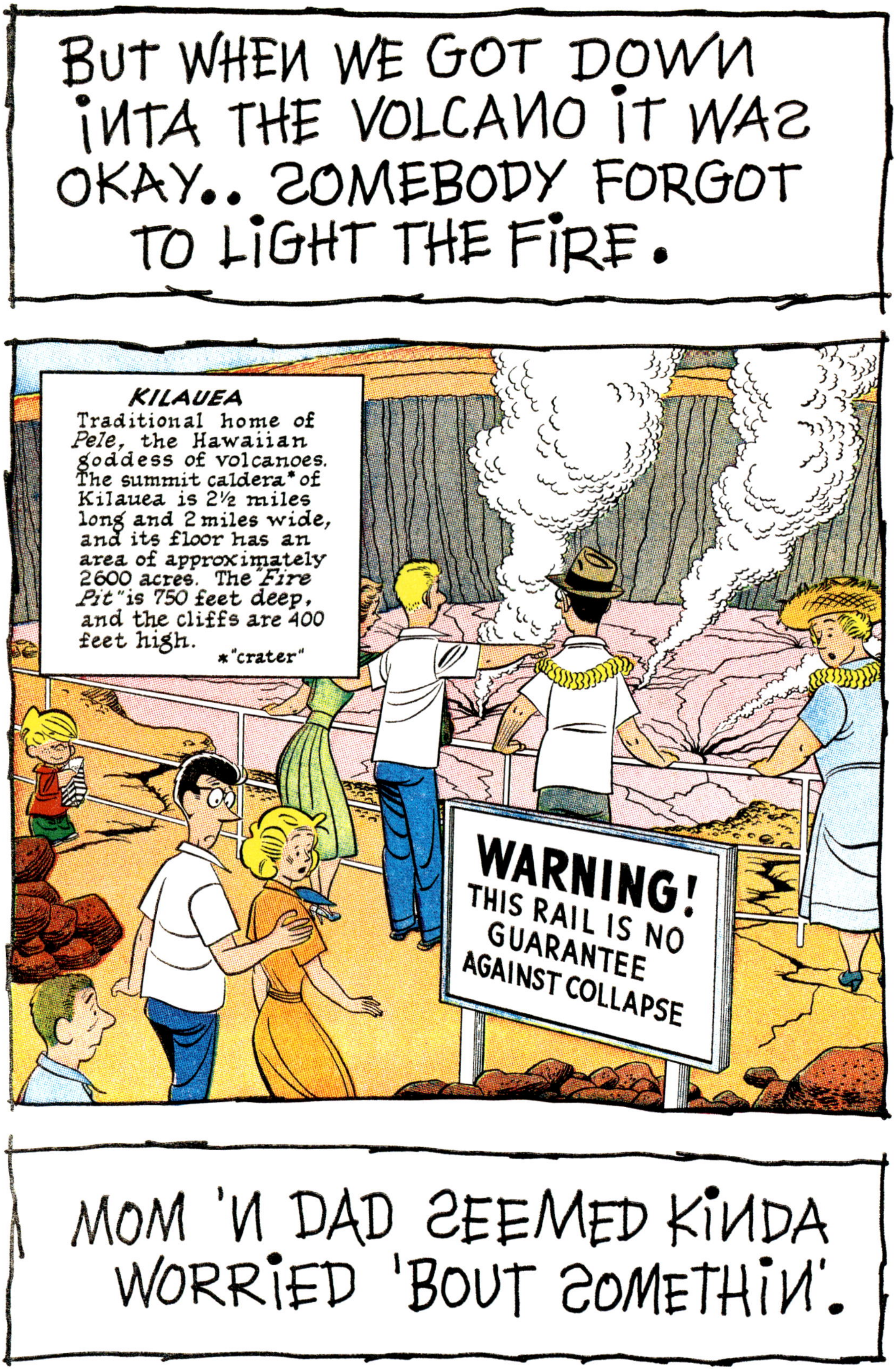
BUT WHEN WE GOT DOWN INTA THE VOLCANO IT WAS OKAY.. SOMEBODY FORGOT TO LIGHT THE FIRE.
KILAUEA
Traditional home of Pele, the Hawaiian goddess of volcanoes. The summit caldera* of Kilauea is 2½ miles long and 2 miles wide, and its floor has an area of approximately 2600 acres. The "Fire Pit" is 750 feet deep, and the cliffs are 400 feet high.
*"crater"
WARNING! THIS RAIL IS NO GUARANTEE AGAINST COLLAPSE
MOM 'N DAD SEEMED KINDA WORRIED 'BOUT SOMETHIN'.

AN WHEN THEY LOOKED IN THE BIG HOLE, THEY GOT WORRIED-ER. MAYBE THEY THOUGHT IT WAS GONNA BLOW IT'S TOP!

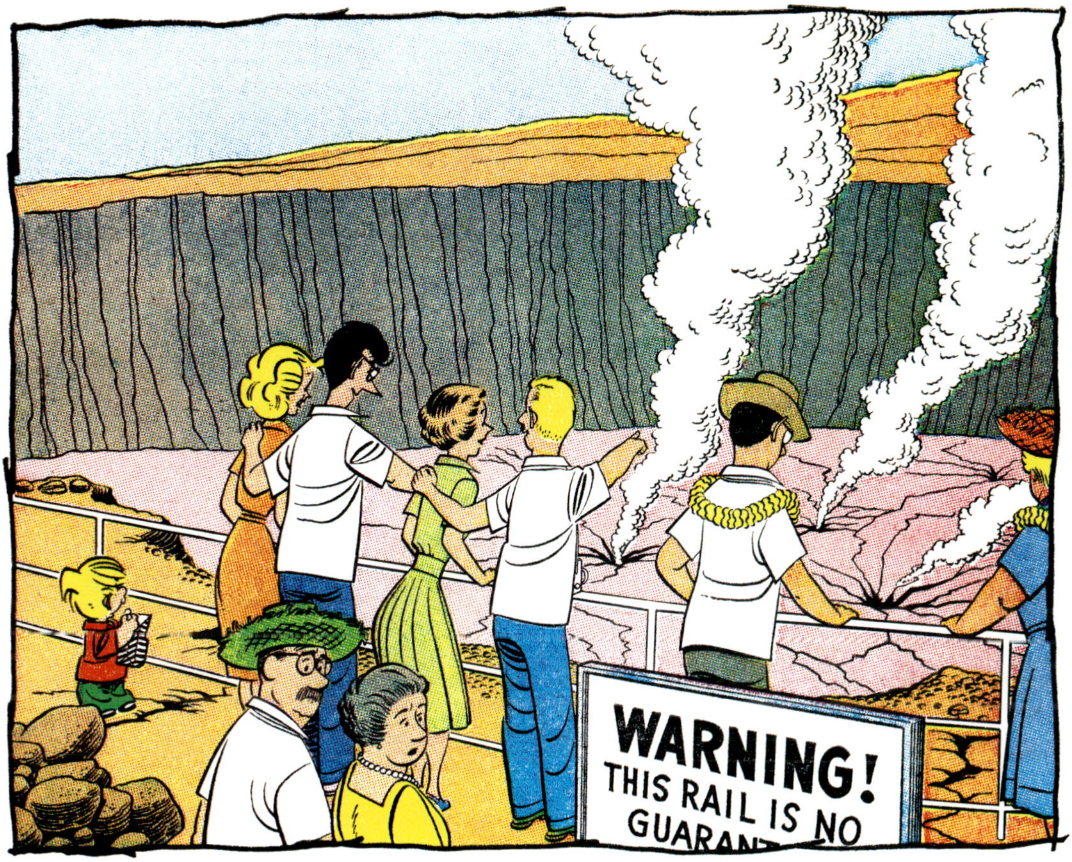
WARNING!
THIS RAIL IS NO

BUT THEY *REALLY* GOT WORRIED WHEN I .....

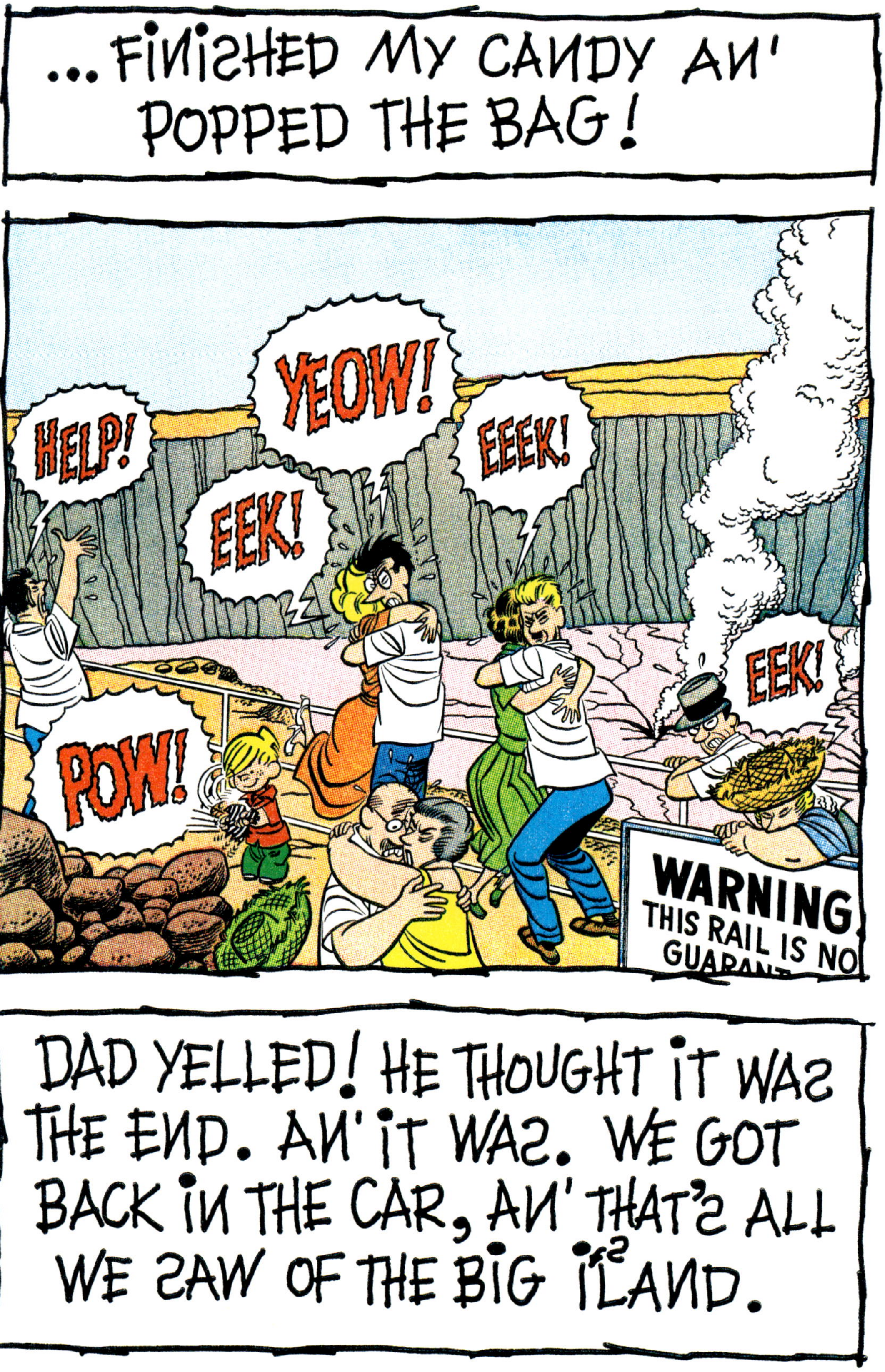
...FINISHED MY CANDY AN' POPPED THE BAG!
HELP!
YEOW!
EEK!
EEEK!
POW!
EEK!
WARNING
THIS RAIL IS NO
DAD YELLED! HE THOUGHT IT WAS THE END. AN' IT WAS. WE GOT BACK IN THE CAR, AN' THAT'S ALL WE SAW OF THE BIG ISLAND.

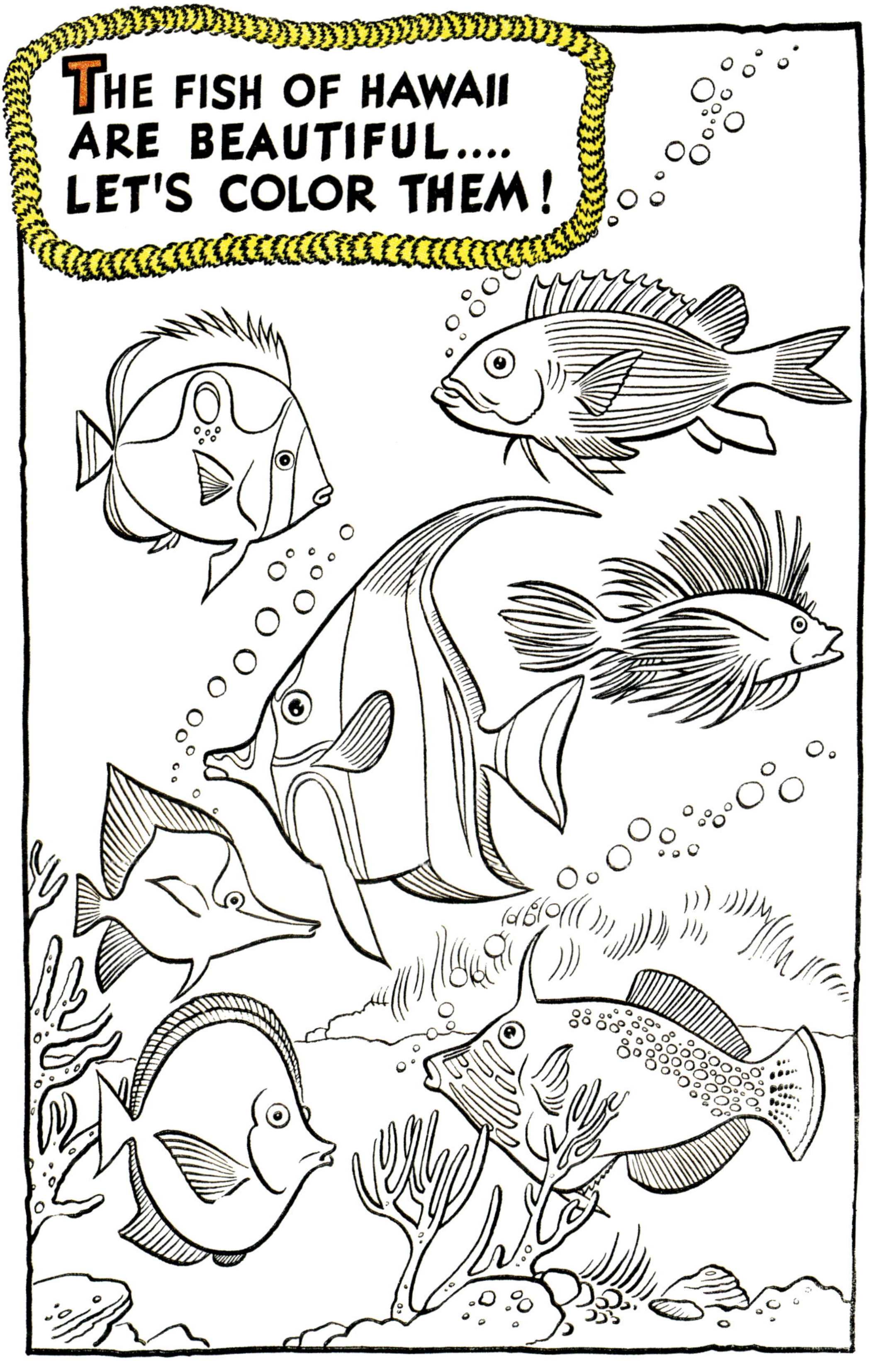
THE FISH OF HAWAII
ARE BEAUTIFUL....
LET'S COLOR THEM!

HERE IS DENNIS.. IN HAWAII.. IN 3D!

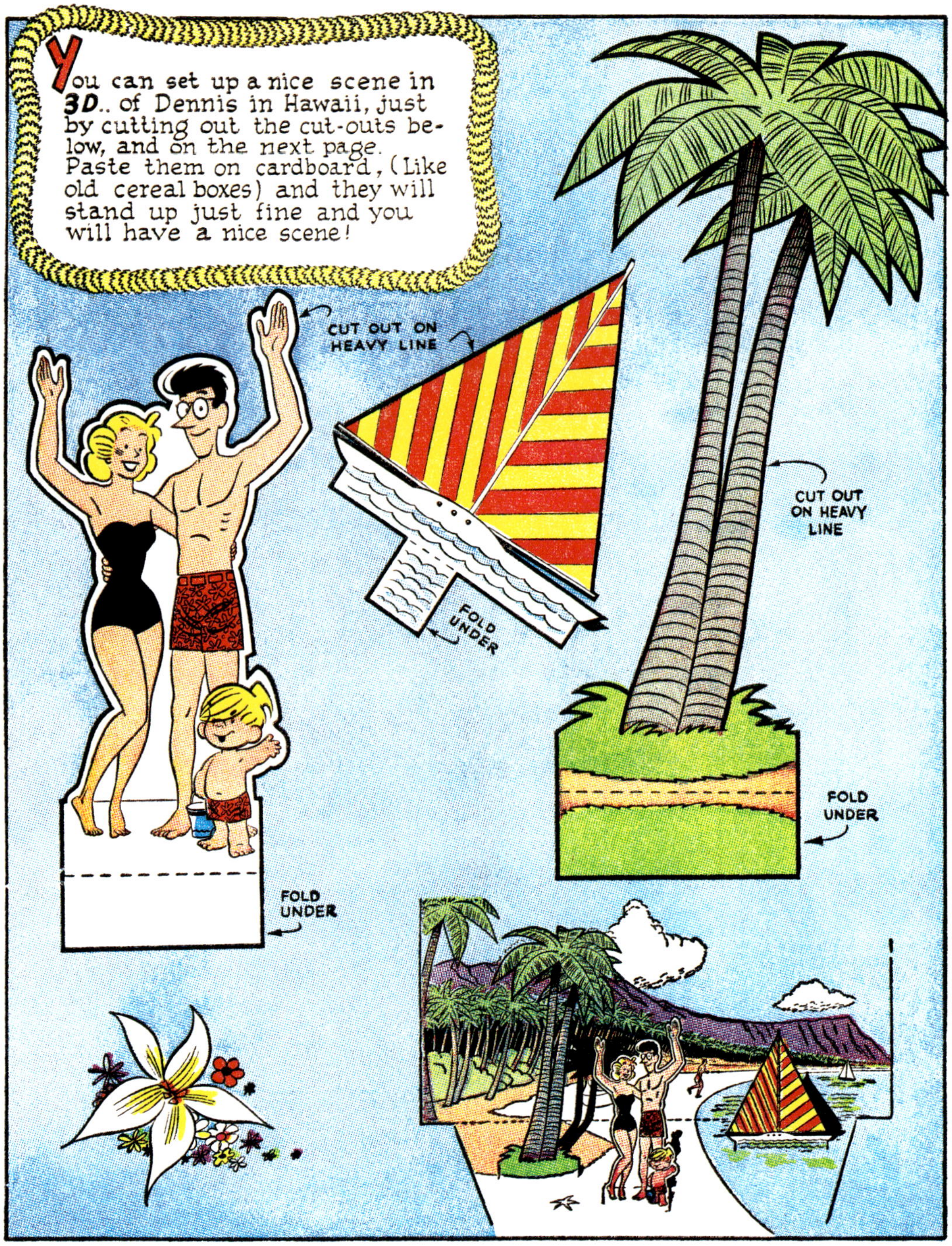
You can set up a nice scene in 3D.. of Dennis in Hawaii, just by cutting out the cut-outs below, and on the next page. Paste them on cardboard, (Like old cereal boxes) and they will stand up just fine and you will have a nice scene!
CUT OUT ON HEAVY LINE
CUT OUT ON HEAVY LINE
FOLD UNDER
FOLD UNDER
FOLD UNDER

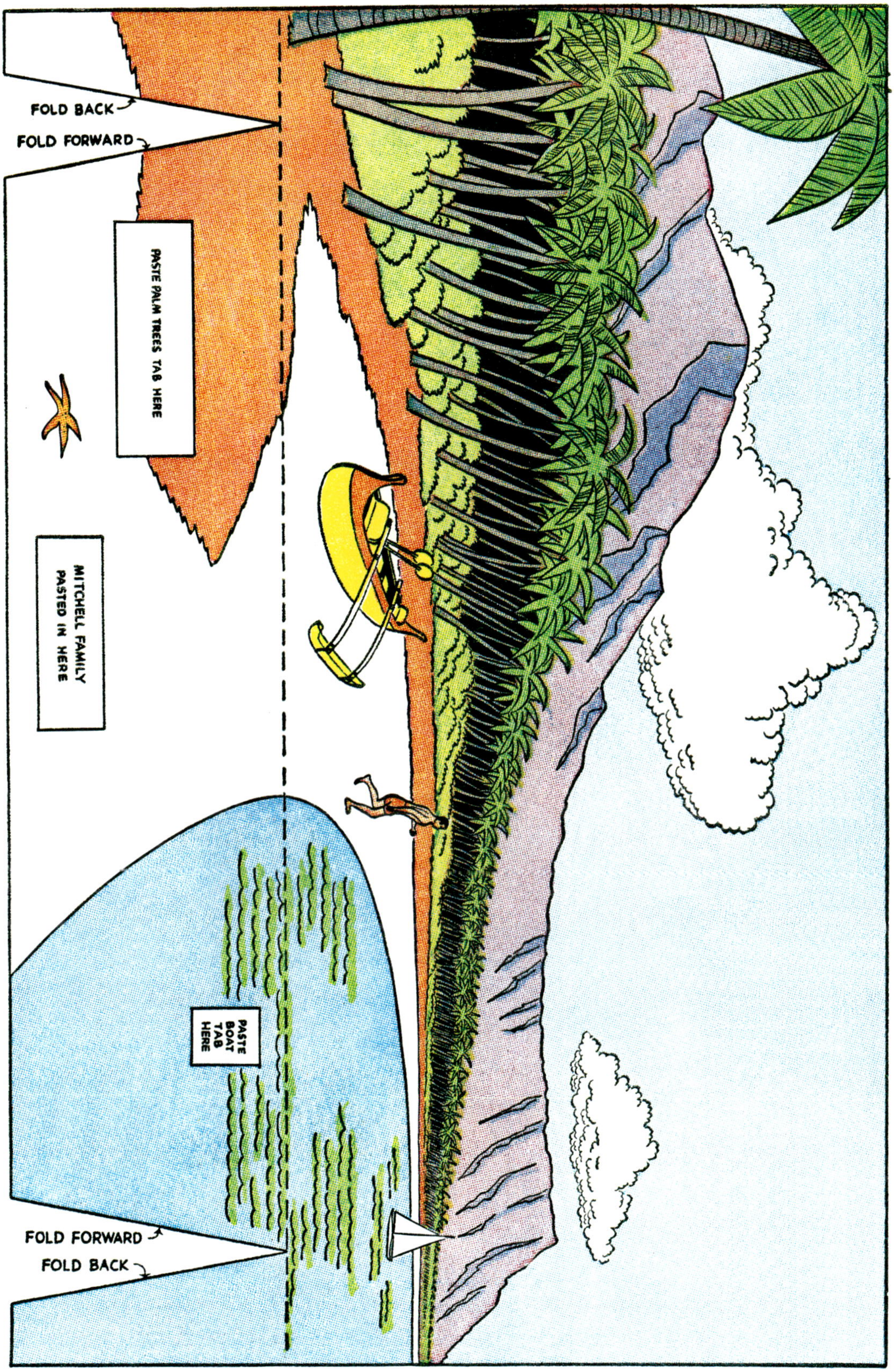
FOLD BACK
FOLD FORWARD
PASTE PALM TREES TAB HERE
MITCHELL FAMILY PASTED IN HERE
PASTE BOAT TAB HERE
FOLD FORWARD
FOLD BACK

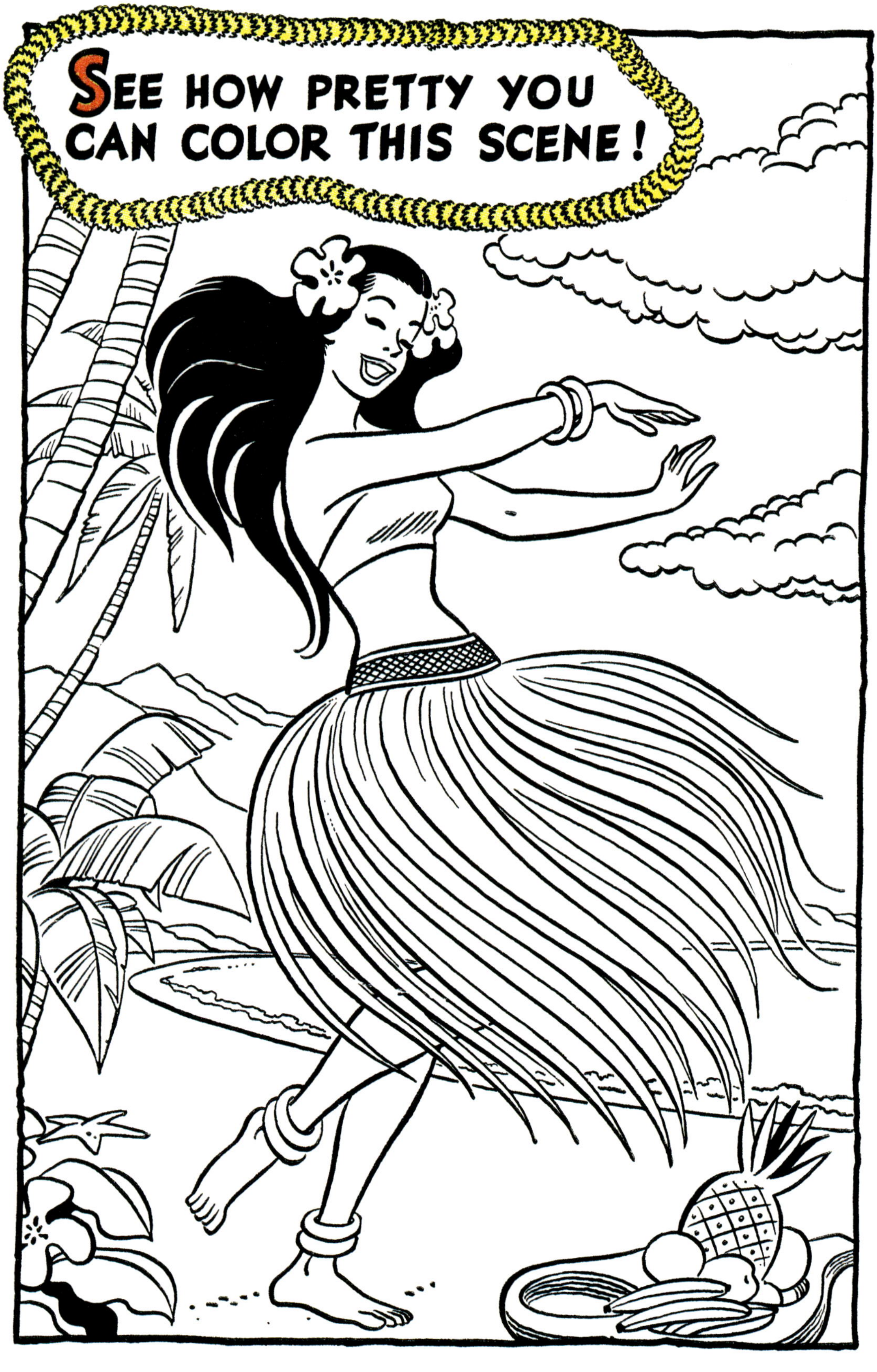
SEE HOW PRETTY YOU CAN COLOR THIS SCENE!

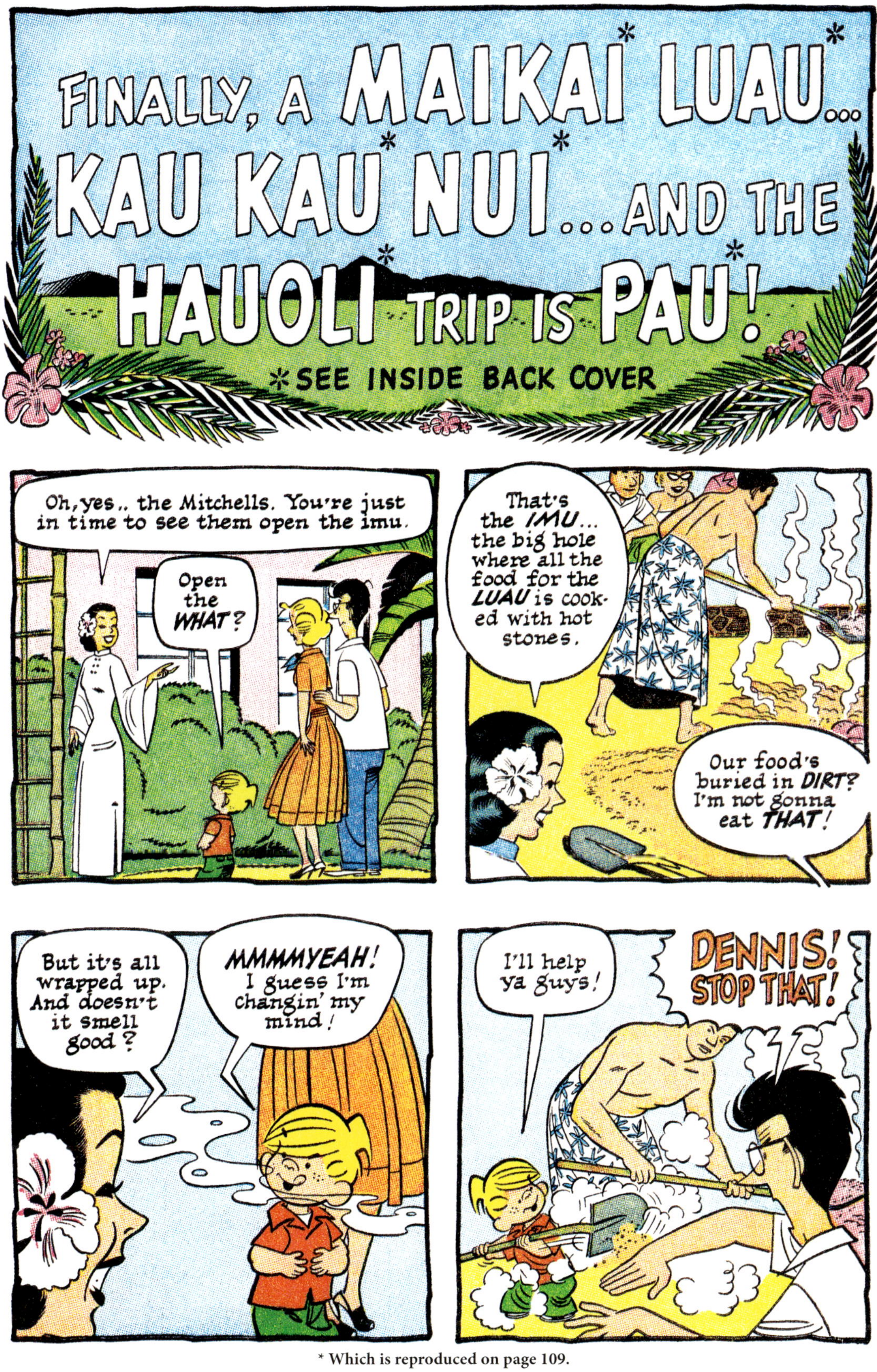
FINALLY, A MAIKAI* LUAU*... KAU KAU* NUI*... AND THE HAUOLI* TRIP IS PAU*!
*SEE INSIDE BACK COVER
Oh, yes.. the Mitchells. You're just in time to see them open the imu.
Open the WHAT?
That's the IMU... the big hole where all the food for the LUAU is cooked with hot stones.
Our food's buried in DIRT? I'm not gonna eat THAT!
But it's all wrapped up. And doesn't it smell good?
MMMMYEAH! I guess I'm changin' my mind!
I'll help ya guys!
DENNIS! STOP THAT!

* Which is reproduced on page 109.

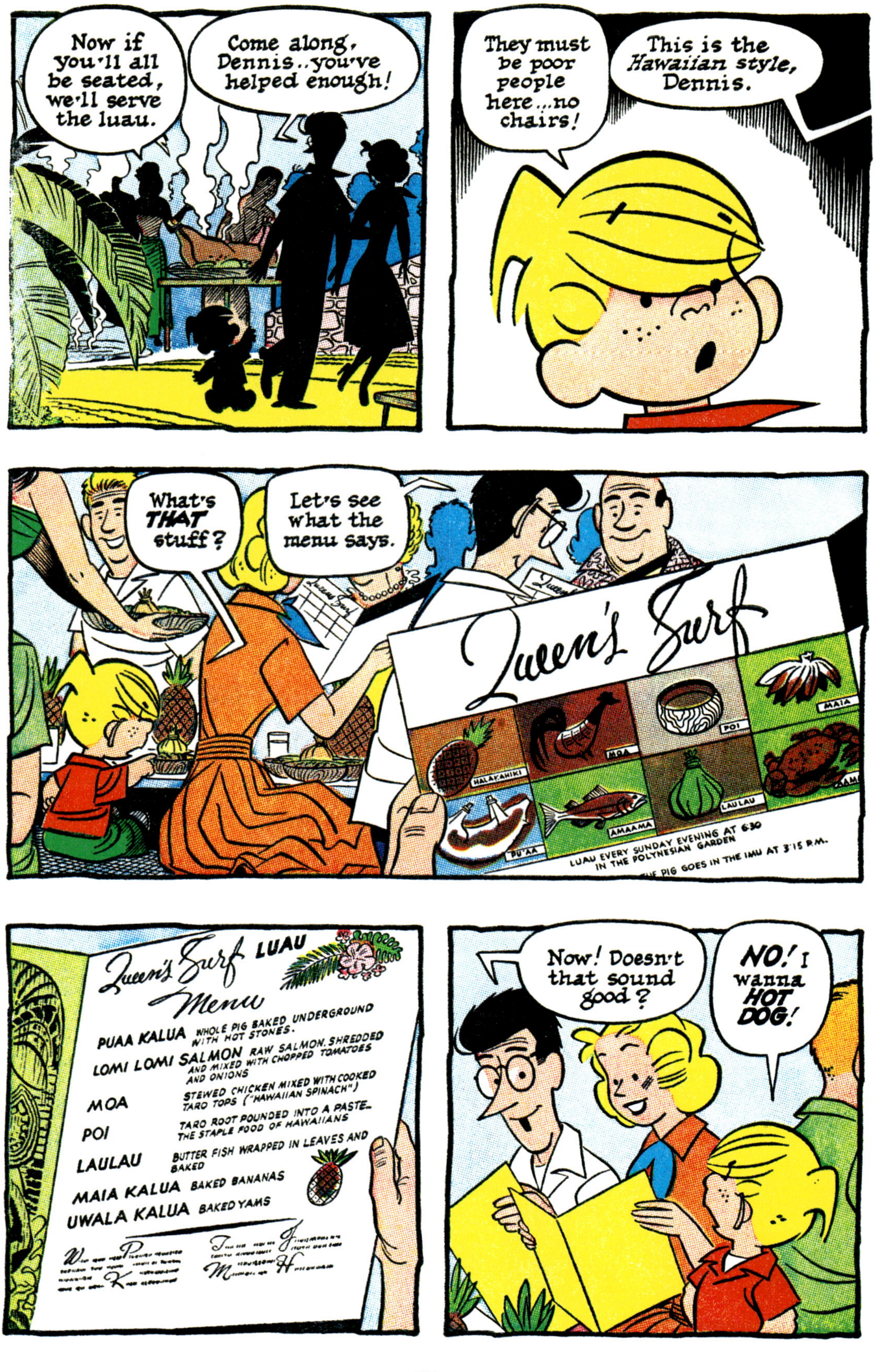
Now if you'll all be seated, we'll serve the luau.
Come along, Dennis..you've helped enough!
They must be poor people here...no chairs!
This is the *Hawaiian style,* Dennis.
What's ***THAT*** stuff?
Let's see what the menu says.
Queen's Surf
MAIA
MOA
POI
HALAKAHIKI
LAULAU
AMAAMA
PU'AA
LUAU EVERY SUNDAY EVENING AT 6:30 IN THE POLYNESIAN GARDEN
Queen's Surf LUAU
Menu
PUAA KALUA WHOLE PIG BAKED UNDERGROUND WITH HOT STONES.
LOMI LOMI SALMON RAW SALMON, SHREDDED AND MIXED WITH CHOPPED TOMATOES AND ONIONS
MOA STEWED CHICKEN MIXED WITH COOKED TARO TOPS ("HAWAIIAN SPINACH")
POI TARO ROOT POUNDED INTO A PASTE.. THE STAPLE FOOD OF HAWAIIANS
LAULAU BUTTER FISH WRAPPED IN LEAVES AND BAKED
MAIA KALUA BAKED BANANAS
UWALA KALUA BAKED YAMS
Now! Doesn't that sound good?
NO! I wanna ***HOT DOG!***

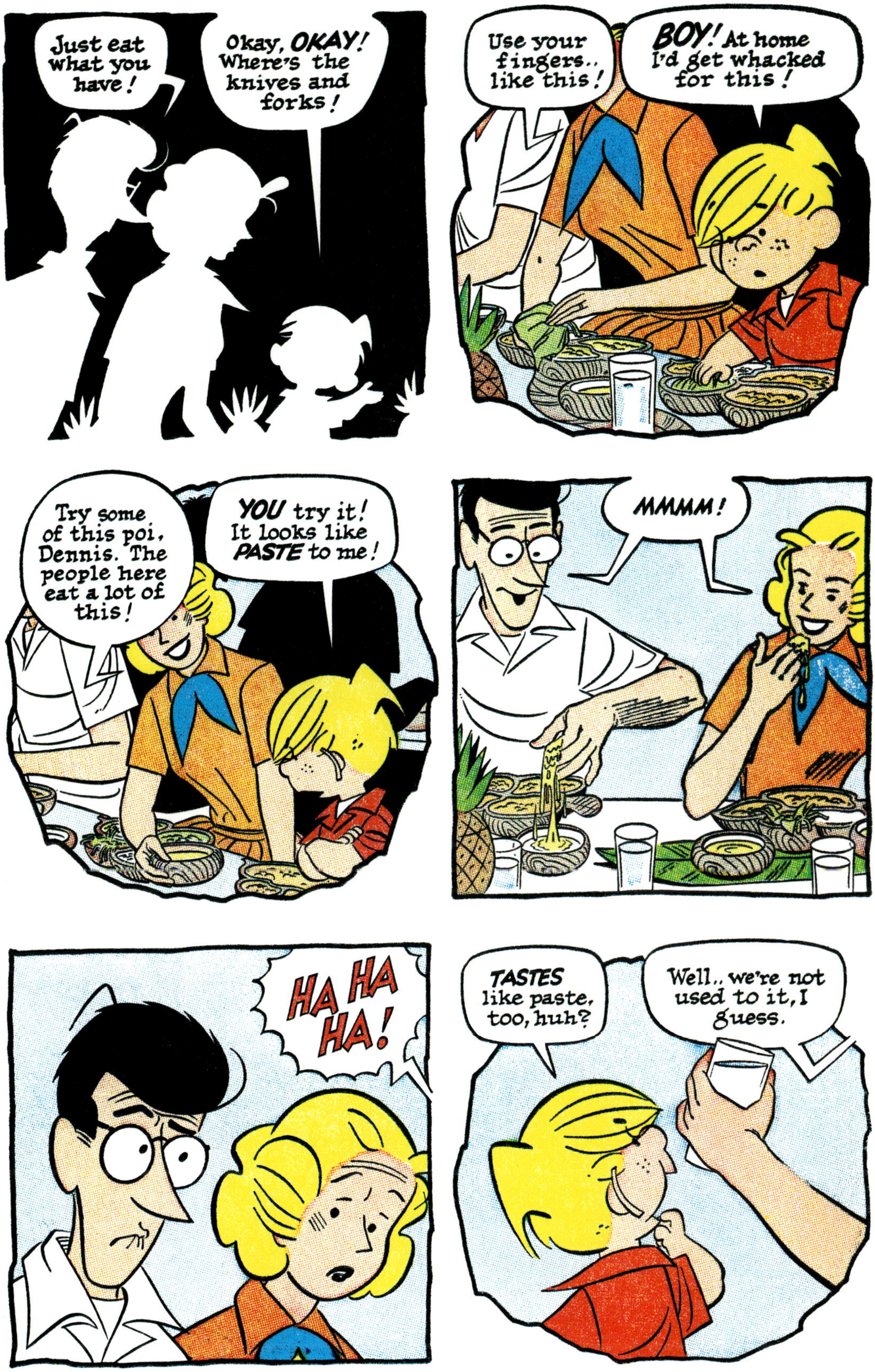
Just eat what you have!
Okay, OKAY! Where's the knives and forks!
Use your fingers.. like this!
BOY! At home I'd get whacked for this!
Try some of this poi, Dennis. The people here eat a lot of this!
YOU try it! It looks like PASTE to me!
MMMM!
HA HA HA!
TASTES like paste, too, huh?
Well.. we're not used to it, I guess.

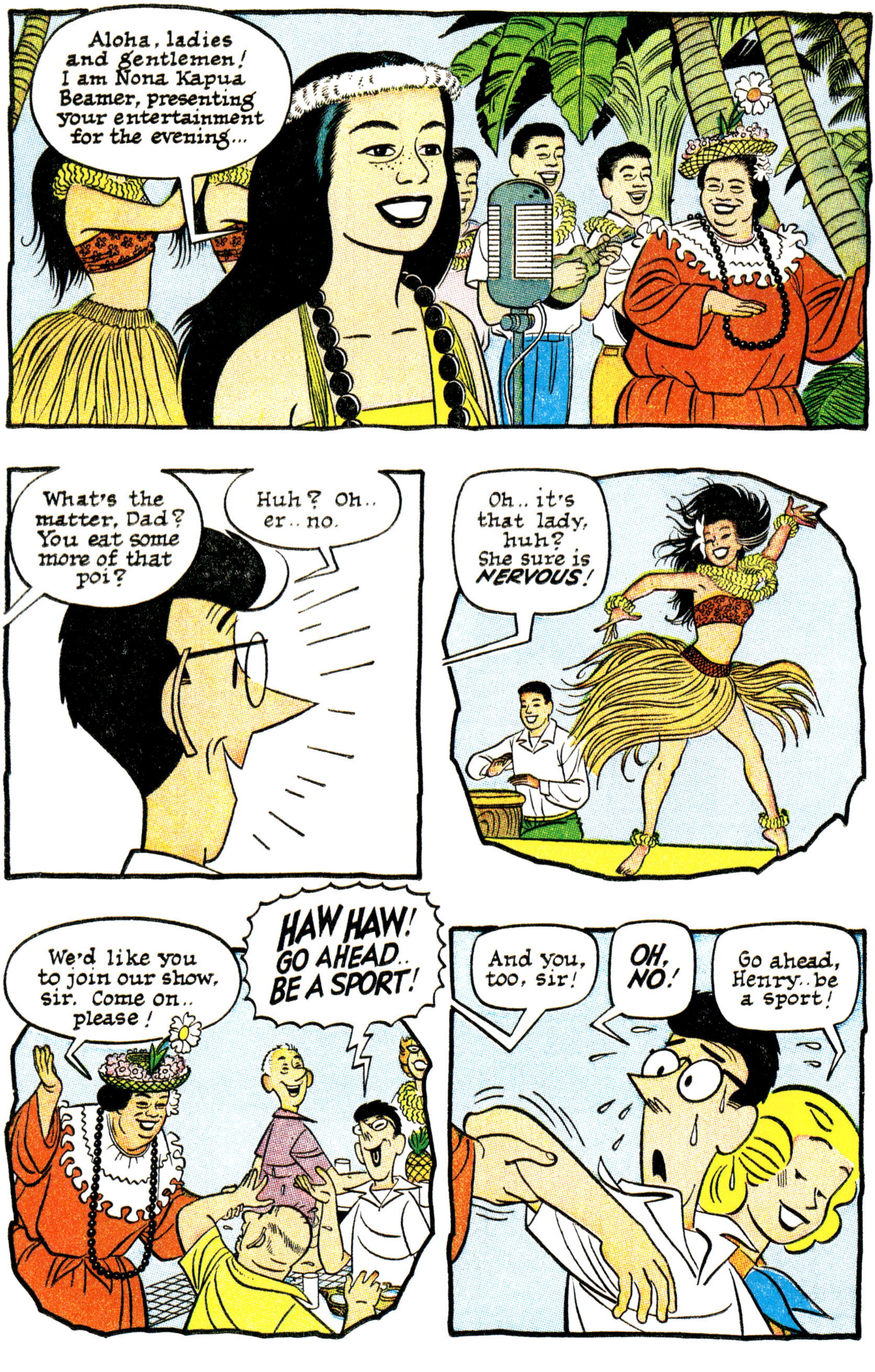
Aloha, ladies and gentlemen! I am Nona Kapua Beamer, presenting your entertainment for the evening...
What's the matter, Dad? You eat some more of that poi?
Huh? Oh.. er.. no.
Oh.. it's that lady, huh? She sure is NERVOUS!
We'd like you to join our show, sir. Come on.. please!
HAW HAW! GO AHEAD.. BE A SPORT!
And you, too, sir!
OH, NO!
Go ahead, Henry.. be a sport!

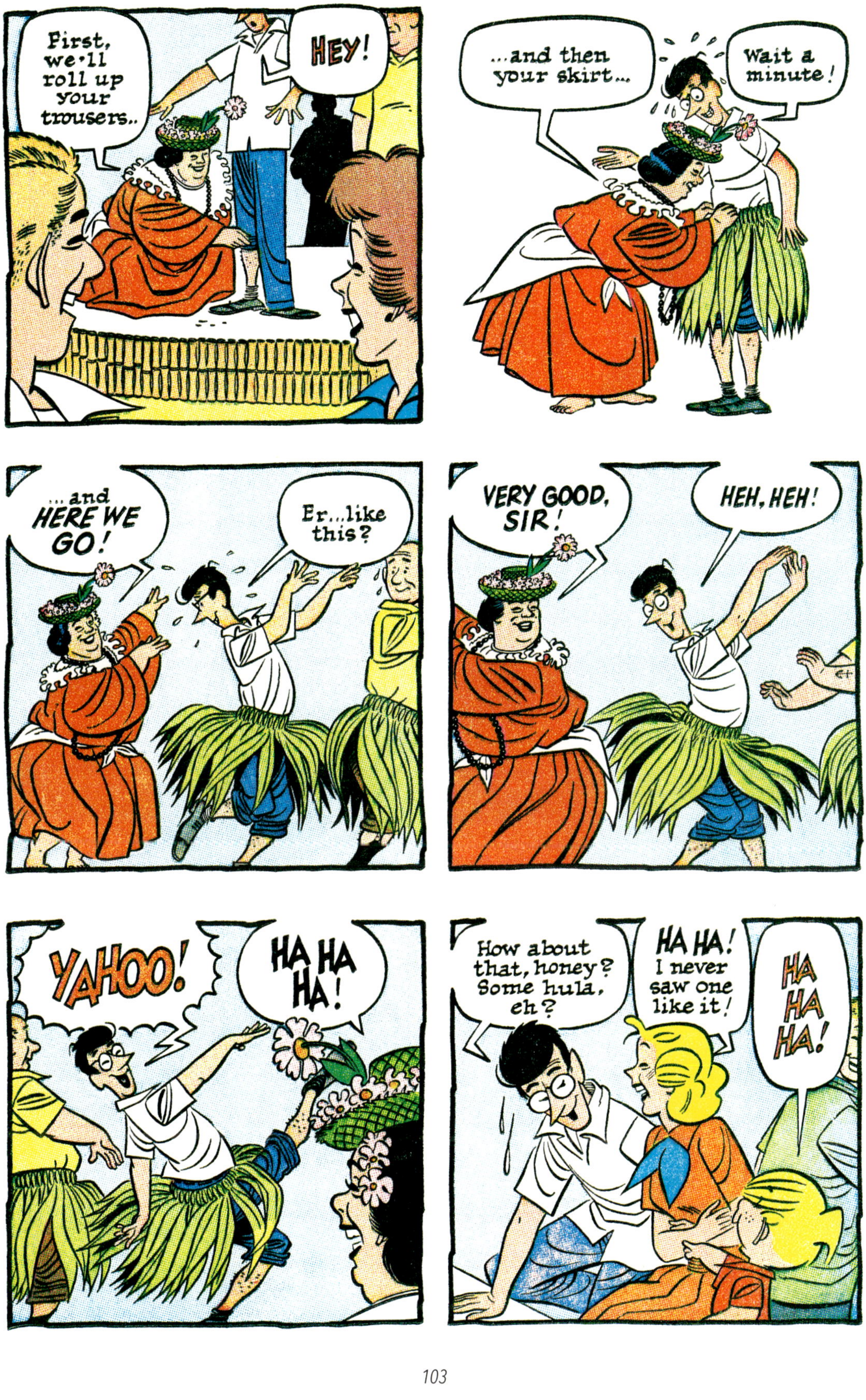
First, we'll roll up your trousers..
HEY!
...and then your skirt...
Wait a minute!
...and HERE WE GO!
Er...like this?
VERY GOOD, SIR!
HEH, HEH!
YAHOO!
HA HA HA!
How about that, honey? Some hula, eh?
HA HA! I never saw one like it!
HA HA HA!

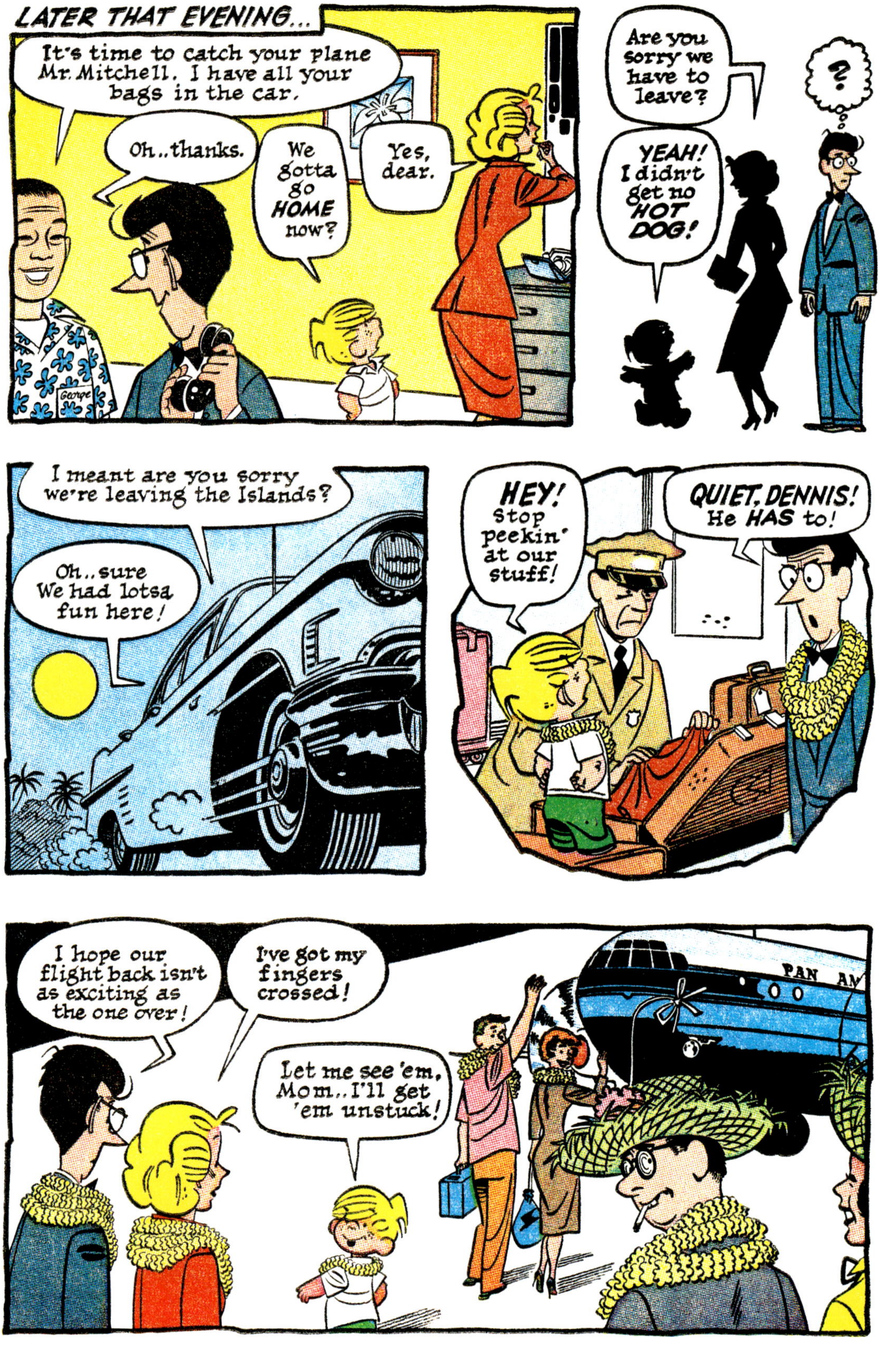
LATER THAT EVENING...
It's time to catch your plane Mr. Mitchell. I have all your bags in the car.
Oh..thanks.
We gotta go HOME now?
Yes, dear.
George
Are you sorry we have to leave?
YEAH! I didn't get no HOT DOG!
?
I meant are you sorry we're leaving the Islands?
Oh..sure We had lotsa fun here!
HEY! Stop peekin' at our stuff!
QUIET, DENNIS! He HAS to!
I hope our flight back isn't as exciting as the one over!
I've got my fingers crossed!
Let me see 'em, Mom..I'll get 'em unstuck!
PAN AM

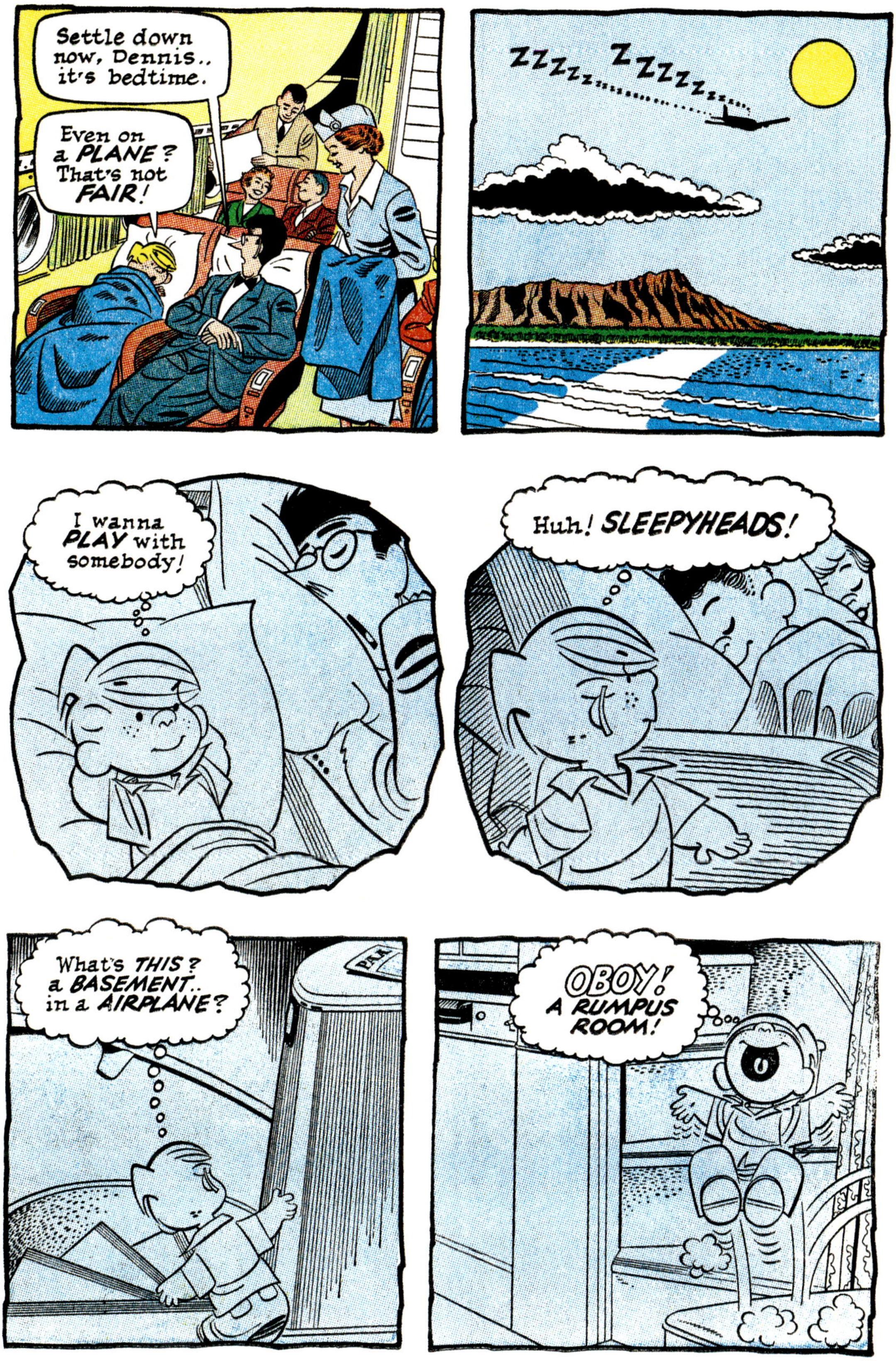

Settle down now, Dennis.. it's bedtime.
Even on a PLANE? That's not FAIR!
ZZZzz ZZZZz
I wanna PLAY with somebody!
Huh! SLEEPYHEADS!
What's THIS? a BASEMENT.. in a AIRPLANE?
OBOY! A RUMPUS ROOM!

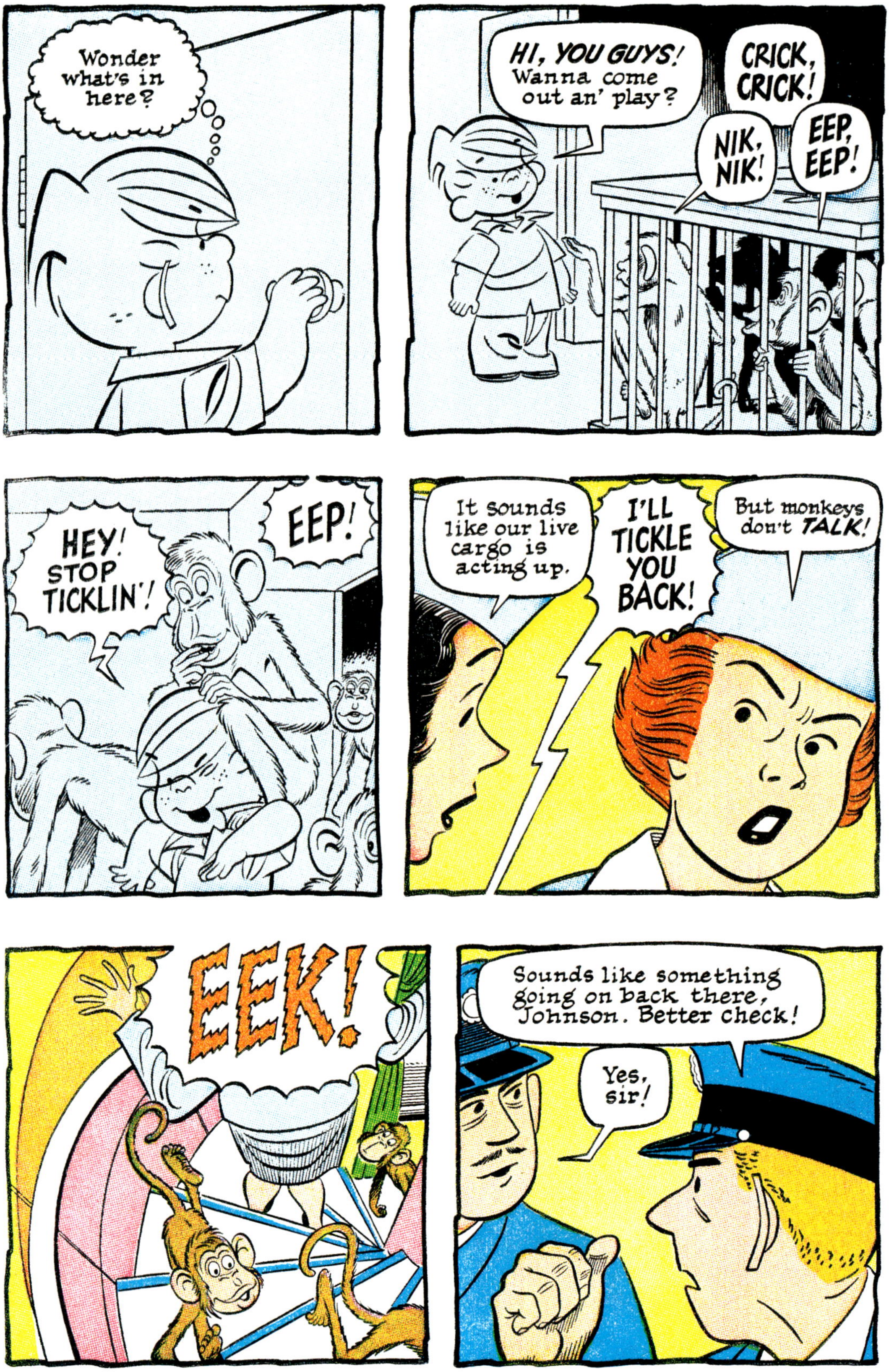
Wonder what's in here?
HI, YOU GUYS! Wanna come out an' play?
CRICK, CRICK!
NIK, NIK!
EEP, EEP!
HEY! STOP TICKLIN'!
EEP!
It sounds like our live cargo is acting up.
I'LL TICKLE YOU BACK!
But monkeys don't TALK!
EEK!
Sounds like something going on back there, Johnson. Better check!
Yes, sir!

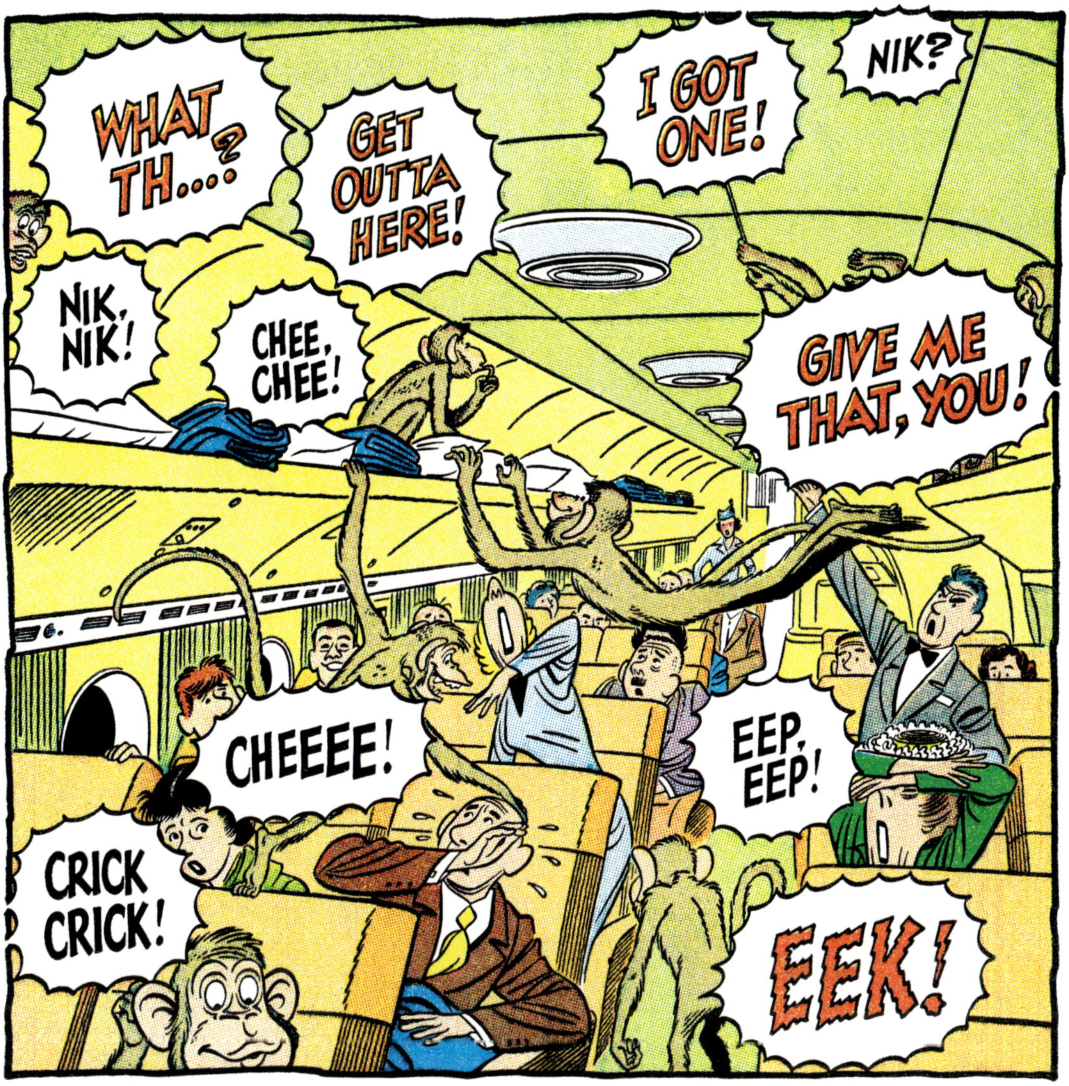
WHAT TH...?
GET OUTTA HERE!
I GOT ONE!
NIK?
NIK, NIK!
CHEE, CHEE!
GIVE ME THAT, YOU!
CHEEEE!
EEP, EEP!
CRICK CRICK!
EEK!

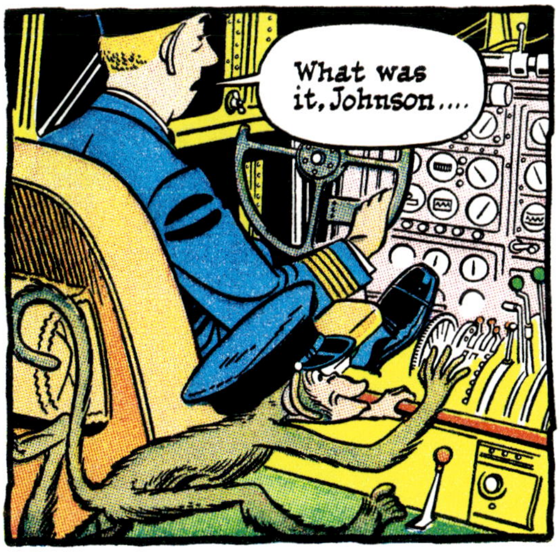
What was it, Johnson....

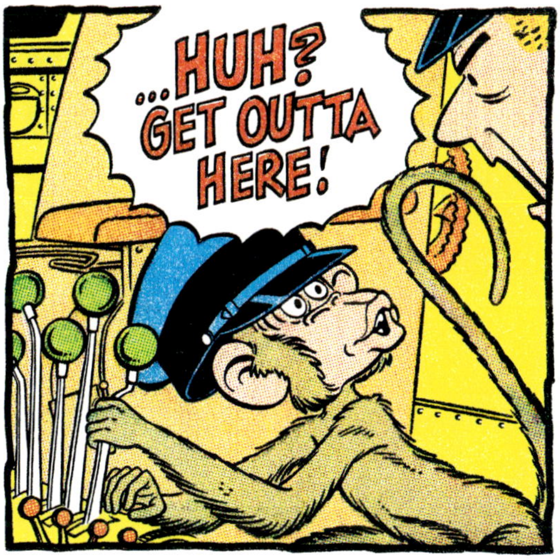
...HUH? GET OUTTA HERE!

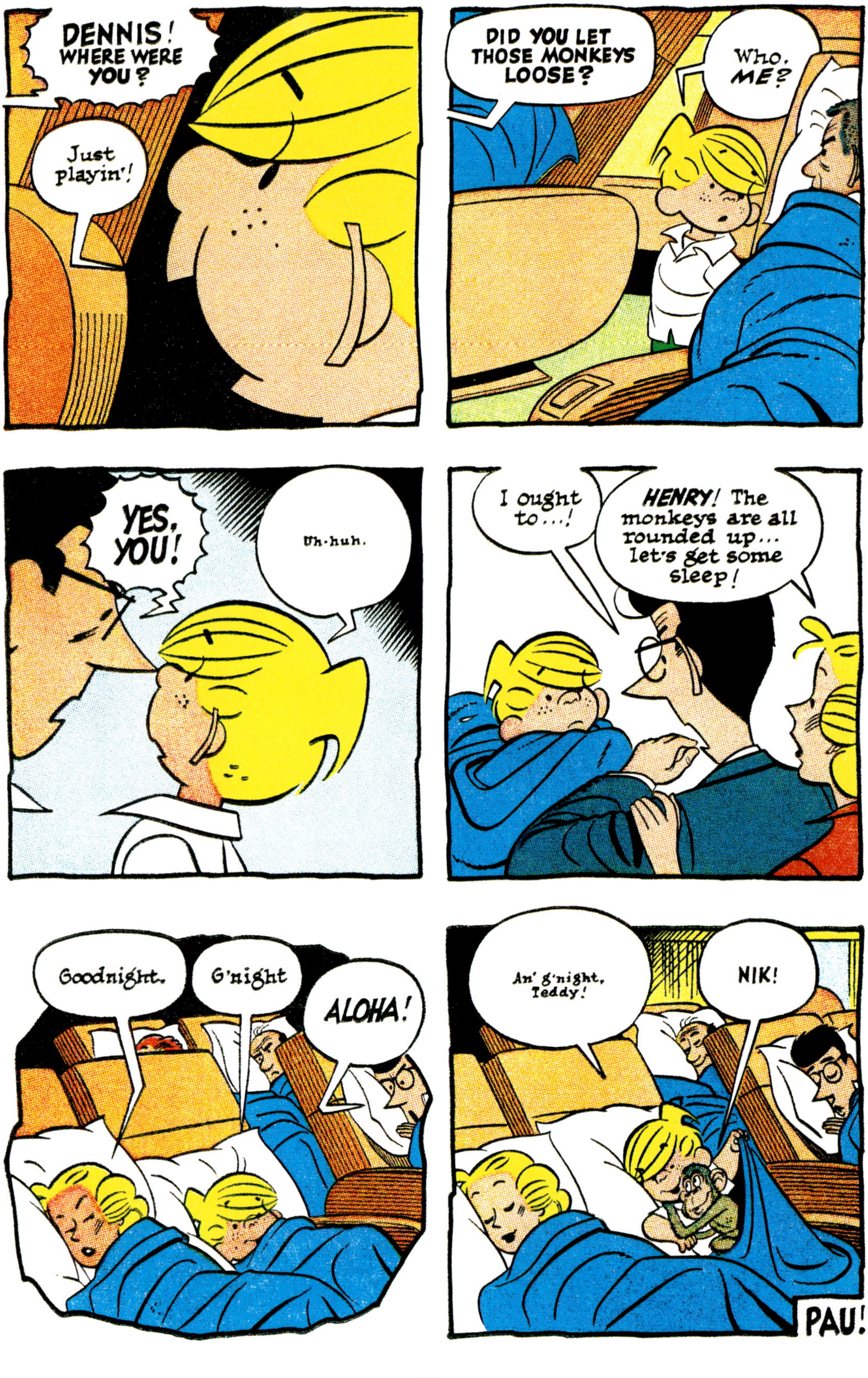
DENNIS! WHERE WERE YOU?
Just playin'!
DID YOU LET THOSE MONKEYS LOOSE?
Who, ME?
YES, YOU!
Uh-huh.
I ought to...!
HENRY! The monkeys are all rounded up... let's get some sleep!
Goodnight.
G'night
ALOHA!
An' g'night, Teddy!
NIK!
PAU!

YOU CAN TALK HAWAIIAN... IT'S EASY!

MOST PEOPLE IN HAWAII SPRINKLE THEIR TALK WITH NATIVE WORDS... AND YOU CAN, TOO! YOU AND YOUR PALS CAN USE HAWAIIAN WORDS AS A **"SECRET LANGUAGE"**, AND NOBODY ELSE WILL KNOW WHAT YOU'RE TALKING ABOUT. HERE ARE SOME OF THE MOST COMMON WORDS, AND HOW TO PRONOUNCE THEM.... **TRY 'EM!**

English	Hawaiian	Pronunciation
Friend	Aikane	Eye-<u>kah</u>-nee
Hello, goodbye	Aloha	Ah-<u>lo</u>-ha
No	Aole	Ah-<u>oh</u>-lay
House	Hale	<u>Ha</u>-lay
Work	Hana	<u>Ha</u>-na
Happy	Hauoli	How-<u>oh</u>-lee
Sleep	Hiamoe	Hee-ah-<u>mo</u>-ey
Sweetheart	Ipo	<u>Ee</u>-po
Money	Kala	<u>Kah</u>-la
Man	Kane	<u>Kah</u>-nay
Forbidden: keep out	Kapu	<u>Kah</u>-poo
Food: to eat	Kaukau	<u>Cow</u>-cow
Child	Keike	<u>Kay</u>-kee
Help	Kokua	Ko-<u>koo</u>-ah
Big meal, feast	Luau	<u>Loo</u>-ow
Thanks	Mahalo	Ma-ha-<u>low</u>
Very much	Nui	<u>Noo</u>-ee
Good, fine	Maikai	My-<u>kay</u>-ee
Fat	Momona	Mo-<u>mo</u>-nah
Tastes good	Ono	<u>Oh</u>-no
Finished	Pau	<u>Pow</u>
Crazy	Pupule	Poo-<u>poo</u>-lay
Woman	Wahini	Wa-<u>hee</u>-nee
Newcomer	Malihini	Ma-lee-<u>hee</u>-nee

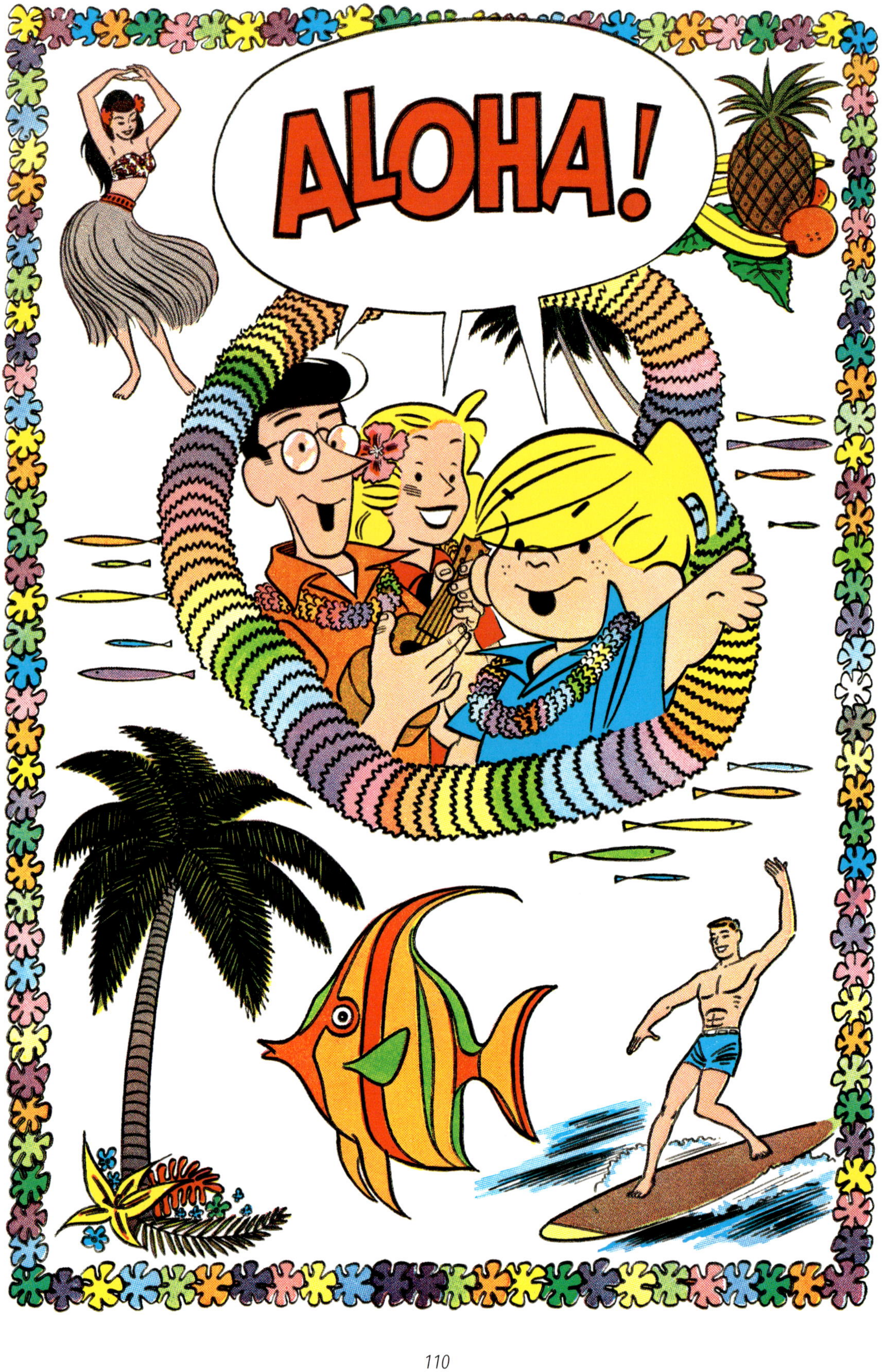
ALOHA!

Drawn From Life: Real Folks Who Snuck Into The DENNIS IN HAWAII Comic!

As with many of Wiseman's other Dennis comics, Al Wiseman included the names and images of his friends, family, co-workers, and acquaintances in DENNIS IN HAWAII. Al's son Jim Wiseman explained, "My dad never gave any advance notice of those people who he often included in his drawings – me included. It was always interesting to see the final comicbook and go through to identify certain people or find that he used the names of real people in his drawings. He also often depicted real locations or businesses – although he usually changed the name of the business – usually changing a letter so that those who knew recognized where it was. The only exception to his rule of not divulging who or what would be in his final drawings was the DENNIS GOES TO MEXICO issue. I got to go along on his research trip where we visited everything that was depicted in the issue. He sketched the whole time and several of the things that Dennis got up to were actual events I was involved in. But even then, while I was aware that he was doing research – it wasn't until the comicbook was released that I was able to recognize particular instances."

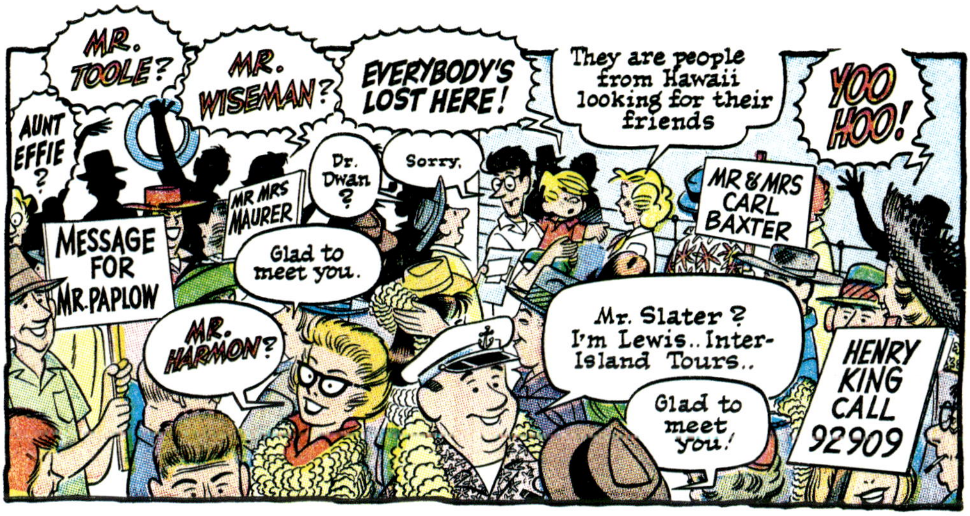
MR. TOOLE?
AUNT EFFIE?
MR. WISEMAN?
EVERYBODY'S LOST HERE!
They are people from Hawaii looking for their friends
YOO HOO!
Dr. Dwan?
Sorry.
MR MRS MAURER
MR & MRS CARL BAXTER
MESSAGE FOR MR. PAPLOW
Glad to meet you.
MR. HARMON?
Mr. Slater? I'm Lewis.. Inter-Island Tours..
Glad to meet you!
HENRY KING CALL 92909

Above: This panel is filled with all sorts of references to people Al knew. Thanks to everyone who helped identify the names on this panel, including Jim & Teresa Wiseman and Mark Arnold.

From left to right (more or less), starting at top:
1) "Mr. Toole"— Fred Toole, writer of the DENNIS THE MENACE comicbooks.
2) "Aunt Effie"— Jim Wiseman said, "No idea who Effie was, hmmm."
3) "Mr. Paplow"— Bob Paplow, 1950's DENNIS THE MENACE cartoonist.
4) "Mr. Wiseman"— Al Wiseman referencing himself.
5) "Mr. and Mrs. Maurer"— Cartoonist-director Norman Maurer and his wife, Joan Howard Maurer, the daughter of Moe from the Three Stooges.
6) "Mr. Harmon"— Bob Harmon, ghost-writer for the Dennis the Menace daily panel.
7) "Dr. Dwan"— Jim Wiseman said, "Doc. Dwan was a retired doctor, who lived in California Hot Springs when the HAWAII book was drawn. Doc's house was near Deer Creek, where my dad would fish."
8) "Mr. and Mrs. Carl Baxter"— Carl and Ann Baxter. Carl was one-third owner in the California Hot Springs resort. According to interviews with Vadis and her daughter, Jan, the Wisemans frequently visited the resort when they lived in nearby Pine Flats, California, circa 1956.
9) "Mr. Slater"— Henry Slater, head of Hallden comics, publisher of DENNIS THE MENACE.
10) "Lewis … International Tours"— Possibly the travel agency that handled Wiseman and Toole's Hawaii visit.
11) "Henry King" is the first and middle name of Dennis creator Henry King Ketcham … better known as "Hank Ketcham."

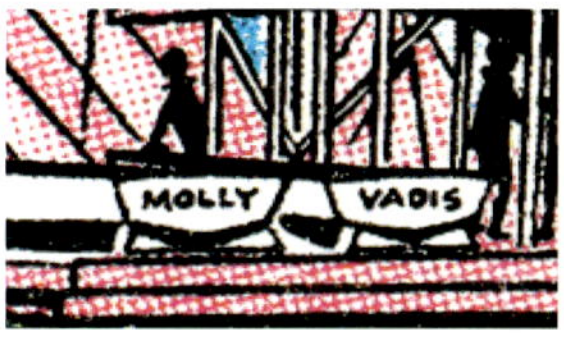
MOLLY
VADIS

Left: "Molly" & "Vadis" (boat names) — Named for Mollie Toole (Fred's wife) and Vadis Wiseman (Al's wife). Fred spelled his wife's name as "Mollie."

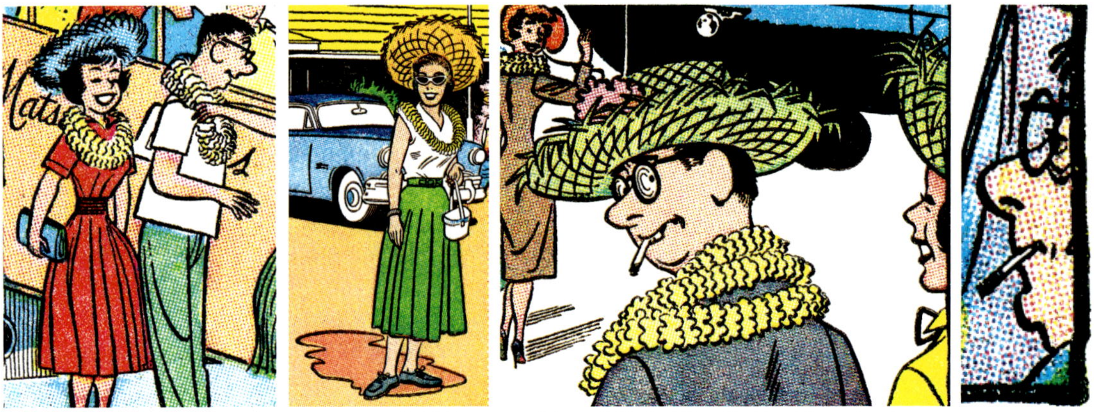

Above: Various images of Al Wiseman and his wife Vadis (Identified by Al's son Jim.)

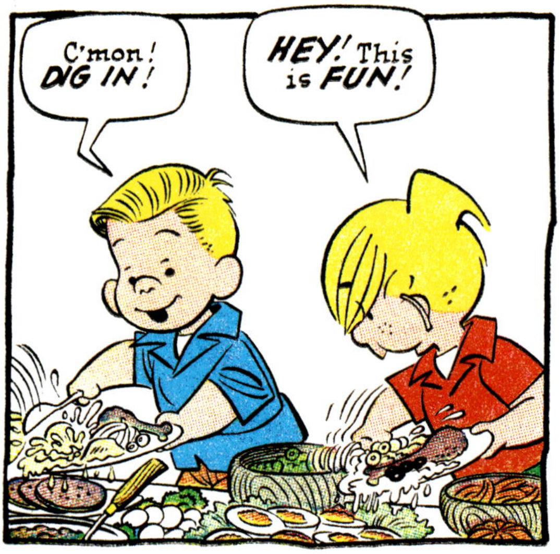
C'mon! DIG IN!
HEY! This is FUN!

Above: Jimmy, the kid in the buffet scene was based upon the likeness of Jim Wiseman, Al and Vadis's son.

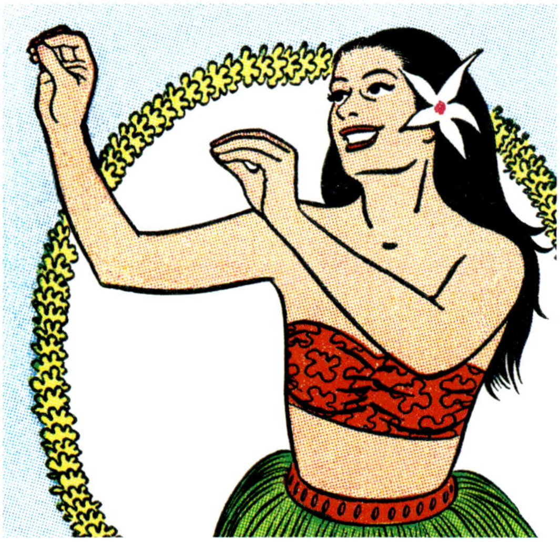

Above: Al and Vadis's oldest daughter, Merrily, posed in Hawaiian Hula dance moves for photos that Al used as reference.

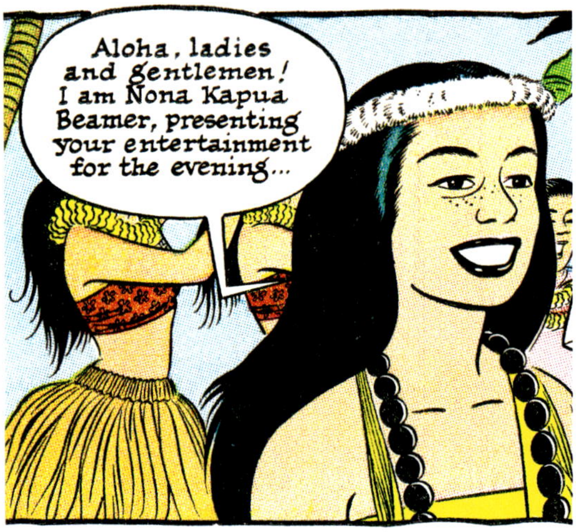
Aloha, ladies and gentlemen! I am Nona Kapua Beamer, presenting your entertainment for the evening...

Above: Winona Kapuailohiamanonokalani Desha Beamer was instrumental in reviving the authentic form of the hula, as opposed to the commercialized "tourist" version.

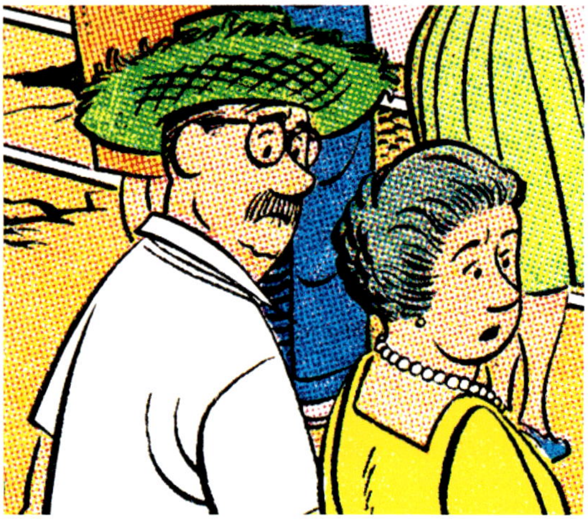

Above: Jim Wiseman thinks this couple is too old to be Fred and Mollie Toole at the time. But he thinks they could be Al's accountant Jack Tostevin and Jack's wife Isabel.

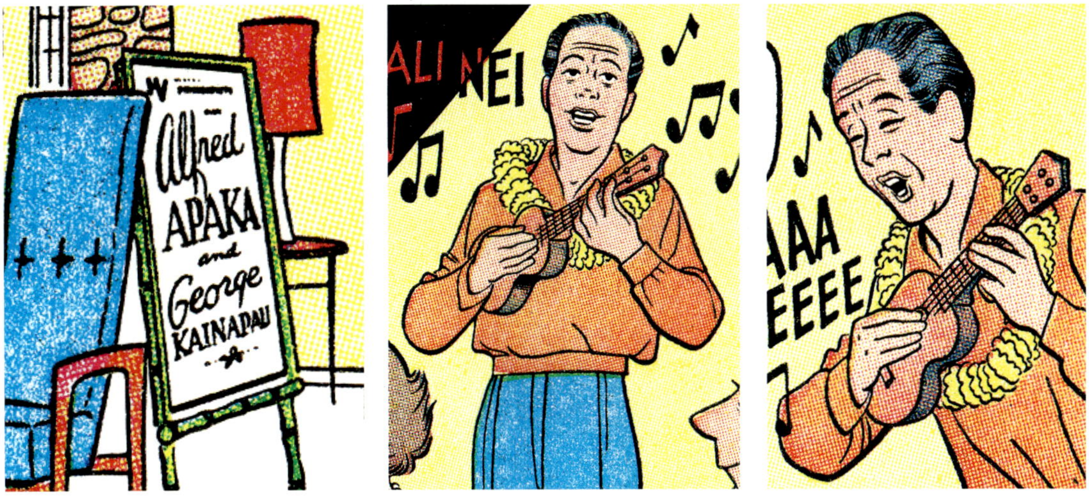
Alfred
APAKA
and
George
KAINAPAU
ALI NEI
AAA
EEEE

Above: The singer featured in the "Dennis on Wahoo" chapter is beloved Hawaiian entertainer Alfred Apaka, one of the most influential performers in the history of Hawaii's popular music. Although he had the chance to become a mainstream crooner, Apaka opted to stay true to his roots and remain in Hawaii. The singer even convinced multimillionaire Henry Kaiser to construct a special showroom for his revue at Kaiser's Hawaiian Village Hotel. Although he's not pictured in the comic, the name "George Kainapau" appears on the lobby billboard. Kainapau was another popular Hawaiian singer of the time who was known for his falsetto voice.

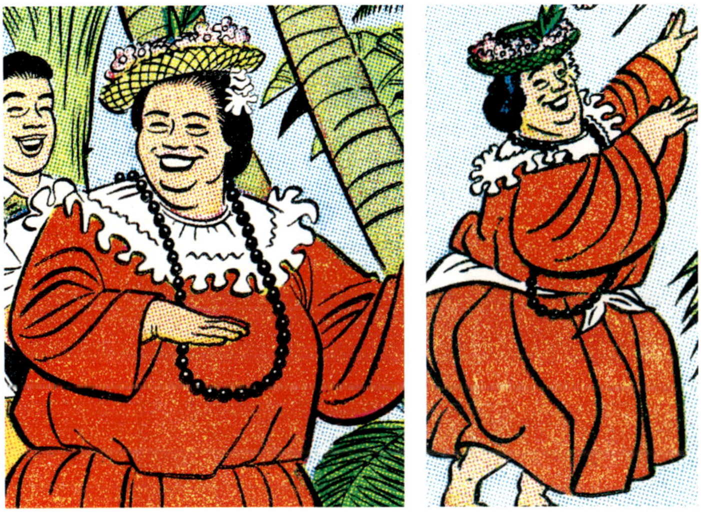

Left: Making the audience part of the show at the luau is Hawaiian singer, hula dancer, actress and comedian Hilo Hattie. Born Clarissa "Clara" Haili, she toured the world and performed in movies and on television. Her acting credits include appearing in the Elvis movie "Blue Hawaii" and guesting on the TV series "Hawaii Five-O."

Right: "Captain Jerry Collins" (Norman Keith Collins) appears as the captain who takes the Mitchells on their tour of Pearl Harbor. As "Sailor Jerry," he later became famous for his influential tattoo artistry.

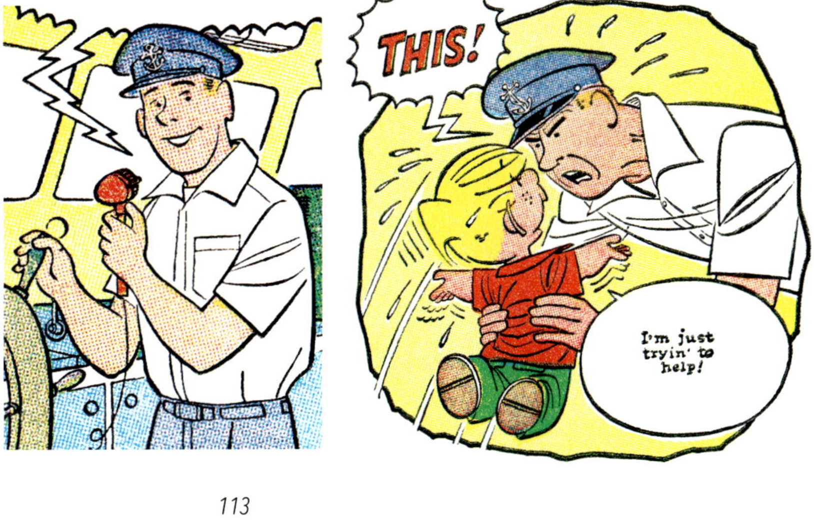
THIS!
I'm just tryin' to help!

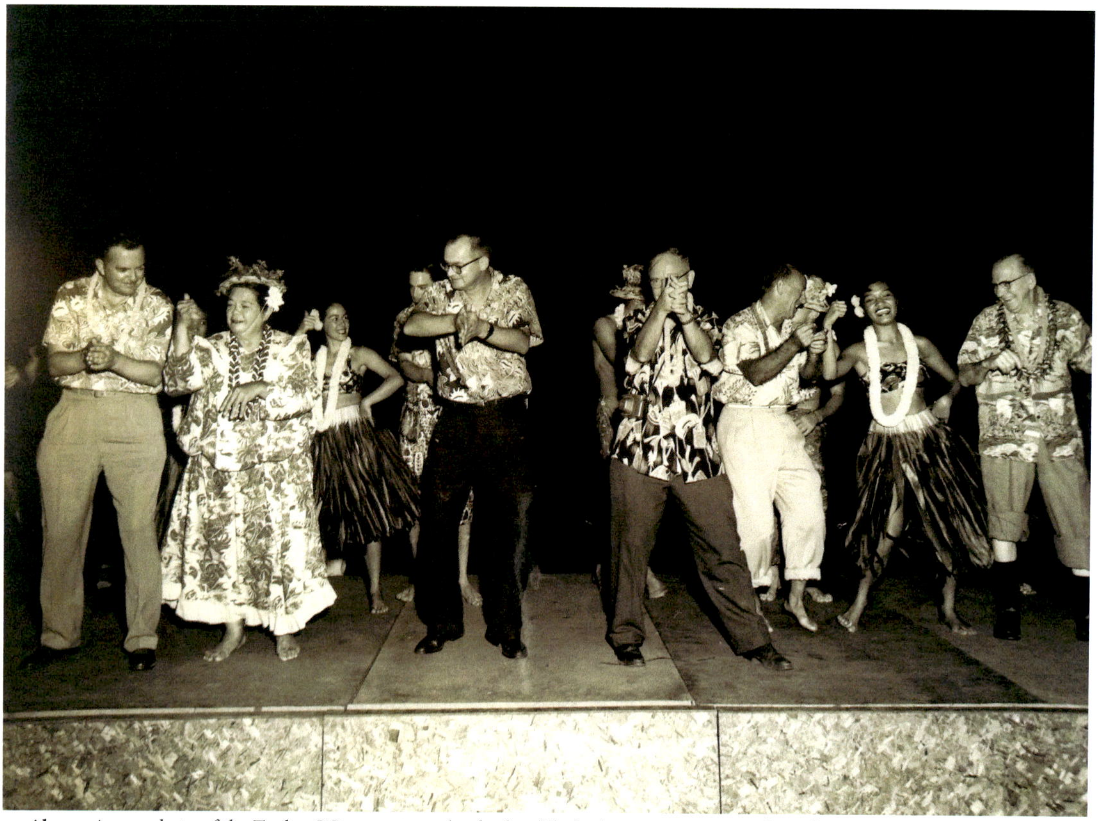

Above: A rare photo of the Toole—Wiseman team (and others) hula dancing onstage at a luau during the 1956 Hawaiian trip. Fred Toole, Hilo Hattie and Al Wiseman are seen on the left. (Photo courtesy of Jim & Teresa Wiseman.)

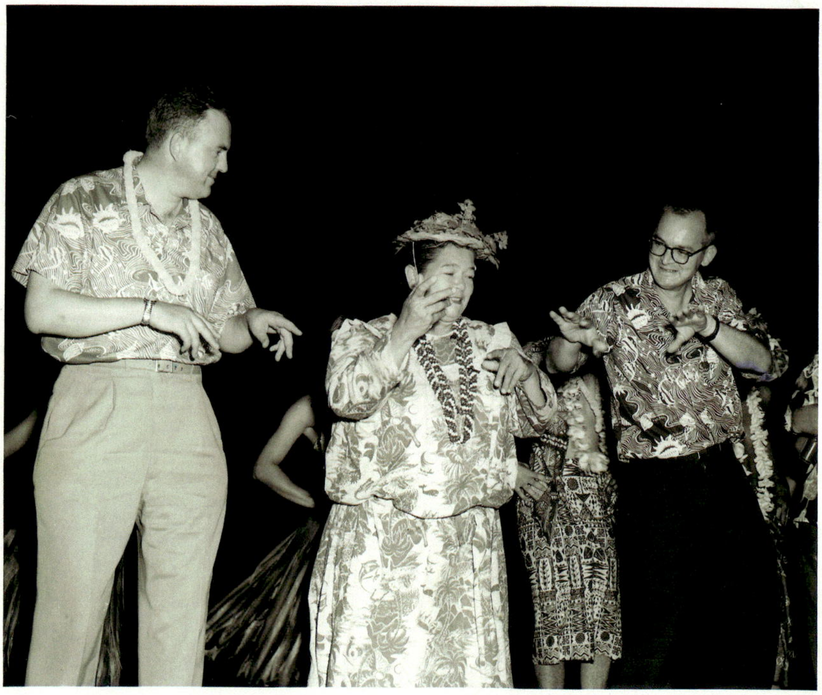

Above: Yet another rare photo — and this one's a closer look at Fred and Al mastering the hula! (Photo courtesy of Jim & Teresa Wiseman.)

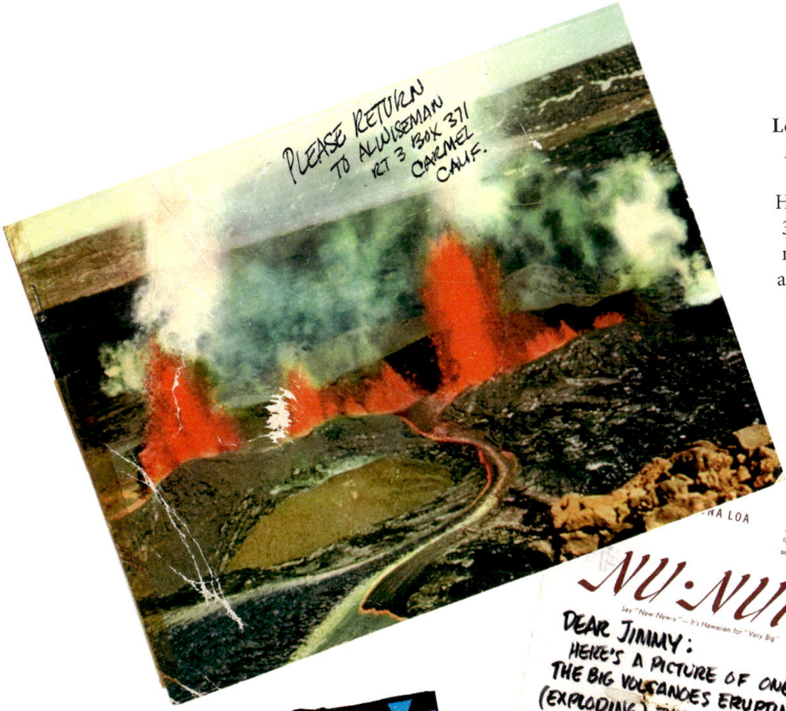
PLEASE RETURN
TO AL WISEMAN
RT 3 BOX 371
CARMEL
CALIF.

Left & below: Both sides of a postcard Al Wiseman mailed to his son, Jim, while Al and Vadis were visiting Hawaii. It was postmarked on August 30, 1956. The photo on the postcard may have been used as reference for a volcano illustration in the DENNIS IN HAWAII comicbook. (Postcard images courtesy of Jim & Teresa Wiseman.)

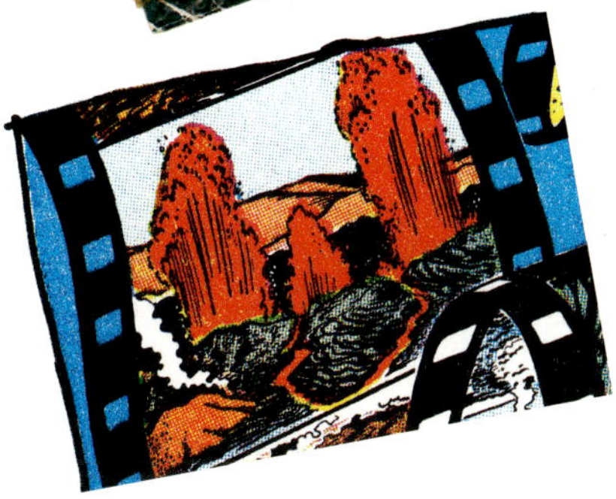

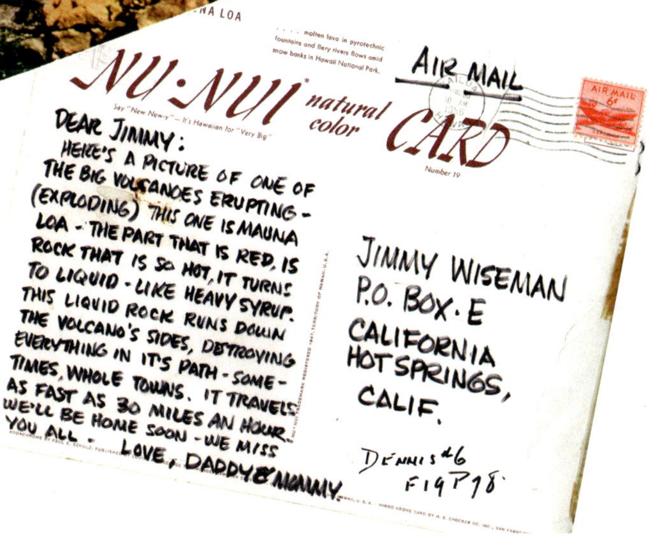
NU-NUI natural color CARD
AIR MAIL
DEAR JIMMY:
HERE'S A PICTURE OF ONE OF THE BIG VOLCANOES ERUPTING - (EXPLODING) THIS ONE IS MAUNA LOA - THE PART THAT IS RED, IS ROCK THAT IS SO HOT, IT TURNS TO LIQUID - LIKE HEAVY SYRUP. THIS LIQUID ROCK RUNS DOWN THE VOLCANO'S SIDES, DESTROYING EVERYTHING IN IT'S PATH - SOMETIMES, WHOLE TOWNS. IT TRAVELS AS FAST AS 30 MILES AN HOUR. WE'LL BE HOME SOON - WE MISS YOU ALL. LOVE, DADDY & MOMMY.
JIMMY WISEMAN
P.O. BOX. E
CALIFORNIA
HOT SPRINGS,
CALIF.

Right: Both sides of a Hawaii National Park membersip card given to Al Wiseman on August 29, 1956. Al's daughter Jan wrote: "Dad got this card when he and Fred Toole went to Hawaii before doing the DENNIS THE MENACE IN HAWAII book. Not sure what it was good for—?"

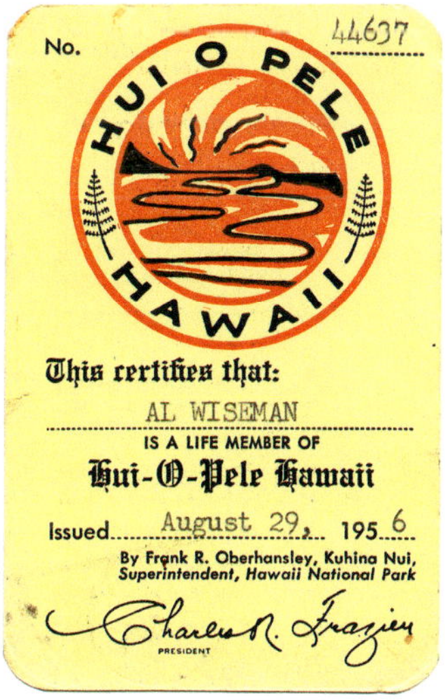
No. 44637
HUI O PELE HAWAII
This certifies that:
AL WISEMAN
IS A LIFE MEMBER OF
Hui-O-Pele Hawaii
Issued August 29, 1956
By Frank R. Oberhansley, Kuhina Nui, Superintendent, Hawaii National Park
PRESIDENT

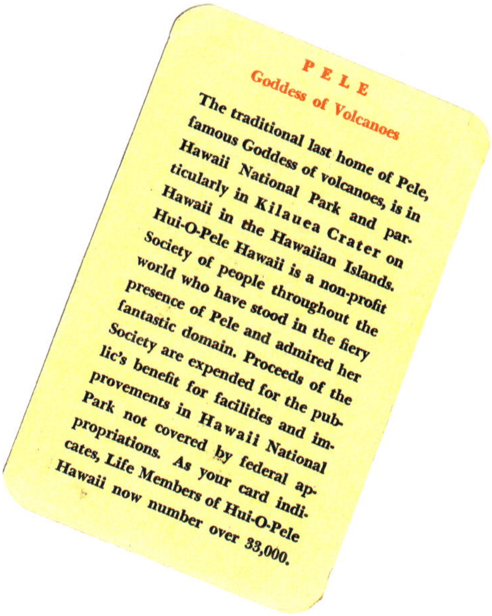
PELE
Goddess of Volcanoes
The traditional last home of Pele, famous Goddess of volcanoes, is in Hawaii National Park and particularly in Kilauea Crater on Hawaii in the Hawaiian Islands. Hui-O-Pele Hawaii is a non-profit Society of people throughout the world who have stood in the fiery presence of Pele and admired her fantastic domain. Proceeds of the Society are expended for the public's benefit for facilities and improvements in Hawaii National Park not covered by federal appropriations. As your card indicates, Life Members of Hui-O-Pele Hawaii now number over 33,000.

A Letter From Al

AL WISEMAN

Dear Joe

mailed a couple of DENNIS THE MENACE books to you right after you called me — Did you ever receive them?

— still banging away on Ketcham characters — and it looks like "old al" will be doing just that for the next twenty years or so — I do all the advertisements bearing Ketchams signature, as well as most of the sunday comic strips. How did you like the Jello billboards?

Just wound up another complete comic book last night — Whew! What a job — but I love it!

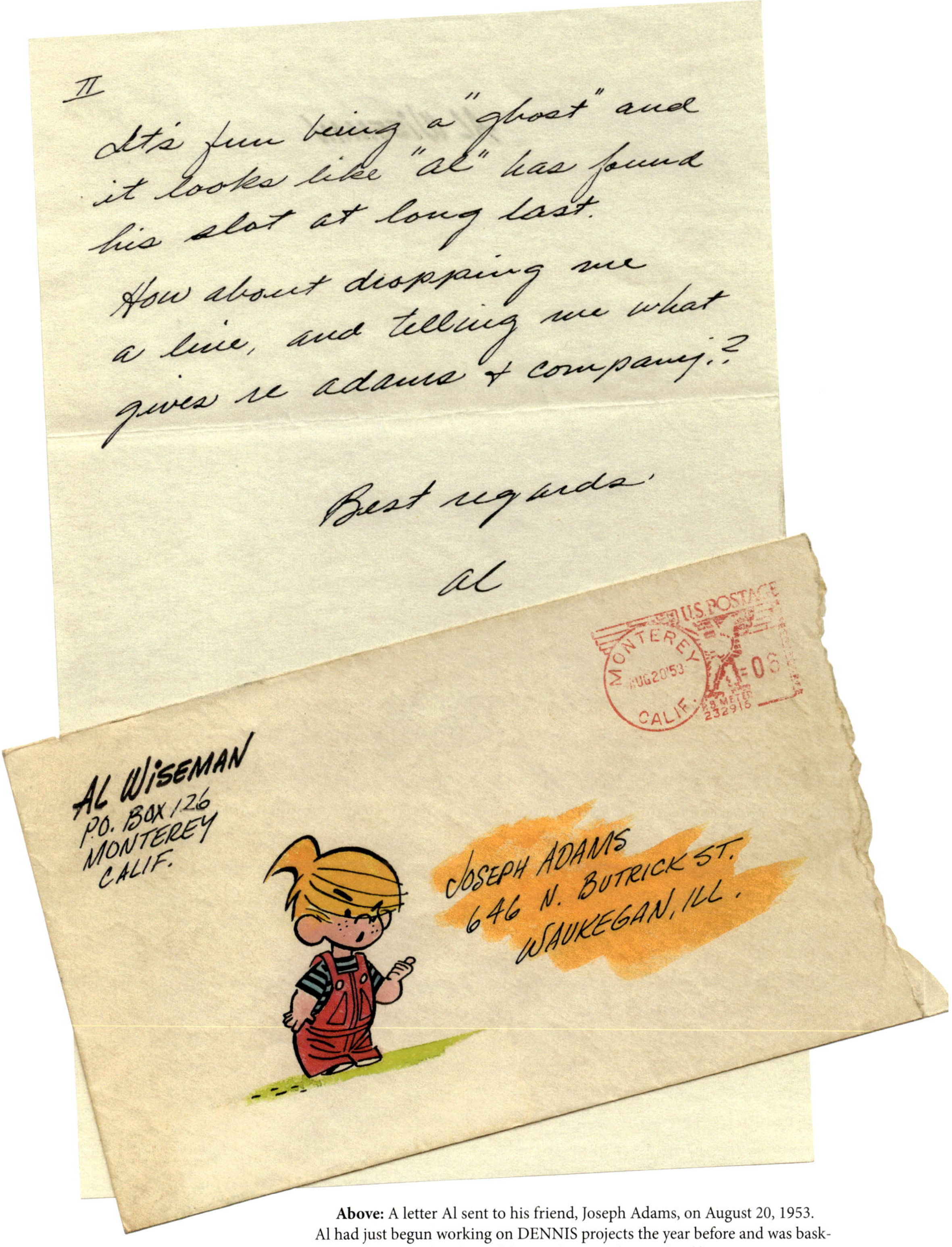

II

It's fun being a "ghost" and
it looks like "Al" has found
his slot at long last.
How about dropping me
a line, and telling me what
gives re adams & company.?

Best regards,

Al

U.S. POSTAGE
MONTEREY
AUG 20 '53
CALIF.
06
PB METER
232916
AL WISEMAN
P.O. BOX 126
MONTEREY
CALIF.
JOSEPH ADAMS
646 N. BUTRICK ST.
WAUKEGAN, ILL.

Above: A letter Al sent to his friend, Joseph Adams, on August 20, 1953. Al had just begun working on DENNIS projects the year before and was basking in the glow of the newly created comicbook's success.

Interview: Hank Ketcham, Creator of Dennis the Menace

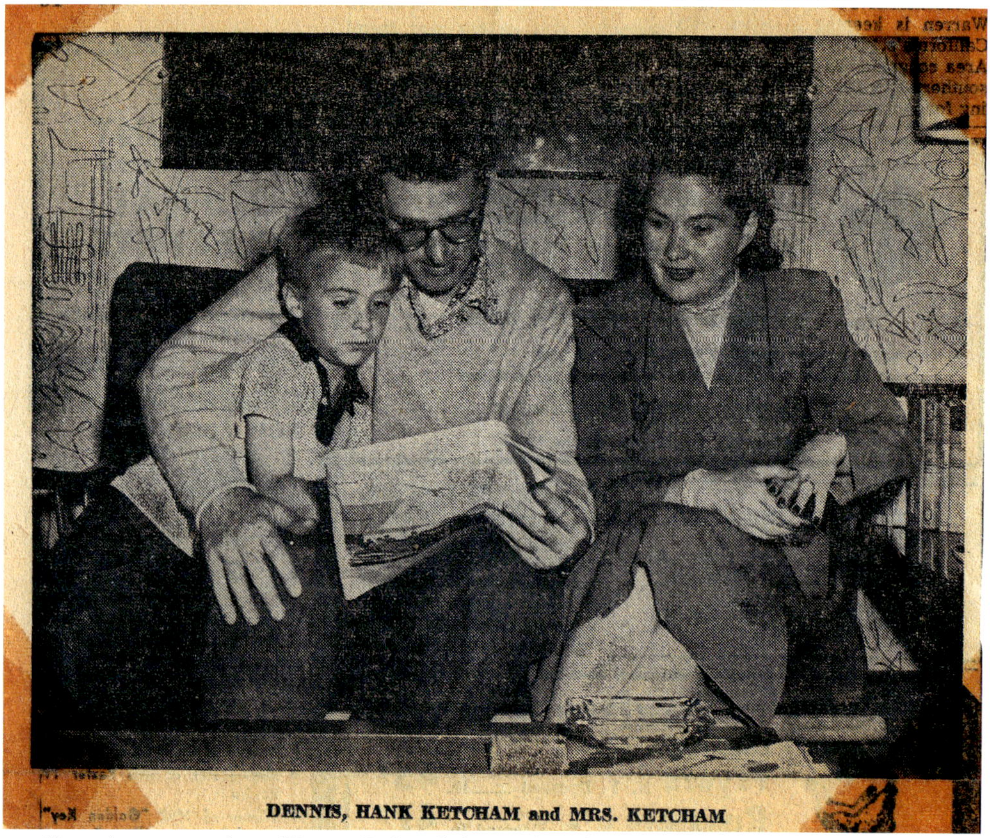

DENNIS, HANK KETCHAM and MRS. KETCHAM

Above: A newspaper photo of Dennis, Hank, and Alice Ketcham that had been taped inside a fan's scrapbook. From the June 18, 1953 Monterey Peninsula Herald.

This is a compilation of two phone interviews I conducted with Hank Ketcham on March 23,1998 and April 7,1999. For our talks, I was mostly trying to gather information about Al Wiseman. Until putting together this book, I hadn't listened to these tapes since the interviews were originally done. My vague memories of our interaction was of me speaking with Hank for a minute or two and then quickly getting off the phone, followed by sending him questions through the mail. I thought there was nothing worth revisiting from our conversations. But recently, my brother Tom was transcribing my tapes for this volume and asked if I wanted to include the Ketcham interview. "Nah," I said, "there's really nothing much there. I wish I had talked to him more." My brother replied, "Umm... I don't know, you should really listen to these. There's a lot here." And there is! I had totally forgotten how friendly Hank was and open to answering my questions. Well, anyway, after all these years, I'm happy to be finally presenting this "lost," never before published interview with DENNIS'S dad, Hank Ketcham!

Bill: Thanks for giving me the opportunity to speak with you. I've got a lot of questions about DENNIS THE MENACE and Al Wiseman. Do you know what work Al did before being employed at your studio?

Hank: He supported himself with freelance stuff a great deal. He'd go out to local merchants and try to get little ads going.

Bill: Do you remember when he started working for you?

Hank: Yeah, it was about 1952.

Bill: That would have been the year before the comicbook came out?

Hank: Yes, that's what he was primarily involved with at that time.

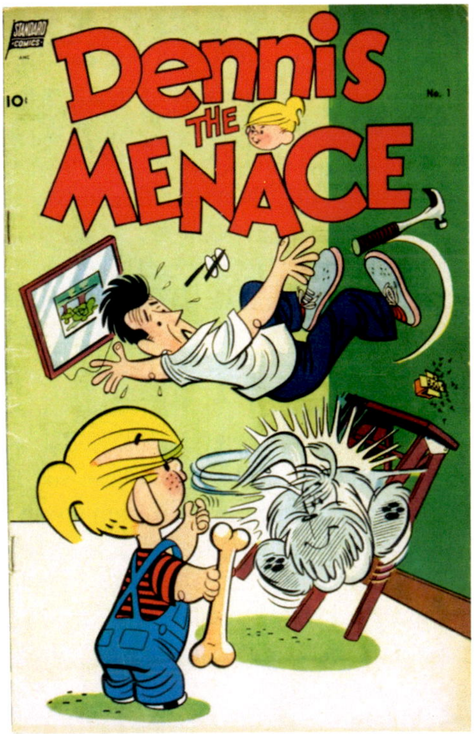
STANDARD COMICS
Dennis THE MENACE
10¢
No. 1

Above. The first issue of the DENNIS THE MENACE comicbook from August, 1953.

Bill: He drew many of the Sundays during the early years, didn't he?

Hank: Some of the time he did the Sundays and did a great job. Fred Toole was the writer that I had. I think I'm probably the only producer who ever sent an artist-writer team on location for a comicbook. I sent them to Hawaii knowing that only looking at post cards or *National Geographics*, they could not grasp at all the substance of the island. So it was important that they be there. And they turned out a tremendous book which was reprinted in nine different languages. And, for many years, people would take the comics with them to the islands as a kind of guidebook for their trips. It got a tremendous kind of reaction. And then we subsequently sent them to Mexico City, and to Washington DC, and then the Tale of Two Cities to London and Paris. So then they were specializing on these specials for a long time. And by doing so, they produced books that had a lot of validity. And people would write to me and thank me, and say they take the books with them when they go on trips. So that was quite something. That was a very flattering result of the whole thing.

Bill: I interviewed Frank Hill recently and he said he had a great time when you sent him to England to get reference for drawing a later travel comic.

Hank: Yeah, right. Until … I think he had an illness in the family and he had to go back.

Bill: He said his daughter fell down somewhere and got a fractured skull.

Hank: That was too bad.

Bill: Frank said you put him up in an amazing hotel. He was very grateful for the trip.

Hank: The boys were good kids and I wanted them to be comfy. And didn't want them to be in a hardship situation.
And they did it. They performed very well.

Bill: Did Fred and Al usually work together as a team when creating comic stories or did they work separately? I mean, did Fred write the book on his own and then send the script to Al?

Hank: Yeah, Fred would have to do that. Of course, in the Islands they worked together. They would go around visiting everything and take notes. But normally a writer will develop his material, then send it along to the artist, who then has to interpret it into graphic form.

It's quite an assignment because the research is so important. But Al was a tremendous artist. And he was a frustrated man that had an ego as large as the Empire State Building. He always wondered why he didn't have his own comic strip. And why people weren't buying his stuff they way he wanted them to.

Bill: It seems like with Al's sense of humor, he really needed a Fred Toole to make his own comics successful.

Hank: Yeah, Al had a very weird sense of humor. Just off-the-wall. What he thought was funny was kind of crude. He needed someone to tone it down a little bit.

Bill: I've got some samples of proposed comic strips and panels he did in the late 1960s and early 1970s. The drawings were superb, but the humor just wasn't there.

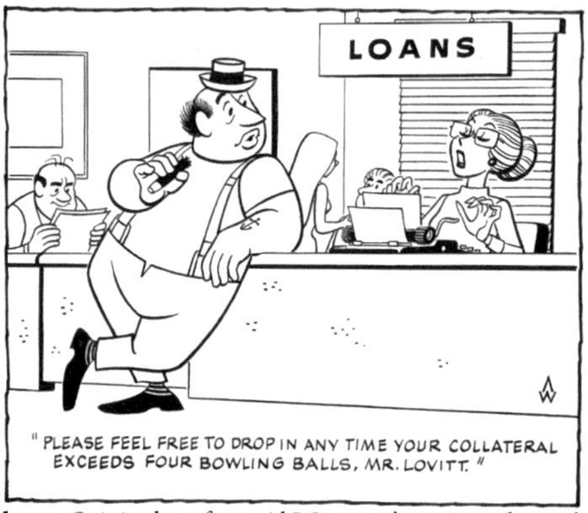
LOANS
" PLEASE FEEL FREE TO DROP IN ANY TIME YOUR COLLATERAL EXCEEDS FOUR BOWLING BALLS, MR. LOVITT. "

Above: Original art from Al Wiseman's proposed 1960's comic panel "THE BLOBS ... GRACE & LOOIE."

Hank: No, that's right. Exactly. He didn't have the intelligence or sense or luck to bring a writer in to develop the material like other people have tried to do. Everything in this world starts with a writer. You can't live without them. It takes the pressure off from staying awake at nights, worrying about what you're going to draw the next day. But, also, you've become an editor. You separate the wheat from the chaff. And then you find a germ here and there. You update it, or if necessary, you change it around. While you're sleeping, you have to have a half a dozen people thinking up ideas. It's worked for me for 50 years

Bill: It's been very successful.

Hank: Because the stuff is fresh. Otherwise you settle for duplicity and mediocrity. A lot of people burn themselves out because they try to do it themselves and it doesn't work.

Bill: It seems that lately, many cartoonists give up their strips after about ten, fifteen years or so.

Hank: I think the stress is just too much for them. I never had that problem. I just gave it up because I'm busy painting. I've done everything. I've climbed every mountain and got all the accolades and prizes that I need. And I wanted to climb another mountain. So I'm doing that now. I'm enjoying it immensely. It's a new career change.

Bill: I just read your autobiography, the "Merchant of Dennis." That's a fascinating book.

Hank: You did?

Bill: Yeah, It's amazing the things you've done.

Hank: Well, yeah. I look at that and say, "Oh my God, did I do that? I don't even remember that." But I've done a lot of stuff since then. I'm glad you had a chance to get the book.

Hank: What is the purpose of your research on Al?

Bill: Some of the earliest comics I remember reading were reprints of the DENNIS THE MENACE comicbooks. When I was a kid, my favorite comicbook was probably DENNIS THE MENACE. Years later, when I first discovered Al's name somewhere, I started doing research to get information on him. I couldn't find any. It seemed like nobody knew anything about Al. I ended up going to a comic convention a couple of years ago and bought some letters Al had sent to a friend in the 1950s. One of the letters mentioned Al's son's name, so I tracked down Jim Wiseman.

Hank: Yeah, he's here in the area somewhere. I believe.

Bill: Jim's been helping me track down other people who knew Al. I've been talking to Vadis.

Hank: That's his wife, first wife.

Bill: Yes, his first wife. And also Sue Dewar.

Hank: Oh, yeah, that's his second wife.

Bill: Plus, I've been speaking with Al's daughters too. I'm just trying to get any information on Al I can.

Hank: You've really gotten a lot of good source material then. Well, you know, he just knew how to draw very well. But he had his terrible personality. And, you know sometimes, he would just do some really crazy things. I was just reading a biography of Jackson Pollock. He makes Al Wiseman look like a YMCA boy. A lot of these creative guys, really, are off-the-wall. I guess in some cases it goes with the territory. Al was a guy … He would go from one extreme to the other with very little moderation.

Bill: I'm also interested in Fred Toole and your whole DENNIS studio. You've had so many people write about you, but many of the people who worked for you are kind of obscure.

Hank: Lee Holley was another fellow that worked with me. He went on to do *Ponytail*.

Then he got into real estate and made a lot of money. And he got into flying. I think, maybe, he's not even drawing anymore. He's living up near San Francisco or Palo Alto or someplace. He's a real neat guy. I felt he quit me too early. He wasn't ready but he sold Ponytail. And it went OK. I wanted to train him a little bit more.

Above: Lee Holley DENNIS THE MENACE original artwork for the 1960 Little Golden Book, "A Quiet Afternoon." (Artwork courtesy of Scott Sheppard.)

Bill: I actually talked to Lee Holley a few weeks ago.

Hank: How is Lee?

Bill: He seems to be doing great.

Hank: Is he in real estate?

Bill: Yeah, he didn't really say what he was doing now but he said he made money in real estate, so he didn't have to work anymore.

Hank: He's not doing any cartooning?

Bill: No, he said he gave that up.

Hank: Is he still flying I wonder? He was flying quite a lot.

Bill: I didn't ask him about that.

Hank: Nice young kid. I liked … He just quit me a little too soon.

Bill: He was saying that he really enjoyed working for you. That there was a pool right next to the art studio. He said he just loved working there.

Hank: Yeah, right. There up in the valley. I had a big pool and a cabana around the pool. That's where we worked. It was a real ideal working condition.

Bill: Lee made a joke that people used to call him the most expensive pool boy in the area. He said he used to clean up a little around there.

Hank: Well, he was a nice boy and I enjoyed working with him. I'm sorry I haven't got a chance to see him since.

Bill: He seems like he's doing well.

Hank: He's living up near Aptos, is he? Or where is that?

Bill: Yeah, he's up there.

Bill: I spoke to Fred Toole's widow, Mollie, a while back but I heard that she's in a retirement home now.

Hank: No, well, It's not a home. It's a retirement … it's not even retirement. It's kind of for people who can't handle things themselves. There's been a lot of people in and around to see her and she's pretty well out-of-it now. She's in her 90s. She can't get into any discussions on things.

Bill: That's too bad, because when I talked to her, she seemed to still have it together.

Hank: Well, she did for a long time. She was very, very sharp. But now she can't see at all. She can't hear very well. So … she's … best, I guess, to be left alone.

Bill: OK, well I appreciate the information. She was wonderful to talk to about Fred.

Hank: As I say with the team, Fred Toole was the glue that held it together because he really was pretty well disciplined. And was a very good writer. And had a great imagination.

Bill: He lasted on the comicbook for a really long time. I guess the whole run, up until the very end of the comic.

Hank: Oh, yeah. He sure did.

Bill: Do you know what Fred did before he worked on DENNIS?

Hank: Well, he was with Bob Barnes up in Santa Cruz area. They had an advertising agency together. I think that's where Al got a hold of them and was doing work for them. I knew Bob better than anyone else.

Bill: Really? What was Bob like?

Above: Signed photo of Bob Barnes. (Back of photo is stamped "1951.")

Hank: He was a marvelous guy. He was in the cartoon business for a long time. He and Ruth were just happy-go-lucky guys who were all over the place. They'd sell a few drawings and go out and they'd buy a used Rolls Royce and have a great time (laughs). He did very well. And then, he decided to settle down and get this advertising agency going, and got a hold of Fred who was writing gags from the East.

Bill: Was Fred writing gags for Bob's comics before working with Bob in their studio?

Hank: He wrote for various artists including Bob. Bob talked him into coming out. So he and Mollie came out from Pennsylvania, actually. Mollie was from Bethlehem. And they came out and settled in Santa Cruz. I got to California in 1948. In October of 1950, I got the idea for the feature. That's how, I think, I really got in touch with Al was through Fred and Bob Barnes. I didn't (put together a studio) until I sold the Sunday page and also the comicbook. It just needed a lot of hands to turn all of that stuff out. And then, I got a hold of Al. Later I decided, well, Fred should be here, too. Because if you need to get into comicbooks, better get Fred here! So I left Barnes high and dry (laughs). I took his boys.

Bill: I heard that Fred Toole was a war hero.

Hank: Well, he said that he walked through France, up to the Mediterranean, and up to Germany. And the Army paid for it (laughs). He was commissioned on the field, I believe. He spent quite a war over there.

Bill: I don't have that much information on Fred. Do you know anyone else I could get in contact with who could help me with anything on him?

Hank: No, I really don't. No, I'm afraid that I can't be of any further help on this.

Bill: So you wouldn't know any of Fred Toole's relatives or anything?

Hank: No … no. They were non-existent as far as I'm concerned. Somewhere in New York they were. And he didn't maintain any kind of communication with them. He was just a whole new boy, as far as I was concerned, when he arrived here. I didn't get into his background too much.

Bill: I found a National Cartoonist Society publication from 1965 where Al said that he met you at S.E.P. after your Navy stints.

AL WISEMAN

FIRST DAYLIGHT: 1918. BAKERSFIELD, CALIF. STARTED DRAWING AT 4. CARTOON FIRST: "FLYING" MAGAZINE, AFTER *YEARS* IN THE ADVERTISING ART BIZ. LUCKY ENOUGH...SOLD MINY MINY CARTOONS TO ALL MAGAZINES. MET HANK KETCHAM AT S.E.P. AFTER OUR NAVY STINTS. MINE IN NEWPORT, R.I. A.V.A. UNIT, AS NEARSIGHTED-INSTRUCTOR-ARTIST. (ONLY SEA DUTY ON THE JAMESTOWN FERRY) WENT BACK INTO ADVERTISING. KETCHAM NEEDED A HACK... HIRED ME.. COMIC BOOKS MAIN MEAT. WON A FEW AWARDS FOR HIM ALONG THE WAY. LIVE IN THE HIGH SIERRAS CALIFORNIA HOT SPRINGS, CALIF. WITH MINE LEETLE ESTONIAN, KIIRA, AND 3 TEENERS, GLENN, JIM, 'N JENNY. WORK TIP: *WORK*. HOBBIES: TROUT FISHING, HUNTING, GOLF. *IF* I COULD LIVE MY LIFE OVER.. I'D SEE TO A SYNDICATED FEATURE OF *MY OWN,* 'BOUT A LIL' BLONDE KID, (AT 4) CHANGE MY NAME TO HANK KETCHAM, AND WEAR CONTACT LENSES.

Hank: At where?

Bill: It's S period, E period, P period. I don't know what he's referring to.

Hank: *Saturday Evening Post.*

Bill: Oh, of course, that's it! Do you remember meeting him there?

Hank: No, I don't. After the Navy ... after the war?

Bill: Yeah, it says, "After our Navy stints."

Hank: No, I was in Washington D.C. Then I went up to Connecticut. On Wednesdays, I would go down and visit the magazine cartoon editors. Could have been that I met him there. I don't recall that meeting, but it could have been. There were a lot of cartoonists down there. Wednesdays was the D-Day to see the art editors, the cartoon editors.

Bill: Did the cartoonists socialize after meeting with the editors?

Hank: Well, afterwards, we'd find a place like the Pen and Pencil over by King Features. And we'd sit down there and have a very liquid lunch. And some of us would attempt to catch the 5:11 home back to Connecticut. It was kind of fun. It was a lot of camaraderie there. We had a good time.

Bill: I loved seeing the 1950's studio photos in the "Merchant of Dennis." It was great seeing you guys interacting.

Hank: Oh, yeah. Well, I used the comicbook as sort of a training ground for the Sunday page.

Bill: There seemed to be various artists contributing to the early Sunday pages and comicbooks, but the art had a strong Al Wiseman touch. Do you remember when Al stopped helping on the Sunday comics?

Hank: I can't remember. No. But I had a number of men who did work on the Sunday page. I went through a whole bunch of them. I even forgot why he quit. It may be that he quit the Sunday page to take over the comicbooks. Because he did a heck of a lot of comicbooks. That production was quite a challenge. And it could have been at that time when I had other men working under my supervision to turn out the Sunday page, while Al ground out the comicbooks. That's probably what happened.

Bill: Yeah. Because, for a while he did a monthly DENNIS comicbook and a bunch of specials along with it.

Hank: Yeah, we had the specials and they were 25 cents at the time (laughs). I was very lucky to have a man of his talent there.

Bill: I've been speaking with cartoonist George Crenshaw, who worked in the DENNIS studio with Al in the 1950's.

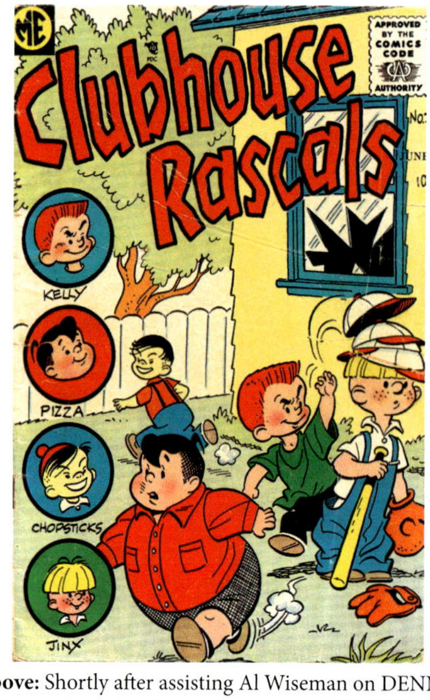
ME
Clubhouse Rascals
APPROVED BY THE COMICS CODE AUTHORITY
KELLY
PIZZA
CHOPSTICKS
JINX

Above: Shortly after assisting Al Wiseman on DENNIS, George Crenshaw began drawing the CLUBHOUSE RASCALS comicbook in 1956.

Hank: Oh, right, yeah.

Bill: George said Al was a good friend, but he basically quit the studio because dealing with Al started getting to him.

Hank: (laughs) Well, I'm glad he blamed Al and not me on the thing.

Bill: George said you were great to work for. He said he couldn't figure out, at the time, why he was quitting. Because it was a great job and he made great money. He said there was no pressure, but he said he'd stay awake at night thinking about Al's problems. He felt that Al's problems were becoming George's problems, too.

Hank: Well, I think that Al did create a lot of atmosphere that was full of friction. He had trouble being an entertainer. His idea of humor was somewhat out of focus. So when he tried to tell a joke or draw a funny cartoon, it just turned out the opposite … wet cold. He was a little weird that way, but he was a terrific artist. Just a fantastic lettering man. He turned out some of the best work we've done. Fortunately he was working with Fred Toole who was doing the writing. I had to whip on Al's back a little bit when he got out of focus. It worked out fine in those days. I'm sorry that he didn't have a better character and could still be with us.

Bill: Yeah, it seems like if he had been able to live his life a little differently, he could have found some sort of happiness or some sort of fame or something.

Hank: Well, that's what he wanted. He knew he was better than everybody and he wanted everybody to know it. And he set out to prove it.

Bill: I was talking to Al's son Jim and he said you had a photographer take reference pictures of him dressed as Dennis. He had blonde hair like the DENNIS character. Do you remember that?

Hank: No, I didn't but I guess his dad did. They did a lot of that. I don't know what Jim is doing now at all.

Bill: I talked to him recently and he's a musician now.

Hank: He's in Carmel, is he?

Bill: Yes, he is. He had a lot of good things to say about you, a lot of good memories. Well, would it be possible for me to mail some questions to you? I'm still trying to research Al Wiseman's life and career.

Hank: Well, certainly …

Bill: OK, great. It's been an honor to talk to you.

Hank: Thank you. I'm pleased of your interest.
And shoot me some questions. I'll do my best to answer.

Bill: Great. I'm amazed I got through to you. You're a hero of mine and I didn't actually think I would get the chance to talk to you.

Hank: Well there it is, it happens. It's the phase of the moon!

Bill: I think so!

Hank: Thank you very much. Nice chatting with you and I'll wait for your letter.

Bill: Thank you. Bye.

Interview: Vadis Davis, Al Wiseman's First Wife

Above: Pictured from left to right: A couple of Hawaiian kids, Al Wiseman, Fred Toole, Vadis Davis, and Mollie Toole during their trip to Hawaii in August and September of 1956. (Photo courtesy of Jim & Teresa Wiseman.)

Al Wiseman's first wife was born Vadis Louise Neve on February 1, 1921 in Wall, Oklahoma. When Vadis was about seven years old, the Neve family moved to California. Vadis met Al in Bakersfield, California. After she and Al divorced, she remarried and became Vadis Davis. Vadis passed away August 11, 2000.

The following is a compilation of six phone interviews conducted with Vadis from March 1998 through April 6, 1999.

Bill: Vadis, thanks for agreeing to talk with me about Al. Let's start with his childhood. What can you tell me about Al's parents?

Vadis: Well, Al's mother and father were divorced after they'd been married for six years. I've been trying to find somebody who knew Al's father because after we were married, I only saw him one time. Al and his father didn't get along very well. So I really didn't see him. Now, I knew his mother really well, but she never talked about Al's father.

Bill: Does artistic ability run in Al's family?

Vadis: His mother could draw. Flowers and things — she used to do that for a little while and then she quit drawing. His full-sister, Betty Janice, died when she was very young. As far as anybody else in the family, he only had the two half-sisters. His oldest half-sister, Trish, was very talented. I'm still very close to my two half-sisters-in-law.

Bill: Your daughter Jan told me that you and Al both liked to dance and that's how you met.

Vadis: Oh, yes, that was why we met. And if he hadn't been a real good dancer, we never would have gone out.

Bill: Oh, really?

Vadis: We both lived up in Bakersfield, and we had this ballroom up there. Every Saturday night, my girlfriend and I went there. We really didn't like to go with anybody else. We didn't want to go with any particular fellow because both of us like to dance too much. We wanted to dance with all of them! (laughs) That was during the jitterbugging days, of course.
Anyhow, Al came over and asked me to dance. I had seen him, you know — watched him. And he was a very, very good dancer. So he came over and asked me to dance. And, we did. After that, every Saturday night, we always went there. Every place we would go — when we went out to parties — Al and I — they wanted us to dance for them.

Bill: What was the name of the place where you met?

Vadis: At the La Granada Ballroom. (There was a La Granada Ballroom in Bakersfield, CA)

Bill: Jan also said you worked at a hospital together.

Vadis: Yes, coincidentally, that's where we both worked. I thought I wanted to be a nurse, but I found that I didn't want to be one. I couldn't — I felt so sorry for the people there, that I just couldn't do it. But anyhow, when we met at the dance, I asked him what he did and he said, "I work at the hospital, at the Kern General Hospital. I do all of their artwork for them." Everything they did at the hospital that needed artwork, he designed everything. Their signs, whatever they needed him to do. It was easy for him!

And anyhow, as I got to know him, I went down to the department where he worked. I'd watch him draw and so forth. And I just felt that he was just so good that I was impressed with him. And we had a lot of fun together.

Bill: Jan told me that shortly after you married Al, you both moved to El Paso, Texas. How did you pick El Paso?

Above: Young Al and Vadis Wiseman. Possibly taken soon after their Sepremder 11, 1941 marraige in Las Vegas, NV. The back of the photo reads, "From Las Vegas to Bakersfeild." (Photo courtesy of Jim & Teresa Wiseman.)

Vadis: Al decided he wanted to go to New York for work, and I thought that was great because that's where he belonged with his talent. That's why he really wanted to leave California. He wanted to go into advertising. And they did make a lot of money in advertising, even then. That was when we headed towards to New York. Of course, years later, after we finally got to New York, that was one of the things he did with his career. I was a couple of months pregnant at the time. We went down to Los Angeles to pick up a car. He had an uncle down there who had a car business, so we borrowed this car. It was a Model T. We got as far as El Paso on our way to New York. And then Al decided, "No, we better not go any farther, because, for one thing, we're almost out of money." We also stayed in Texas because Al thought maybe we shouldn't go any farther because of my pregnancy. He was afraid that something might happen.

The first night when we got close to El Paso, rather than spend the money for a motel, we stopped and he built a sort of a tent-like thing on the ground there. He was very creative. So we spent the first night in that area sleeping under the stars. And we went on into El Paso. He said, "Well, I think we'll stay here for a while till I make some money. I'll get a job and we'll stay until the baby is born." And so, I said, "Well, OK." We looked in the telephone directory and found some advertising agencies. And there was one that Al had heard of. So, he said, "OK, that's the one I'll choose!"

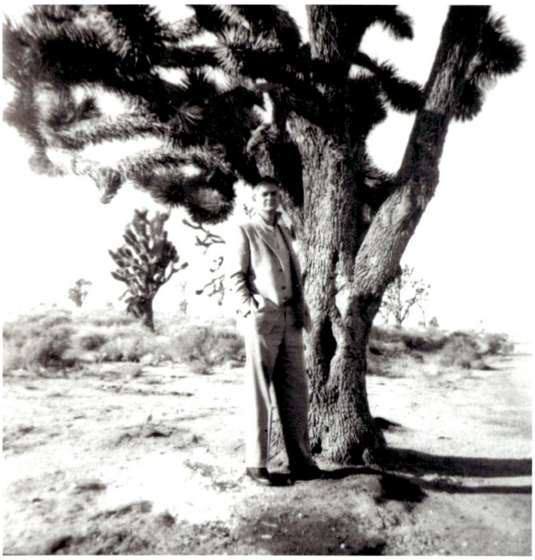

Above: Al Wiseman standing in the Mojave Desert, circa 1941. (Photo courtesy of Jim & Teresa Wiseman.)

So we went out to the park and sat on the benches and he made some drawings. What he did, he made some roughs of different things. He did one drawing sample of shoes and two or three other ones. I don't know whether anybody knows it, but drawing shoes is very very hard. Al then went up to the advertising agency Mithoff & White. He just went in and he showed them his drawings. They wanted him to start working for them immediately. Al told them that he didn't have any money. And they said, "Well, if you'd like, we'll advance money to you." So they did. He worked with them all the time that we were in El Paso. With Mithoff & White, he did a lot of advertising stuff that was his own. Originals which they liked very much. He always had ideas. That's one thing that he had — plenty of original ideas! We stayed in a motel. In that day and age you could stay in a motel for a dollar. These were the days of five cent hamburgers. We stayed in this motel for about three weeks because we were running out of money. We lived in El Paso until after the baby ... well actually, I lost that baby when I was six months along.

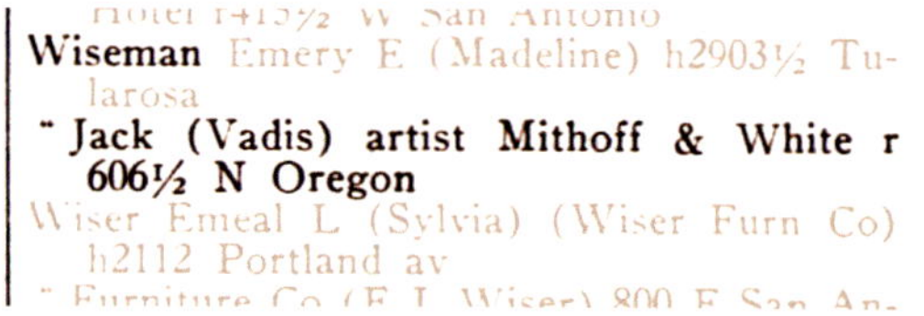

Wiseman Emery E (Madeline) h2903½ Tularosa
" **Jack (Vadis) artist Mithoff & White r 606½ N Oregon**
Wiser Emeal L (Sylvia) (Wiser Furn Co) h2112 Portland av

Above: Al and Vadis' listing in the 1941 El Paso, Texas, city directory. Al's parents called him by the nickname "Jack" when he was a baby and he kept using the name until about 1943.

Bill: How long did you stay in El Paso?

Vadis: We were there for a year. And I lost the first baby while we were there, then I became pregnant with Merrily. Before she was ready to be born, we went back to California. Because Al didn't want to stay in El Paso. We travelled a bit — we went across the border into Mexico to Juarez. Then we went back to California. Because of me being pregnant again, I couldn't drive. At that time, my doctor didn't want me to go back by car. The only way I could go was on a train. So I went back to California by myself. And I went back first to stay with Al's parents (Al's mother & Al's stepfather) in California. Then, Al and my brother, who was back there, came back to California in this little Model A Ford we had. It rained almost all the way back, and also it had snowed in Texas. By the time they got back home … they arrived that night with both of their faces covered with blisters from that wind and so forth. I was at his mother's when Al pulled up into the driveway and he turned the car engine off. So the next morning they went out to get in the car to to move it, as it was in a parking area where it shouldn't have been. They went out to get into the car and both of the front tires were flat. And then Al couldn't get the car started. It wouldn't start. So it got them there and died. It did its part.

Bill: I sent you copies of some black and white drawings Al did during World War Two. Do you know anything about them?

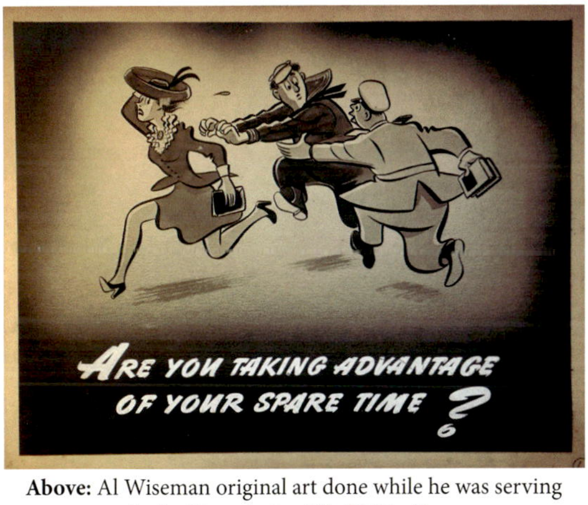
ARE YOU TAKING ADVANTAGE
OF YOUR SPARE TIME ?

Above: Al Wiseman original art done while he was serving in the Navy during World War Two.

Vadis: Those were what he did when he was working for Douglas Aircraft, down in Long Beach. And some of the others are what he did later, when he went in the Navy. But, I didn't see any of those at the time. He had done those for the Navy newspaper. You know how they have their little newspapers? Well, I know that's what he did while he was in the Navy. He never said anything about that artwork. But I know that's what he would have done — I recognize the style.

Bill: So when Al worked for Douglas Aircraft that was before he was in the Navy?

Vadis: Oh, yes. He and another fellow, Frank Adams worked together. Frank is also a cartoonist and he has done many things in cartooning. He has been in magazines and so forth. He lived in Lake Arrowhead. After the war, I took our two girls back to Newport, Rhode Island, where Al was getting out of the Navy. And then from Newport, we moved to Connecticut.

Bill: What kind of work was Al doing at the time?

Vadis: Al was in *The Saturday Evening Post*, *Colliers*, all those magazines.

Bill: So Al had cartoons in *The Saturday Evening Post*?

Vadis: Oh, yes. I went to all of the magazine offices showing Al's work. Every magazine there was in New York! Eldon Dedini and Hank Ketcham were two of the cartoonists that I met at the offices. And Gus Arriola, too, amongst others. They would take me when I would go every week. None of us had any money, so we would all get into a taxi and everybody would pay their part. We'd also go have lunch and we'd talk. The first time I went, they bought lunch for me. Eldon is very nice. Also, Al had worked with an advertising agency. He had this gal who represented him. She got all the jobs for him. He did a lot of ads. Oh, did you get in touch with any of the cartoonists down in Carmel?

Bill: Yes, I actually spoke with Hank Ketcham. And I got his number from …

Vadis: From Sue? (Al's second wife)

Bill: Yeah, Sue gave me his secretary's number. And the secretary gave me Hank Ketcham's number. I'm going to write to him. He was very nice.

Vadis: Oh, he is. He's very nice.

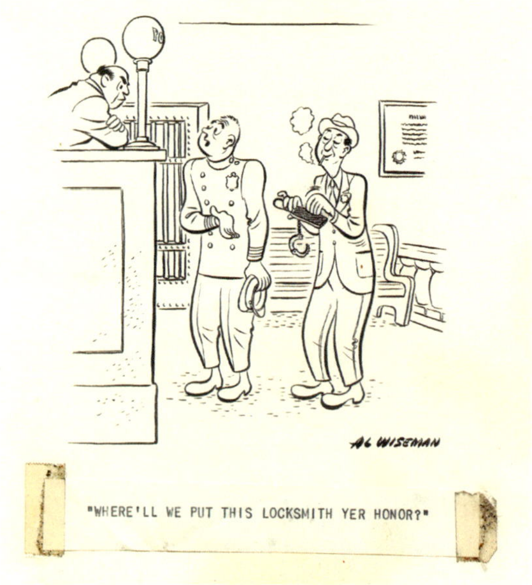
AL WISEMAN
"WHERE'LL WE PUT THIS LOCKSMITH YER HONOR?"

Above: An example of Al's gag cartoon artwork that Vadis would shop around to cartoon editors at New York City based magazines.

Bill: And I talked to Gus Arriola.

Vadis: He is a very wonderful person.

Bill: Yeah, and he said that I could write to him too so I'm going to do that.

Vadis: I think that would be a very good idea.

Bill: And I also spoke with Eldon Dedini. He was great to talk to!

Vadis: Yes, he is. He was one of the cartoonists who was with Hank when I met the cartoonists who were going around to magazine offices. And Eldon's wife is just very nice. And so is ... well, they're all nice. It's just the life that most of them led, it wasn't the type of life that I wanted to lead. I had too many things to do in life. And … but, they're all very good people. But in the life that they led, which Al and I did too, there was a great deal of drinking going around. Because there were parties, parties, parties. Most of them had been very poor, but suddenly had too much money, like Al and Hank. They get into a business like that and they make all kinds of money, but then they don't quite know how to handle it. They don't know what to do with all that money. So they just spend it, spend it. That was one of Al's problems with me and the two kids. I just didn't want to spend the rest of my life like that. I didn't want my children, our children, to keep living under those conditions.

Bill: What would Al spend money on?

Vadis: He had to have a new… oh, one of those little convertibles that were coming out at the time. And on golf. And quite a bit on booze. He could always find something to spend money on.

Bill: You told me that you knew Hank Ketcham's first wife.

Vadis: Yes, Alice, yes.

Bill: What was she like?

Vadis: Well, she was a very … I loved Alice very much. But in the life that they led … Al and I did, there was a great deal of drinking going around. Because there were parties, parties, parties. I told you when I met Hank, it was at *The Saturday Evening Post*. We lived not very far from them. Al loved to play golf and Hank loved to play golf. And so, on the second time when I went in, at *The Saturday Evening Post*, Hank was there. We had lunch. He wanted to know, "Does Al play golf?" And I said yes. Hank said, "Well, why don't you come over this weekend so we can go play golf. And you and Alice — you can meet Alice and do whatever you want." I said, "That's fine. I'll tell him, because he'll be happy to have somebody that likes to play golf as much as he does."

Above: Friends gather at Al Wiseman's art studio in 1949. From left to right: Ruth Barnes, Alice Ketcham, Vadis Wiseman, Al Wiseman and cartoonist Bob Barnes. (Photo courtesy of Jim & Teresa Wiseman.)

So that's how we met. The next day was a Saturday, so I told Al. He was happy about it. Then I got a babysitter for Merrily and Jan and we went over there. I liked Alice very, very much. She was six or seven months pregnant at that time. We went over next Saturday and I stayed with Alice because she couldn't go out and play or anything. We were still there when Dennis was born. We went over when Alice came home from the hospital. Alice and I became rather close. I could sorta see what was going on as far as their circumstances were concerned. So she talked and I listened to her, but that's all. I'm just, I'm always a good listener. I knew her well enough that I knew it was never going to work.
With Dennis, when they had a lot of parties, and when you'd go over — Al and I would go over quite often. Sometimes I would go alone. And they would always send Dennis back to his bedroom and close the door. And tell him he couldn't come out.

Bill: Jan was telling me that Dennis's bedroom had a massive amount of toys in it. She said he had a TV set in there.

Vadis: Oh, he did. He had everything. They had all the toys. And just everything for him. So, when they had company and he had to go to his room, he had plenty of things to play with. But he really didn't want to stay in his room, of course. He would just come out sometimes. But he'd have to go back to his room. And I know that there were a lot of friends that would have liked to know Dennis. And he didn't. As I said, I don't even know where he is today. I know that he got married. And I think they bought some property. They had sort of a ranch. But I just don't know, I don't have any idea of where he is.
So anyhow, it's too bad, to be the person who ... if it wasn't for him, there wouldn't have been a "Dennis." It always made me feel very bad because they could have been a little different with him than what they were. And Dennis was always away, going to some school. He used to come down and stay with his "Aunt" Vadis quite often. And, as he got older, he just left home. He finally got married. I don't know ... I haven't heard anything about Dennis for a while. So he went in the Navy. Then he decided that he wanted to be on his own, definitely. So he stayed back in ... I don't know whether it was Minnesota. Or someplace back there. It's been so darn long.

Bill: I was just wondering why you and Al left the New York area to go back to California.

Vadis: We lived in Connecticut for about seven months when Al made up his mind that he wanted to go back to California. So Al's mother came to Connecticut and took the two girls (daughters Merrily and Jan) back home to California with her. And that's when we moved into New Rochelle (New York). We were there for two and a half months, until Al finished up doing what he had to do. And then we went back to California. So were were in California for the rest of the duration that we were married. We moved all over California, of course (laughs). We lived down in Woodland Hills, which is right out of Los Angeles. Then we moved up to the California Hot Springs. That's quite an event too.

Bill: When Al first moved back to California, what projects was he working on?

Vadis: Al went into business with another cartoonist, Walt Bohrer, when he came back from the East Coast. They went into business together in Santa Cruz. You probably haven't heard of him but he's very good. And he's put out about three books where he did in his own writing and so forth. He was interested in flying and he flew with some of the most famous fliers that ever were on this earth. His sister was the first woman who ever parachuted!

Bill: Is Walt still around?

Vadis: Yes, I'll try to find his number for you.

Bill: Great. Thanks! You mentioned that, after you moved back to California, Al drew his own greeting cards.

Vadis: Yes.

Bill: Do you have copies of those, by any chance?

Vadis: No, I don't, because I thought he was going to continue doing those. He sold them- I sold them like crazy! And when they wrote that they needed more, well then, he decided, no, he didn't want to do those anymore. It was "too much work." But it really wasn't. Not for him. So no, I don't have any. I never had any of those because they were all sold. And that was when the children were small. So it's been a long, long time.

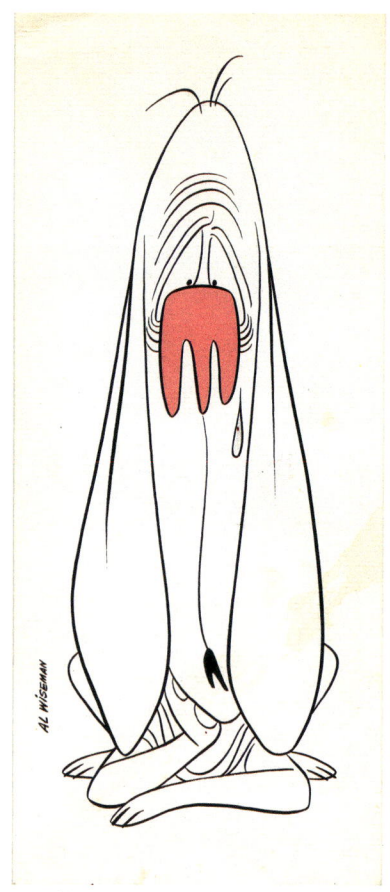

Above: One of the greeting cards Al drew and Vadis helped sell in the mid-1950s. (Courtesy of Al's daughter, Jan Pisciotta.)

Bill: I think you told me at one point that Hank Ketcham used to use Jim as a model for Dennis.

Vadis: Yes, this was when Jim was … let's see … about four and five and Hank used to have a lot of DENNIS products going on. They used to take a lot of pictures out in Pebble Beach. And Jim wore DENNIS clothes. He and Hank got along very well. Hank would use Jim because he couldn't do it with his son Dennis, who was too old by that time. And Jimmy, my son, was always, he was just a little ham from the time he was born. He was on stage in two minutes. Never knew what he was going to do. But he was always a very good kid. So Hank liked Jim. Hank would always call me and ask me if he could borrow him, and have Jim wear his "Dennis the

Menace" clothes. So Jim was a model for those clothes too. That's how much he sort of looked like "Dennis."

Above: A photoshoot with Jim Wiseman as DENNIS THE MENACE. (Photo courtesy of Jim & Teresa Wiseman.)

Bill: He had blonde hair, I guess?

Vadis: Oh, yes. Very blonde. So many people have said when he was little, how much he looked like the character. Of course he doesn't anymore. But he still has a wonderful sense of humor and he's a wonderful musician. I don't have any of those photos. I don't know whether Hank would even have any. I doubt very much. Jim also posed for Al because he did look quite a bit like the character. Al used to use him all the time. I'm going to make a copy of one of the pictures that I have of Jim when he was very young. You'll see, how much, that he really looked like the character. He even had the little hair that stuck up.

Bill: The cowlick?

Vadis: Yeah, Jim had that (laughs). So that made it easier, too. And of course, he had the Dennis the Menace clothes. They were very nice and very cute. Some of the cartoons Al did of Dennis, he used Jim and Merrily as reference. Merrily was used for his Hawaiian book. She was his model for the Hula dancing girl, and so forth.

Bill: You told me that the Ketchams wanted Jim to test for the role of Dennis?

Vadis: Yes, Hank wanted Jim to take the role of Dennis for TV.

Bill: In the TV show?

Vadis: In the first TV show. Jim wanted to do that. But you know, I didn't feel comfortable about it. I didn't really want him to do that. Not to be involved in that, because I didn't know how that would work out. And also how he would be treated. Every time that Hank would come over, they would talk back and forth about Jim playing Dennis. They'd tease each other. Hank would kid around with Jim. Well, I sort of had things in mind that he should be doing as a boy. I wanted him to be involved in sports and in music and things at school. So maybe it was wrong for me to do that — to tell Hank that I didn't want him to do that. Maybe it was wrong because maybe it would have made a difference in Jim's future. But I don't know. I'd rather have spent the time with him. And I wanted him to be with us, not someplace else. It would mean moving south. We did move south, but that was much later.

Bill: So Jim was younger than Dennis Ketcham?

Vadis: Yes. Uh-huh. A couple of years younger. And, of course, Dennis and Jim always played together. And they got along really good. But, as Dennis got a little older, they sent him away to Montebello [Montevallo??] near Los Angeles, to a private school. So Dennis wasn't with his parents a great deal of

the time. I used to have him down quite often because Alice would go to lunch with friends quite often. So I would arrange for her to drop off him at our place. Then he would have Jim to play with.
So they did. I always just hoped that things would change for him. But he finished, well, all the way through high school away from home. I don't know if it was in Santa Monica. I'm not sure. I don't remember. But then he was home on holidays. But without Dennis, there wouldn't be a "Dennis the Menace." Very definitely.

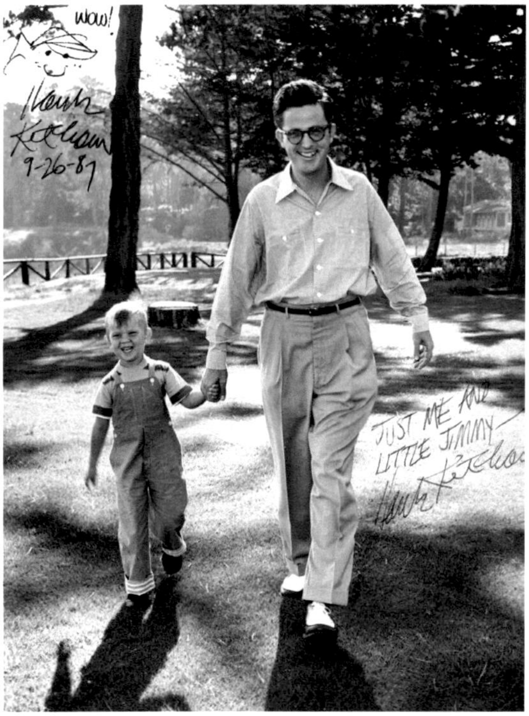

wow!
Hank Ketcham
9-26-87
JUST ME AND
LITTLE JIMMY

Above: A pic taken during a DENNIS THE MENACE photo-shoot with Hank Ketcham and Jim Wiseman. Hank originally signed this photo in the mid-1950s and signed it again for Jim in 1987. (Photo courtesy of Jim & Teresa Wiseman.)

Bill: You went with Al to Hawaii when he and Fred were doing research for the DENNIS IN HAWAII comic, right?

Vadis: Right.

Bill: And do you remember any...?

Vadis: Oh, yes. Fred, Mollie, Al and I went.

Bill: And did you have a good time there?

Vadis: Oh, yes. Yes, I had a wonderful time. That was where he got all the information, you know, for the book. It was all ... he captured everything when we were there. And there were pictures of when we were at a Luau, which were very good. And it was especially good because Al and Fred got up and did, sort of, the hula on the stage that they had. And I do have those pictures but heaven only knows where they are right now. But I wish I could ... I'll see if Merrily can find those for me.

Bill: OK, great.

Vadis: And I would send them to you.

Bill: Thank you. It sounds like Al was always having adventures. Was it fun being married to a cartoonist?

Vadis: I had always wished that he would have grown up a little bit after we had our children and realize that he had responsibilities. Maybe Al shouldn't have had children. Then he could have done what he wanted to do. I always wanted him to spend some time with the kids. And he did once in a while. But he wanted them to do everything his way. I just feel when I tell you things that you'll understand more about him. The only thing that meant anything to him really was his drawings, his cartooning. That was the only thing he lived for. And a lot of artists do that. I'm very familiar with that part of it. But when you have a family and children, you have to be a parent. He really didn't know how to do that. So the children loved him. But they couldn't ... he didn't want to spend any time with them.
And he just wanted them to do exactly what he said. He wanted them all to be artists like he was. My life was very interesting. If only I could have tolerated all the parties. I couldn't

quite do that because I needed to spend more time with my children. And so our marriage ending was just one of those things that happens.

Bill: When did you get married to your second husband?

Vadis: In 1961. He passed away seven years ago. Ward and I had such a wonderful life because we enjoyed all the same things. Ward liked to travel, so we traveled. I had always wanted to go — especially to Switzerland, New Zealand, Greece and those places. When we went there, he was like a tour guide. I had a very wonderful time with him. I still … I can't … I still … We just had a very special life with each other. I wish everybody could have a life as happy as I was with him. And he liked children. He meant a great deal to me and to them. He worked for Pacific Tel (Pacific Telephone and Telegraph) until he retired from there. We went to Micronesia when he retired, where he helped build telephone systems and so forth. And I taught school there. I taught Micronesians English and so forth.
It was marvelous. Such a wonderful experience where we went. And seeing what could be done! I felt so wonderful because I was able to help him. I even got seven (ten) of my students into vocational school. They had never been off that island. I just enjoyed it so much.

Bill: I talked to Jim earlier and he gave me contact info for Al's second wide, Sue Dewar.

Vadis: She is an artist also. She doesn't do anything professional anymore. But she did. She drew quite a bit of stuff for magazines and so forth. So I think she would be good to talk to. We're very good friends and she loves my children. She never had children herself.

Bill: Did you keep up with Al's career at all after your divorce?

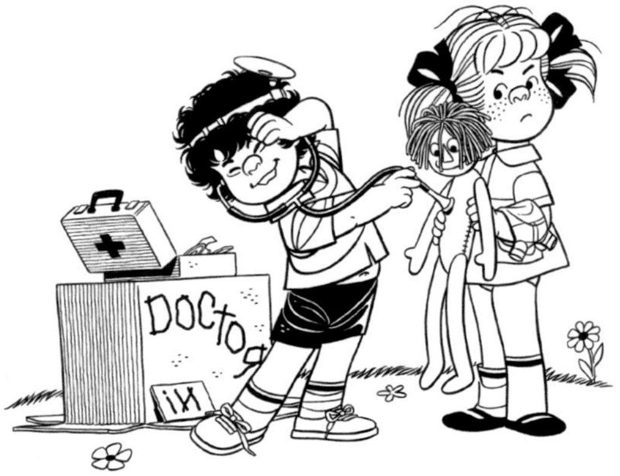
DOCTOR

Above: An Al Wiseman illustration done after he stopped working on DENNIS THE MENACE.

Vadis: He did so many commercial ads. He did those after we were divorced. He went back to doing that, after he quit working with Hank. He had some good contacts. He could have had someone represent him like he did when we were in New York, but he didn't. His agent back then, she had no problems selling his stuff. And all the magazines wanted his work. He just had quite a life with his talent. He didn't do exactly what he should have done. I always wanted him to do children's books, because it was so easy for him to work with drawing children. And he didn't really have too many that he used as models, because he could just look at kids and he could draw like he did.

Bill: I was wondering, when was the last time you saw Al or had any contact with him?

Vadis: The last time I saw him was in 1960, no it was… 1963. That was when he came over he wanted to get Jim. He wanted Jim to go with him to Washington.

Bill: Do you know what happened when Al died? Was he in Salt Lake City?

Vadis: Salt Lake City … That's where it was. He went fishing and had a heart attack on the way back home.
Bill: Was he driving and had a heart attack?

Vadis: Yes, Yes. And on the way home, he had an accident. He ran off the road and had a heart attack. So that was what happened to him.

Bill: Did he die from the heart attack or from the accident?

Vadis: He had a heart attack. But the accident would have left him crippled. That would have been very hard for him if he couldn't fish and do the things he liked to do. It would have been very hard for him to not be able to do that. So I always feel that there's a reason for things that happen. And that was too bad. Because he had so much he had planned in his life.

Above: Al sketches during his 1956 trip to Hawaii. (Photo courtesy of Jim & Teresa Wiseman.)

Bill: Did anyone from Al's family attend his funeral? Was Al married at the time?

Vadis: My children, Merrily and Jim, went back for his funeral. And this gal, which I was happy that I didn't know her, because Merrily and Jim, you know, they were there for a week. And they wanted to know about their father. What he had been doing and so forth, about these last few years. And she wouldn't talk too much to them. And Merrily and she were talking. And Jim went in to his father's studio. And he'd never had any of his father's work. And his father never would give him anything. So Jim walked in there and saw several things on the wall. And he wanted one just to have so he took it off the wall. And he, when he started back in the living room, she went to the door and saw that he had taken that down. And she told him, "Get out of this room. You're not supposed to be in here. And you leave those things alone." Jim asked her if he could have it. And she said no. And so what happened is she sold all of those. Which that was OK, too. Maybe I would have done the same thing if I were in her shoes. Because I'm sure Al didn't have any money.
So, anyhow, that was the end of that. The woman was not very kind to them. So they have no idea what she did with his any of his stuff. But I do know, that I was told, a long time ago, before they went back there that she had sold a lot of his cartoons for the Catholic church and to raise money. He gave them to her. She asked for them and she got them. That's what happened. What he did after that, anything that he did, she had. They were in Idaho for a while, I know. I don't know and I'm sure they were in other places too. Because Al didn't like to be still very long. He was always very restless. And that he couldn't help. We all went along with it. He didn't really have a great many friends but because he had to have everything his way. Men don't like that. They like for all to be equal. They like to get along. And not have one person that everybody has to cow-tow to that person.
I think about him often. I always felt that Al was one of the most talented artists that I've

ever known. And everybody else also felt the same way. I think it's so sad that somebody had so much talent and that's what happens to him in life. Maybe I could say that he never grew up. And was always a little boy. Al could have done so many things. He was so talented. Very, very. I guess that's why people who see his work — they don't know him, but they always enjoy looking at his work. And … Well, I just feel … I always felt bad that he couldn't do more with his talent than what he did. And he could have made a lot of people very happy with some of the stuff that he did. He made them happy anyhow.

Bill: Yes.

Vadis: They all liked his work. All the cartoonists and artists really liked his work. They felt it was … that he was the best that there was. And I think he was.

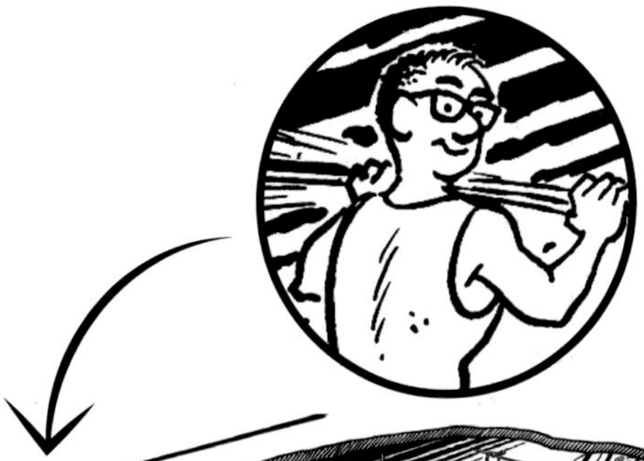

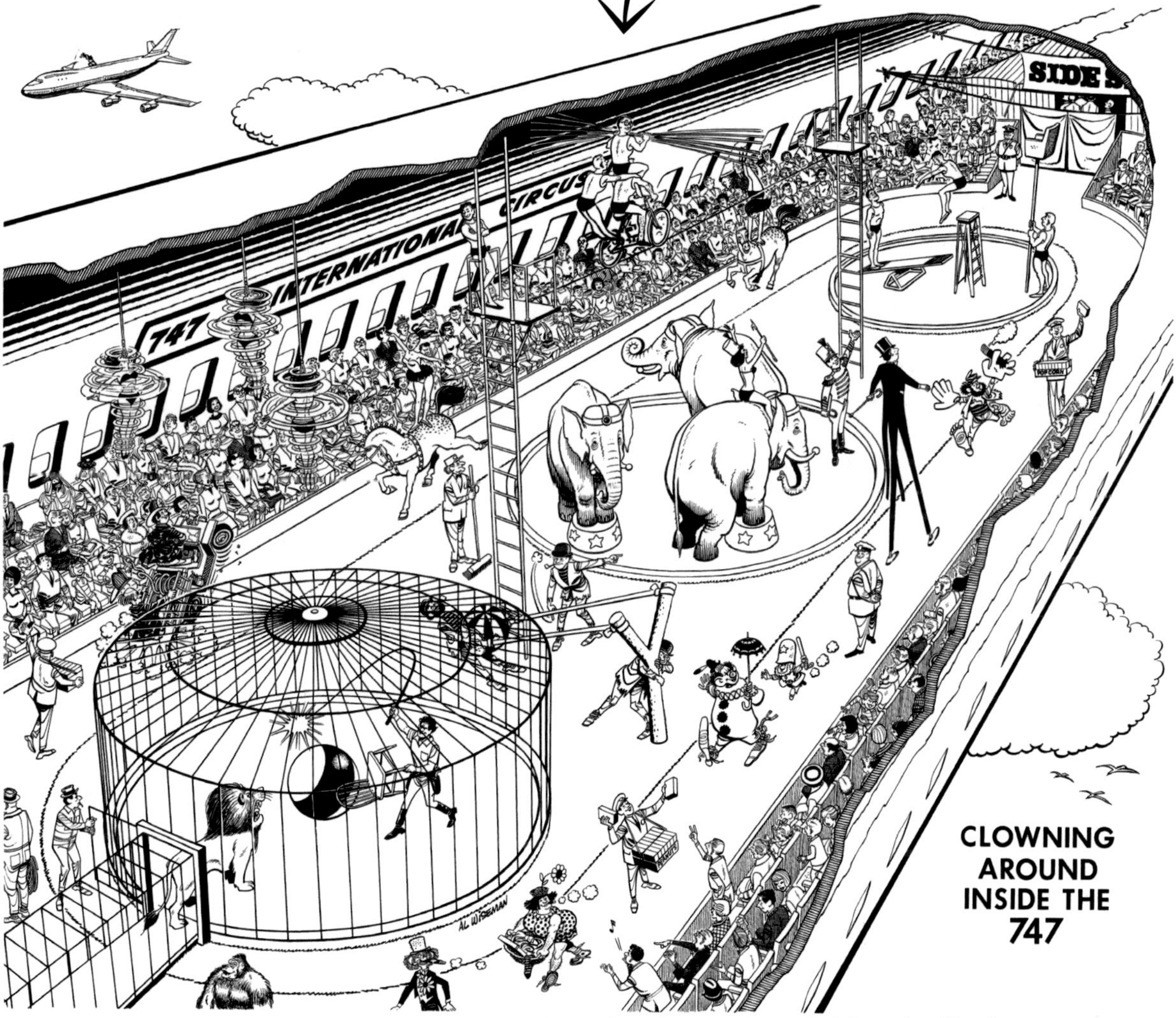
747
INTERNATIONAL CIRCUS
CLOWNING AROUND INSIDE THE 747

Above: One of the series of amazingly detailed 747 airliner drawings Al created while employed by The Boeing Company, circa 1967. (Note that Al drew himself balancing at the top of the tightrope bicycle.)

Interview: Mollie Toole, Fred Toole's Wife

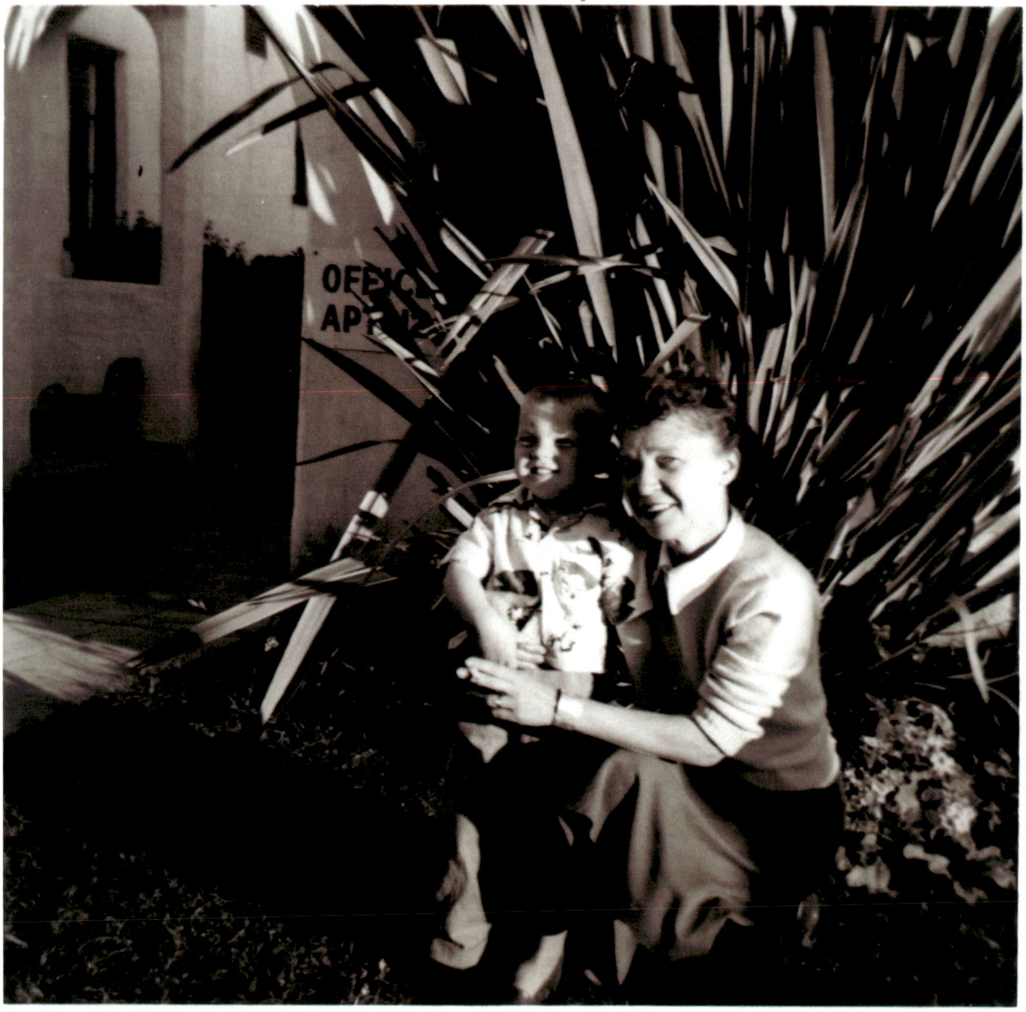
OFF
AP

Above: Jim Wiseman and Mollie Toole in Santa Cruz, California, 1951. (Photo courtesy of Jim & Teresa Wiseman.)

The following is a compilation of three phone interviews conducted with Mollie on March 21, 1998, April 8, 1998 and April 1, 1999.

"Mollie" Toole was born Mary Canam Groman on August 7, 1908 in Bethlehem, Pennsylvania. On March 2, 1947, she married Fred Toole, then a gag writer for cartoonist Bob Barnes. Fred Toole died on December 9, 1993 at the age of 80. Mollie passed away on October 25, 2003 at the age of 95.

After my conversations with Mollie, I learned some additional facts about her. Mollie had served in the WAVES (Women's branch of the U.S Navy: "Women Accepted for Volenteer Emergency Services") from November 6, 1942 until September 11, 1945. Also, in their first year of marraige, Mollie gave birth to her and Fred's only child, Frederick William Toole Jr. According to Pennsylvania records, the boy died of congenital atelectasis some eight hours after his birth at St. Luke's Hospital.

Bill: To begin with, Mollie, could you tell me about Fred's life and career before he started writing the DENNIS comicbooks?

Mollie: Hmmm… I don't know anything much about Fred's life before he came out of the army. His father had a confectionery shop and Fred was in business with his father for a while. They made the most fabulous home-made ice cream and frozen pies. At Christmas time, they made those peppermint canes. All this was hand-done and no substitutes at all. Everything was made from scratch and everything was the purest material that they could get their hands on.

Bill: That sound fun (Mollie laughs). Well, it sounds like fun, anyway!

Mollie: Well, he didn't mind the work. Fred was supposed to take over and work with his dad. But Fred had a step-mother that was…. well, Irene came along in the picture, and he was no longer required. He could work for them but it was not going to be a partnership.

Bill: So Fred moved on to other work? When did you meet him?

Mollie: Oh, I previously knew him. In fact, he lived with us when he came to Bethlehem to work with his dad in the confectionary shop. We had a tremendously big house. It was just my father, and mother. And me. My brother had gone off to college. So Mr. Toole (Fred's father) asked my mother whether Fred could come and stay with us until Fred found a place to live. He said, "You have that big house …"

Above: A current photo of Mollie Toole's childhood home in Bethlehem, Pennsylvania.

So, of course, my mother said, "Well, I'll have to ask Mr. Groman (Mollie's Father.) We never had any people staying with us. So my dad, well, he guessed it was alright until Fred found a place to live. Well, he never found a place to live until he went into the service.

And then when Fred came back, he called and asked if he could come out and see my mother. So he did. She asked him if he wanted to come back, as his room was still there. And he said "No," he was going to stay at the hotel. And the reason was that he wanted to stay at the hotel because if he lived in our house he couldn't ask me to go out on a date. Oh, Fred was very proper. Very proper. And the first Christmas when we were going together, he gave me a bottle of champaign and apologized because he said, "I can't give you anything personal." No, Fred was a very proper young man.

Bill: And he was a war hero during World War II?

Mollie: Yes, he had a *Croix de guerre* and, I think, three Purple Hearts.

Bill: What did Fred do in the war? What

did he do to earn the purple hearts?

Mollie: They sent him to "cooks and bakers school." Well, he came out of "cooks and bakers school" and was handed a gun. And he was sent in the infantry. He never saw the inside of a kitchen. He never saw the inside of a kitchen, except for the ones that they used to cook their K rations.

Bill: Did Fred ever talk about the war to you?

Mollie: Fred never talked about it unless the question came up from somebody else asking — unless we had a guest who had been in the service. If I got anything it was like pulling teeth. He never talked about unpleasant things. After the war was over, he conducted a class — he conducted a reserve program in Bethlehem for anybody in the service. A seminar for retired military. It was strictly a local thing. One story he did tell me was that, one day at the front lines, one kid came up to him and said, "Lieutenant, would you tell me? Show me how to load this rifle?" The kid had just came from bootcamp and had to ask how to load a rifle. Unless the poor kid was so scared of the darn rifle that he couldn't think.

Bill: When did you marry Fred?

Mollie: 1947.

Mollie: We would have been married 50 years back in March. I think that's right. Yeah? Is that right?

Bill: Yeah. Last March. From the time you met him, was Fred mostly interested in comics and cartoons or did he just like humor writing?

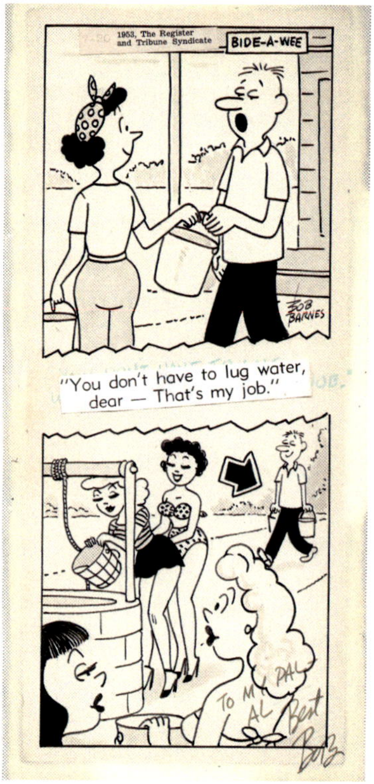
1953, The Register and Tribune Syndicate
BIDE-A-WEE
BOB BARNES
"You don't have to lug water, dear — That's my job."
TO MY PAL AL Best Bob

Above: An Original 1953 Bob Barnes comic given to Al Wiseman. "To My Pal Al, Best Bob."

Mollie: I don't know that he wrote anything else other than cartoons. He wrote gags for the late Bob Barnes, who later did the cartoon *"The Better Half,"* for many years. In fact, that's how we came out here to California. Bob asked him to come out. Bob was going to open an advertising agency in Santa Cruz, but he didn't know much about Santa Cruz. He had passed through there several times. He thought it looked like a nice little town. But Santa Cruz, as you probably know, back then-that was in 1950 — was no more ready for an advertising agency than Iwo Jima. Santa Cruz was not ready for an advertising agency. It was strictly a retirement town. So Fred and Bob had an advertising agency there. We were there for about a year. And Bob decided to go back East. We stayed in Santa Cruz. In fact, we managed a motel for three years, I think.

Bill: What was Bob Barnes like?

Mollie: Bob Barnes was Bob Barnes. That's … (laughs) … he was one of a kind. He tried to be as tough as he could. And it turns out that underneath all that gruff-toughness — he had a heart as big as the world. If he liked you, nothing's too good for you.

Bill: And did Fred stay in contact with Bob after he left the advertising agency?

Mollie: Oh, yes. Uh-huh. And I still kept in contact with his wife.

Bill: What is her name?

Mollie: Ruth. They're both gone.

Bill: When did Fred meet Hank?

Mollie: Well … Fred met Hank … We had met Hank when we lived in Santa Cruz with Bob Barnes. Around that time, Hank decided he was going to try doing a DENNIS comicbook. Bob had referred Fred to Hank. Because Hank was talking to Bob Barnes and he said he was looking for a writer. Bob said, "I think I have a man for you and I think Fred Toole is the man." So Hank called Fred one day, and he chatted with him, and asked him if he'd be interested in writing the comicbook. That was just up Fred's alley — exactly what he would like to do. Fred called me and said "Let's give it a go." So we talked it over one night, like we did everything else. That's how we hooked up with Hank.

Bill: Did Fred start with the comic strip or did he immediately start into the comicbook?

Mollie: He started on the comicbook and doing some PR work. "PR work" — that's what Hank called taking care of all the fan mail and things like that.

Bill: How did Hank and Fred get along?

Mollie: Very well. Very well. Fred, and Hank, and Alice and I, the four of us, we got along very well socially. Whether Fred and Hank had anything during the day, it never turned up at nighttime. After 4pm that was the end of it. So they had an excellent relationship.

Bill: So Fred and you got together with Hank a lot socially?

Mollie: Oh, yes. Yes, indeed. Particularly when his first wife, Alice, was living.

Above: Friends of Fred & Mollie — Al Wiseman, Bob & Ruth Barnes, Alice Ketcham and Vadis Wiseman in 1949 (Courtesy of Jim & Teresa Wiseman).

Bill: What was Alice Ketcham like?

Mollie: Alice was charming. She was very pretty, very friendly. She and I were very close friends. She always said I was an older sister whenever she spoke of me. I was her big sister. She was a very sweet woman. Very generous. Very generous. I knew Alice from the early days. She was a very, very, very sweet girl. I have a pearl choker that Alice gave me. Because, if I said I liked anything she had on — in the way of jewelry and things of that type- she got me wearing it. Because she'd take it off and say, "Here. You can have this." No, she was a very generous woman.
Of course, you learned how Hank got the title of Dennis the Menace?

Bill: Yeah, from his wife Alice.

Mollie: One day Hank was at his desk, getting ready to work, and Alice came in. Dennis had been particularly naughty that morning. She came in flying into the room and she said, "Hank, your son Dennis is a Menace!" It lit that bulb in Hank's head and... whoop, there it is! Hank wanted to do a kids' comic panel, but he couldn't get a title for it. And the fact is that he wanted to do a kids' daily when he came out of the Navy, but he just couldn't find the right title. So it was Alice who came up with it. Once she threw that at him, that was it. That's where the story kind of started.

Bill: (laughs) That's great. And did you know Dennis well?

Mollie: Yep.

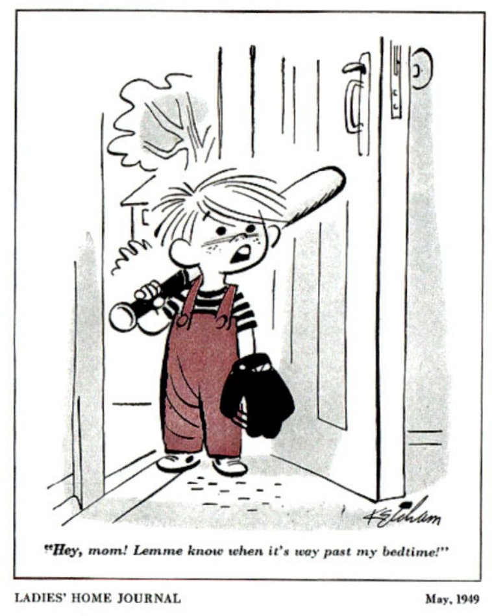
"Hey, mom! Lemme know when it's way past my bedtime!"
LADIES' HOME JOURNAL
May, 1949

Above: A pre-Dennis comic from Hank Ketcham

Bill: What was he like?

Mollie: He was a little devil (both laugh).

Bill: Was he kind of hyperactive?

Mollie: Who? Dennis? Oh, yeah. Very hyper (laughs). You never knew what he was going to do next. Some of the things that DENNIS did in the comics were actually true. I think there's one story which was true. He went in their bathroom and I guess he was upset because they wouldn't let him do something. I don't know why. But he got hold of a lipstick. The bathroom paint was a beautiful shade of yellow. Well, when he got finished, it was a beautiful shade of red and yellow. Oh, he had made it a mess. I think that was in one of the comicbooks. It had to be!

Bill: I would think so! Pretty funny.

Mollie: Not too fun for his parents, though. He was a mischievous little devil. I think he was three years old when we met him, and met Hank and Alice.

Bill: Did Fred ever get ideas from the real Dennis?

Mollie: Well … sure. 'Cause you see, Fred was working up there at Hank's ranch in Carmel Valley. And their offices were right by the swimming pool. Oh, yes. Fred got a lot of his ideas from Dennis. But the majority of them were after Dennis got a little bit older. Hank and Alice separated, as you know. And Dennis went with his mother. So consequently, Fred didn't see as much of him. The contact between Fred and Dennis had not been what it had been before.

Bill: Did you keep in contact with Dennis at all then?

Mollie: Not really. We saw him before because the fact of the proximity of the office and everything was up at the ranch. Hank had a ranch up there in the Valley. He had a studio there for Fred and for himself. And a swimming pool which was delightful. That was a delightful place to work! It was a ranch — it was a big, big ranch. It wasn't a little two-by-four thing.
Oh, no, this was a real ranch. It wasn't an operating ranch, of course. He had a couple of horses for riding. I don't know whether Alice rode. Actually, I don't know if Hank rode either. But I know that he had his own keeper, and his own gardener and everything. They lived right there on the ranch. I forget their names.

Bill: Did you ever swim at their pool?

Mollie: Yes, indeed. We were not just the scruffy employees. We were very close friends with Hank. We were often up there for dinner with them. And they were often down to dinner with us. Oh, yes, we socialized together.

Bill: What did Fred think of Al Wiseman's art?

Mollie: I never asked him. Al's work was beautiful. It was so precise and everything. When he drew a building, every brick was laid like it really was laid in reality. If a brick was supposed to be laid this way, he laid that brick that way. Nothing jagged, or exaggerated, nothing comic about it. And it looked more photographic than it seemed like a freehand drawn job. Did you get that impression of the books?

Bill: Yeah, everything was always perfect.

Mollie: Absolutely. Al was so very precise about everything.

Bill: Very technical.

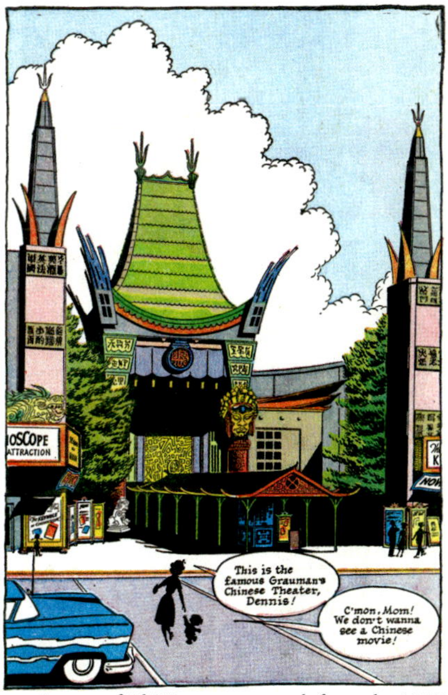
This is the famous Grauman's Chinese Theater, Dennis!
C'mon, Mom! We don't wanna see a Chinese movie!

Above: A page of Al Wiseman artwork from the 1959 comic DENNIS THE MENACE IN HOLLYWOOD.

Mollie: Fred said that Al was not actually a cartoonist. I think architectural work was more his line. 'Cause he used to complain about Fred. He used to say, "Well, Fred makes these things so difficult. And gets into my pocket." Because, if he was drawing a brick house, every brick was drawn precisely. And, of course, it took him longer to draw a page.

Bill: But he seemed to enjoy drawing it.

Mollie: Yeah, he did. Uh-huh.

Bill: And especially for the travel books like HAWAII — then he put in a lot more detail than the regular comics.

Mollie: Oh, gee, I would be sure to say this that Al Wiseman was a terrific artist, though. But this was a comicbook and Al's rendition was too "artistic." I don't know … it took away from the funny side.

Bill: Did Fred get along with Al?

Mollie: Oh, yeah. Uh-huh.

Bill: So they were friends?

Mollie: Sure. We were sociable with everybody on the staff.

Bill: Was Al fun to be around in a social situation?

Mollie: Oh, yes, he was. Uh-huh.

Bill: There's a 1950s story where Dennis meets a comicbook artist — Al Wiseman. And Al brings Dennis back to his studio where Fred Toole is working there. I was wondering if Fred and Al actually worked together much in the studio.

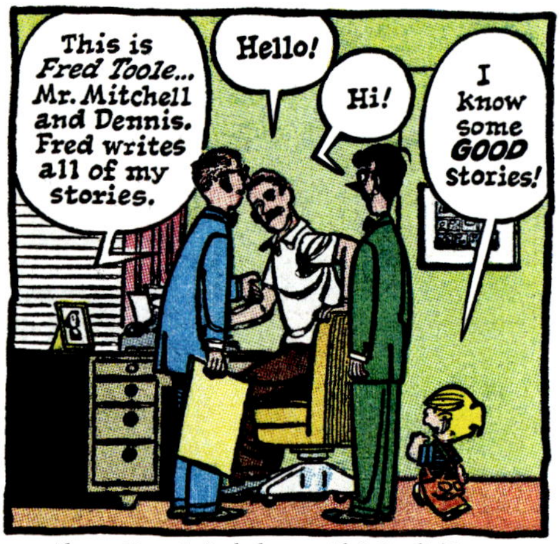
This is Fred Toole... Mr. Mitchell and Dennis. Fred writes all of my stories.
Hello!
Hi!
I know some GOOD stories!

Above: Dennis & dad meet Al & Fred! (From DENNIS THE MENACE #30, September 1958.)

Mollie: Oh, yes. Uh-huh. They started out together. Fred and Al worked together from the first DENNIS book to the last book with Al quitting. Al started a succession of artists who worked on the comicbooks. We got along very well with Al and his wife.

Bill: That was Vadis?

Mollie: Yeah. We got along. Al could be very generous.

Bill: Oh, really, how so? How was he generous?

Mollie: Well, in things … One time I was complaining about my vacuum cleaner. And the next thing I know, we had a new vacuum cleaner. Oh, yeah, yes. He could be very generous.

Bill: Was Fred proud of his work on DENNIS?

Mollie: Oh, yes, yes. Indeed.

Bill: Fred wrote a massive amount of DENNIS stories. That's a lot of writing.

Mollie: It was. It was a lot.

Bill: Did he work around the clock sometimes?

Mollie: No, he worked 9 to 4. He started at work at 9:00 in the morning … took an hour for lunch … and stopped working about 4:30. He had himself settled down to so many pages a week. And also, once in a while, he did DENNIS things like the Grimm's Fairy Tales which were public … what do you call it that anyone could use it?

Bill: Public domain?

Mollie: Yeah, that. Sometimes he used things that were public domain and put them in a DENNIS type story.

Bill: I remember there were DENNIS stories with characters like Ali Baba...

Mollie: Yeah, sometimes. But, usually they were Fred's original ideas. Very few of them weren't.

Bill: Do you know if Fred wrote out a full script that he sent to the artists?

Mollie: Yes. He wrote the script and then gave them to Al. In the beginning, when Al drew them.

Bill: Did Fred have to submit the scripts to Hank Ketcham for approval?

Mollie: Oh, yes. Well, he was the only one that had to OK it. It was Hank's baby. Fred didn't have anybody other than Hank to check his books. Except for his wife, to check for spelling sometimes (laughs).

Bill: Did Hank make many changes?

Mollie: Oh, sometimes Hank could be a very tough taskmaster. And other times, it was fine. But, by and large there was very little that Hank changed. Very little. He had to make a couple though, don't you think (laughs)? Hank supervised everything, and of course, Fred would have the book finished and the three of them would sit down and discuss it. And see what changes Hank would like to make. Or Fred might suddenly get another idea that fit in somewhere in the book.

Bill: So the three of them would sit down? That would include Al, too?

Above: A 1950s Ketcham studio photo from Hank's 1990 book "The Merchant Of Dennis The Menace."

Mollie: Sometimes. It was mostly Hank and Fred, though.

Bill: Did Fred technically work for the syndicate, and not Hank directly?

Mollie: Uh huh. He worked with Hank,

though the syndicate paid him, I believe. I never asked — this was Fred's department.

In fact, Bob Hall, who was the president of the syndicate, was here one time. And they were out back discussing finances, and what-not. I excused myself and Bob said, "Well, you should stay and hear this." I said, "That is between Fred and you, not me. I handle our finances, but anything other than that is up to Fred, not me."

Bill: So Fred worked in Hank Ketcham's studio. Was there ever a time when he started working at home?

Mollie: Oh, no. He worked in the studio the whole time.

Bill: Oh, the whole time?

Mollie: Even the time that Hank was in Geneva, Fred's studio was up in Carmel Valley. Not at home. The only time he worked at home was when he did the crossword puzzles after he retired. I take that back — Fred did work at home when he was writing for Bob Barnes. He did that when we lived back East. Everything with Fred was scheduled. He scheduled everything that he had to do. So it would be done on time and all that. He was a very conscientious young man. Those DENNIS books were pretty much a part of his life. They had to be. He tried to get them five pages a week. Then he'd come home and we'd have dinner.

Bill: It seems like when Fred was writing DENNIS, he really captured what it was like to be a kid. How did Fred get ideas? Were there relatives or neighborhood kids around? Or did he remember things from his childhood?

Mollie: You see Fred was an extremely brilliant man. So maybe some of it was observation. I never thought to ask him how. I just took it for granted that Fred could do it. I said one time, "I think Fred can do anything he puts his mind to." He wasn't around kids much at all. It was strictly his imagination, and not anything from his childhood. There's only one story that I say was brought on by the neighborhood kids. We had a picket fence and one day Fred went out and on the pickets were written the names of all these little kids. All in childish print. Fred asked them if they had done it. Of course they "didn't," you know. But signing the fence proved that they did. What he did, he made them go home — each one of them.

They all went home and had to come back with a bucket of water, and a scrub brush, and whatever they had to scrub it off. It was so funny seeing all these kids lined up out front scrubbing the front of our picket fence. Their parents were standing on the other side of the street and one of them came over and said, "Fred, that was the best thing you could have done!" They never did it again.

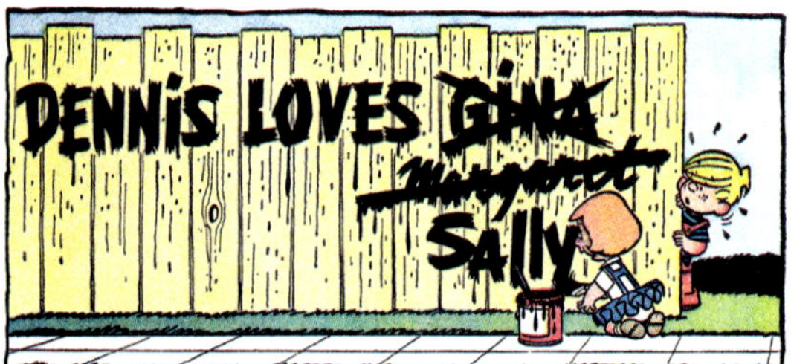
DENNIS LOVES GINA
Sally

Above: Some fence painting (From DENNIS THE MENACE #39, November 1959).

Bill: So did he use that idea in a DENNIS story?

Mollie: I think that was in one of the comics.

Bill: Did Fred ever get to meet his fans? Did people come up to him and tell him how much they enjoyed his writing?

Mollie: No, it rarely happened. Because you see, there was never much publicity about Fred or Al. There wouldn't have been many pictures that the fans would have seen that they recognized. When I married Fred, I had no idea how comicbooks or cartoons or anything were done. Before I knew anything about the business, I gave the main cartoonist the full credit for doing all of it — the captions and everything. I never thought that somebody else might write the captions and another artist might draw them. It never entered my head. With DENNIS, I would have given Hank credit for all of it. For everything. They were all under the name "Hank Ketcham." After I was married to Fred I realized that this was not so. All the books were written by Fred, which I could never understand. I never — It took me years to get it in my head. Why, if Fred wrote it, why didn't he get any credit for it? I finally realized that this is not the way things happen.

Bill: Nobody seems to know that much about Fred. He seems kind of invisible since his name wasn't listed in most of the comicbooks.

Mollie: Well, except for those couple that had pictures of Fred and Al, I don't think I remember Fred's name being in the book. I'm not saying they weren't, but I don't recall his name being used much. Just like the scripts for the DENNIS dailies and whatnot — they never had anybody else's name used. They were just plain "Hank Ketcham." That's just the way the business goes. None of the originators of most comics could possibly have done everything — the strips, the Sunday pages and the books.

Bill: What did you think of the travel books? Do you remember Fred writing the Hawaiian and Mexican books, when Al and Fred went together on vacation with the families?

Mollie: I don't remember that Mexican book well. I don't remember it, but I do remember the Hawaiian book. They gave Fred credit for it. If you remember they also published a photo of Fred. They have some silly pictures of that Hawaiian trip, believe me (laughs). Some really funny ones with Fred and Al Wiseman trying to learn the Hula.

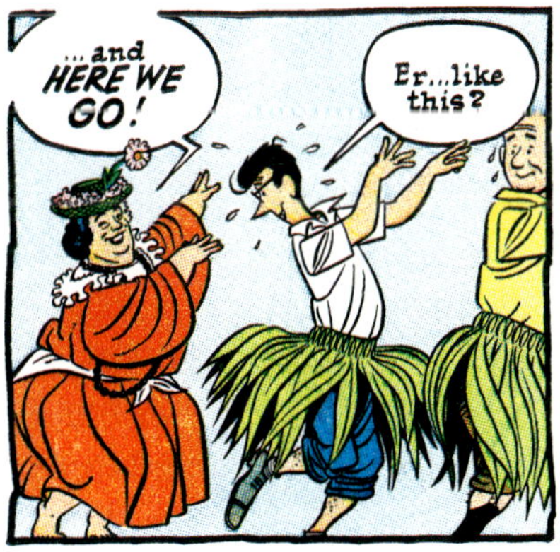

...and HERE WE GO!
Er...like this?

Bill: (laughs) So was Al there mainly to take pictures so he could draw them up?

Mollie: I guess it was so that Al would have the flavor of something. See, we were up together on the first one, to Hawaii.

And then he didn't go with us to Mexico. He waited until the Mexican script was already written. He went down after Fred had done it. But after the HAWAII book, Hank would OK the script, and then they sent Al. Which was a much better way, because if they went together they'd come up with the same stuff.

Bill: So this way they would get different ideas?

Mollie: That is why I think it was. I tried not to get into the business too much. And I'm trying to think … no, Al didn't do the Paris or London books. Or any of the stories that were done when we were on cruises. For those, Fred and I went on alone. If he planned to write … oh … DENNIS IN ENGLAND or something like that, he'd go through the whole thing in his head. And then he'd write it down on paper in pencil. Then type it. And gave it to the gal who collected it at the studio. And she took the scripts down and had them printed to give to the artist. (Cartoonist) Frank Hill went to London and Paris with us, for research. He came home in a hurry because his mother-in-law called home frantically that one of the babies was quite sick. So they packed up and left. I think that was London. I'm not sure.

Bill: Yeah, I talked to him and he said he had to leave early because his child was sick. Did Hank Ketcham ever go with you for the vacation comics research?

Mollie: No.

Bill: Do you have any interesting stories about when you were visiting these places?

Mollie: Truthfully, it was a lot of work and play. Oh, we always had a good time. We always enjoyed the social end of it, too. But the object was not to get too involved too much with the social stuff and still have time to do a half-way decent book. So much research, of course. We took slides and bought them back for Al to work with. But for the non-travel books, those were completely out of Fred's own head.

Bill: So Fred would use a typewriter for his finished scripts?

Mollie: Uh-huh. He used a typewriter most of the time for everything.

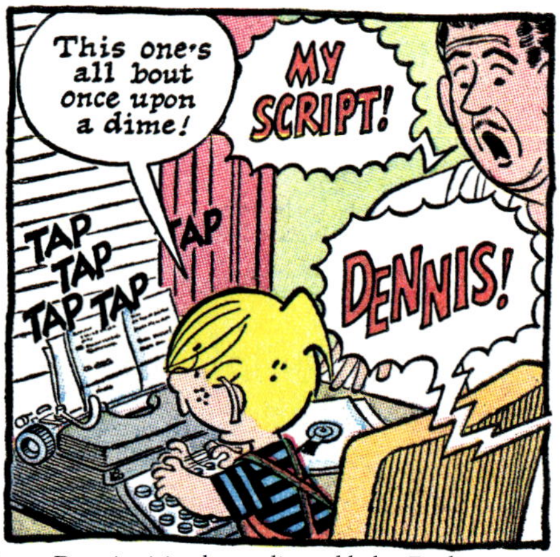
This one's all bout once upon a dime!
MY SCRIPT!
TAP TAP TAP TAP TAP TAP
DENNIS!

Above: Dennis visits the studio and helps Fred on a script. (From DENNIS THE MENACE #30, September 1958.)

Bill: And do you remember Fred walking around Hawaii, getting ideas and writing them down?

Mollie: Oh, he always did. Even before he was doing DENNIS, even when he was doing the cartoons. We'd go for a drive on a Sunday afternoon. He always had his pencil and a pad of paper. Every travel book was written from experience. Anytime we had a book that was set in Hawaii, Canada or … you know … anyplace, those were written after visiting the area.

Bill: I'm sure you enjoyed going on the DENNIS vacations.

Mollie: Oh, of course. Of course! I was his go-fer.

Bill: How would you be his go-fer?

Mollie: I'm the one that had to go and get him coffee on the trips. I carried his notebooks and everything else as he was too busy taking pictures. So he'd give me the film and I'd have it developed. Then he'd start writing his book.

Bill: Sounds like he needed you there and you helped him a lot.

Mollie: Well, he thought so.

Bill: It seems like so much of what Fred wrote was technically correct. Like when Dennis would visit a TV studio, it seems like Fred knew a lot about soundstages.

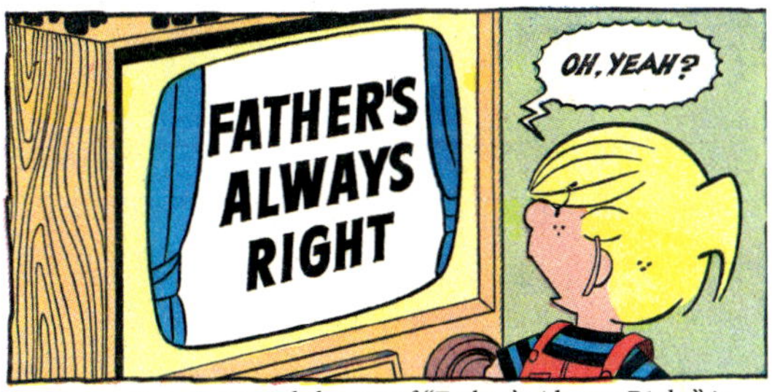
FATHER'S ALWAYS RIGHT
OH, YEAH?
Above: Dennis visited the set of "Father's Always Right" in the 1959 DENNIS THE MENACE IN HOLLYWOOD comic. Perhaps Fred and Mollie Toole visited the real-life set of "Father Knows Best"?

Mollie: Oh, yeah. When we went down to Hollywood, I think were were down there for four days, three or four days. We met several people who were in a show. I forget what show they were doing in the TV studio.

Bill: Did you ever help come up with ideas for DENNIS stories?

Mollie: Nope, that was Fred's department. It was my department to see that he didn't go in debt. The house is my job. And the backyard, and the front yard, and all of that writing was Fred's job.

Bill: What types of DENNIS stories did Fred enjoy writing the most?

Mollie: He enjoyed every one he wrote. He enjoyed his work as much as a man could possibly enjoy his job. He was very happy doing it. Once we met a psychologist, one night at a party, who asked Fred what he did. So Fred told him. And the psychologist said, "Why do you do that?" (Mollie laughs) Fred said, "Because I enjoy doing it."

Bill: Well, what DENNIS books do you think Fred was most proud of?

Mollie: The Bible books, I think. He also liked the travel books. They gave him the chance to see what was on the other side of the world. He enjoyed the first Christmas book. And the one in a shoe store. I have a picture … or had a picture … of the first Christmas book they did. Fred and I had gone up there for dinner that night. And, after dinner, everyone sat around talking and finally one of them said, "Why don't we work on a Christmas book?" So that's how that was started. But not every time that they did a book did Hank sit in.

Bill: If I understand correctly, Fred took over the DENNIS studio when Hank moved to Switzerland around 1960 or so?

Mollie: Yes he did. He took over. Sometimes he sent copies of paperwork so Hank could check and see if there was anything he would like to include, exclude, or add to.

Bill: How did Fred feel about taking on that much responsibility?

Mollie: Oh, he didn't mind at all. As long as my husband could do something with his brain, he would be happy as could be. Fred was basically a brilliant man. He was asked to join the MENSA society. Unfortunately, he failed it on one question. It was a question on California history going way, way back. He had everything but one question correct, and the woman who monitored the quiz said it was not a fair question for people who were not native Californians and had been here a short time. "Fred," she said, "You did remarkably well considering that you weren't born and raised in California." Of course, that was a blow to his ego, but they were sorry that he didn't quite make it.

Bill: Was Fred funny in person? Did he have a good sense of humor when you were talking to him?

Mollie: If you met him, you would never know he wrote comicbooks. Mentally, he was a very serious good man. Someone said to him one time, "Gee, you're not particularly funny, Fred." He said, "I get paid for being funny" (laughs).

Bill: I guess Fred didn't have time to work on any other writing while he was working on DENNIS?

Mollie: No. That was enough.

Bill: Did he ever want to create his own comic strip?

Mollie: Yes, he did and I could have kicked him. He thought up this comic about an egg. He had Al draw it and he submitted it. Not to the Hall Syndicate, I don't know who they submitted it. And they bought it. It was the only one he did. And I could have kicked him. I said, "How many of the artists sell their very first cartoon to the first person they showed it to?"

Bill: And this was … ?

Mollie: I think it was Fred proving he could do it and that's all he cared about.

Bill: Huh? And did they create a whole bunch of strips or just one at the time — for a sample?

Mollie: I think he only sent one or two, but the thing that I was always amazed about was that it was picked up the very first time. You know, he had proven to himself that he could do it and that's all he cared about.

Bill: That's a shame because, from looking at Al Wiseman's later artwork, it was obvious he needed a writer. There were some strips he did in the early 1970s where the jokes didn't make a whole lot of sense. And it seems if Al was able to work with Fred on a strip, that it would have been successful.

THE BLOBS... GRACE AND LOOIE
AL WISEMAN
COMICS
" YOU SAY SOMETHIN', LOOIE? "

Above: Al Wiseman's proposed 1960s comic panel "The Blobs ... Grace & Looie." The promotional materials for this comic proclaimed: "Created To Make Any Reader Laugh... And Like Himself Better!"

Mollie: Yeah, The thing about Fred was that he was perfectly happy working with Hank. As I say, that was Fred.

Bill: Would you have copies of that "Egg" strip anywhere?

Mollie: No. And it just would have been a panel. He could have had his own panel or strip or whatever it turned out to be. I wouldn't be surprised if he had never said anything about it to anybody, except Al of course. And ... (pause) I have an old crumpled up two dollar bill. I never even knew it existed until Fred died and he had it all tucked in his wallet. It was so old, I couldn't read the date on it. Wouldn't have done any good anyway. But I often wondered, is that what they paid him? Was the two dollar bill what they paid him for his single little cartoon. I'm not even sure that that's where it came from. I didn't know he had it until after he passed away. Because one thing we never did — I never knew what Fred had in his wallet and he never knew what I had in mine. No way.

Bill: Did Fred ever keep in contact with Al Wiseman after Al stopped working on DENNIS?

Mollie: Oh, sure

Bill: Yeah?

Mollie: Yeah.

Bill: So they would like talk on the phone?

Mollie: Yeah. Uh-huh. They weren't as close as they were when they were working, but they still kept in touch with each other.

Dennis the Menace
P O. DRAWER BB
CARMEL VALLEY, CALIFORNIA 93924

Dec. 21, 1977

Dear Al:

Since you may have heard about these, I thought you might like to see how we "got religion" with these books put out by a religious publisher, and sold in bookstores instead of newsstands.

I think they are the high point of something which might never have got off the ground without you in the first place.

I was going to get them bound, but wanted to get them to you before Christmas, so maybe you can get a printer there to bind them if you wish.
If bound, they go (and read) in this order:-
Moses
Jesus
David
Joseph
The Girls
More About Jesus

All the best......

Fred.

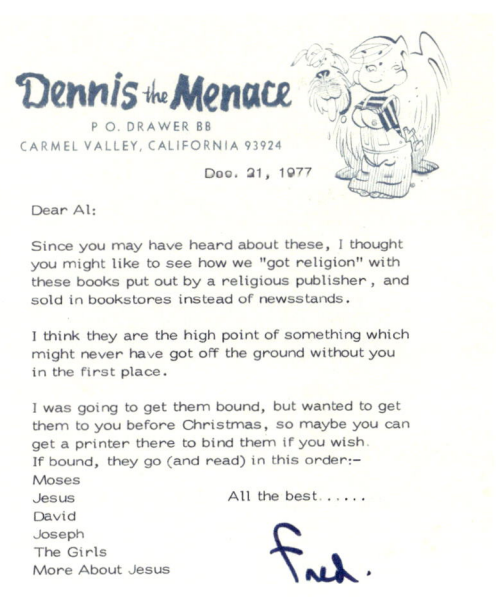

Above: A 1977 letter from Fred Toole to Al Wiseman.

Bill: When Fred retired, was he ready to stop working on DENNIS or ... ?

Mollie: Well, he worked on all the books as far as they went. I don't remember that they continued after Fred passed away.

Bill: Yeah, I don't think they did.

Mollie: I don't think so. But after Al left there were a number of artists that worked on the DENNIS comicbooks. Oh, gosh … I don't know how many. There was Bob Paplow, but he passed away long before Fred did. Then for a while there was Frank Hill. And a fellow by the name of O'Brien. And I think, I believe, Ron Ferdinand worked on the comicbook, but I couldn't swear to that. I kind of lost track because, for a while it seems, they switched artists quite a bit. Quite a number of them in there. They weren't there long enough to make a big impression. Actually, even though I should have known, sometimes I couldn't tell the difference. Of course the … oh … I can't think, what was his position … oh, well, the head man at the syndicate. I think it was Paul …

Bill: Bob Hall?

Mollie: Yeah, Bob Hall. He said near the end of the DENNIS run that those books are "alright, but they're too damned educational."

Bill: How can you be too educational?

Mollie: I don't know. I don't know. Fred couldn't see any reason why anything could be considered too educational. They were very very good. The teachers around here used the comicbooks in school. But then they were discontinued

Bill: It seems like they sold pretty well.

Mollie: Yes they did. Yes they did. Then toward the end is when they … oh, how should I put it? When all the comics became a little rougher. And a little more … well, all the comicbooks had changed.

Bill: Where they weren't as innocent?

Mollie: The comicbooks then began to change their format entirely. That's when the kids began getting into real trouble. When they changed from the more or less innocent type to the getting wilder.

Bill: What year did Fred stop writing DENNIS?

60¢
13
NOV
MARVEL COMICS GROUP
Dennis the Menace

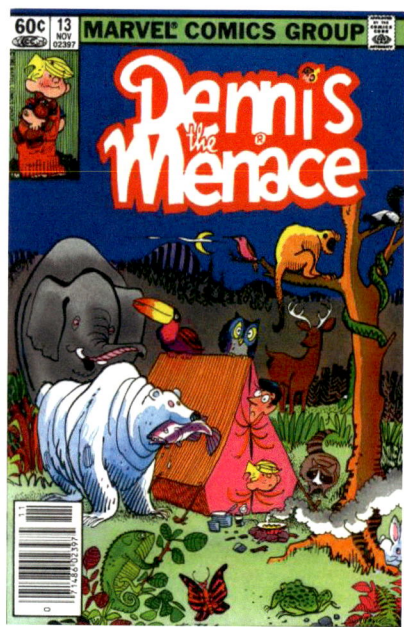

Above: The final issue of the DENNIS THE MENACE comicbook, from November 1982, also contained Fred Toole's final DENNIS scripts. Cover by Hank Ketcham.

Mollie: When they did the last one. He did them from the very first to the very last. I think he retired … in the early 80s. Maybe 81, 82. That's the last comicbook he wrote and that's the last one that was ever published. After that, he worked with Hank for about a year doing PR work and things of that sort.

Bill: And did Fred write anything after DENNIS?

Mollie: Well, no. After DENNIS, then he began constructing crossword puzzles. He started doing them very shortly after he retired. His crossword puzzles were a regular feature in *The New York Times*, the daily ones. Fred was a brilliant man.

Bill: Did he enjoy working on those?

Mollie: Yes, indeed. He worked on them like he did everything else. He'd get up in the morning and he work in back. Our guest room became Fred's office room. He worked at his desk from about 9:30 till about 12 … or 12:30. Then I got him hooked on a half-hour soap opera. And for lunch we watched the half-hour soap opera. Then he was back at his desk until 4:30 in the afternoon when I'd make him stop so we could watch our other show.

Bill: Did he continue on with crossword puzzles for a number of years?

Mollie: Uh-huh. I really couldn't tell you when he stopped doing it.

Bill: Did Fred ever ask you for advice on his crossword puzzles?

Mollie: Oh, yeah. I helped Fred with many of his crossword puzzles.

Bill: Did he retire from that, too, before he passed away?

Mollie: Semi-retired. He didn't do all of them. His eyes began to get weak.

Bill: When did Fred pass away?

Mollie: December 9, 1993.

Bill: Could I ask... how did Fred die?

Mollie: He had a stroke … a stroke … and he lived for four months after that. And the day Fred died... but anyway... when Hank went into the office the next day and told the kids, Ron said Hank's eyes filled with tears. And he just turned around and went into his office. So they were very, very close.
Did you read the … what was it? The first … it would have been the 40 years. He had written a book for the first 40 years of doing Dennis the Menace.

Dennis the Menace
HIS FIRST
40
YEARS
Hank Ketcham

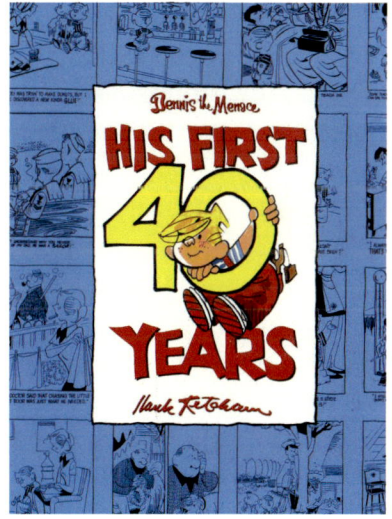

Above: Hank Ketcham's 1991 book "Dennis The Menace: His First 40 Years."

Bill: Yes.

Mollie: Yeah, Hank apologized one time. He said, you know, he wrote one book, a biography. And he could write only so many words. So he had planned to continue and do the next book … to finish it up. He didn't have room to do anything much about Fred in the first book. But he wanted to write more about Fred in the next one … to finish up the later part of his career.

Bill: I was hoping to see more about Fred and Al in Hank's autobiography "Merchant of Dennis." (1990) But it was nice to see the photos of both that were in there.

Mollie: We're still very good friends. And Hank's present wife, Rolande, is a delightful woman. She's an Austrian. And she is a lovely woman. In fact, she comes to see me almost every day. She has ever since I've been here. And she hasn't lost her accent yet.

Mollie: Hank now is doing oil paintings. And they're excellent, beautiful things. He was having a show, I think it was in San Francisco. He's already sold a number of his paintings. He did one for me to hang in my room here. It was an abstract. And I tell you, everybody looks at it and says, "Now what in the world does that mean?" (Bill and Mollie laugh).

Bill: That's great.

Mollie: And they have a son, Scott. I forget what college he goes to. It's down south somewhere. I think he has another year, maybe two.

Bill: Is there anything else you'd like to say about Fred?

Mollie: Well, I could tell you one thing … Fred and I would have been married 52 years the second of March. And, I'll tell you, in all that time, we did not have one cross word. If I wanted something one way, and he wanted it another, it was discussed. And if we couldn't settle it, we just forgot about it.

Bill: Yeah, from everything I've heard, he was a great guy.

Mollie: Oh, he was.

Bill: And I … I just really love Fred's writing on the DENNIS comic.

Mollie: Too bad you never met Fred.

Bill: Someone showed me a photo of him later in his life and I thought he looked a little bit like Mr. Wilson.

Mollie: That's what somebody else said. Well, that was after he gained weight. I could tell you, 'cause he only weighed 145 pounds when we were married. When he passed away, he weighed 180.

Bill: He looked like a really nice man.

Mollie: Oh, he was. He was nice … he was a wonderful man. And that's not just his wife speaking. And, as I said, we never had a cross word. I remember Ruth Barnes was sitting in a bar somewhere on one of their trips to visit us. Ruth said somebody had asked her about Fred and she told him what she knew. Ruth said to her, "I don't understand. His wife says that they never had any kind of a confrontation. They were always discussing things and if they couldn't agree they'd table it." The other girl looked at Ruth and said, "You know, that woman is either a liar or they had the dullest marriage ever!" (Mollie laughs) So I guess to have a good marriage, you had to be scrapping all the time, huh?

Bill: (laughs) I guess so!

Mollie: I hope I haven't gotten things out of context. After all — I run around telling people that women never tell their age — but I'm 90 years old. And I'm pretty sure I got everything in the right context (laughs).

Bill: I'm sure you did. Well, Mollie, it's been a pleasure speaking with you.

Mollie: Well, thank you. It was pleasant to talk to you.

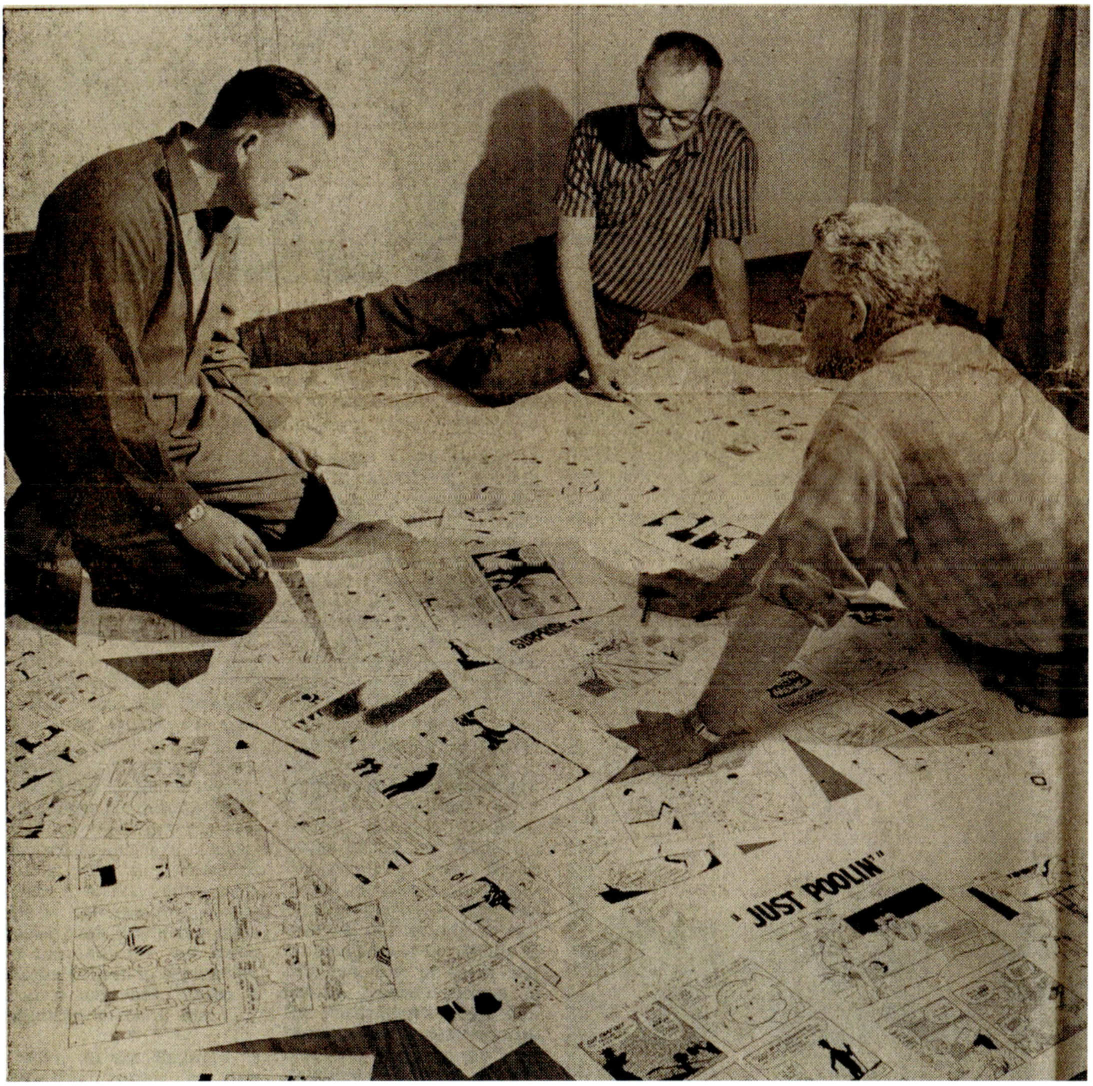
"JUST POOLIN'"

Above: A photograph from *The Monterey Peninsula Herald*, Peninsula Life section, Saturday, November 14, 1959. "Fred, Al and Bruce (Ariss) sit on the floor of Al's home surrounded by completed and already published pages of DENNIS comicbooks."

Artistry Of Two Men Creates Dennis Comicbooks.

(Article from *The Monterey Peninsula Herald* Peninsula Life, Saturday, November 14, 1959. Courtesy of Jim and Teresa Wiseman.)

Above: "Al Wiseman contemplates with satisfaction a drawing of Dennis he made at his desk in Carmel."

Two million readers will be chuckling over the Christmas adventures of that loveable 4 ½ year old moppet, Dennis. Meanwhile, two men who write the script and draw the wispy-haired, freckled Dennis encased in comicbooks will have completed another 100 page book, DENNIS THE MENACE IN HOLLYWOOD, that is to delight readers the world over during the summer of 1960. And, in all probability, when the Christmas book hits the newsstands, the two artists will be in Mexico, writing new script and drawing new DENNISes for the edification and entertainment of MENACE fans in a book designed for the later part of 1960.

The artists: Al Wiseman, who failed his high school art course, and Fred Toole, who wrote gags in his spare time from long ago jobs with the phone company and on a chicken ranch.

Creation of DENNIS THE MENACE comicbooks is a serious, time-consuming profession in which Al and Fred insist upon maintaining a standard that has won them Congressional Record mention ("wholesome interest and entertainment value"); an outstanding citation award from the Boys Clubs of America; a seven year record of never having a single page rejected by the Comic Code Authority for containing any objectionable material; innumerable and enthusiastic endorsements from educators; the Spanish translation DANIEL EL TRAVIESO, is used for extra reading material at the Army Language School; DENNIS IN HAWAII gets classroom perusal by sixth graders at La Mesa School; plus grateful letters from hundreds of parents.

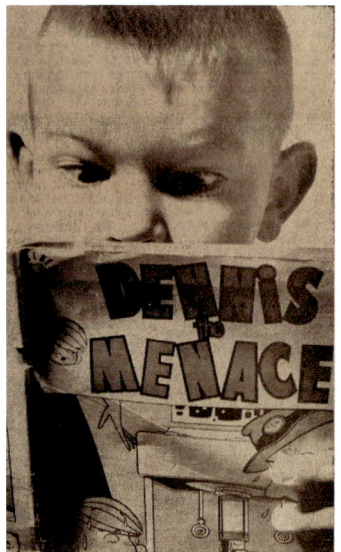

Left: "This is the chief reward for the Wiseman-Toole-Ariss combine gets from its work — the delighted and wholehearted enjoyment of youthful readers." (The kid pictured here is none other than Al's son Jim.)

One of their prize possessions, though, is

the letter from an 18 year old in Santa Fe, New Mexico, who describes himself as an avid comicbook reader. "I was amazed," Norman van Tilbergen wrote, "that all this educational material included without sacrificing any of the characteristic wholesome humor that I always expect (and receive) in a DENNIS comic… It is publications such as this that raise the comicbook in the eye of the public from a level of indifference or disgust to one of esteem and admiration…"

Al, who draws the comicbook DENNIS (the daily cartoon continues to be done by DENNIS creator, Hank Ketcham) works in his Carmel studio-home. A stickler for accuracy, Al works early (sometimes at 4 or 5 o'clock in the morning) and late to translate into drawings the Dennis antics described in the script written by Fred Toole.

known to his fans) probably has more of his work viewed by the public that almost any other artists, with the exception of Dennis's creator, Hank Ketcham.

Above: "Al takes to his files after the script conference. There he can find photographs, clippings, models for almost anything called for by Fred's script."

Above: "Al Wiseman sits at this Rube Goldberg-type machine for some of the work required in the production of a comicbook. Formally known as a Camera Lucida, but affectionately referred to as Lucy, the machine will enlarge or reduce the proportions of any picture placed on its accordian-pleated maw."

Al's interest in cartooning began at just about the same time Al did. It's been a lifelong passion and that bit about failing art in high school resulted from the fact that his instructor wouldn't let him draw cartoons. "Uncle Al" (that's how he's

Al's teammate, Fred Toole, came west from Brooklyn at the instigation of Bob Barnes, now a Carmel Valleyite turning out his own comic strip but then an owner of an advertising agency in Santa Cruz. When Bob went East to sell his syndicated feature, Fred took over the agency and he and Al, its art director, began an association that continues successfully today. Fred has his own home in Del Rey Oaks but works from the 61-acre Carmel Valley ranch that houses Hank Ketcham's home and the cabana-studios in which Fred turns out script and handles public relations and correspondence. (There, too, work Lee Holley who does the Sunday Dennis cartoon strip, and Arch Garner, who devises the Dennis toys, games and puppets.) Since he and Al conceived the DENNIS comicbook idea in 1953, Fred has accepted only two outside suggested stories for use in the books. The 40th has just been published and Fred has No. 43 nearly completed.

The Wiseman-Toole team turns out six 36-page DENNIS comics every year, several 100-page "extras" each year, plus occasional specials such as the book campaign in for Safety at the behest of the National Safety Council and one entitled "Dennis and Dirt" — no strangers they — for the Soil Conservation Society of America.

The two man team recently was upped to three when Bruce Ariss joined Al at the Carmel studio — Bruce's career has covered every phase of the arts. He has written, edited, illustrated magazines; he has served as art director for advertising agencies in San Francisco; he has designed and written for radio and TV; he has written, directed and acted in plays. And he has done production designing for the movies in Hollywood; work that he finds closely parallels his present job with Al Wiseman.

While his uncles Al, Fred and Bruce bend over their steaming typewriters and drawing boards Dennis capers through colorful pages in all corners of the world, emitting his embarrassingly honest observations in French, Afrikaans, Spanish, Swedish, Danish, Finnish, Italian, Dutch, German, Portuguese, Japanese. And English.

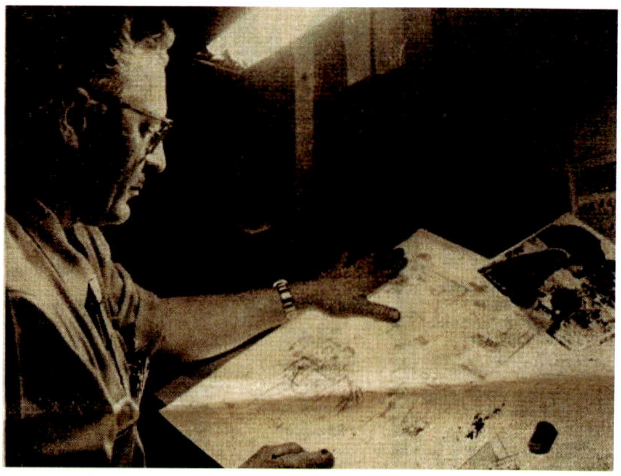

Above: "Bruce Ariss is the most recent addition to the Wiseman-Toole team. He has his drawing board in Al's Carmel studio where his work, much as it was when he was production designer for the movies, is to draw "roughs" that are later filled in by Al. In Hollywood Bruce broke the script down into roughs, establishing the scenes, sequences and positions of the characters. Bruce has designed and decorated sets for television (including some for "I Love Lucy"). Many of his own paintings and murals decorate homes and business houses in this area. Almost every phase of the arts intrigues Bruce and has captured his attention at one time or another during the years. And in his spare time he has built the rambling 22 room home on Huckleberry Hill — where he is recognized as the unofficial mayor. In that home, designated by John Steinbeck as a 'triumph over architecture.' Bruce lives with his novelist-wife, Jean (author of "The Quick Years") and their five children.

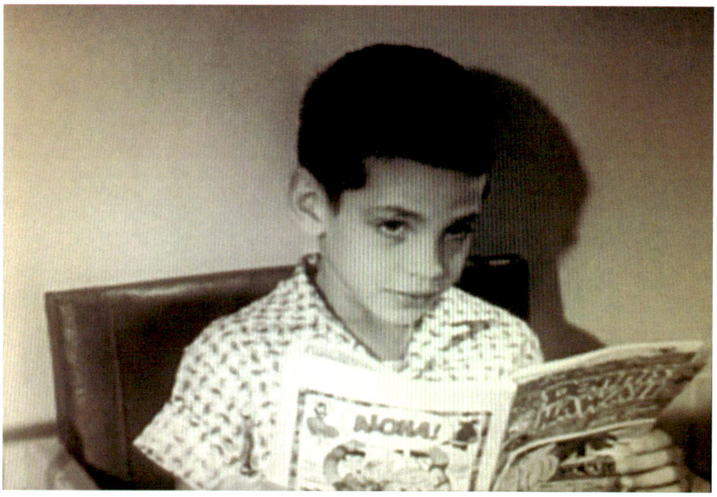
ALOHA!

Left: This photo has nothing to do with the above newspaper article. It's a still from a 1950s public domain film clip that shows a kid walking into a barber shop and picking up a DENNIS IN HAWAII comic to enjoy. Courtesy of Shaun Clancy, who used the film clip in a documentary he produced about ARCHIE COMICS titled "Archie's Betty."

Comics Show What Fred Toole Thinks About

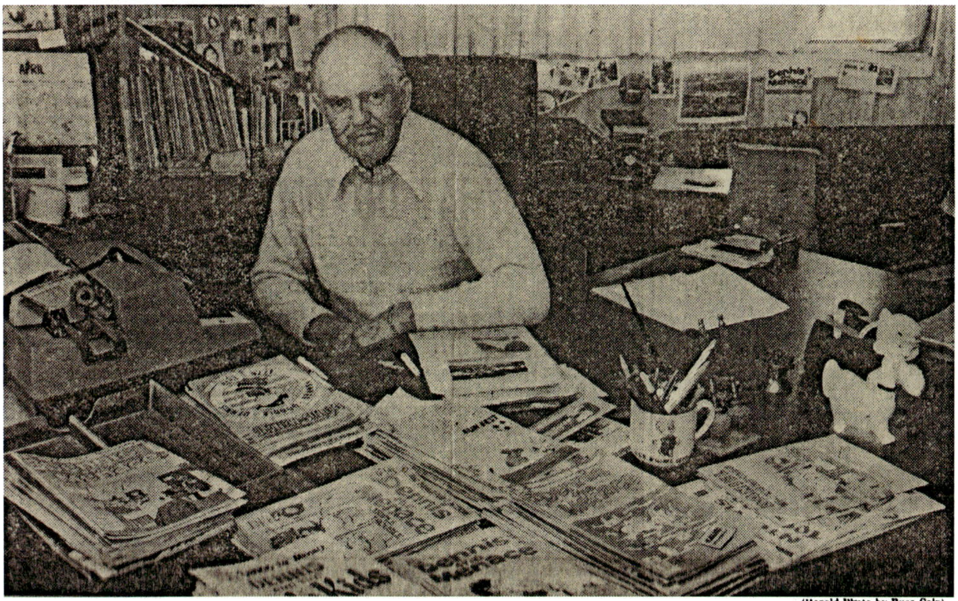

(Herald Photo by Russ Cain)

FRED TOOLE WITH SOME OF HIS COMIC BOOKS AND DENNIS (RIGHT)
. . . Dennis the Menace 'has calmed down quite a bit' of late

All you have to do is read a Dennis the Menace comic book to find out what 66-year-old Fred Toole of Del Rey Oaks thinks about.

For the last 28 years, this innocent-looking man has been dreaming up many of the situations that drive Mr. Wilson wild.

The comic books for which he writes the scripts have a circulation of 250,000 in the United States and are translated into a number of foreign languages, including Portuguese, Greek, Swedish, French, Finnish and Spanish.

The cartoon that runs in The Herald and other newspapers continues to be handled by Dennis' creator, Hank Ketcham, who also lives on the Peninsula.

It all began in 1952, the year after Ketcham started his now-famous comic strip.

"It occurred to me it would make a

HANK

good comic book, so I worked up a book for Ketcham and he approved it," Toole recalls.

His first office was in downtown Monterey and his second at Ketcham's Carmel Valley ranch, where Toole moved to work in about 1960.

In 1961, when Ketcham sold his ranch, Toole moved to his present office in Carmel Valley Village. There he writes scripts three days a week and sends them to an artist in Connecticut for illustrating.

In addition to the regular comic book series, which consists of 12 editions a year, Toole writes a religious series in which Dennis explains the Bible.

From his Del Rey Oaks home, where he has lived for 22 years, Toole commutes to the Carmel Valley office over Los Laureles Grade, which he describes as "a lovely drive."

Some of his time is spent responding to fan mail, such as the letter he received recently from a 13-year-old Canadian boy.

"I always try to be like Dennis," the boy wrote. "I've been a fan of Dennis since I was 5, and he's still my favorite.

"I even named my dog Ruff—I like Dennis so much that some call me Dennis at school, and I don't mind."

Many of the children who write in send photos of themselves, and Toole responds with a picture of Dennis.

Toole says his ideas for Dennis' adventures just sort of come naturally: "I guess I'm just a child at heart."

He and his wife of 33 years have no children—"Just Dennis, you might say."

According to Toole, Dennis isn't as mischievous as he was in the early days: "He's calmed down quite a bit—I guess we all have."

Above: A Fred Toole interview from the May 18 1980, *Monterey Peninsula Herald*. This clipping was sent to Al Wiseman's daughter, Jan. Fred wrote, "Janis — Mollie said you missed this article. Famous overnight!" Notice that Fred replaced the misquoted "me" with "Hank."

1949: Al Wiseman Becomes Jack Chapman!
(But Not Really, Probably.) By Jim Wiseman

(Thanks to Shaun Clancy for scanning this article from his copy of *The American Cartoonist* magazine!)

Jack Chapman, we hardly knew ye! Bill Alger so kindly forwarded me this autobiographical article my dad wrote (from the Oct-Nov, 1949 issue of *The American Cartoonist* magazine.) I'd never seen it and was quite amused to read – particularly since it was published the year I was born. Yes – I'm that "Jungle Jim" who was busy stacking up the diapers at the time. As far as I know this article was an example of my dad's humor – funny but with an underlying bite to it. No – he never legally changed his name – Al Wiseman being his name throughout his life – with a few *nom de plumes* or aliases thrown in every now and then. I think his message was two-fold – one, he felt his particular brand of humor (the stories) were underappreciated and secondly, how frustrating it was as an artist to be pigeon-holed into a particular type. Looking at the timing this was just about the time that my dad was looking at setting up a new business – an advertising agency in Santa Cruz which, presumably would allow him to get more into copy – and factor in some of those gag stories that the editors had previously chosen to reject. Being just a baby I'm not sure whether the agency was a success or not but from the time I do have memories of living in Santa Cruz – he was always Al Wiseman and continued to be Al until he died… at least as far as I know. So if there are any old stories about Jack Chapman – I hope to hear about them someday.

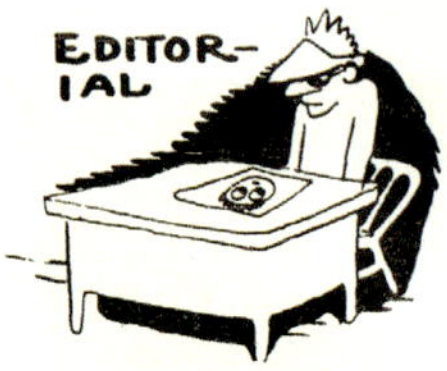

EDITOR-
IAL

We are glad to be able to bring you this issue's profile of Jack Chapman, who will be remembered by most of our older readers as Al Wiseman. Jack is one of those none too occasional fellows who is equally at home in any kind of drawing, from drafting up a locomotive, to a magazine ad, to a gag cartoon. And with a control of medium which makes the work of most of us look as if it were done blindfolded at three paces. As Bob Barnes says,he can use about anything from a kalsomine brush to a toothpick. Barnes and Chapman are now both living up by Monterey Bay, and are about to start work on an ad agency which will operate out of Santa Cruz.

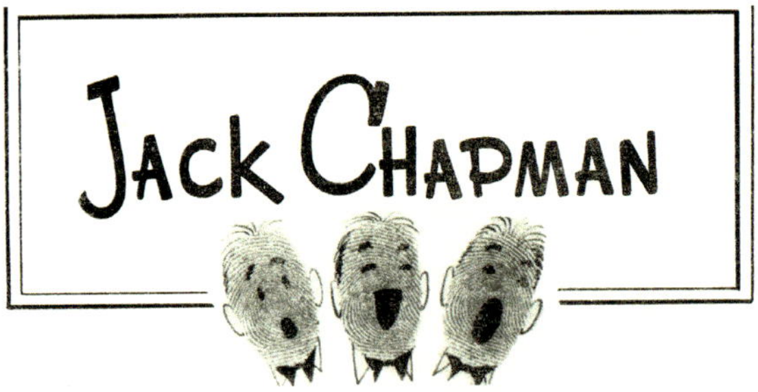

JACK CHAPMAN

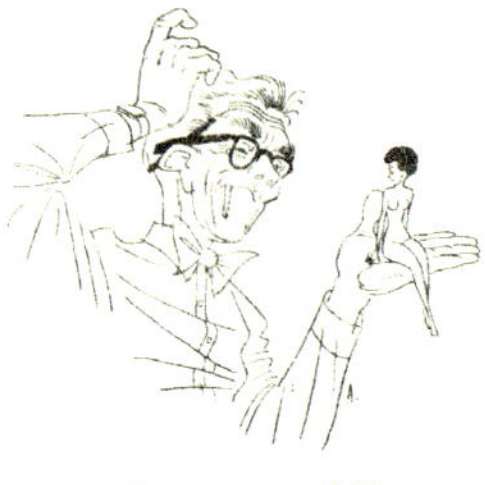

Jack Chapman was Al Wiseman. --- the name switch was necessary, that I might more easily avoid bill collectors, keep from being mis-hailed as Weeesmannn, Wisenkamp or Wiseguy, and to help me chide myself into turning out some funny gags for a change.

After 15 years of licking envelopes and changing drawing styles, it finally dawns on me that editors are sensitive too and are still looking for FUNNY GAGS. I thought Al Wiseman turned out a lot of good gags, but now I know why they (the editors) didn't buy. More often than not the "snapper" was hidden in a grandiose display of pen or brush technique..... He sold a few, but I'll bet Jack Chapman does a lot better.

I really haven't any regrets,----- I'd rather draw than eat. Often do. I get funny gags all the time, and I'm the first one to tell my gagwriters so.

Learned to draw just as the double conversation gag went over the horizon. For years I drew nothing but desert islands. Gradually worked into a shape where prison cells and door gags came easy; then-- saayyy, didn't the D'Conversation come back in a hurry--- just like women's bucket hats. Anyway, I learned to draw everything from Aard-

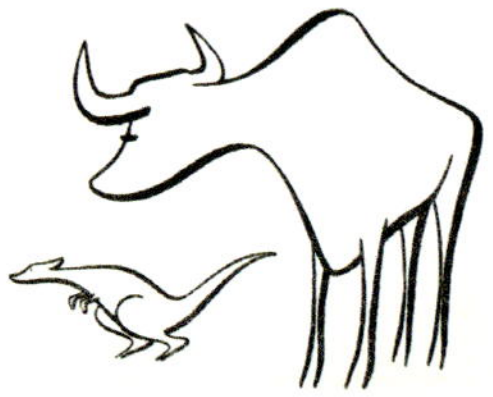

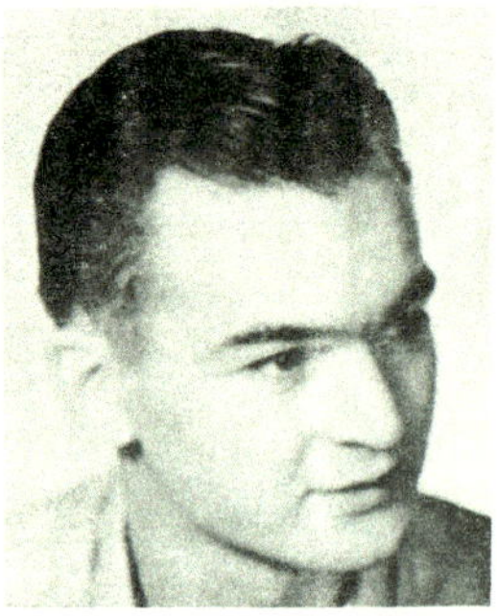

varks to Zebras. Why not, in spite of remarks by a few of my contemporaries about my 'photographic memory' I have a very complete morgue. Not ashamed to use it either, although drawing from life itself is a lot more fun.

While I'm no Rembrandt, I did get into a rut on drawing; and it still hurts me, even though Jack Chapman's gags are a lot simpler and funnier. Editors have a way of continuing to pass up a guy's stuff once the habit is formed, no matter what the cartoonist comes up with. Under the name Jack Chapman (a legal change, incidentally) I am approaching the cartoon business with a much healthier attitude than Al Wiseman ever had. Really not out to deceive anyone--- just out to produce saleable gags.

This was supposed to be a profile; okay then, profile: I am 31, tall, Married to a nice little "Okie". We have three children- Merrily, Janice, and 'Jungle' Jim. Can't see more than five feet, but it's all right, because I'm not such a hot-shot at golf anyway. Like working late at night because it keeps my neighbors wondering why I never leave in the mornings..........Will you excuse me now? Jungle Jim can really stack up the diapers... then too, I have to get out a batch of roughs.

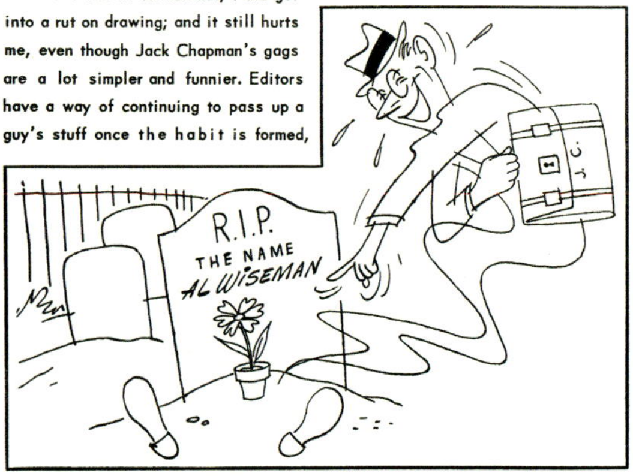

R.I.P.
THE NAME
AL WISEMAN

1967: Al Wiseman Works For Boeing

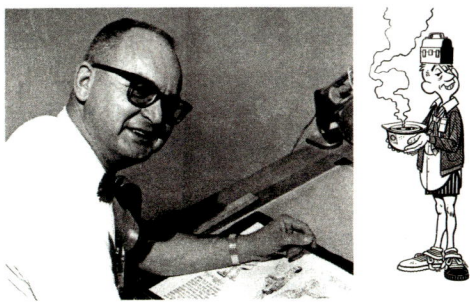

Al Wiseman and friend

Cartoonist Ken Alvine shared an office with Al Wiseman at Boeing around 1967 and supplied this wonderful article and images from Boeing's *Everett Flyer* newsletter. Thanks, Ken!

Al Wiseman is the artist-humorist who created "Ev Rett" and the 747 concept on page two of this issue. For 13 years Wiseman did all of creator Hank Ketcham's "Dennis the Menace" comic books and commercial by-products of that popular feature.

Wiseman joined The Boeing Company in March of last year as motion picture art director for the SST Division. He is now graphic designer and art director for 747 Presentations and Proposals.

Of his new cartoon character created expressly for for the Everett Flyer, Wiseman said, "Ev Rett is is not meant to be the typical Boeing employee. He is, however, a combination of everyone's faults and idiosyncracies. Ev is a paradox. His situations will seem to contradict the way something should be done, yet his temporary confusion will suggest the right way."

Wiseman sold his first cartoon to the Saturday Evening Post when he was in the Navy during World War II. He went on to become one of the top freelance gag cartoonists in the country.

"EV" RETT
AL WISEMAN

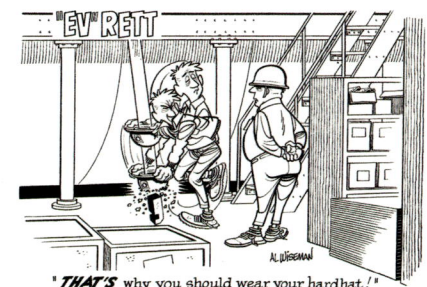

"*THAT'S* why you should wear your hardhat!"

EVERETT FLYER

PUBLISHED BY EMPLOYEE AND MANAGEMENT COMMUNICATION | E-1800 PHONE 655-3114 M.S. 1A-55

EDITOR JIM MARINER — ART AND LAYOUT DICK TUCKER — PHOTOGRAPHERS RED RAE, TOM TOWNSEND

THE BOEING COMPANY

COMMERCIAL AIRPLANE DIVISION — EVERETT BRANCH

Below: Al snuck some familiar faces into the bowling scene. Can you spot Alice Mitchell, Martha Wilson, George Wilson, and Al Wiseman?

Big cash prizes! BOWL IN 747 SEATTLE TO BANGKOK JACKPOT DOUBLES
Meanwhile...up forward...where the hockey game is in progress....

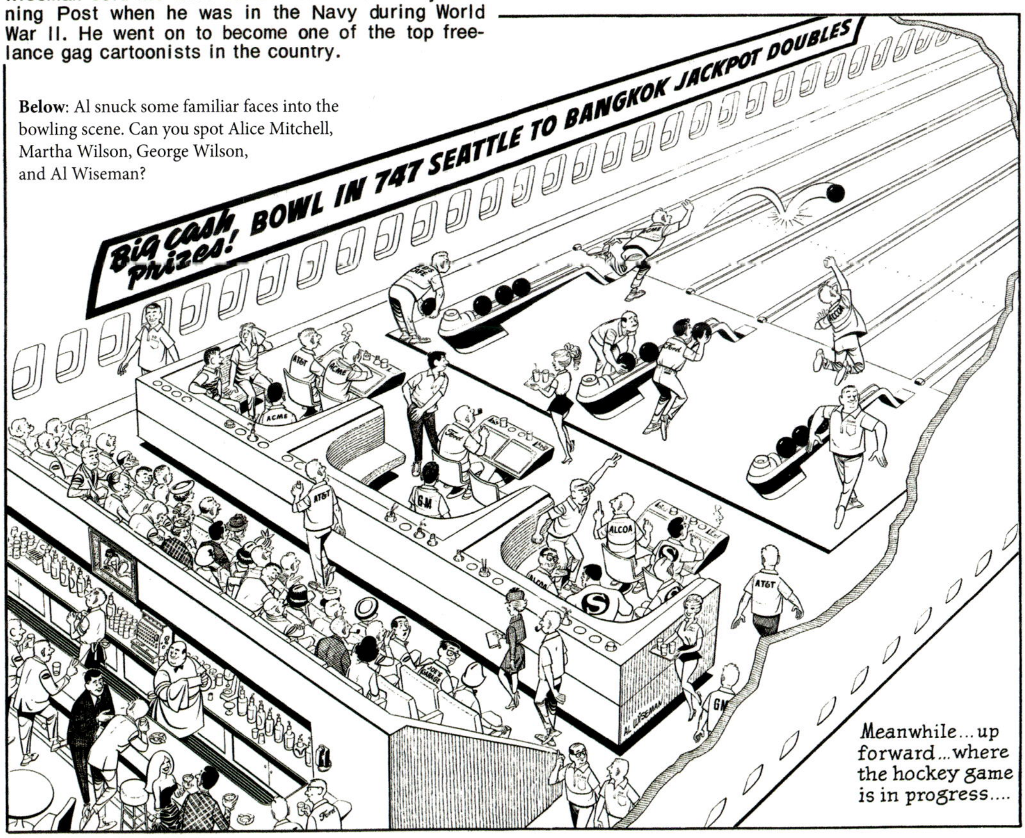

This concept of the 747 may be an exaggeration, but the jetliner's cabin will be undeniably spacious and comfortable.

Portfolio of Al Wiseman Original Art

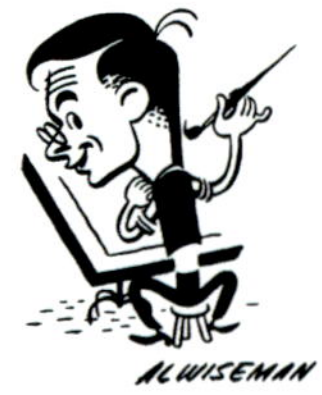
AL WISEMAN

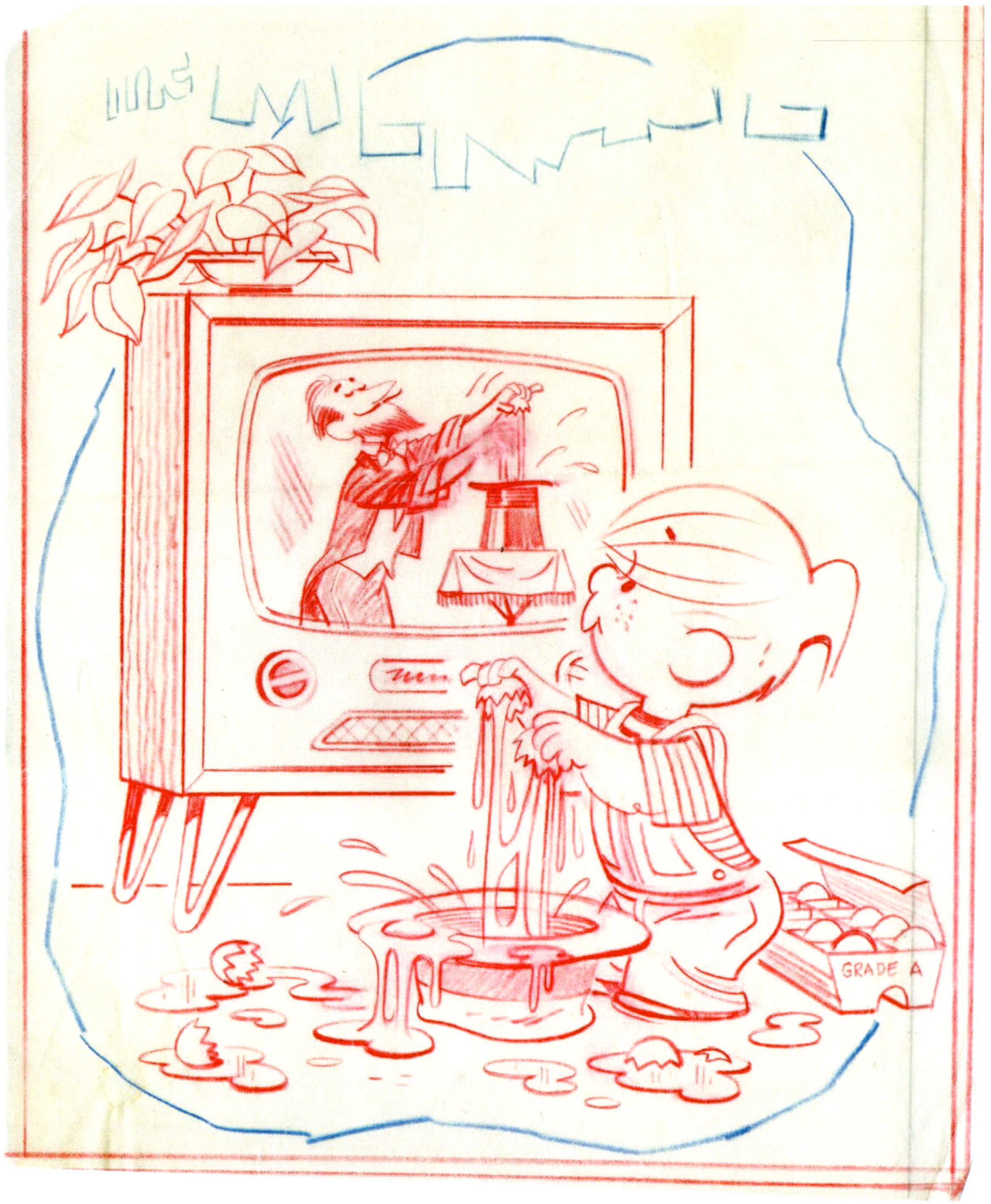
GRADE A

Above: Al Wiseman pencil rough for the cover of DENNIS THE MENACE #12, September 1955. (Courtesy of Jim & Teresa Wiseman.)

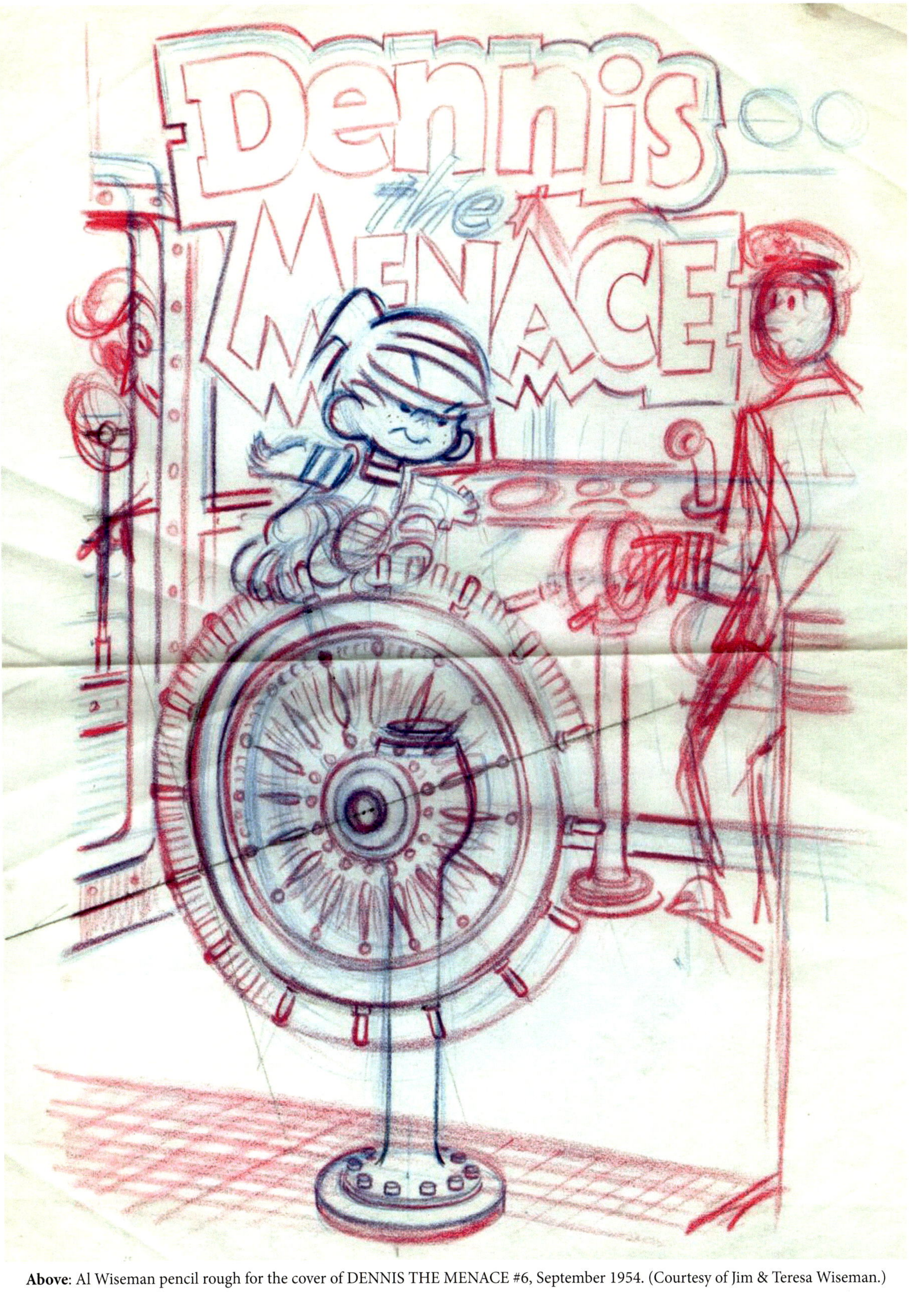
Dennis
the
MENACE

Above: Al Wiseman pencil rough for the cover of DENNIS THE MENACE #6, September 1954. (Courtesy of Jim & Teresa Wiseman.)

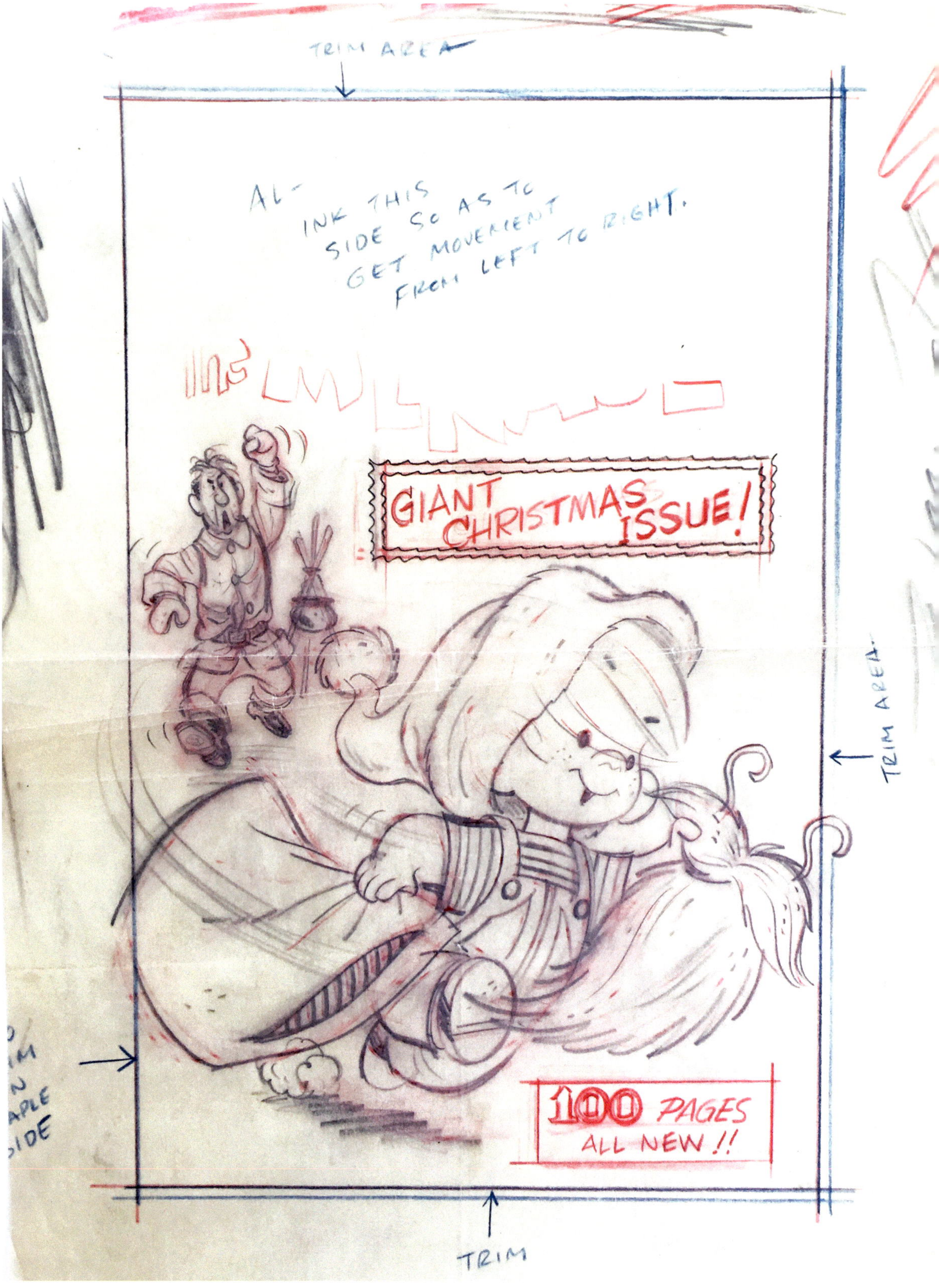
TRIM AREA
AL- INK THIS SIDE SO AS TO GET MOVEMENT FROM LEFT TO RIGHT.
GIANT CHRISTMAS ISSUE!
TRIM AREA
100 PAGES ALL NEW !!
TRIM

Above: Al Wiseman pencil rough for the cover of DENNIS THE MENACE GIANT CHRISTMAS ISSUE #1, January 1955.

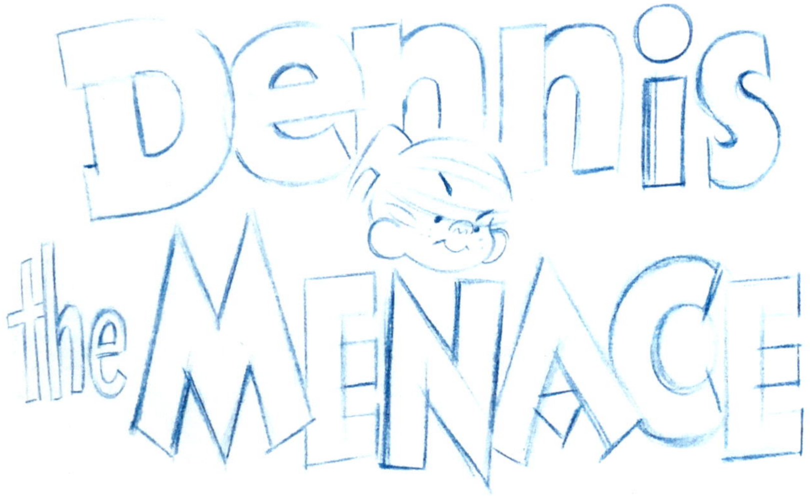
Dennis
the MENACE

Above: Al Wiseman pencil rough of the DENNIS THE MENACE comicbook logo.

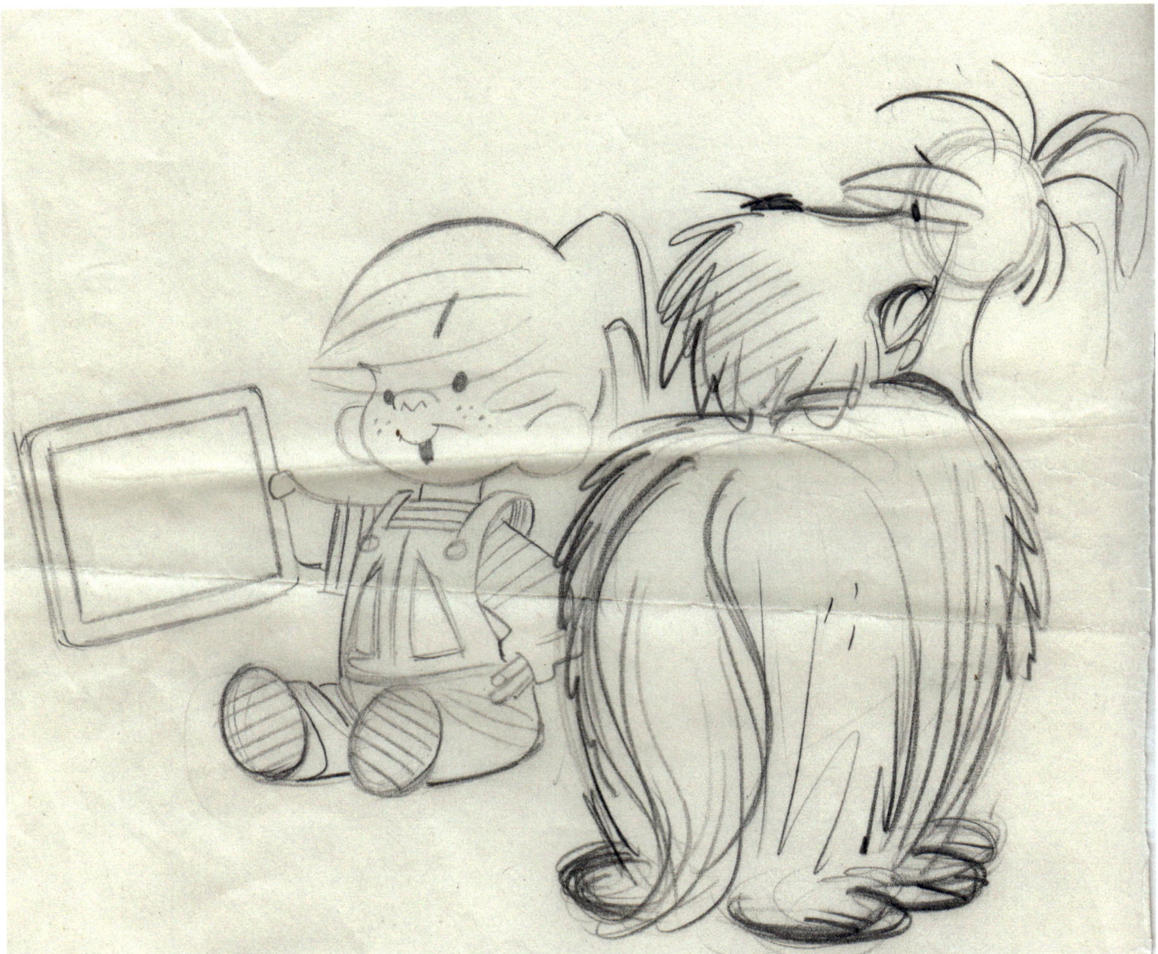

Above: Al Wiseman pencil rough for 1950s DENNIS THE MENACE mechandising.

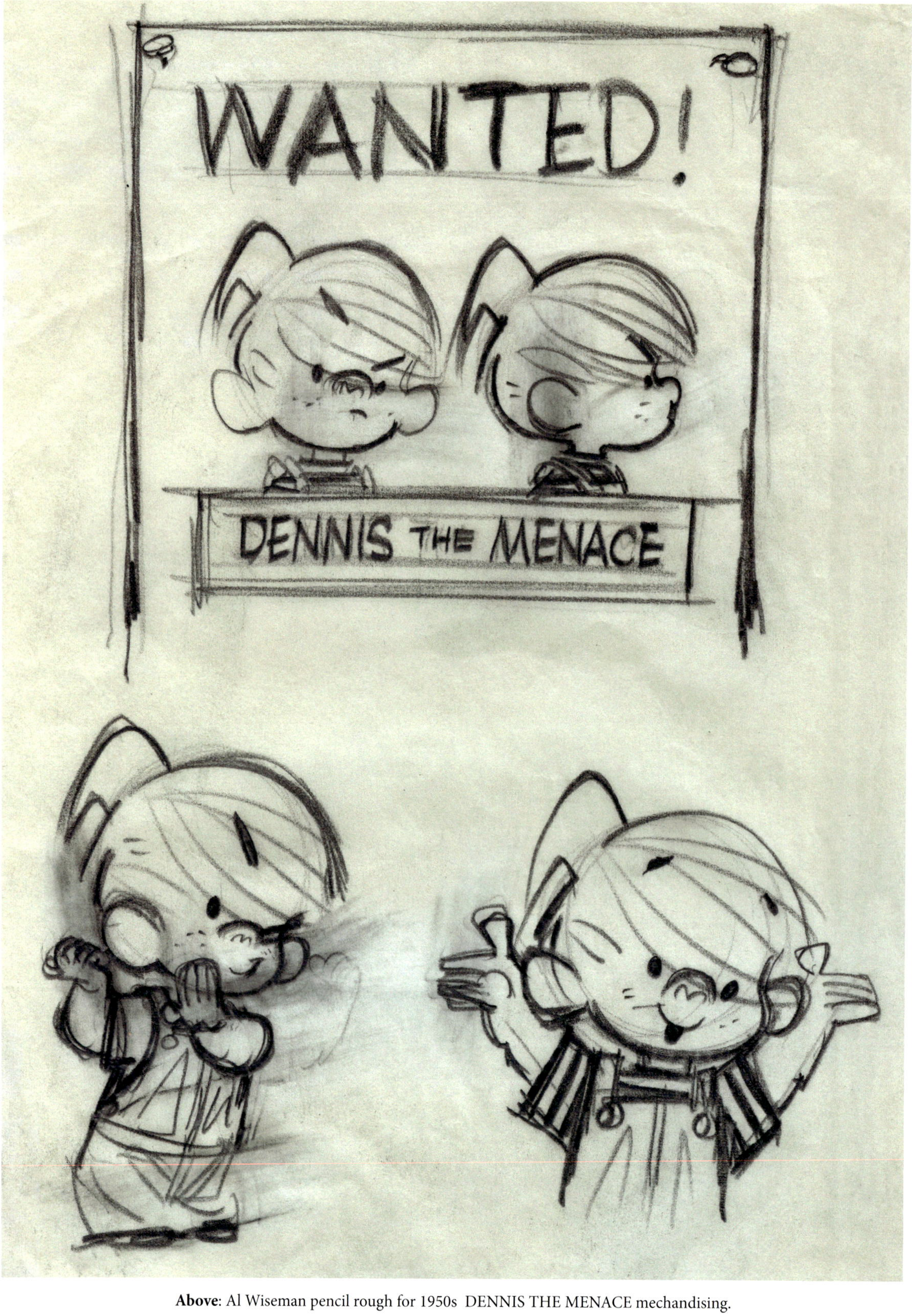
WANTED!
DENNIS THE MENACE

Above: Al Wiseman pencil rough for 1950s DENNIS THE MENACE mechandising.

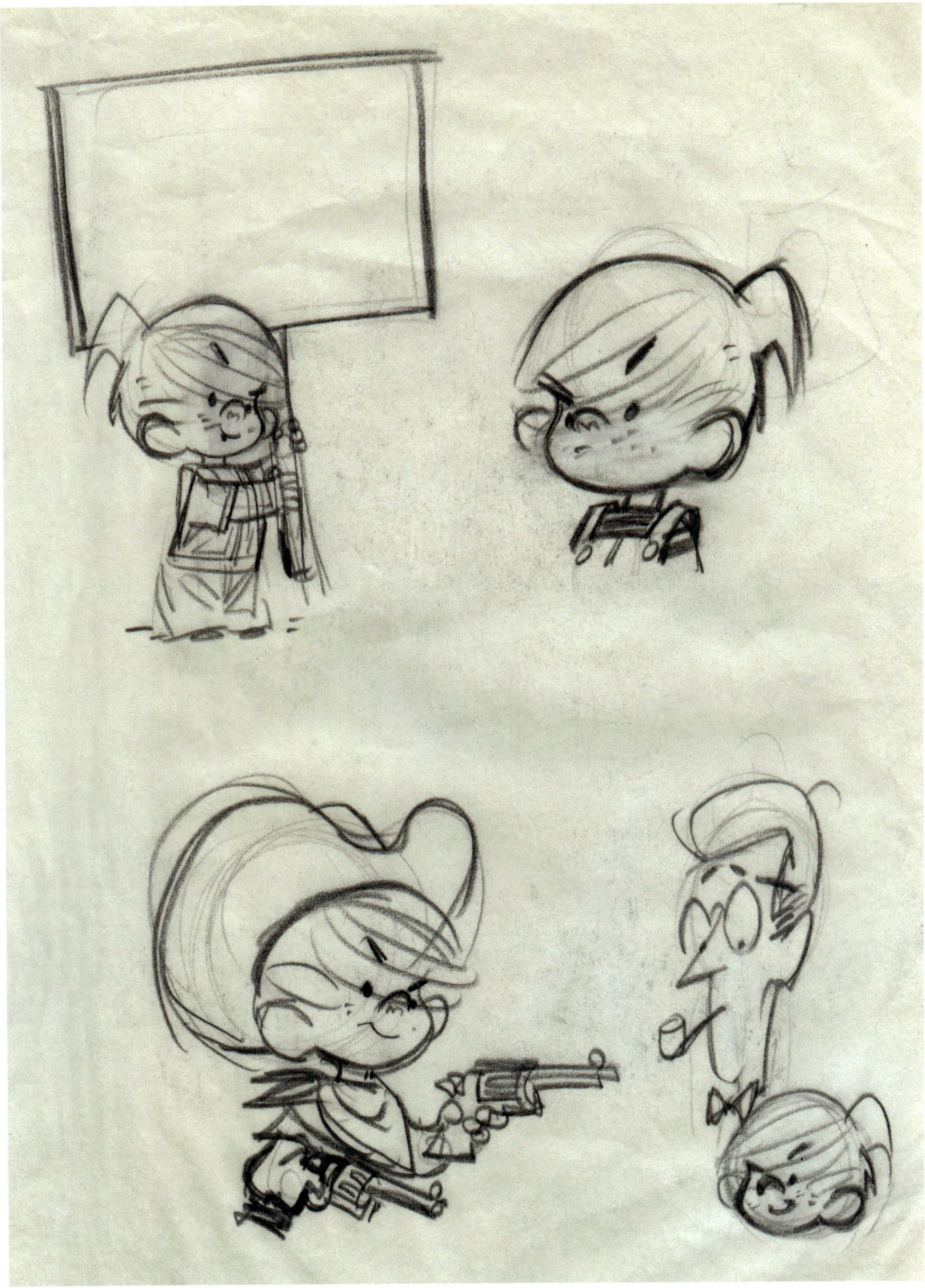

Above: Al Wiseman pencil rough for 1950s DENNIS THE MENACE mechandising.

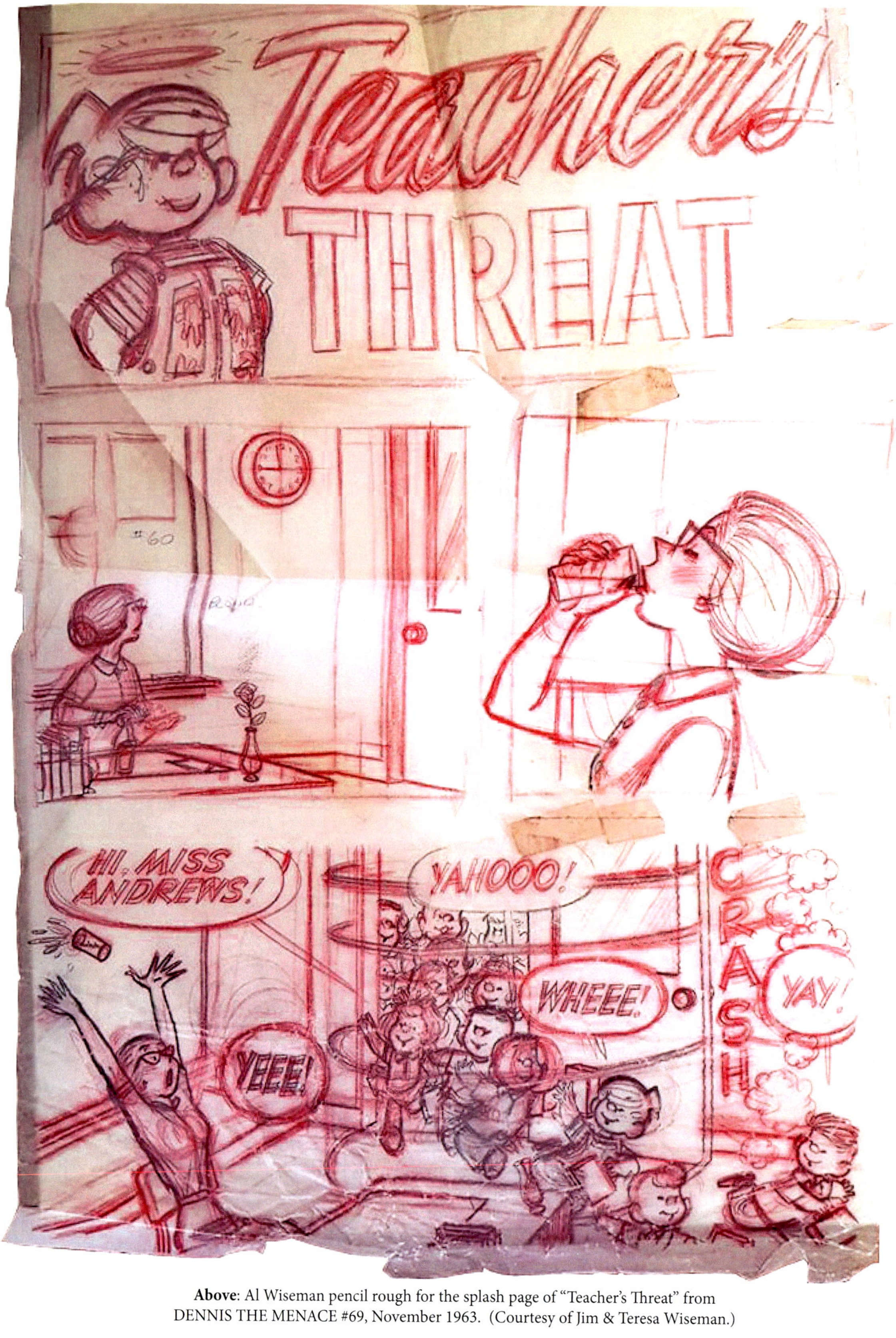
Teacher's
THREAT
HI, MISS ANDREWS!
YAHOOO!
CRASH
WHEEE!
YAY!
YEEE!

Above: Al Wiseman pencil rough for the splash page of "Teacher's Threat" from DENNIS THE MENACE #69, November 1963. (Courtesy of Jim & Teresa Wiseman.)

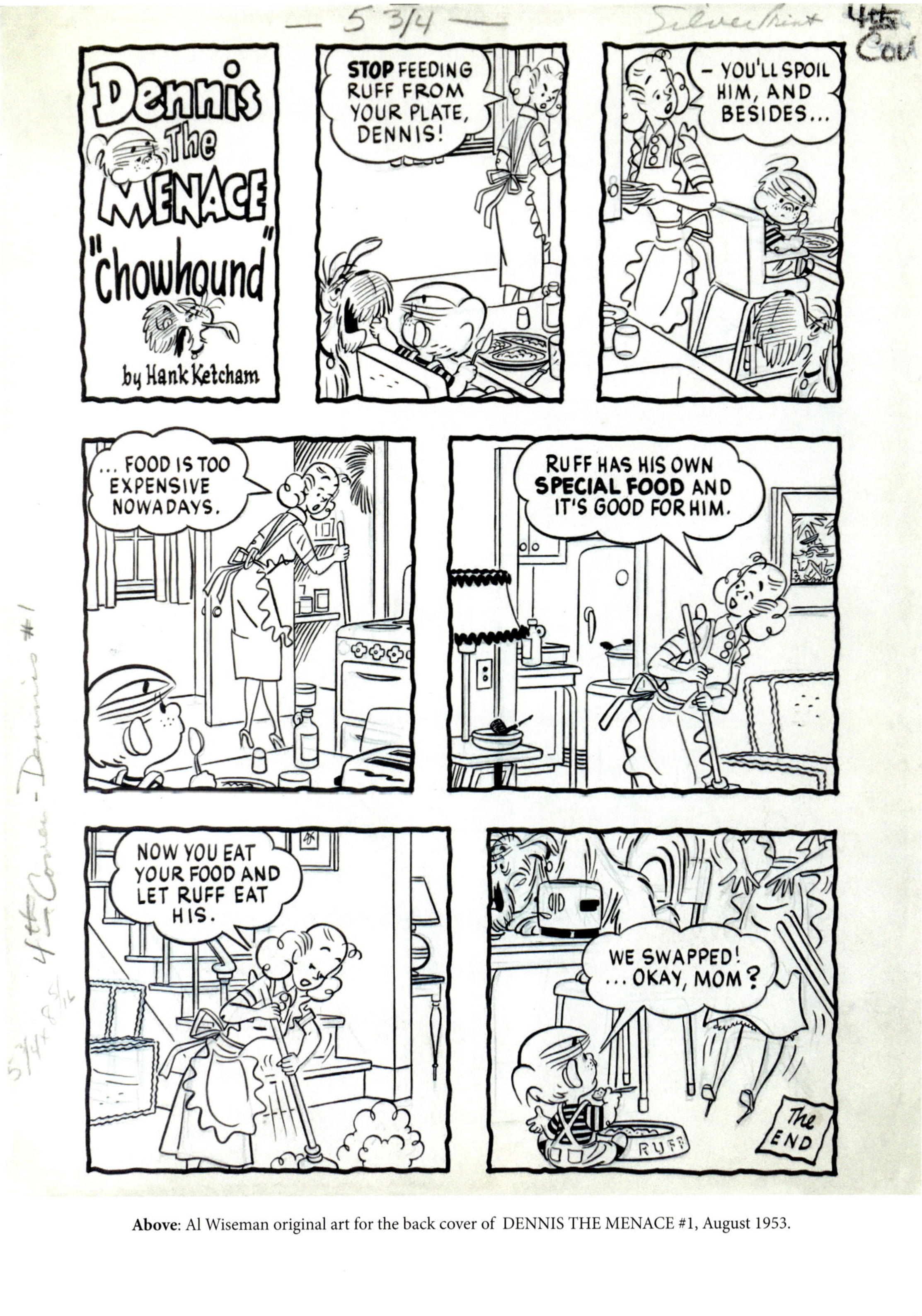
— 5 3/4 —
Silverprint
4th Cov
Dennis The MENACE
"Chowhound"
by Hank Ketcham
STOP FEEDING RUFF FROM YOUR PLATE, DENNIS!
– YOU'LL SPOIL HIM, AND BESIDES...
... FOOD IS TOO EXPENSIVE NOWADAYS.
RUFF HAS HIS OWN SPECIAL FOOD AND IT'S GOOD FOR HIM.
NOW YOU EAT YOUR FOOD AND LET RUFF EAT HIS.
WE SWAPPED! ... OKAY, MOM?
RUFF
The END

Above: Al Wiseman original art for the back cover of DENNIS THE MENACE #1, August 1953.

Above: Hand-painted color guide for the back cover of DENNIS THE MENACE #1, August 1953.

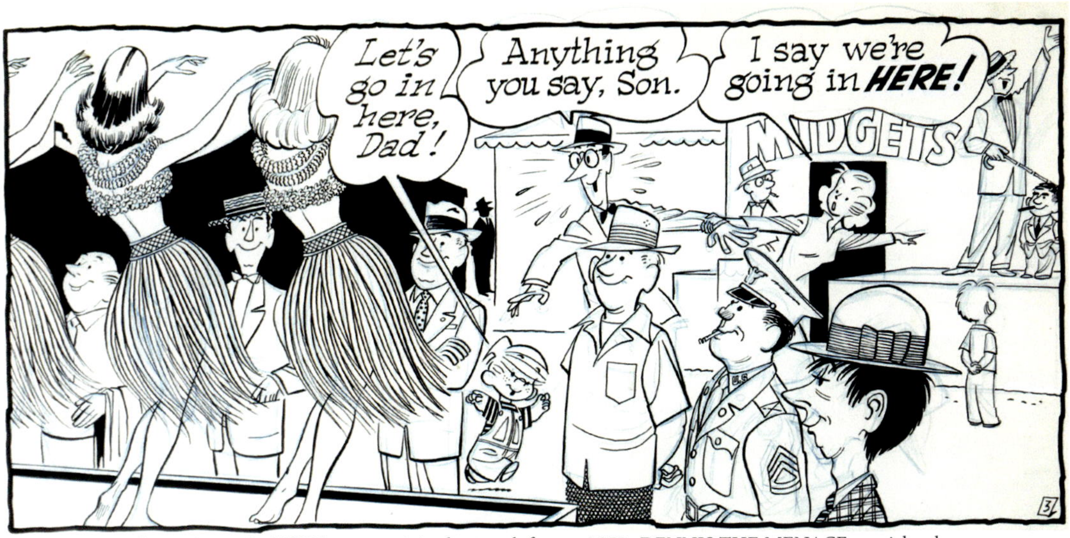
Let's go in here, Dad!
Anything you say, Son.
I say we're going in HERE!
MIDGETS
3

Above: A panel of Al Wiseman original artwork from a 1950s DENNIS THE MENACE comicbook.

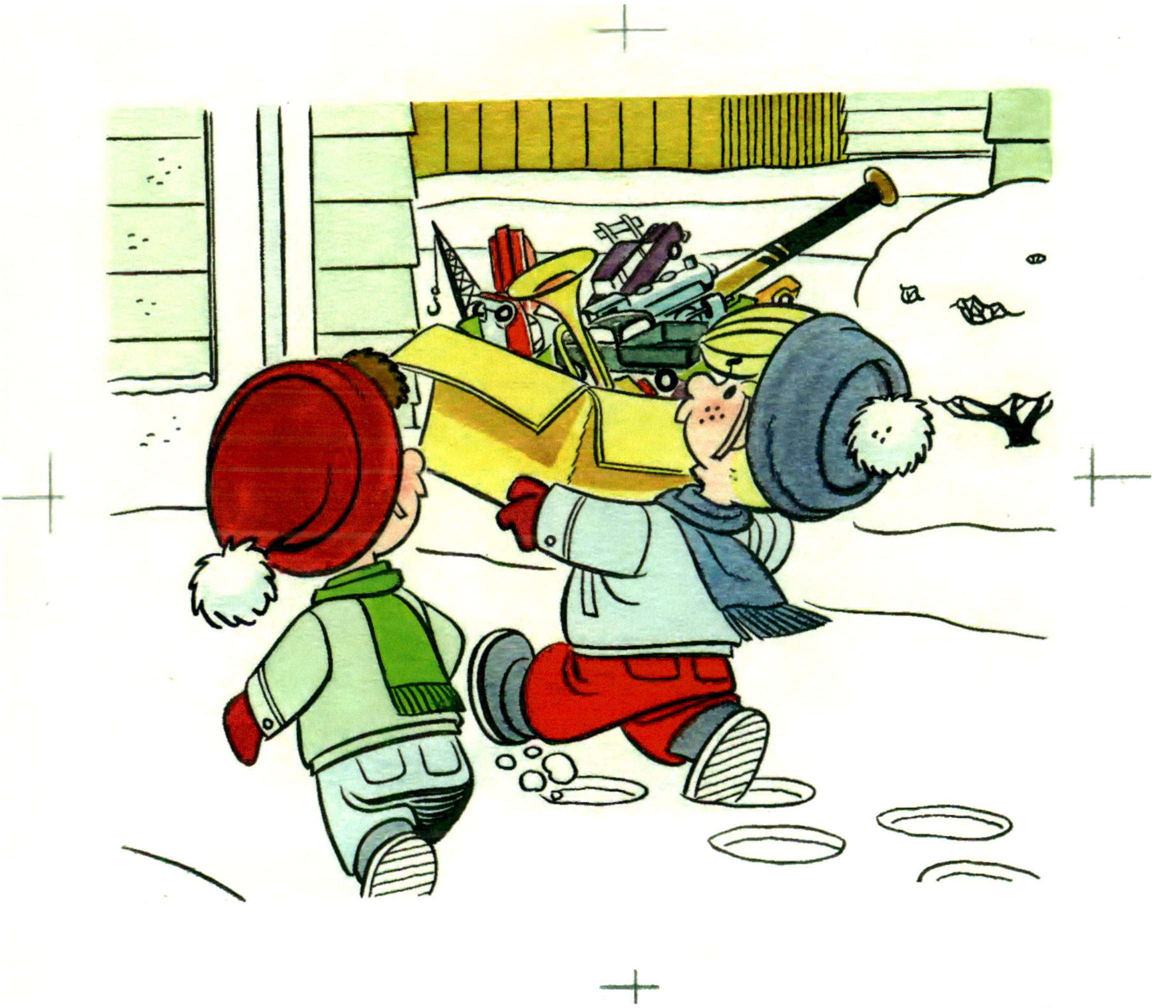

Above: Al Wiseman original artwork for the 1961 Little Golden Book "Dennis The Menace Waits For Santa Claus."
(Artwork courtesy of Scott Sheppard.)

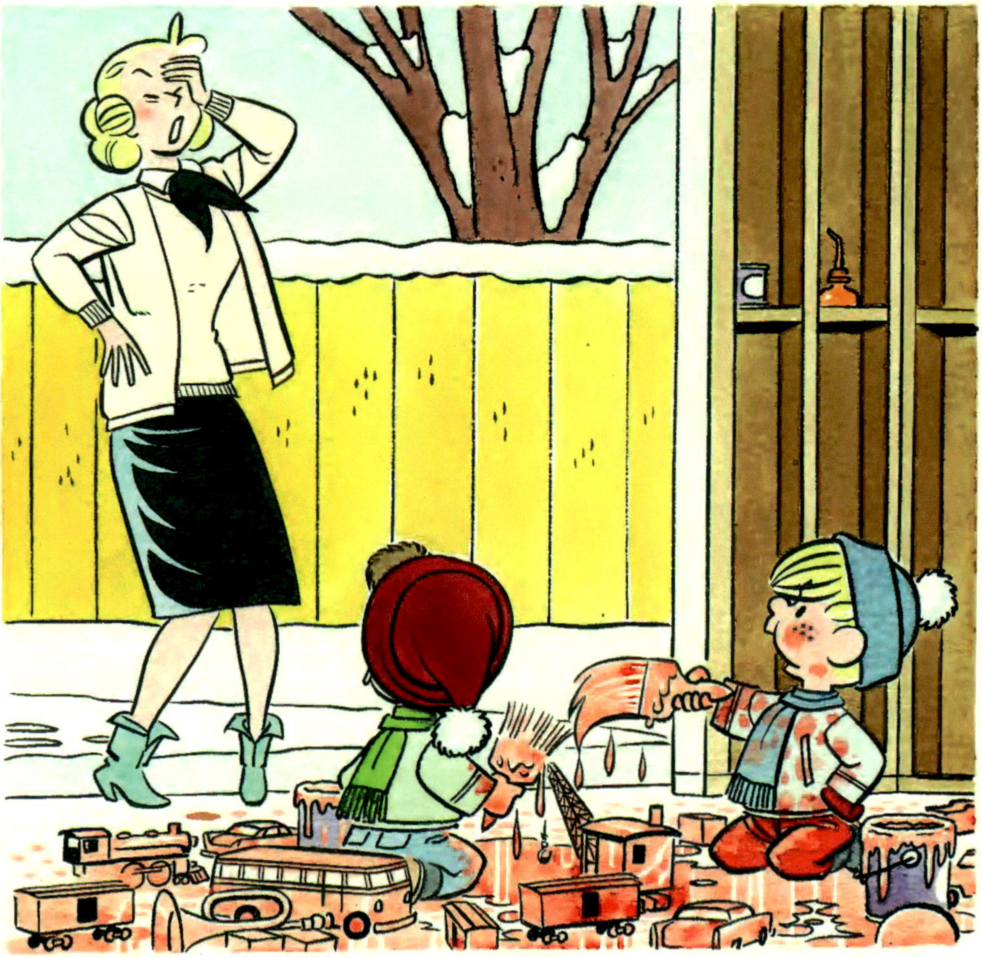

Above: Al Wiseman original artwork for the 1961 Little Golden Book "Dennis The Menace Waits For Santa Claus."
(Artwork courtesy of Scott Sheppard.)

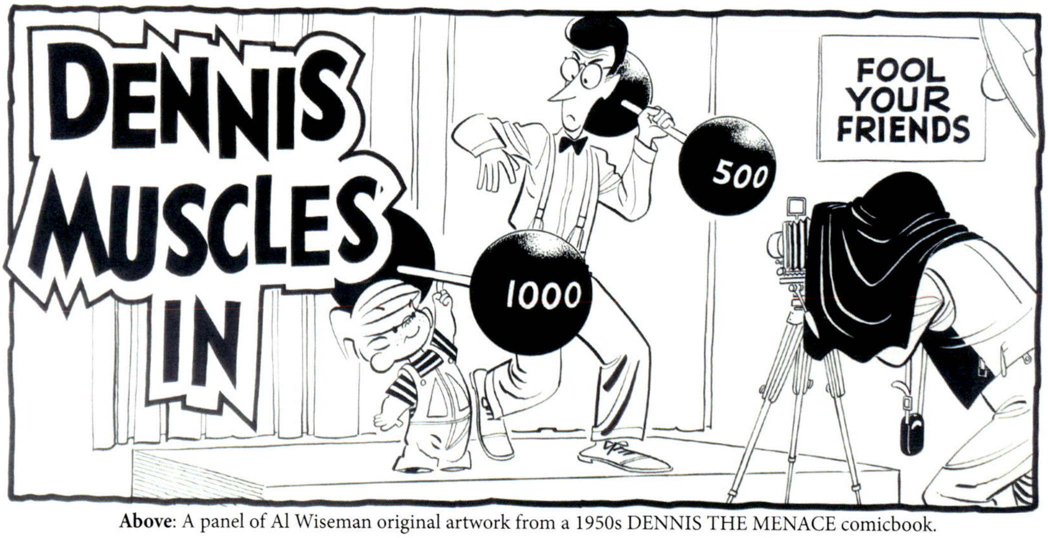

DENNIS MUSCLES IN
FOOL YOUR FRIENDS
500
1000

Above: A panel of Al Wiseman original artwork from a 1950s DENNIS THE MENACE comicbook.

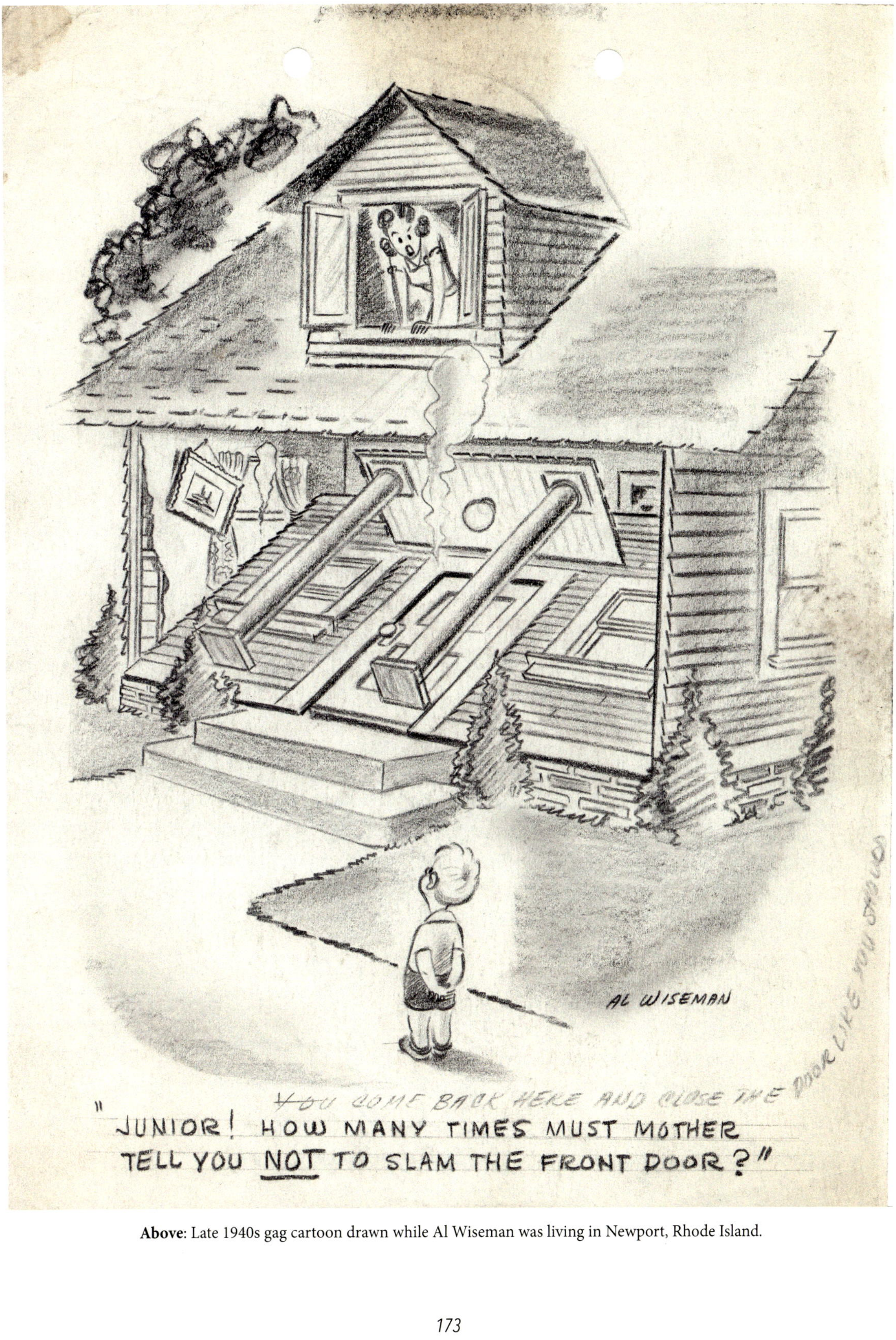
AL WISEMAN
"YOU COME BACK HERE AND CLOSE THE DOOR LIKE YOU SHOULD
"JUNIOR! HOW MANY TIMES MUST MOTHER TELL YOU NOT TO SLAM THE FRONT DOOR?"

Above: Late 1940s gag cartoon drawn while Al Wiseman was living in Newport, Rhode Island.

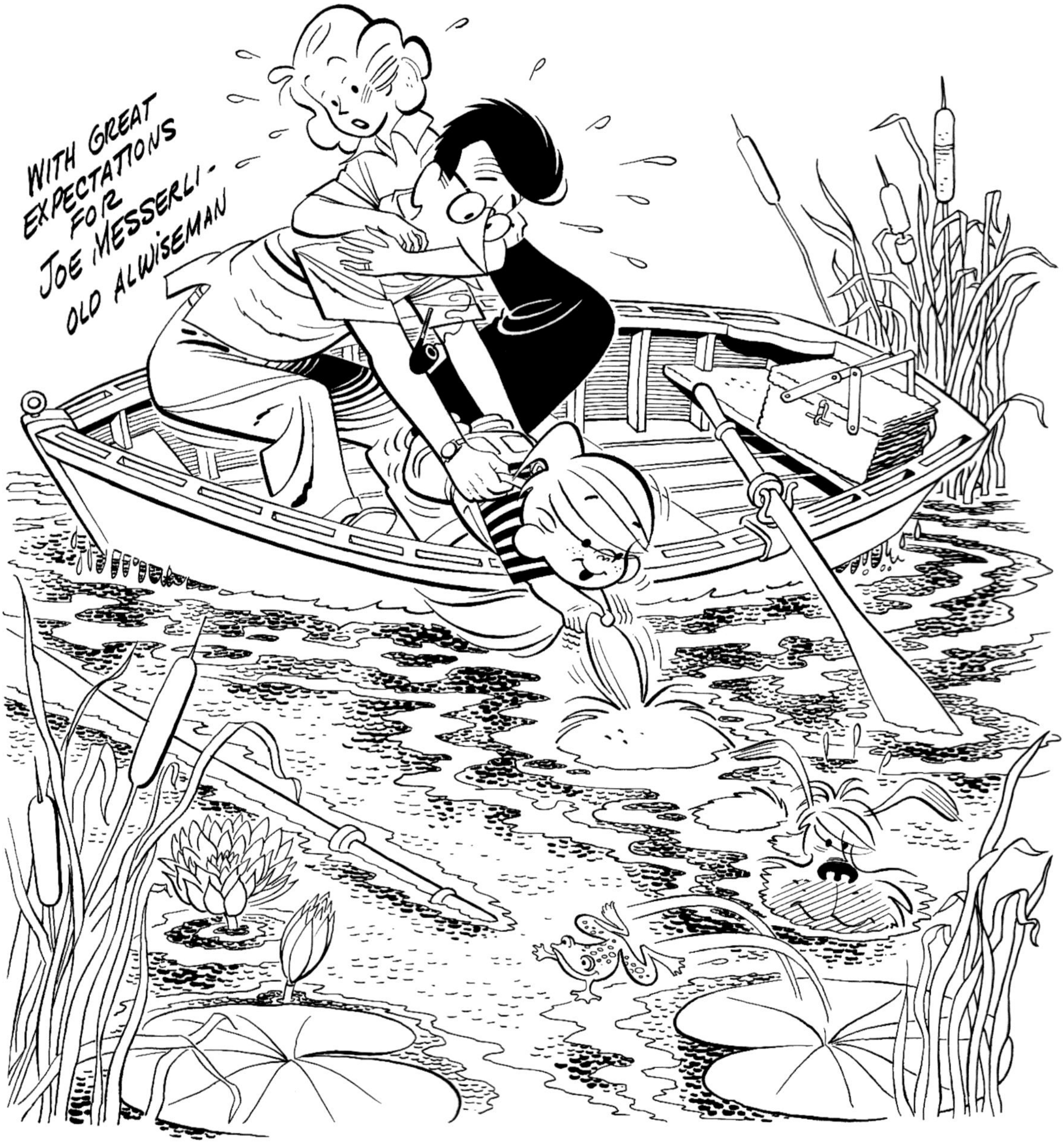
WITH GREAT EXPECTATIONS FOR JOE MESSERLI - OLD AL WISEMAN

Above: 1950s Al Wiseman original artwork for an unpublished DENNIS cover. Al's cartoonist friend Joe Messerli sent me (Editor Bill Alger) this scan in 2008. Joe wrote, "Got an HP scanner. Finally! Here's an original Al cover that was never used (powers-that-be decided on something else). Al asked if I wanted it and I said, 'Sure!'"

Interview: Frank Hill

In 1969, an updated version of DENNIS IN HAWAII appeared with new pages drawn by cartoonist Frank Hill. Greg Beda conducted this interview with Frank in 2017.

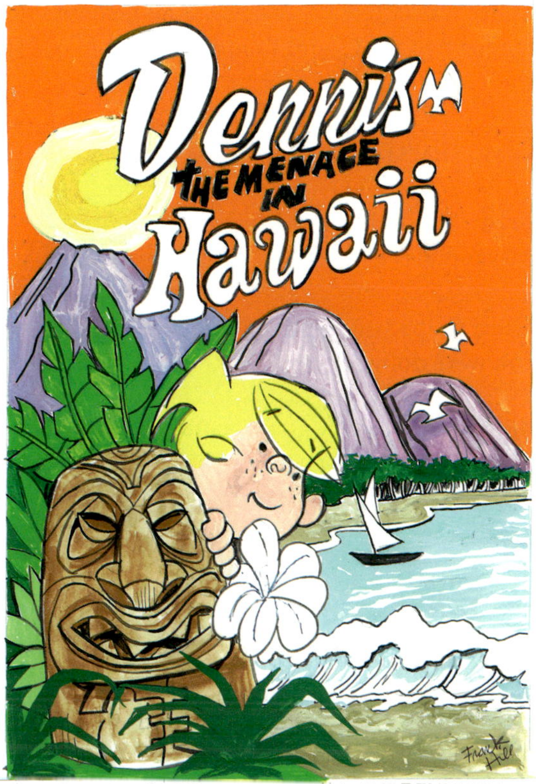
Dennis
THE MENACE
IN
Hawaii
Frank Hill

Above: Frank Hill's re-creation of his 1969 DENNIS IN HAWAII comicbook cover. (Courtesy of Greg Beda.)

Greg: Did you go to Hawaii to do these stories?

Frank: No, I didn't. Fred Toole always gave me lots of reference material, whether I was there or not. He would give me yards of stuff. Photographs, a lot of 8 by 10 photographs, and local folders and promotional stuff. I had lots of reference material and I understood Hawaii. I just followed his script, and if I couldn't remember, I would look at reference material. We [Fred Toole and Frank Hill] went to both London and Paris and we stayed at the King V Hotel, which was the headquarters for the Nazis when they were there. A beautiful hotel. I don't know how much a night it cost, but Hank popped for it. It was elegant, along the *Champs-Elysées*. It was for both [travel books]: we spent a week in London and a week in Paris.

Greg: Was that on the same trip?

Frank: Yes. London first and then Paris.

Greg: When you were drawing these stories, was it difficult to meet the deadlines?

Frank: Well, that's when Carol and I were first married. We were living in Aptos. I was doing as many as six pages in a day.

Greg: Penciling, inking, and lettering.

Frank: (Laughs) And guess what we got paid? We got paid 35 dollars a page for pencil, ink, and letter. I could do six pages... I was drinking lots of Coke back then because Coke had caffeine and sugar. I learned that from Al. Al Wiseman was the best draftsman that I ever knew. My pencils had to go back to Zurich for approval. I used to keep an elaborate scrap pile. I had three cabinets full. I had somebody helping me, getting magazines and all that stuff. I'm sure that I had a file folder that thick full of Hawaii, and Fred provided some more. And I'd been there and I had pictures I'd kept. Hank was a stern taskmaster. I had to send my roughs to Switzerland and when they came back before I opened it I would look and see the Swiss postage stamp which says Helvetia. And to this day when I see a Helvetia stamp I break out in a sweat. He'd say "I'd get this back to you sooner, but I couldn't find a toilet paper roll the right size."

Greg: You would send him the roughs of the stories? These were on tissue.

Frank: Yeah, on tissue. And then they'd come

back and I'd put them on 2 ply on a light table and ink them.

Greg: Earlier you were saying you could do six pages a day — penciling, inking, and lettering — but wouldn't the pencils already be done at a previous time?

Frank: You're right, you're absolutely right. I'd already done the pencils. I'd do ink and lettering, six in a day.

Greg: You've done a lot of material in your life. What would you like to be most remembered for? Is it DENNIS THE MENACE? Is it *Short Ribs*? Is it something else?

Frank: Through my involvement with Frank O'Neil [ghosting *Short Ribs*], bit by bit I was doing more of it while his name was still on it. He had his alcohol problem that just tore him up. The last eight years [of *Short Ribs* were signed Frank Hill], I go back and look at those pages [strips] and I think they're still funny. But somebody didn't obviously. At one time, there were almost 600 clients.

Greg: You had said that Hank Ketcham had made you a better artist. What did you learn from Hank Ketcham?

Frank: I learned from Hank Ketcham discipline. And — I remember drawing a fire plug on a corner where Dennis is walking by and he just read me the riot act. It was lunch time and he and Ron Ferdinand and I were out and I had a sketchpad. I took a sketch of a fire plug in Monterey and I went back and did it and it was pretty good. Hank didn't even look at it and said "Don't try to tell me you're doing another screwed up, poorly drawn fire plug?" and Ron said "Look at it, Hank." And he looked at it and said "I'll be damned." [Frank laughs] Anytime I ever got a positive, the word he'd always use was it's "cute." If it was cute, that was OK, but other adjectives were pretty fiery.

Greg: He had a high standard. He wanted you to rise above.

Frank: Yeah. And he was generous in many ways. When we had the earthquake here, this house was in terrible disarray, and he paid me for two weeks and I didn't have to go over there.

Greg: That's really good. When was that?

Fred: '89. That's when I was going to Monterey.

Greg: In '89 you weren't doing comicbooks, you were doing other things.

Frank: We were doing his daily and Sundays.

Greg: You helped on the dailies and Sundays in '89?

Frank: Yes. Not on the dailies, just the Sundays.

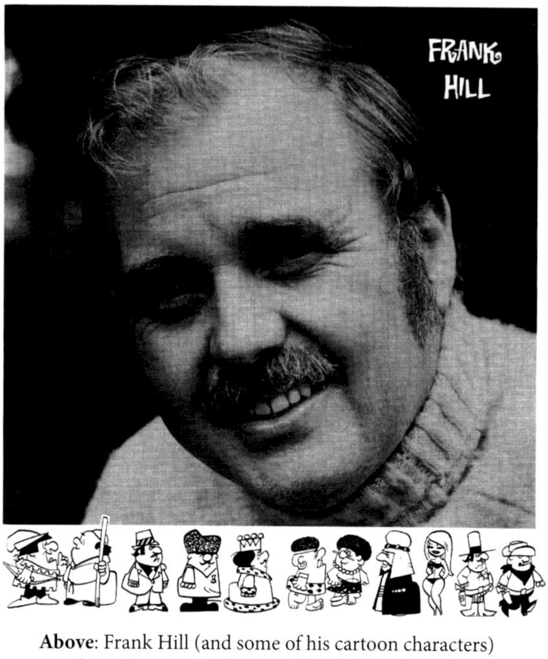
FRANK HILL

Above: Frank Hill (and some of his cartoon characters) from the cover of CARTOONEWS #12 (1976).

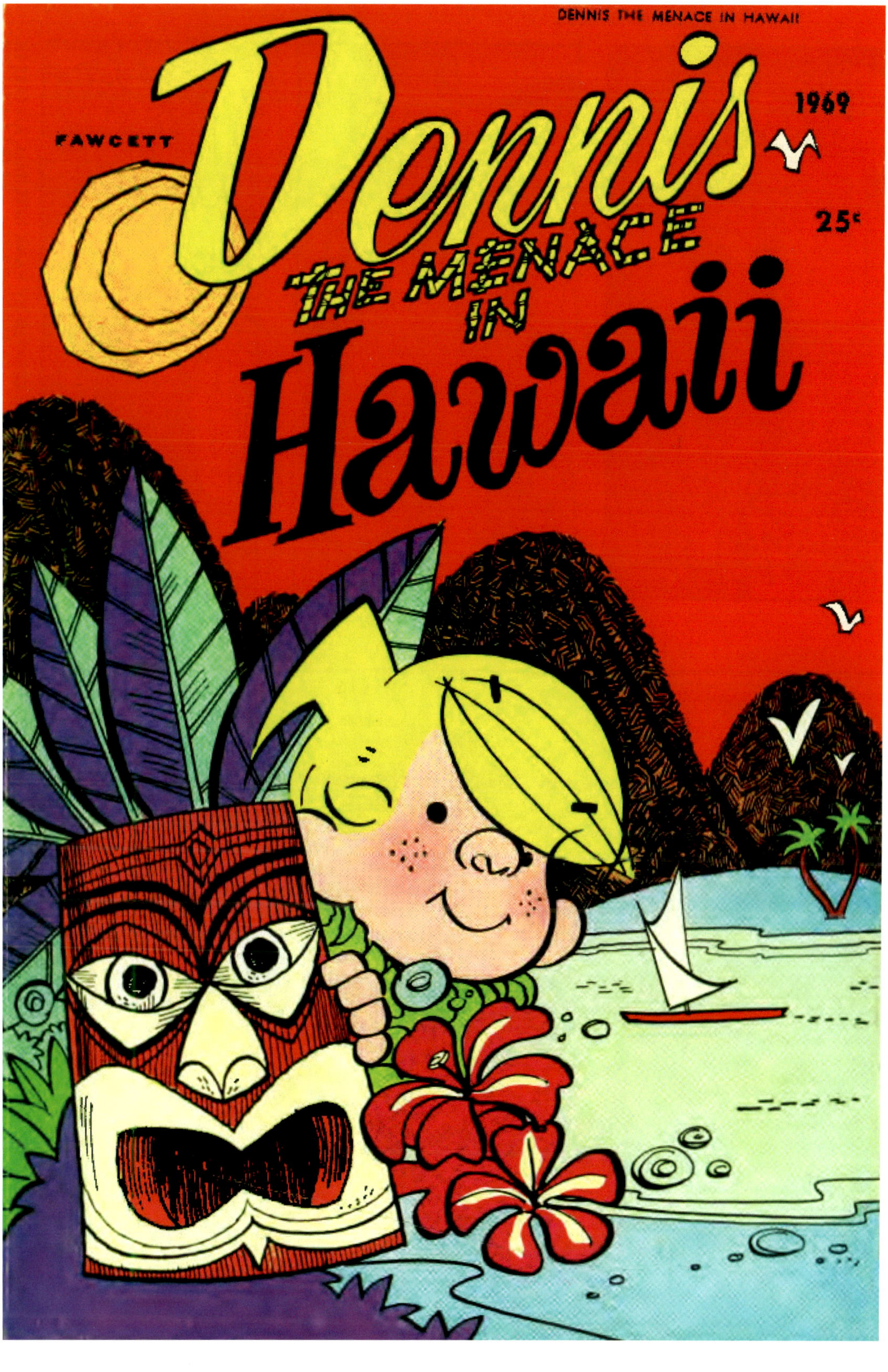
DENNIS THE MENACE IN HAWAII
FAWCETT
Dennis
THE MENACE
IN
Hawaii
1969
25¢

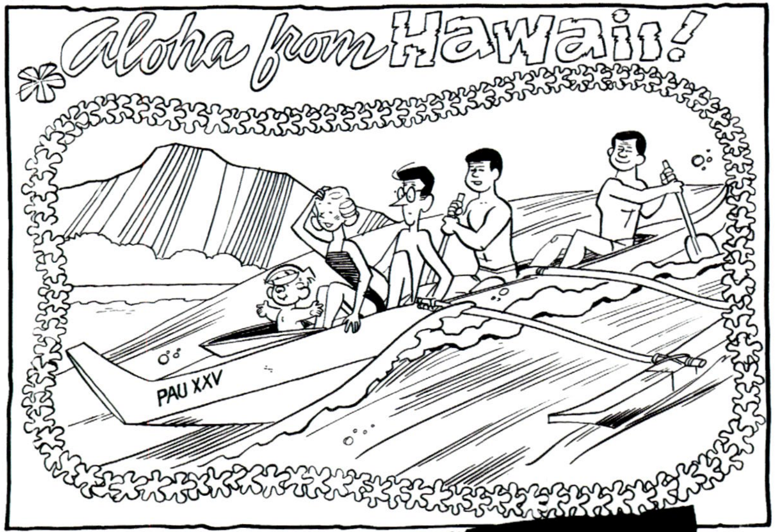
Aloha from Hawaii!
PAU XXV

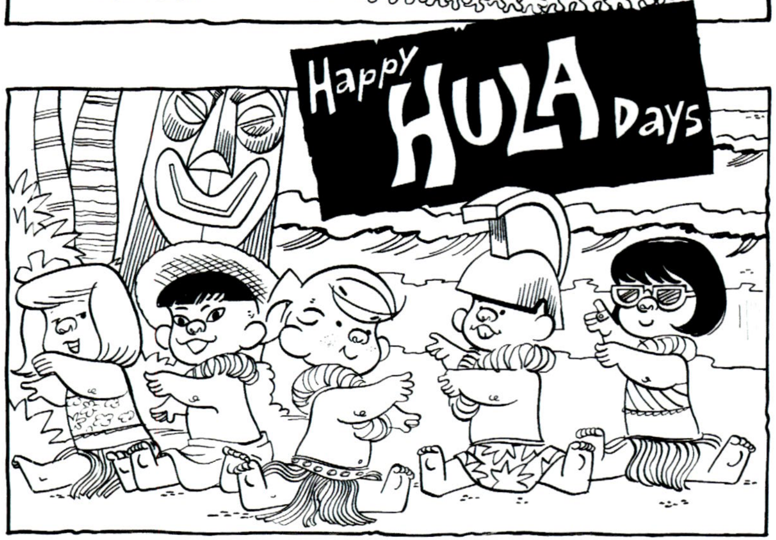
Happy HULA Days

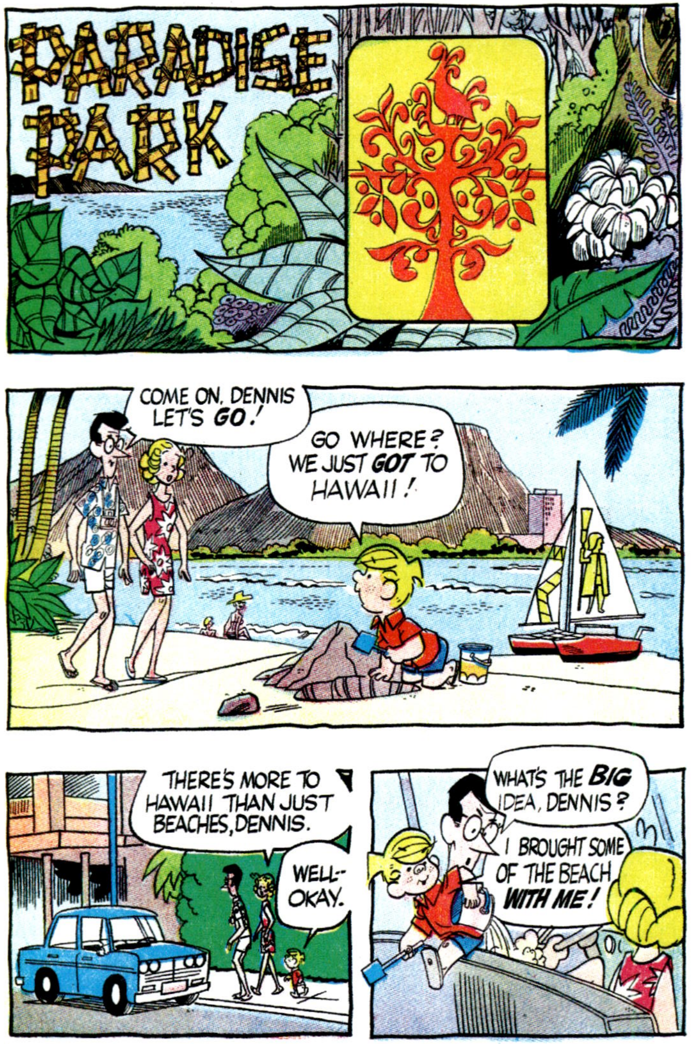
PARADISE PARK
COME ON, DENNIS LET'S GO!
GO WHERE? WE JUST GOT TO HAWAII!
THERE'S MORE TO HAWAII THAN JUST BEACHES, DENNIS.
WELL-OKAY.
WHAT'S THE BIG IDEA, DENNIS?
I BROUGHT SOME OF THE BEACH WITH ME!

"DENNIS THE MENACE", CREATED BY HANK KETCHAM, APPEARS IN OVER 700 NEWSPAPERS . . . IN 43 COUNTRIES . . . IN 14 LANGUAGES!

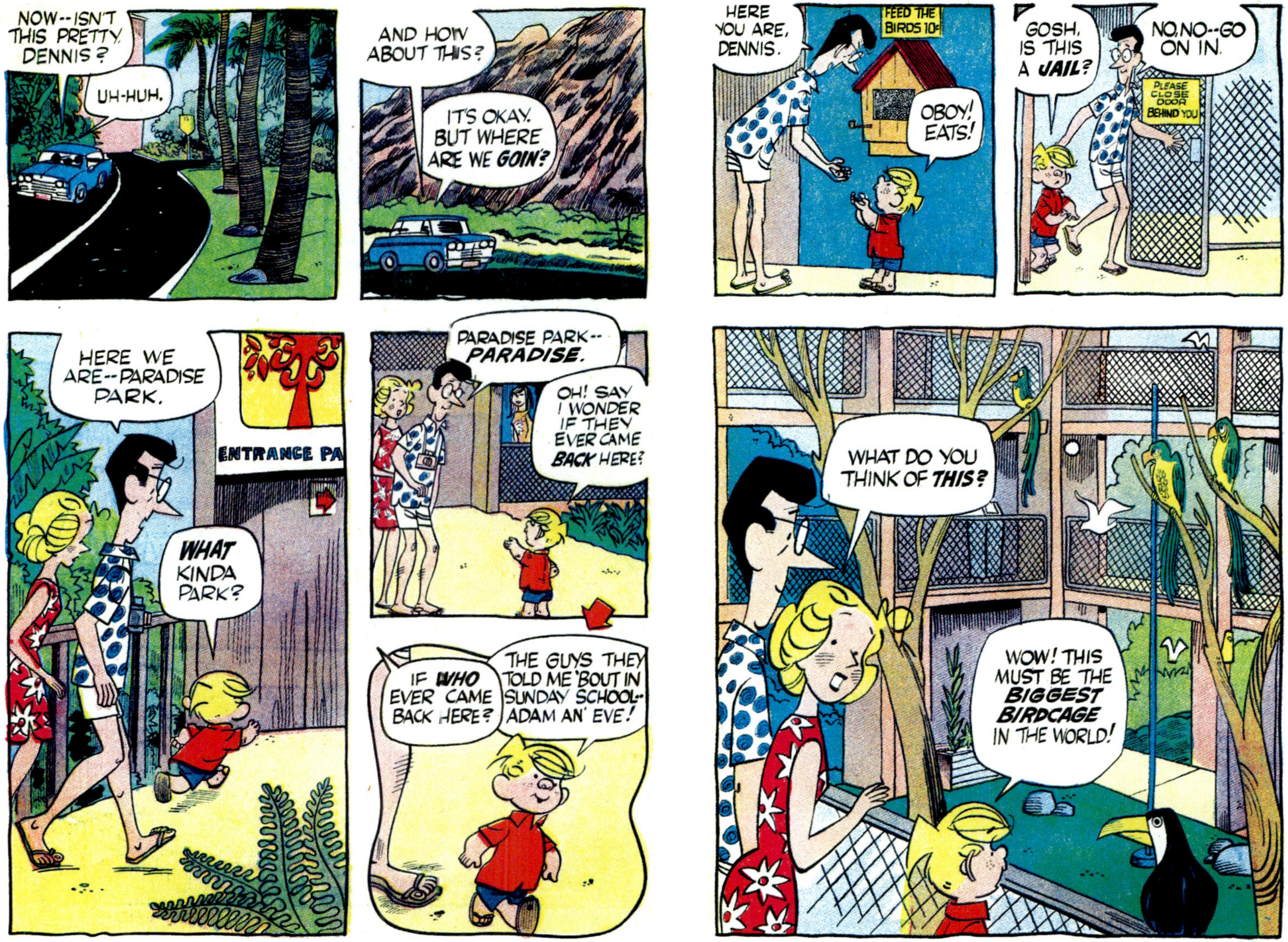

NOW--ISN'T THIS PRETTY, DENNIS?
UH-HUH.
AND HOW ABOUT THIS?
IT'S OKAY. BUT WHERE ARE WE GOIN'?
HERE WE ARE--PARADISE PARK.
ENTRANCE PA
WHAT KINDA PARK?
PARADISE PARK--PARADISE.
OH! SAY I WONDER IF THEY EVER CAME BACK HERE?
IF WHO EVER CAME BACK HERE?
THE GUYS THEY TOLD ME 'BOUT IN SUNDAY SCHOOL--ADAM AN' EVE!
HERE YOU ARE, DENNIS.
FEED THE BIRDS 10¢
OBOY! EATS!
GOSH, IS THIS A JAIL?
NO, NO--GO ON IN.
PLEASE CLOSE DOOR BEHIND YOU
WHAT DO YOU THINK OF THIS?
WOW! THIS MUST BE THE BIGGEST BIRDCAGE IN THE WORLD!

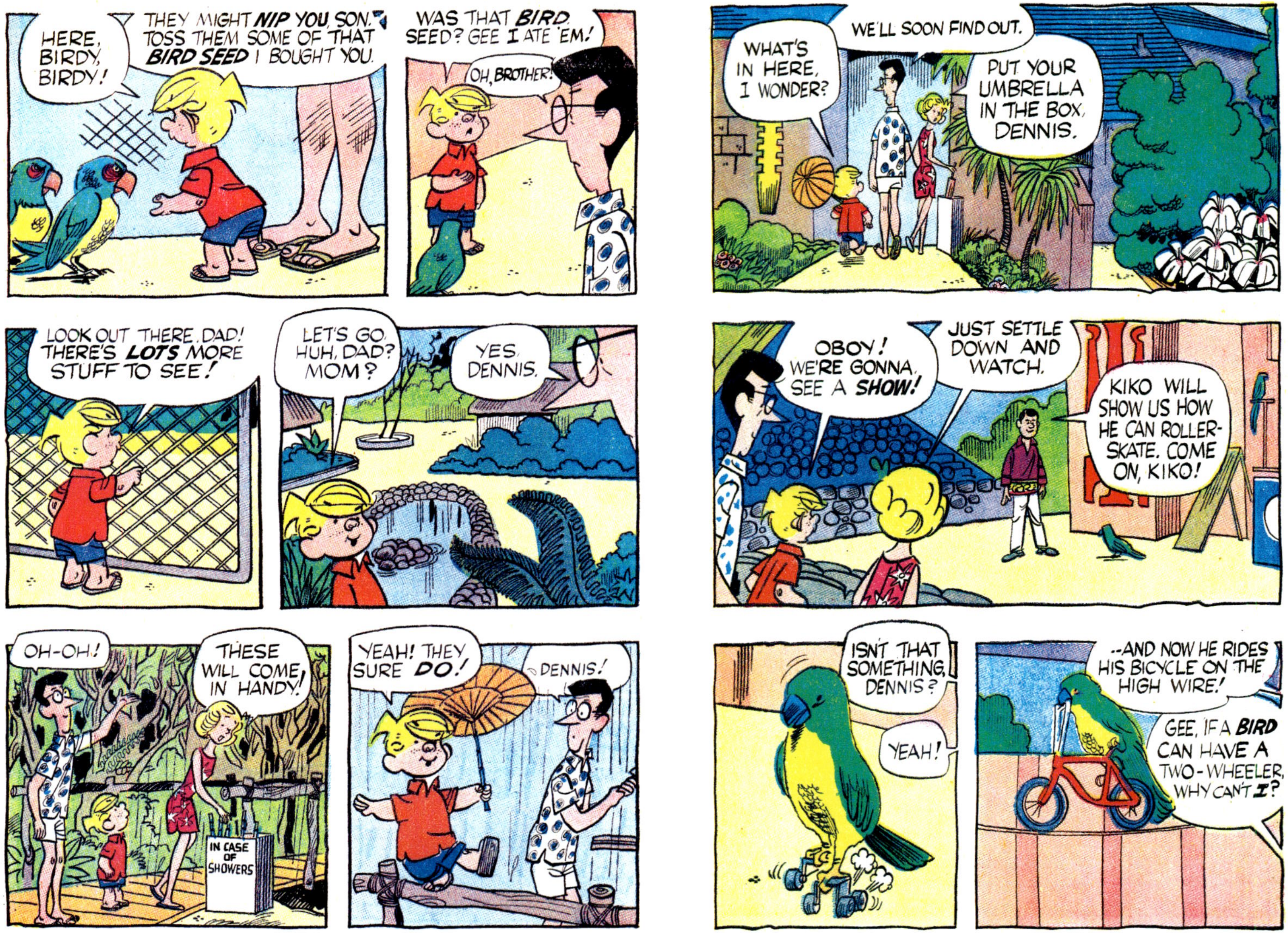
HERE, BIRDY, BIRDY!
THEY MIGHT **NIP YOU**, SON. TOSS THEM SOME OF THAT **BIRD SEED** I BOUGHT YOU.
WAS THAT **BIRD** SEED? GEE **I** ATE 'EM!
OH, BROTHER!
LOOK OUT THERE, DAD! THERE'S **LOTS** MORE STUFF TO SEE!
LET'S GO, HUH, DAD? MOM?
YES, DENNIS.
OH-OH!
THESE WILL COME IN HANDY!
IN CASE OF SHOWERS
YEAH! THEY SURE **DO**!
DENNIS!
WHAT'S IN HERE, I WONDER?
WE'LL SOON FIND OUT.
PUT YOUR UMBRELLA IN THE BOX, DENNIS.
OBOY! WE'RE GONNA SEE A **SHOW**!
JUST SETTLE DOWN AND WATCH.
KIKO WILL SHOW US HOW HE CAN ROLLER-SKATE. COME ON, KIKO!
ISN'T THAT SOMETHING, DENNIS?
YEAH!
--AND NOW HE RIDES HIS BICYCLE ON THE HIGH WIRE!
GEE, IF A **BIRD** CAN HAVE A TWO-WHEELER, WHY CAN'T **I**?

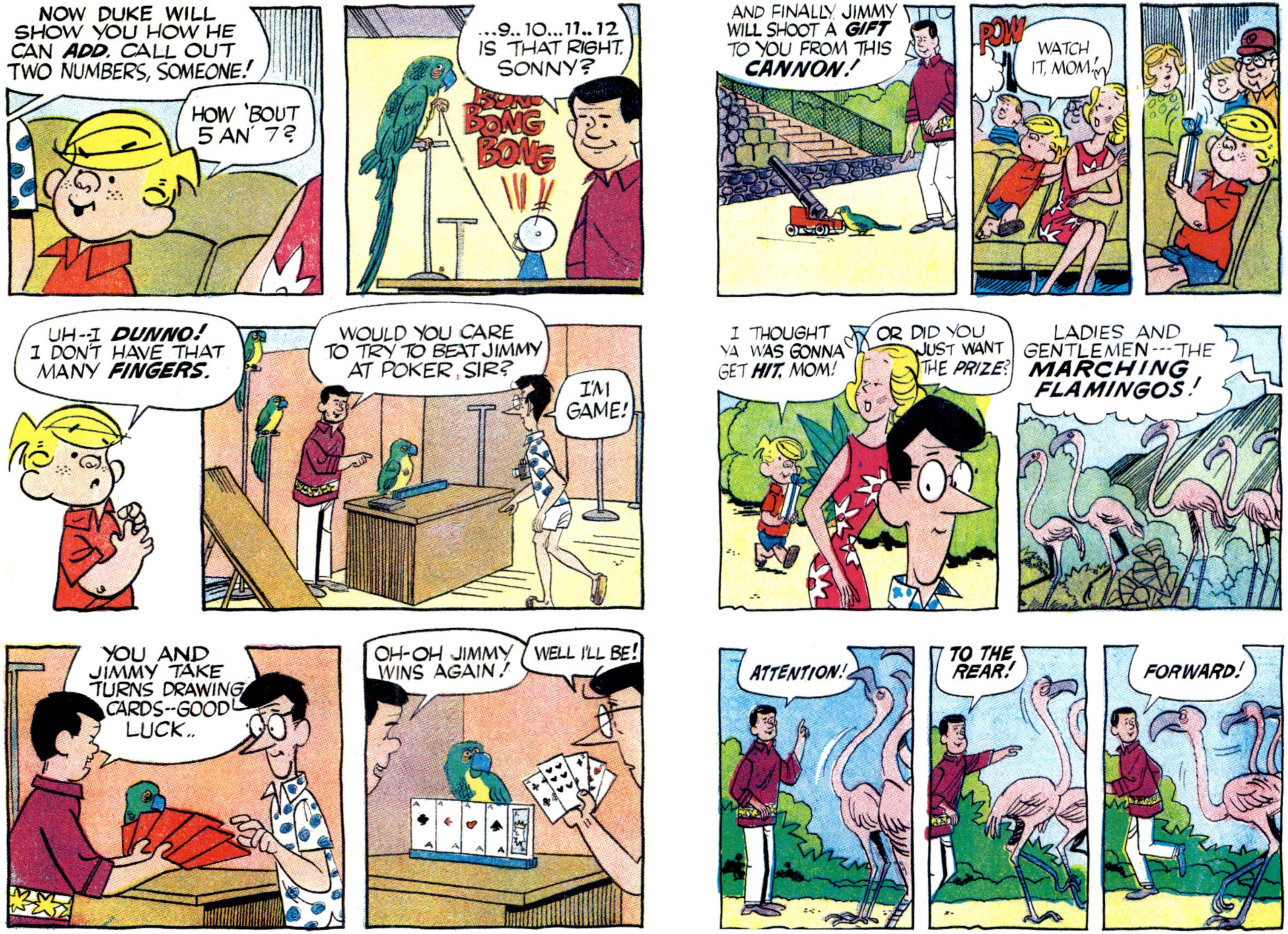

NOW DUKE WILL SHOW YOU HOW HE CAN ***ADD***. CALL OUT TWO NUMBERS, SOMEONE!
HOW 'BOUT 5 AN' 7?
...9..10...11..12 IS THAT RIGHT, SONNY?
BONG BONG
UH--I ***DUNNO!*** I DON'T HAVE THAT MANY ***FINGERS.***
WOULD YOU CARE TO TRY TO BEAT JIMMY AT POKER, SIR?
I'M GAME!
YOU AND JIMMY TAKE TURNS DRAWING CARDS--GOOD LUCK..
OH-OH JIMMY WINS AGAIN!
WELL I'LL BE!
AND FINALLY, JIMMY WILL SHOOT A ***GIFT*** TO YOU FROM THIS ***CANNON!***
POW
WATCH IT, MOM!
I THOUGHT YA WAS GONNA GET ***HIT,*** MOM!
OR DID YOU JUST WANT THE ***PRIZE?***
LADIES AND GENTLEMEN---THE ***MARCHING FLAMINGOS!***
ATTENTION!
TO THE REAR!
FORWARD!

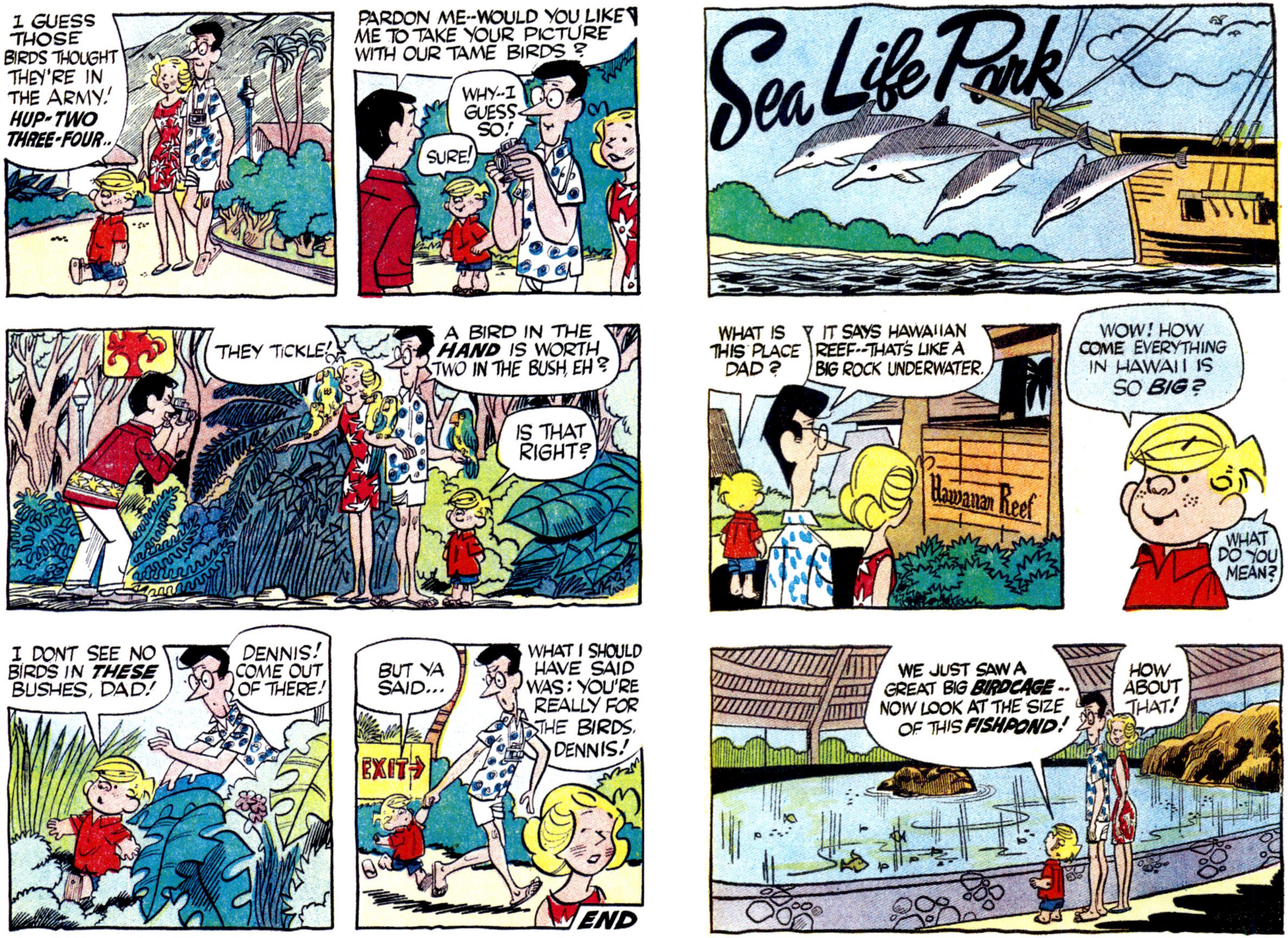

I GUESS THOSE BIRDS THOUGHT THEY'RE IN THE ARMY! HUP-TWO THREE-FOUR..
PARDON ME--WOULD YOU LIKE ME TO TAKE YOUR PICTURE WITH OUR TAME BIRDS?
WHY--I GUESS SO!
SURE!
THEY TICKLE!
A BIRD IN THE HAND IS WORTH TWO IN THE BUSH, EH?
IS THAT RIGHT?
I DONT SEE NO BIRDS IN THESE BUSHES, DAD!
DENNIS! COME OUT OF THERE!
BUT YA SAID...
WHAT I SHOULD HAVE SAID WAS: YOU'RE REALLY FOR THE BIRDS, DENNIS!
EXIT
END
Sea Life Park
WHAT IS THIS PLACE DAD?
IT SAYS HAWAIIAN REEF--THAT'S LIKE A BIG ROCK UNDERWATER.
Hawaiian Reef
WOW! HOW COME EVERYTHING IN HAWAII IS SO BIG?
WHAT DO YOU MEAN?
WE JUST SAW A GREAT BIG BIRDCAGE -- NOW LOOK AT THE SIZE OF THIS FISHPOND!
HOW ABOUT THAT!

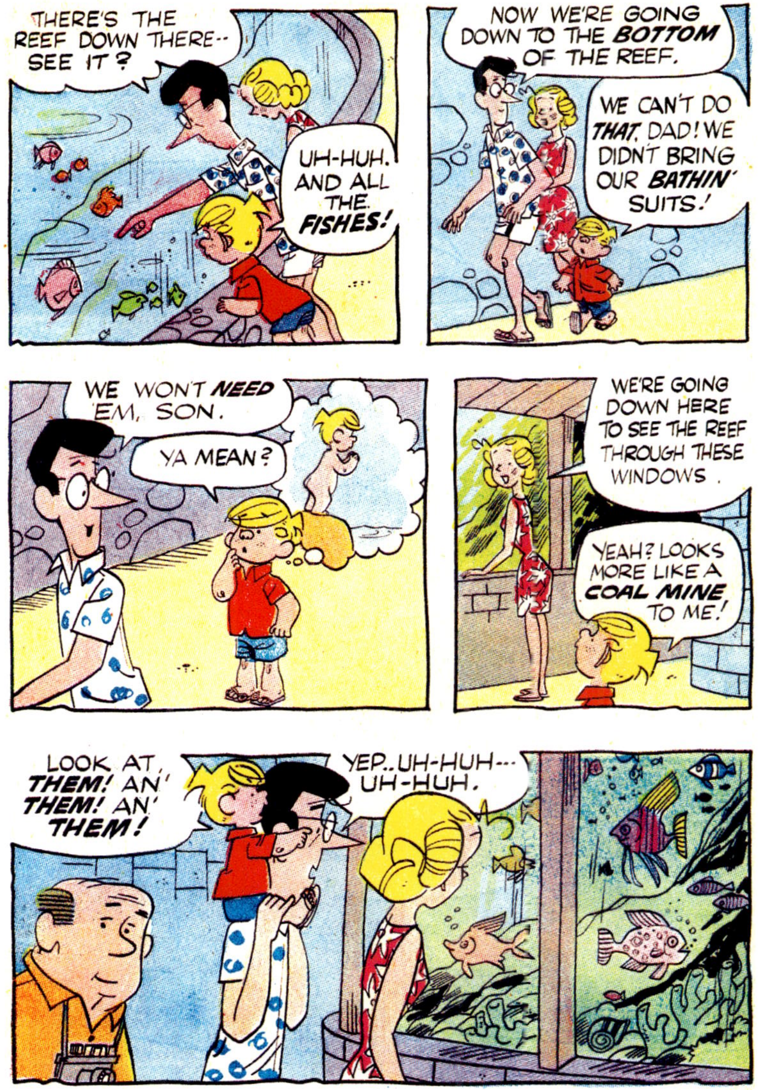
THERE'S THE REEF DOWN THERE-- SEE IT?
UH-HUH. AND ALL THE FISHES!
NOW WE'RE GOING DOWN TO THE **BOTTOM** OF THE REEF.
WE CAN'T DO **THAT**, DAD! WE DIDN'T BRING OUR **BATHIN'** SUITS!
WE WON'T **NEED** 'EM, SON.
YA MEAN?
WE'RE GOING DOWN HERE TO SEE THE REEF THROUGH THESE WINDOWS.
YEAH? LOOKS MORE LIKE A **COAL MINE** TO ME!
LOOK AT **THEM!** AN' **THEM!** AN' **THEM!**
YEP..UH-HUH--- UH-HUH.

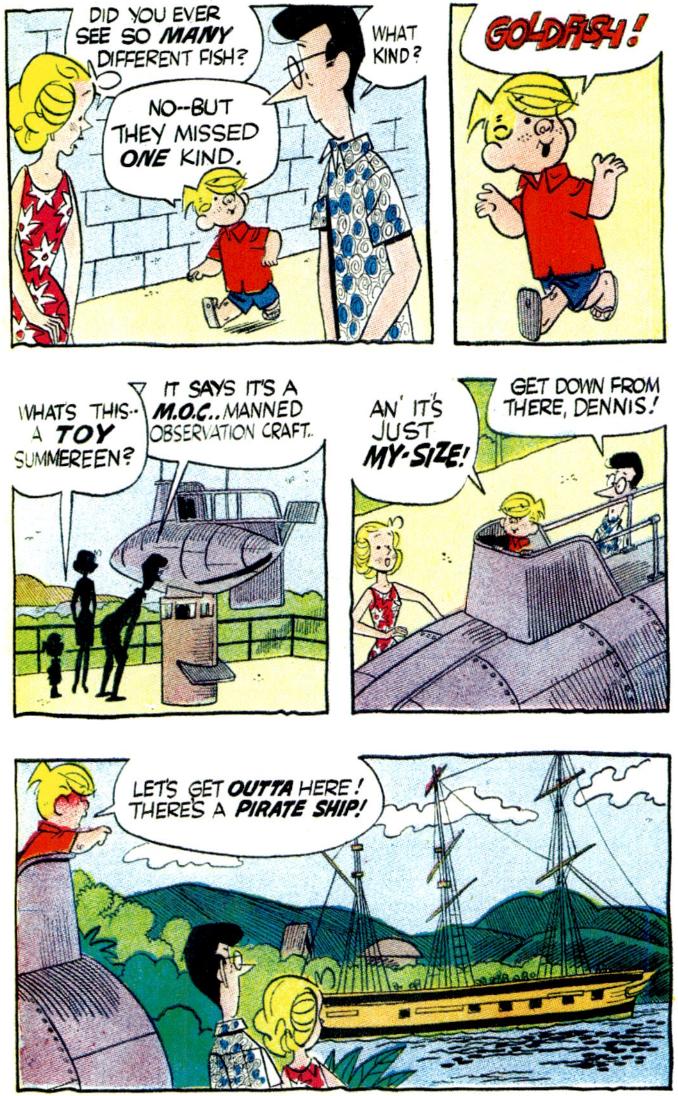
DID YOU EVER SEE SO **MANY** DIFFERENT FISH?
NO--BUT THEY MISSED **ONE** KIND.
WHAT KIND?
GOLDFISH!
WHAT'S THIS-- A **TOY** SUMMEREEN?
IT SAYS IT'S A **M.O.C.**.. MANNED OBSERVATION CRAFT..
AN' IT'S JUST **MY-SIZE!**
GET DOWN FROM THERE, DENNIS!
LET'S GET **OUTTA** HERE! THERE'S A **PIRATE SHIP!**

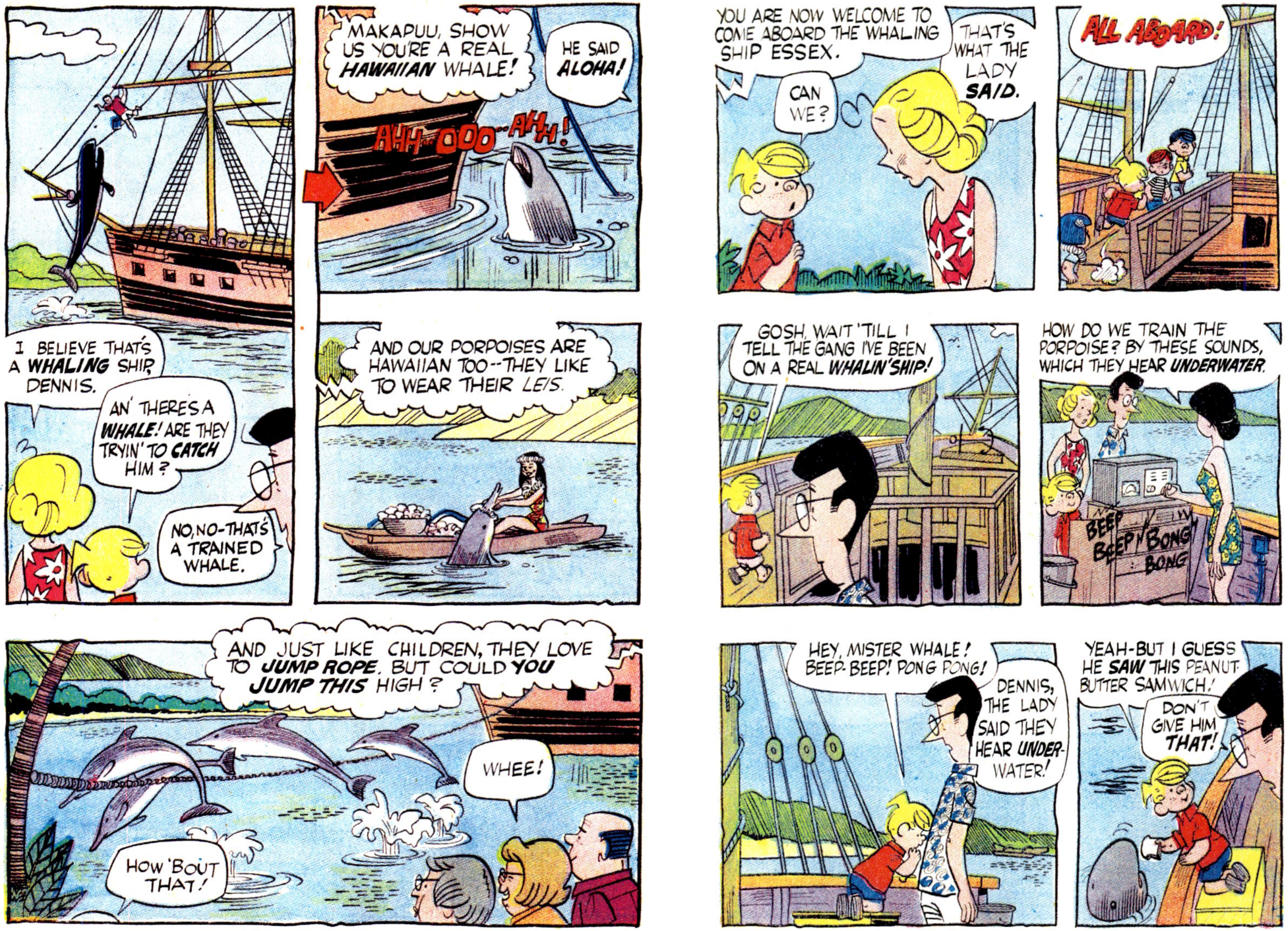
I BELIEVE THAT'S A WHALING SHIP, DENNIS.
AN' THERE'S A WHALE! ARE THEY TRYIN' TO CATCH HIM?
NO, NO-THAT'S A TRAINED WHALE.
MAKAPUU, SHOW US YOU'RE A REAL HAWAIIAN WHALE!
AHH-OOO-AHH!
HE SAID ALOHA!
AND OUR PORPOISES ARE HAWAIIAN TOO--THEY LIKE TO WEAR THEIR LEIS.
AND JUST LIKE CHILDREN, THEY LOVE TO JUMP ROPE. BUT COULD YOU JUMP THIS HIGH?
WHEE!
HOW 'BOUT THAT!
YOU ARE NOW WELCOME TO COME ABOARD THE WHALING SHIP ESSEX.
CAN WE?
THAT'S WHAT THE LADY SAID.
ALL ABOARD!
GOSH, WAIT 'TILL I TELL THE GANG I'VE BEEN ON A REAL WHALIN' SHIP!
HOW DO WE TRAIN THE PORPOISE? BY THESE SOUNDS, WHICH THEY HEAR UNDERWATER.
BEEP BEEP BONG BONG
HEY, MISTER WHALE! BEEP-BEEP! PONG PONG!
DENNIS, THE LADY SAID THEY HEAR UNDER-WATER!
YEAH-BUT I GUESS HE SAW THIS PEANUT-BUTTER SAMWICH!
DON'T GIVE HIM THAT!

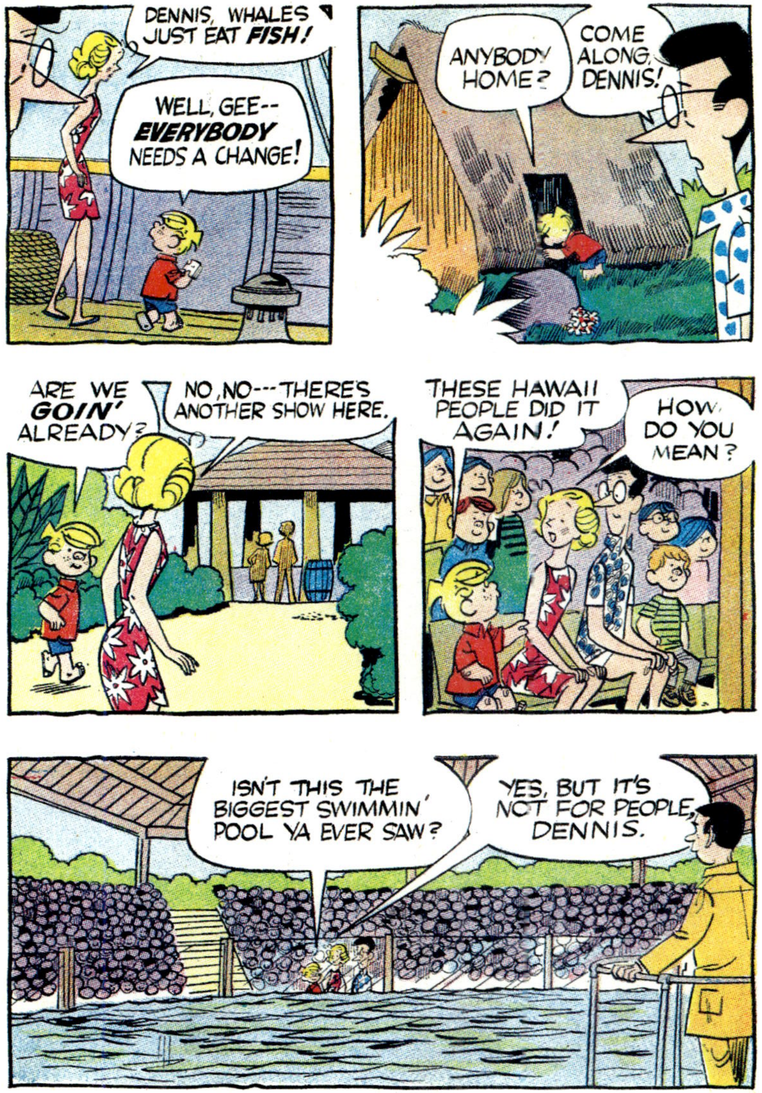
DENNIS, WHALES JUST EAT **FISH**!
WELL, GEE-- **EVERYBODY** NEEDS A CHANGE!
ANYBODY HOME?
COME ALONG, DENNIS!
ARE WE **GOIN'** ALREADY?
NO, NO---THERE'S ANOTHER SHOW HERE.
THESE HAWAII PEOPLE DID IT AGAIN!
HOW, DO YOU MEAN?
ISN'T THIS THE BIGGEST SWIMMIN' POOL YA EVER SAW?
YES, BUT IT'S NOT FOR PEOPLE, DENNIS.

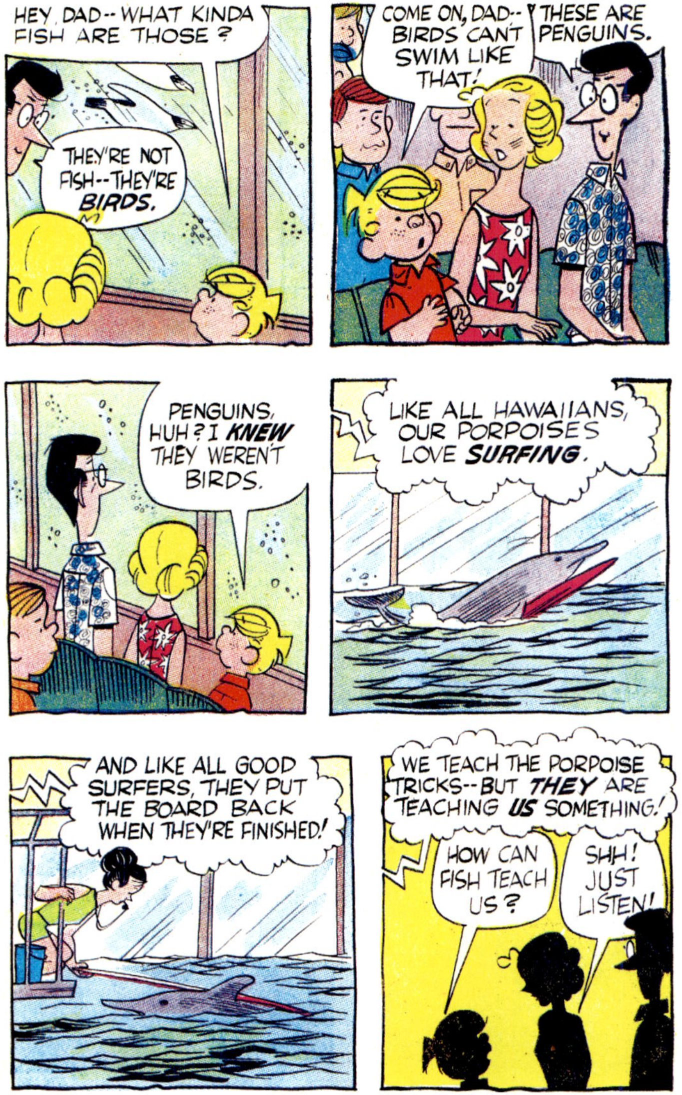
HEY, DAD--WHAT KINDA FISH ARE THOSE?
THEY'RE NOT FISH--THEY'RE **BIRDS.**
COME ON, DAD-- BIRDS CAN'T SWIM LIKE THAT!
THESE ARE PENGUINS.
PENGUINS, HUH? I **KNEW** THEY WEREN'T BIRDS.
LIKE ALL HAWAIIANS, OUR PORPOISES LOVE **SURFING**.
AND LIKE ALL GOOD SURFERS, THEY PUT THE BOARD BACK WHEN THEY'RE FINISHED!
WE TEACH THE PORPOISE TRICKS--BUT **THEY** ARE TEACHING **US** SOMETHING!
HOW CAN FISH TEACH US?
SHH! JUST LISTEN!

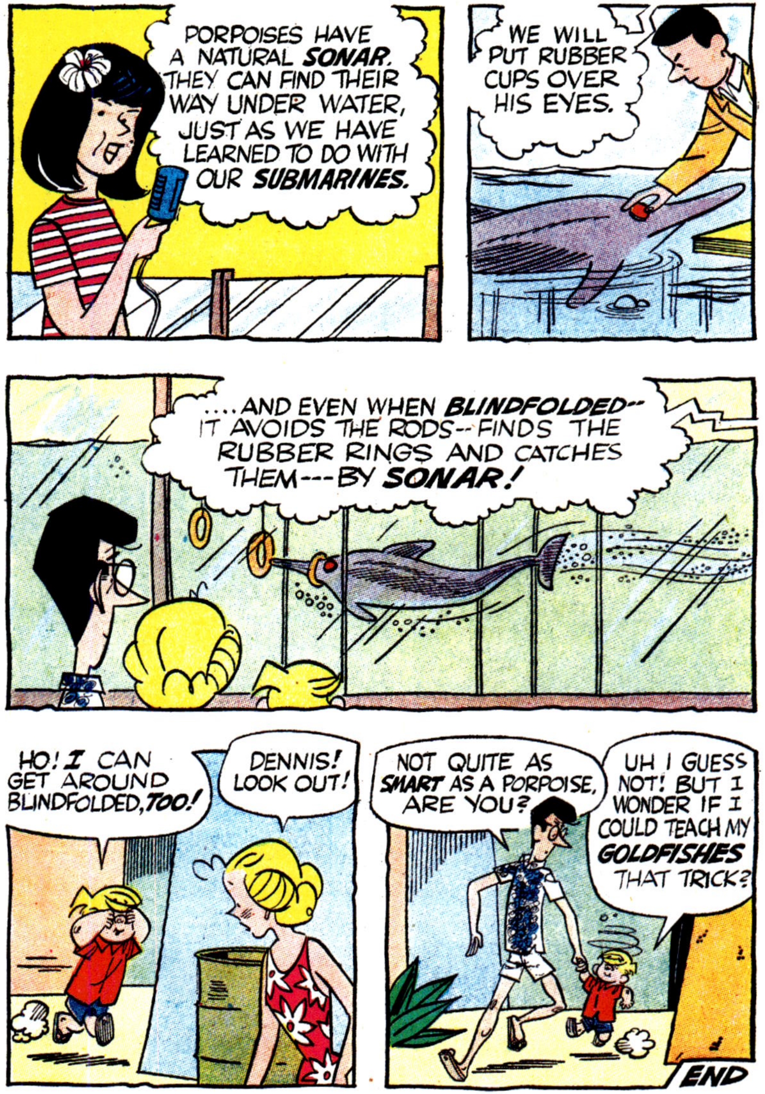
PORPOISES HAVE A NATURAL SONAR. THEY CAN FIND THEIR WAY UNDER WATER, JUST AS WE HAVE LEARNED TO DO WITH OUR SUBMARINES.
WE WILL PUT RUBBER CUPS OVER HIS EYES.
....AND EVEN WHEN BLINDFOLDED-- IT AVOIDS THE RODS-- FINDS THE RUBBER RINGS AND CATCHES THEM---BY SONAR!
HO! I CAN GET AROUND BLINDFOLDED, TOO!
DENNIS! LOOK OUT!
NOT QUITE AS SMART AS A PORPOISE, ARE YOU?
UH I GUESS NOT! BUT I WONDER IF I COULD TEACH MY GOLDFISHES THAT TRICK?
END

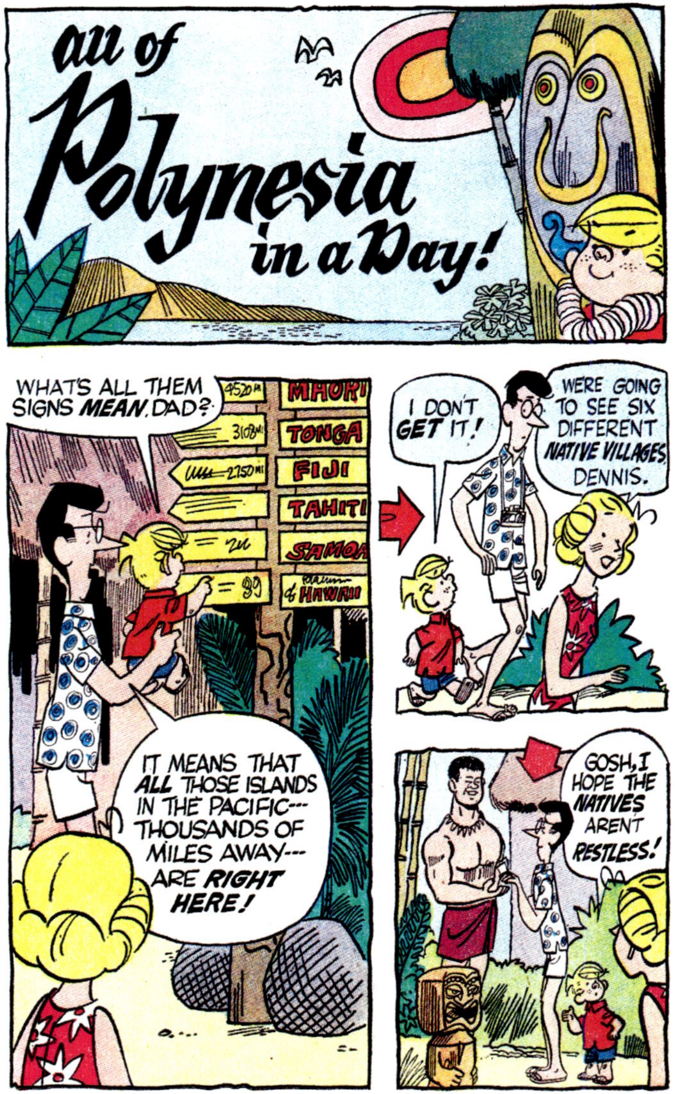
all of Polynesia in a Day!
WHAT'S ALL THEM SIGNS MEAN, DAD?
MAORI
TONGA
FIJI
TAHITI
SAMOA
HAWAII
IT MEANS THAT ALL THOSE ISLANDS IN THE PACIFIC--- THOUSANDS OF MILES AWAY--- ARE RIGHT HERE!
I DON'T GET IT!
WE'RE GOING TO SEE SIX DIFFERENT NATIVE VILLAGES, DENNIS.
GOSH, I HOPE THE NATIVES AREN'T RESTLESS!

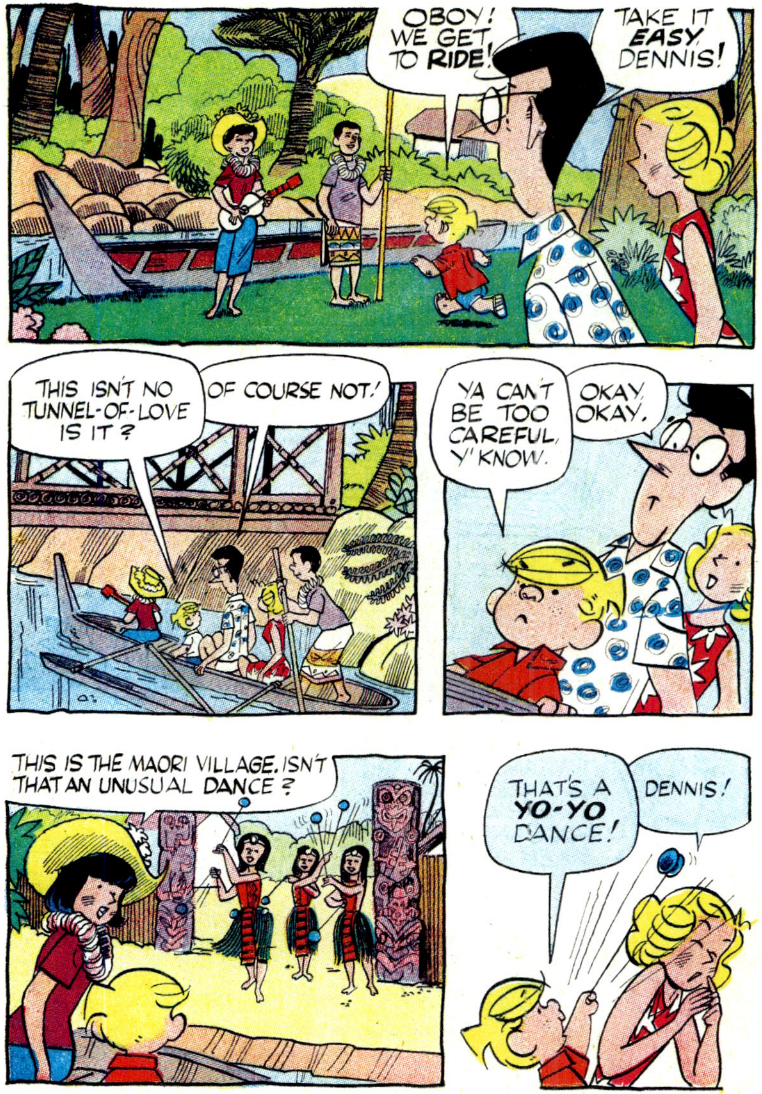
OBOY! WE GET TO RIDE!
TAKE IT EASY, DENNIS!
THIS ISN'T NO TUNNEL-OF-LOVE IS IT?
OF COURSE NOT!
YA CAN'T BE TOO CAREFUL, Y'KNOW.
OKAY, OKAY.
THIS IS THE MAORI VILLAGE. ISN'T THAT AN UNUSUAL DANCE?
THAT'S A YO-YO DANCE!
DENNIS!

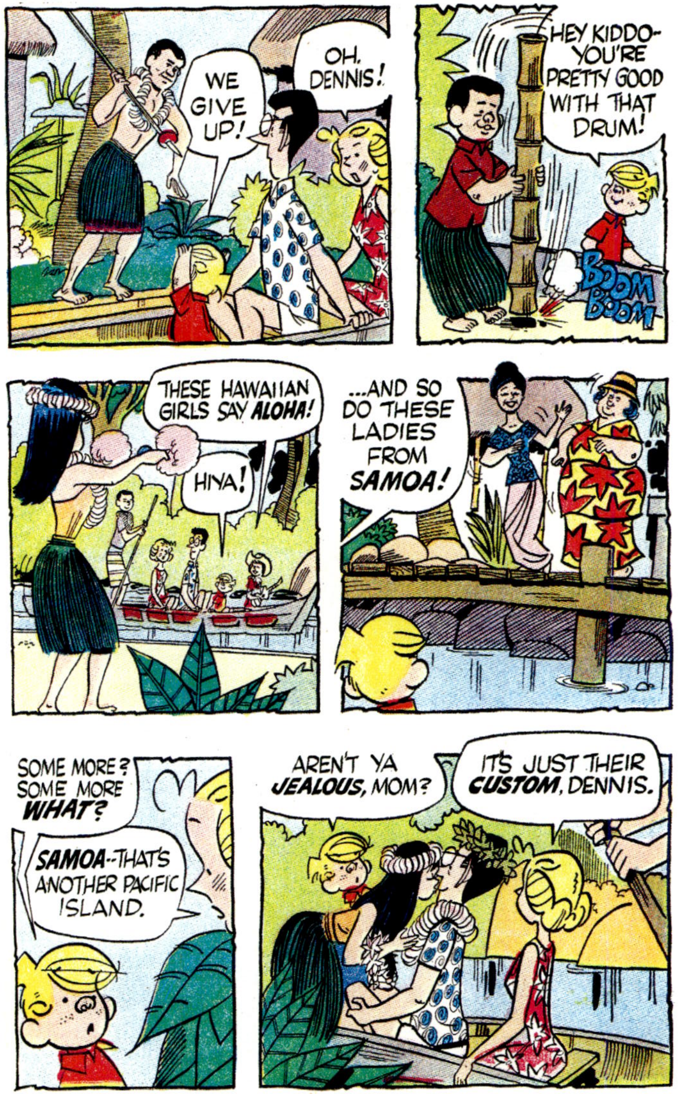
WE GIVE UP!
OH, DENNIS!
HEY KIDDO- YOU'RE PRETTY GOOD WITH THAT DRUM!
BOOM BOOM
THESE HAWAIIAN GIRLS SAY ALOHA!
HIYA!
...AND SO DO THESE LADIES FROM SAMOA!
SOME MORE? SOME MORE WHAT?
SAMOA--THAT'S ANOTHER PACIFIC ISLAND.
AREN'T YA JEALOUS, MOM?
IT'S JUST THEIR CUSTOM, DENNIS.

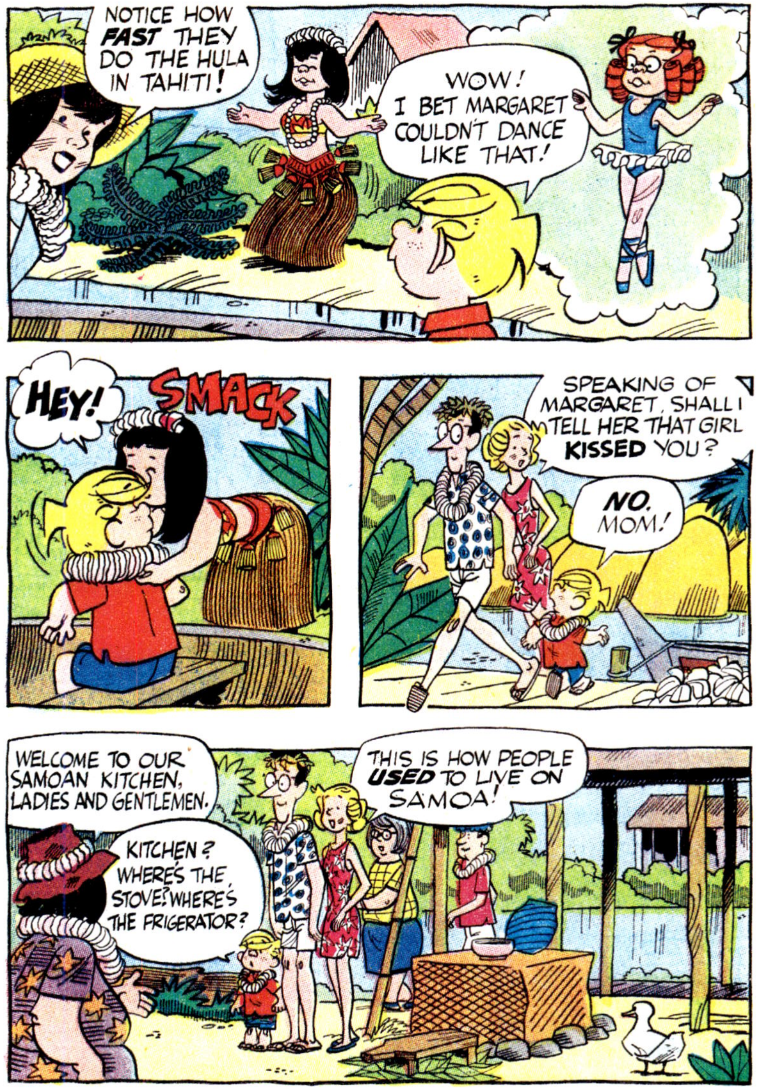
NOTICE HOW **FAST** THEY DO THE HULA IN TAHITI!
WOW! I BET MARGARET COULDN'T DANCE LIKE THAT!
HEY!
SMACK
SPEAKING OF MARGARET, SHALL I TELL HER THAT GIRL **KISSED** YOU?
NO, MOM!
WELCOME TO OUR SAMOAN KITCHEN, LADIES AND GENTLEMEN.
THIS IS HOW PEOPLE **USED** TO LIVE ON SAMOA!
KITCHEN? WHERE'S THE STOVE? WHERE'S THE FRIGERATOR?

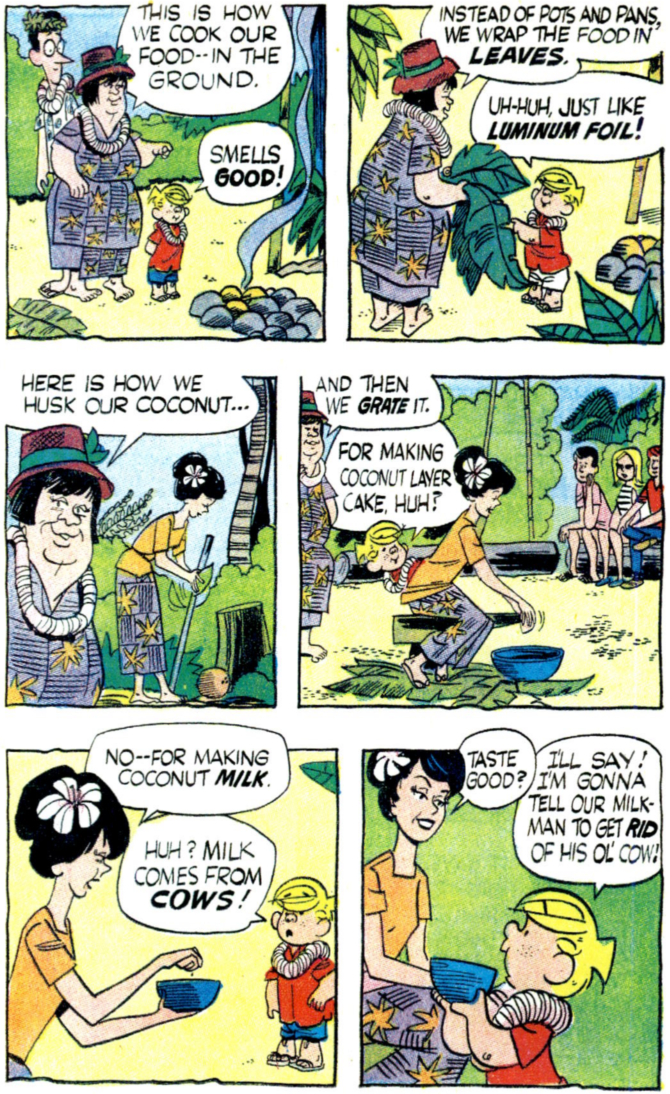
THIS IS HOW WE COOK OUR FOOD--IN THE GROUND.
SMELLS **GOOD!**
INSTEAD OF POTS AND PANS, WE WRAP THE FOOD IN **LEAVES.**
UH-HUH, JUST LIKE **LUMINUM FOIL!**
HERE IS HOW WE HUSK OUR COCONUT...
AND THEN WE **GRATE** IT.
FOR MAKING COCONUT LAYER CAKE, HUH?
NO--FOR MAKING COCONUT **MILK.**
HUH? MILK COMES FROM **COWS!**
TASTE GOOD?
I'LL SAY! I'M GONNA TELL OUR MILK-MAN TO GET **RID** OF HIS OL' COW!

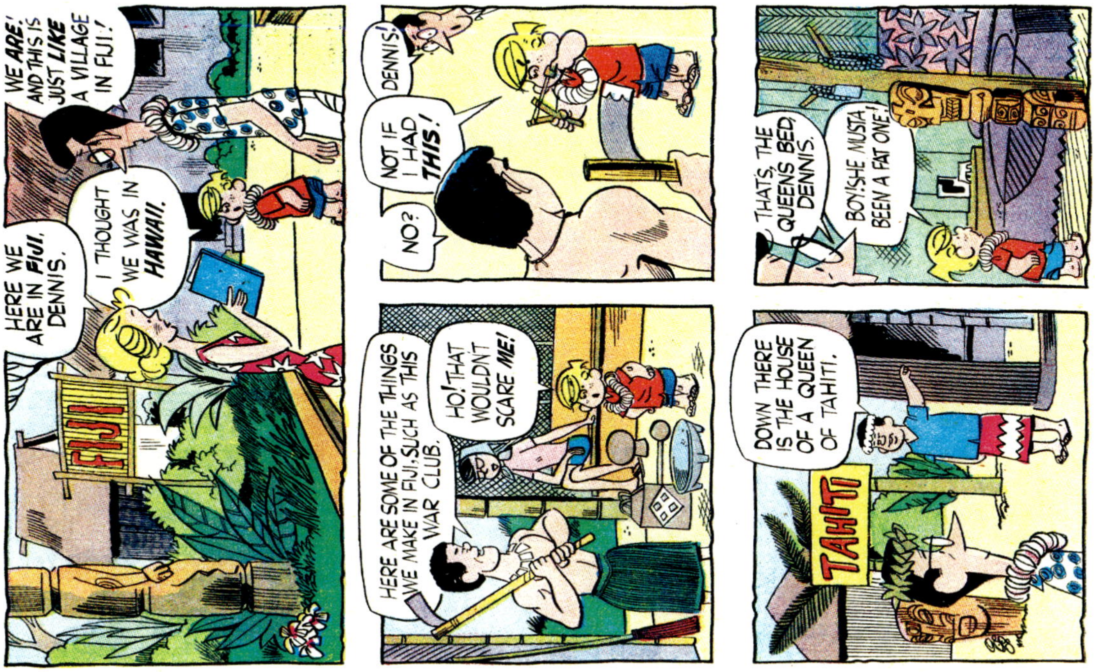
HERE WE ARE IN FIJI, DENNIS.
I THOUGHT WE WAS IN HAWAII.
WE ARE! AND THIS IS JUST LIKE A VILLAGE IN FIJI!
FIJI
HERE ARE SOME OF THE THINGS WE MAKE IN FIJI. SUCH AS THIS WAR CLUB.
HO! THAT WOULDN'T SCARE ME!
NO?
NOT IF I HAD THIS!
DENNIS!
DOWN THERE IS THE HOUSE OF A QUEEN OF TAHITI.
TAHITI
THAT'S, THE QUEEN'S BED, DENNIS.
BOY! SHE MUSTA BEEN A FAT ONE!

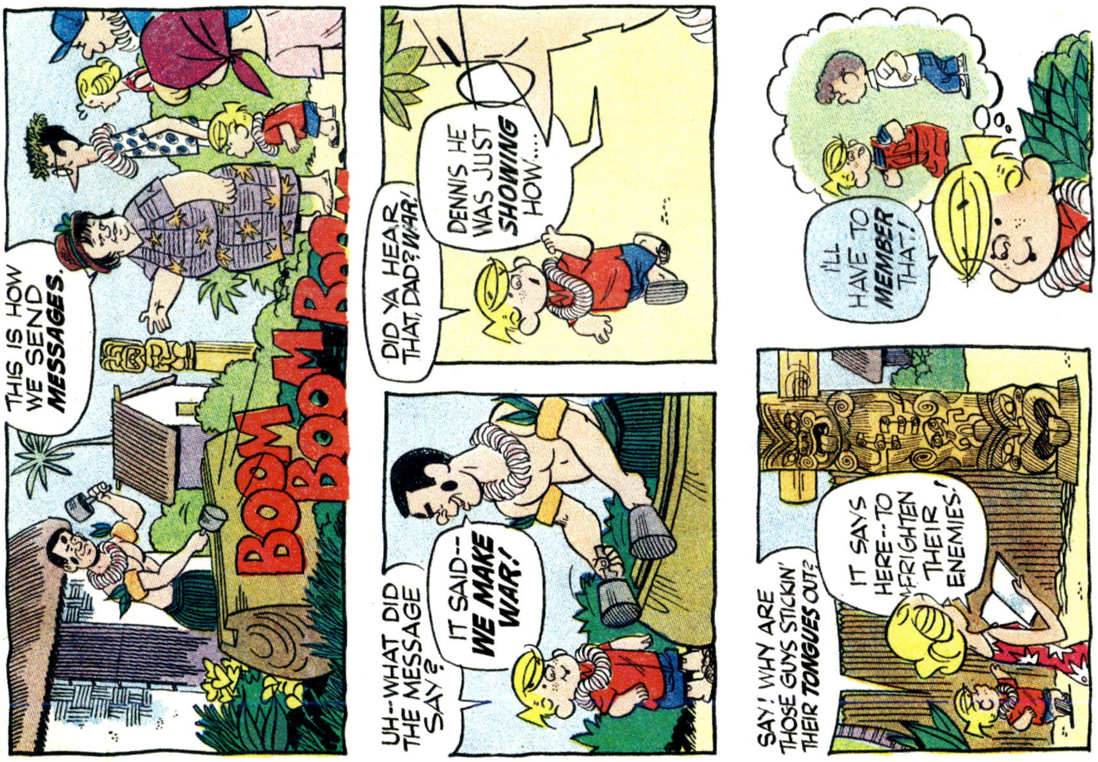
THIS IS HOW WE SEND MESSAGES.
BOOM BOOM BOO
UH--WHAT DID THE MESSAGE SAY?
IT SAID-- WE MAKE WAR!
DID YA HEAR THAT, DAD? WAR!
DENNIS HE WAS JUST SHOWING HOW....
SAY! WHY ARE THOSE GUYS STICKIN' THEIR TONGUES OUT?
IT SAYS HERE--TO FRIGHTEN THEIR ENEMIES!
I'LL HAVE TO MEMBER THAT!

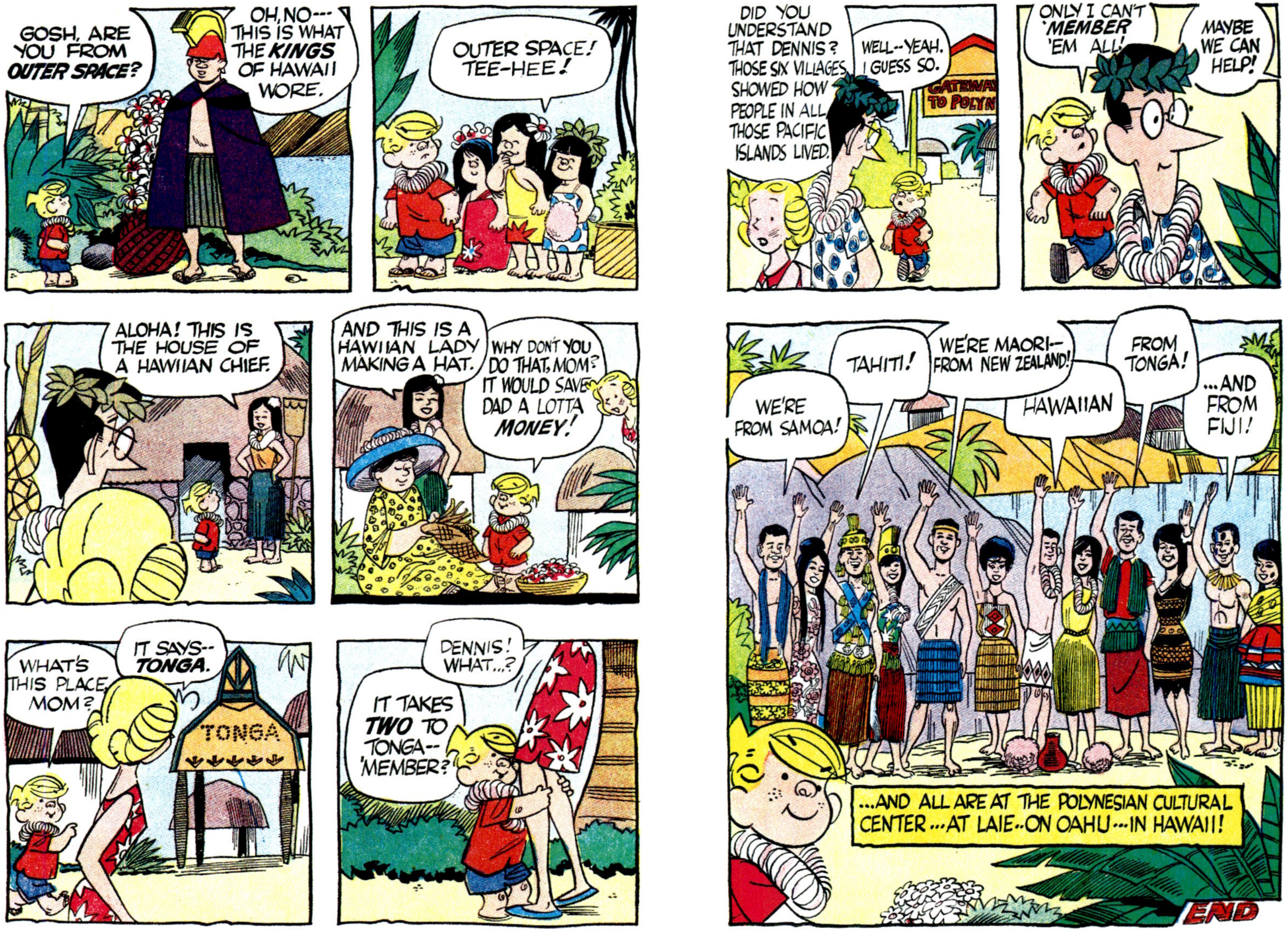
GOSH, ARE YOU FROM **OUTER SPACE?**
OH, NO--- THIS IS WHAT THE **KINGS** OF HAWAII WORE.
OUTER SPACE! TEE-HEE!
ALOHA! THIS IS THE HOUSE OF A HAWIIAN CHIEF.
AND THIS IS A HAWIIAN LADY MAKING A HAT.
WHY DON'T YOU DO THAT, MOM? IT WOULD SAVE DAD A LOTTA **MONEY!**
WHAT'S THIS PLACE, MOM?
IT SAYS-- **TONGA.**
TONGA
DENNIS! WHAT...?
IT TAKES **TWO** TO TONGA-- 'MEMBER?
DID YOU UNDERSTAND THAT DENNIS? THOSE SIX VILLAGES SHOWED HOW PEOPLE IN ALL THOSE PACIFIC ISLANDS LIVED.
WELL--YEAH. I GUESS SO.
GATEWAY TO POLYN
ONLY I CAN'T **'MEMBER** 'EM ALL!
MAYBE WE CAN HELP!
WE'RE FROM SAMOA!
TAHITI!
WE'RE MAORI-- FROM NEW ZEALAND!
HAWAIIAN
FROM TONGA!
...AND FROM FIJI!
...AND ALL ARE AT THE POLYNESIAN CULTURAL CENTER...AT LAIE..ON OAHU...IN HAWAII!
END

In The Year 2000: Dennis Returns To Hawaii!

by Ron Ferdinand & Marcus Hamilton

In the year 2000, history repeated itself as Hank Ketcham sent DENNIS Sunday comic artist Ron Ferdinand and DENNIS daily panel artist Marcus Hamilton to Hawaii for inspiration to create a new vacation storyline. Here's the complete series of nine-dailies and two Sundays.

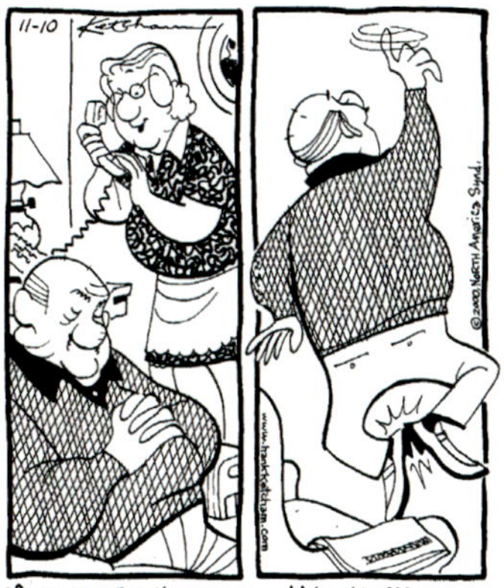
11-10
Ketcham

"GEORGE! THE MITCHELLS ARE GOING TO HAWAII!"

"ALOHA-HA! ALOHA-HEE!"

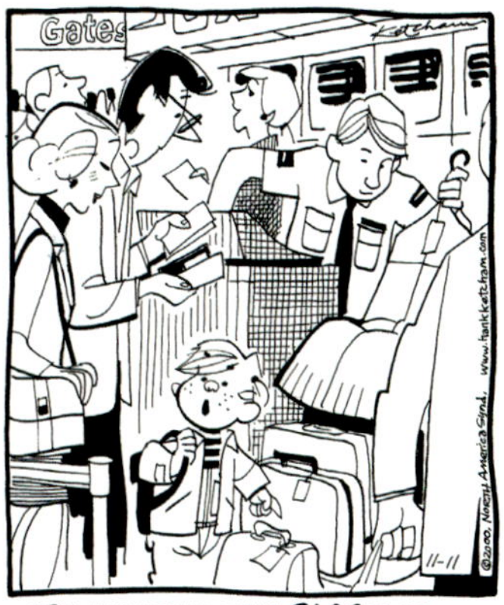
Gates
Ketcham
11-11

"TELL HIM WE WANT OUR BAGS TO GO TO HAWAII, TOO!"

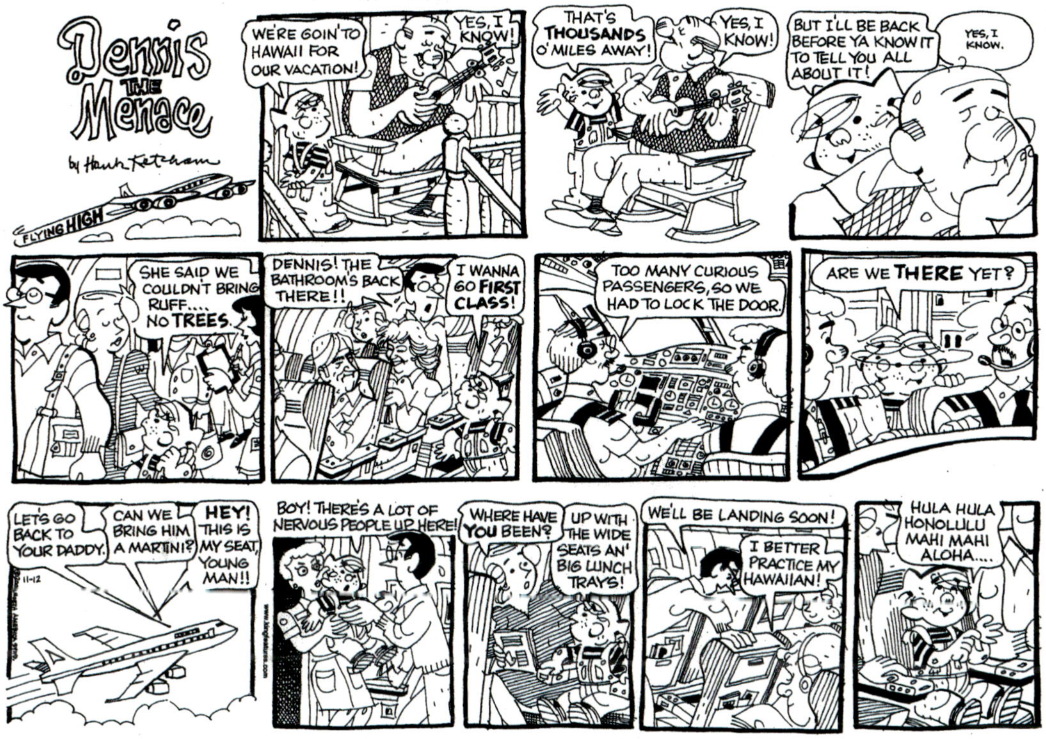
Dennis the Menace
by Hank Ketcham
FLYING HIGH
WE'RE GOIN' TO HAWAII FOR OUR VACATION!
YES, I KNOW!
THAT'S THOUSANDS O' MILES AWAY!
YES, I KNOW!
BUT I'LL BE BACK BEFORE YA KNOW IT TO TELL YOU ALL ABOUT IT!
YES, I KNOW.
SHE SAID WE COULDN'T BRING RUFF.... NO TREES.
DENNIS! THE BATHROOM'S BACK THERE!!
I WANNA GO FIRST CLASS!
TOO MANY CURIOUS PASSENGERS, SO WE HAD TO LOCK THE DOOR.
ARE WE THERE YET?
LET'S GO BACK TO YOUR DADDY.
CAN WE BRING HIM A MARTINI?
HEY! THIS IS MY SEAT, YOUNG MAN!!
11-12
BOY! THERE'S A LOT OF NERVOUS PEOPLE UP HERE!
WHERE HAVE YOU BEEN?
UP WITH THE WIDE SEATS AN' BIG LUNCH TRAYS!
WE'LL BE LANDING SOON!
I BETTER PRACTICE MY HAWAIIAN!
HULA HULA HONOLULU MAHI MAHI ALOHA....

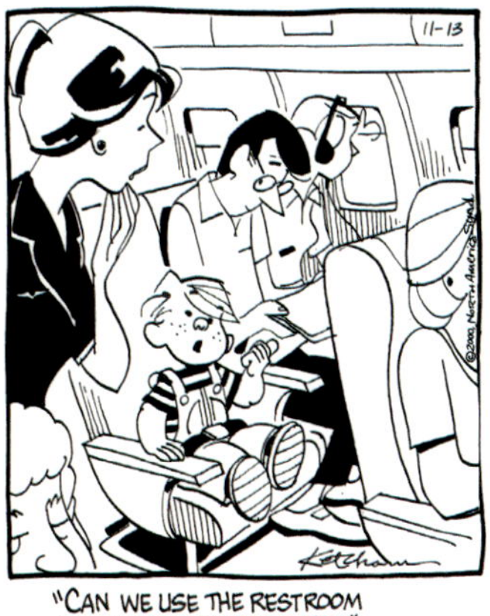
11-13
Ketcham

"CAN WE USE THE RESTROOM WHEN WE FLY OVER CITIES?"

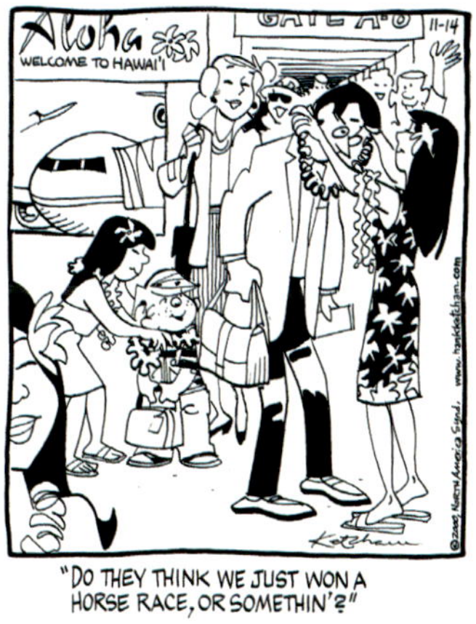
Aloha
WELCOME TO HAWAI'I
11-14
Ketcham

"DO THEY THINK WE JUST WON A HORSE RACE, OR SOMETHIN'?"

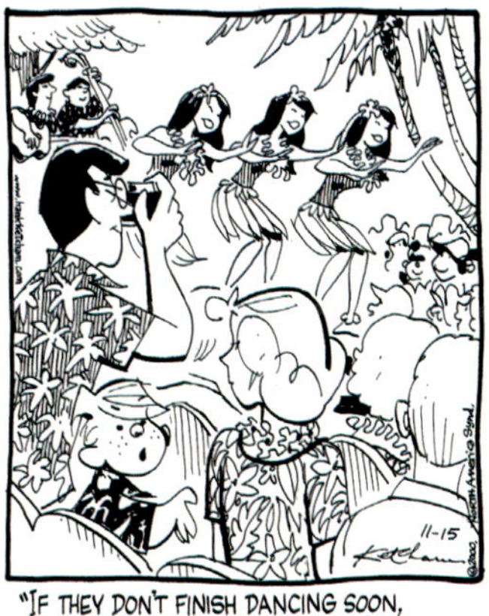
11-15
Ketcham

"IF THEY DON'T FINISH DANCING SOON, DAD'S GONNA RUN OUT OF FILM!"

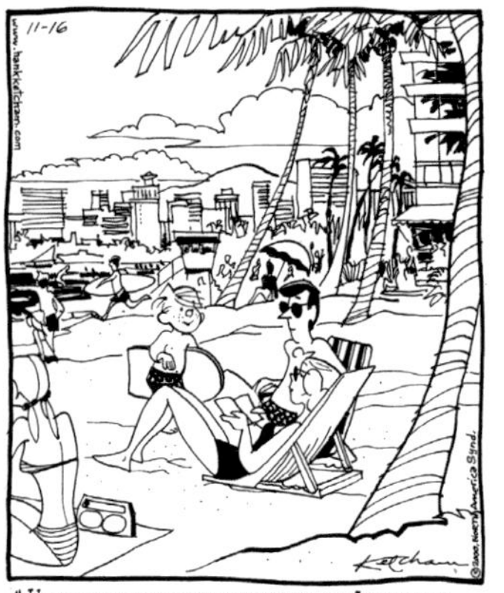

"I'D LIKE TO LIVE HERE IF IT WEREN'T SO FAR FROM MRS. WILSON'S KITCHEN."

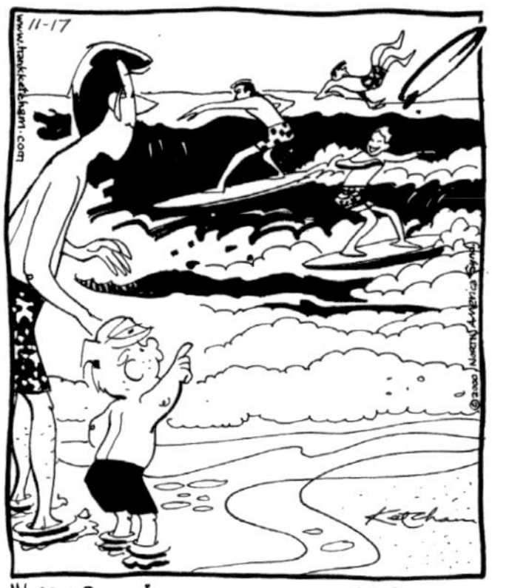

"LOOK, DAD! I SHOULDA BROUGHT MOM'S IRONING BOARD!"

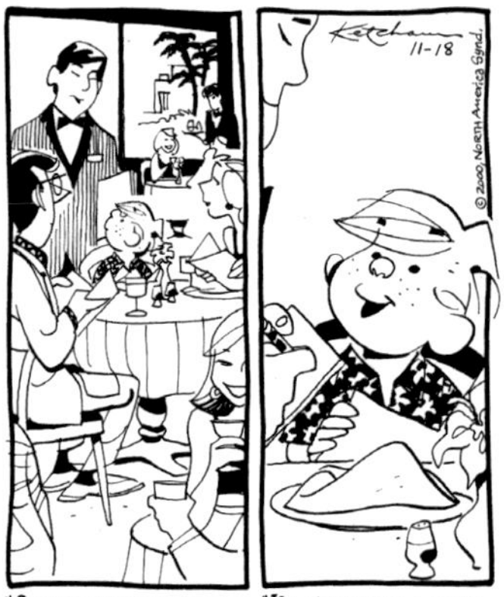

"OUR SPECIAL TODAY IS FRESH OPAKAPAKA AND MAHI MAHI."

"I'LL JUST HAVE A GOOD OL' AMERICAN HAMBURGER."

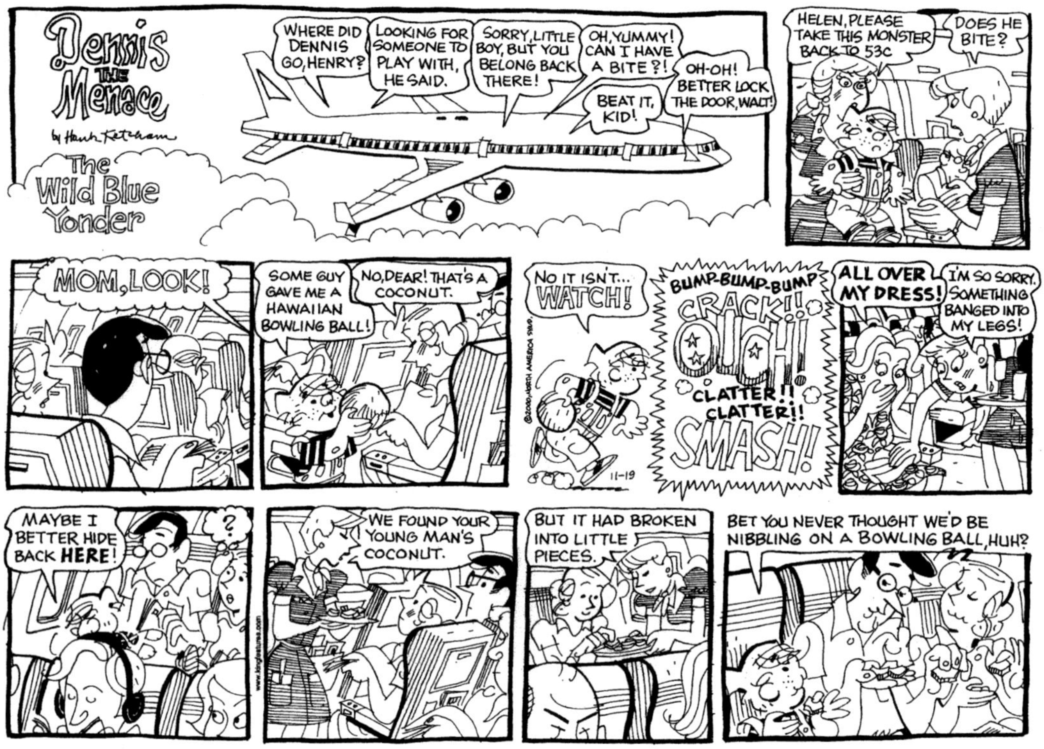
Dennis the Menace
by Hank Ketcham
The Wild Blue Yonder
WHERE DID DENNIS GO, HENRY?
LOOKING FOR SOMEONE TO PLAY WITH, HE SAID.
SORRY, LITTLE BOY, BUT YOU BELONG BACK THERE!
OH, YUMMY! CAN I HAVE A BITE?!
BEAT IT, KID!
OH-OH! BETTER LOCK THE DOOR, WALT!
HELEN, PLEASE TAKE THIS MONSTER BACK TO 53C
DOES HE BITE?
MOM, LOOK!
SOME GUY GAVE ME A HAWAIIAN BOWLING BALL!
NO, DEAR! THAT'S A COCONUT.
NO IT ISN'T... WATCH!
BUMP-BUMP-BUMP
CRACK!!
OUCH!
CLATTER!! CLATTER!!
SMASH!
ALL OVER MY DRESS!
I'M SO SORRY. SOMETHING BANGED INTO MY LEGS!
MAYBE I BETTER HIDE BACK HERE!
?
WE FOUND YOUR YOUNG MAN'S COCONUT.
BUT IT HAD BROKEN INTO LITTLE PIECES.
BET YOU NEVER THOUGHT WE'D BE NIBBLING ON A BOWLING BALL, HUH?

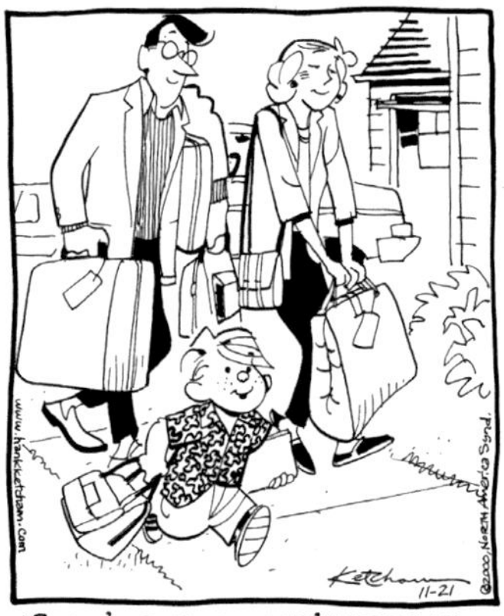

"BOY, IT'LL BE NICE KNOWIN' WHERE I AM WHEN I WAKE UP TOMORROW!"

Ron Ferdinand: "Hank sent Marcus and me and our wives to Hawaii in 2000 for a Hawaiian series. He sent us there for research and, if I remember correctly, both my Sundays were on the plane going and coming. LOL! We went to Don Ho's restaurant and he was SITTING there. I did a sketch of us with Don."

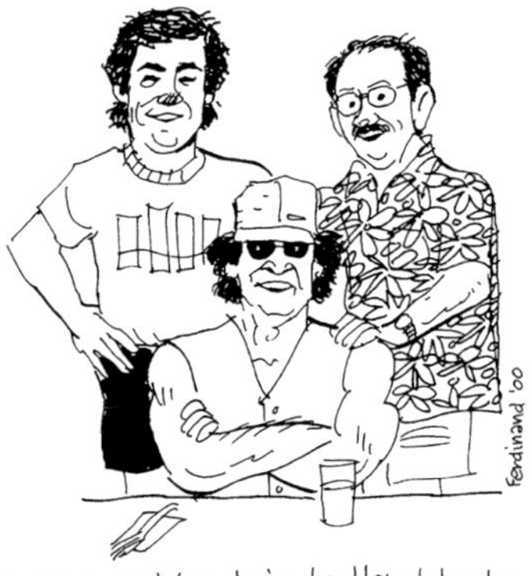

And what would a trip to Honolulu be without an audience with Don Ho? (At least we think it was him.)